OXFORD STUDIES IN DEMOCRATIZATION

Series editor: Laurence Whitehead

• • • • • • • • • • • • • • • • • •

THE DEMOCRATIC DEVELOPMENTAL STATE

OXFORD STUDIES IN DEMOCRATIZATION

Series editor: Laurence Whitehead

••••••••••••••••••

Oxford Studies in Democratization is a series for scholars and students of comparative politics and related disciplines. Volumes will concentrate on the comparative study of the democratization processes that accompanied the decline and termination of the cold war. The geographical focus of the series will primarily be Latin America, the Caribbean, Southern and Eastern Europe, and relevant experiences in Africa and Asia.

OTHER BOOKS IN THE SERIES

Human Rights and Democratization in Latin America:
Uruguay and Chile
Alexandra Barahona de Brito

The New Politics of Inequality in Latin America:
Rethinking Participation and Representation
Douglas A. Chalmers, Carlos M. Vilas,
Katherine Roberts Hite,
Scott B. Martin, Kerianne Piester,
and Monique Segarra

The Bases of Party Competition in Eastern Europe:
Social and Ideological Cleavages in Post Communist States
Geoffrey Evans and Stephen Whitefield

Citizenship Rights and Social Movements:
A Comparative and Statistical Analysis
Joe Foweraker and Todd Landman

Regimes, Politics, and Markets:
Democratization and Economic Change in Southern and
Eastern Europe
José María Maravall

Democracy Between Consolidation and
Crisis in Southern Europe
Leonardo Morlino

Electoral Systems and Democratization in
Southern Africa
Andrew Reynolds

The International Dimensions of Democratization:
Europe and the Americas
Laurence Whitehead

The Democratic Developmental State

Politics and Institutional Design

....

Edited by

MARK ROBINSON

and

GORDON WHITE

OXFORD UNIVERSITY PRESS
1998

Oxford University Press, Great Clarendon Street, Oxford OX2 6DP
Oxford New York
Athens Auckland Bangkok Bogotá Buenos Aires Calcutta
Cape Town Chennai Dar es Salaam Delhi Florence Hong Kong Istanbul
Karachi Kuala Lumpur Madrid Melbourne Mexico City Mumbai
Nairobi Paris São Paolo Singapore Taipei Tokyo Toronto Warsaw
and associated companies in
Berlin Ibadan

Oxford is a registered trade mark of Oxford University Press

Published in the United States
by Oxford University Press Inc., New York

© the several contributors 1998

The moral rights of the authors have been asserted

First published 1998

British Library Cataloguing in Publication Data
Data available

Library of Congress Cataloging in Publication Data
The democratic developmental state : politics and institutional design
/ edited by Mark Robinson and Gordon White.
p.   cm. — (Oxford studies in democratization)
1. Democracy—Economic aspects.   2. Economic development—
Political aspects.   3. Democracy—Case studies.   4. Economic
development—Case studies.   I. Robinson, Mark, 1951– .
II. White, Gordon, 1942–1998.   III. Series.
JC423.D44174   1998   320.9172'4—dc21   98-35998
ISBN 0-19-829382-8

1 3 5 7 9 10 8 6 4 2

Typeset by Graphicraft Limited, Hong Kong
Printed in Great Britain
on acid-free paper by
Bookcraft (Bath) Ltd
Midsomer Norton, Somerset

....

Dedication

....

As this volume was going to print we received the tragic and unexpected news that Gordon White had passed away having suffered a major stroke. Within hours of Gordon's death, messages of condolence flooded in from all parts of the world, from his many friends and colleagues, and others who had been influenced by his teaching and research. This was rich testament to his intellectual reach and energy, which touched the hearts and minds of large numbers of the global academic community.

Gordon was first and foremost an acclaimed Sinologist, having published many books and articles about the politics and political economy of the Chinese state. He was also very much a student of comparative politics, and avidly pursued new and compelling routes of intellectual enquiry, immersing himself in contemporary theoretical debates, while at the same time grounded in careful empirical enquiry. This approach underpins the collective research endeavour that gave rise to the various chapters which constitute this book.

Much of the impetus for this collection came from Gordon, reflecting his creative ability to conceive of and nurture compelling new ideas and intellectual agendas. His critical and inquisitive demeanour, and willingness to challenge received wisdom, was a source of inspiration for us all. We dedicate this volume to Gordon's memory; may his creative and combative spirit live on.

M.R.

······················

Preface and Acknowledgements

······················

THE idea for this book arises from a conviction that the literature concerned with democracy and development has been running into a dead end. Efforts to demonstrate a conclusive relationship in either direction have proved either empirically suspect or theoretically deficient. Moreover, it has become evident that established and emergent democracies in the developing world have major shortcomings in terms of institutional depth and political legitimacy. Their developmental performance has often been disappointing, whether judged in terms of growth or equity. The political priorities and material needs of poor and marginalized citizens do not loom large in their development agendas. These concerns give rise to the argument that effective developmental states require an appropriate blend of political conditions and institutional structures to shape developmental outcomes in productive and equitable ways.

This collective research endeavour brings together contributions by a group of IDS Fellows in the Governance and Democracy Programme and other scholars associated with the Institute. It was made possible through generous funding provided by the UK Department for International Development (DFID—formerly the Overseas Development Administration), as part of its Accountable Grant to the IDS. It follows on from an earlier project, also funded by DFID, which sought to analyse critically the nature and substance of the democratization process in developing countries in the 1980s and early 1990s (R. Luckham and G. White (eds.), *Democratization in the South: The Jagged Wave*, Manchester: Manchester University Press, 1996). This volume is going into print as we embark on the third of our collaborative research ventures, *Strengthening Democratic Governance in Conflict-Torn Societies*, in which we examine the effectiveness of democratic political institutions and their role in conflict prevention and post-conflict reconstruction.

We would like to acknowledge the varied contributions that made this book possible. Our thanks go to the series editor Laurence Whitehead for encouraging us to pursue this project, and for including it as part of the OUP Democratization series. Thanks are also due to Sophie Ahmad and Jackie Pritchard of the OUP editorial team for speedy and efficient processing of the volume. At IDS we would like to acknowledge warmly the contributions of Julie McWilliam and Glenis Morrison in typing, revising, and collating the manuscript.

M.R.
G.W.

Contents

List of Contributors   xi

Introduction   1
Mark Robinson and Gordon White

PART I. THE DEMOCRATIC DEVELOPMENTAL STATE

1. Constructing a Democratic Developmental State   17
   Gordon White

2. Forms of the Democratic Developmental State: 52
   Democratic Practices and Development Capacity
   Adrian Leftwich

3. Death without Taxes: Democracy, State Capacity, and   84
   Aid Dependence in the Fourth World
   Mick Moore

PART II. POLITICAL INSTITUTIONS AND SOCIAL FORCES

4. Democratization and the Developmental State: 125
   The Search for Balance
   James Manor

5. Democracy, Participation, and Public Policy: 150
   The Politics of Institutional Design
   Mark Robinson

6. The Developmental Implications of Federal Political   187
   Institutions in India
   Rob Jenkins

7. Democratic Institutions and Development in   215
   Post-apartheid South Africa
   Nicoli Nattrass and Jeremy Seekings

PART III. DEEPENING DEMOCRACY

8. 'Fiddling with Democracy': Translating Women's　　　245
   Participation in Politics in Uganda and South Africa
   into Gender Equity in Development Practice
   Anne Marie Goetz

9. Democratization and Sustainable Rural Livelihoods　　　280
   Susanna Davies

10. Are There Alternatives to Liberal Democracy?　　　306
    Robin Luckham

Index　　　　　　　　　　　　　　　　　　343

....

Contributors

....

Susanna Davies is a Fellow of the Institute of Development Studies, University of Sussex. Her recent research has compared how civil society and the state support or undermine rural livelihoods in dryland India and sub-Saharan Africa.

Anne Marie Goetz is a Fellow at the Institute of Development Studies, University of Sussex. Her research interests include developing a gendered perspective on the state and on the structure and institutions of democratic politics. In her published work she has investigated gender-sensitive approaches to understanding public institutions, for instance in her edited book *Getting Institutions Right for Women in Development* (Zed Press, 1997). She is currently undertaking theoretical and empirical research on women's engagement in formal politics and in civil society in Uganda and South Africa.

Rob Jenkins is Lecturer in Politics at Birkbeck College, University of London. He is the author of the forthcoming *Democracy and the Politics of Economic Reform in India* (Cambridge University Press). His research interests span political economy, electoral politics, and the politics of nationalism. Jenkins is currently researching local anti-corruption initiatives and other movements for government accountability in India with Anne Marie Goetz.

Adrian Leftwich is a Senior Lecturer in Politics at the University of York, where he specializes in the politics of development. He has published a variety of articles, books, and edited collections on politics and development, including *Redefining Politics* (Methuen, 1983), *New Developments in Political Science* (Elgar, 1990), and *Democracy and Development* (Polity, 1996). He is currently completing a study to be published by Polity Press as *States of Development* in 1999.

Robin Luckham is a Research Associate (formerly Fellow) of the Institute of Development Studies, University of Sussex. He has written extensively on the military institutions in developing countries, focusing in particular on the problems of bringing them under democratic control. He has co-edited (with Gordon White) an IDS book on *Democratization in the South: The Jagged Wave* (Manchester University Press, 1996).

James Manor is a Professorial Fellow of the Institute of Development Studies, University of Sussex. He has taught South Asian and comparative politics at Yale, Harvard, London, and Leicester universities.

Mick Moore is a Fellow of the Institute of Development Studies, University of Sussex, and has recently been Visiting Professor at the Massachusetts Institute of Technology. He is a political economist who specializes in issues of the state, governance, and the relationships between government and private capital in poor countries.

Nicoli Nattrass is an Associate Professor in the School of Economics at the University of Cape Town. Her recent publications include articles on growth and unemployment, and a textbook on *Macroeconomics: Theory and Policy in South Africa* (Cape Town: David Philip, 1997). She is currently working on a book on the labour market and welfare policy (with Jeremy Seekings) and on an edited volume on unemployment and the labour market (with Murray Leibbrandt).

Mark Robinson is a Fellow of the Institute of Development Studies, University of Sussex. His current research interests are on political participation and public policy, the contribution of foreign aid to the strengthening of civil society in Africa, and the role of civic organizations in the provision of public services. He is also editor of *Corruption and Development* (Frank Cass, 1998).

Jeremy Seekings is a Senior Lecturer in the Sociology Department at the University of Cape Town. He is the author of *Heroes or Villains? Youth Politics in the 1980s* (Johannesburg: Ravan, 1993), and *The UDF: A History of the United Democratic Front in South Africa, 1983–1991* (Johannesburg: Ravan, forthcoming). He is also working on a study of the transformation of South Africa's lower courts, an edited collection comparing Nigerian and South African politics (with Abdul Raufu Mustapha), and a book on labour market and welfare policy (with Nicoli Nattrass).

Gordon White was Professorial Fellow at the Institute of Development Studies, University of Sussex, at the time of his death in April 1998. He was a China specialist and author of numerous books and articles on the politics and political economy of development. His recent publications include *Riding the Tiger: The Politics of Economic Reform in Post-Mao China* (Macmillan, 1993), *In Search of Civil Society: Market Reforms and Social Change in Contemporary China* (with Jude Howell and Shang Xiao-yuan, Clarendon Press, 1996), and *Democratization in the South: The Jagged Wave* (edited with Robin Luckham, Manchester University Press, 1996).

....

Introduction

....

MARK ROBINSON and GORDON WHITE

Much of the debate in recent years concerning the developmental significance of new democratic states is premised on the assumption that democracy and socio-economic development are complementary. This is in marked contrast to the dominant consensus which endured from the late 1960s through to the mid-1980s which held that developmental progress in poor societies could best be assured by strong states under the tutelage of authoritarian regimes. The empirical justification for this view lay in the palpable success of some newly industrializing countries in Latin America and East Asia, most of which were governed by authoritarian regimes of various ideological hues. Democracy was perceived to be a luxury that was feasible only in countries which had achieved some measure of developmental success, embodied in sustained economic growth and high living standards. Democratic politics were considered to be a barrier to sustained development since unbridled political competition could generate demands which could not be accommodated within existing political institutions and prevailing resource constraints.

This view lost credibility in the face of a number of developments in the late 1980s and early 1990s. First, the developmental success of a small group of established democracies (Botswana, Malaysia, and Mauritius) demonstrated that democracy (albeit in a formal, procedural sense) and development were not inherently incompatible (Leftwich in this volume).[1] Second, the patent developmental failure of the vast majority of authoritarian regimes in Africa and Latin America demonstrated that only a particular variant of this type of regime—the developmental state—could successfully promote sustained economic growth, under a highly contingent set of political and institutional conditions that were not easily replicable elsewhere (Sørensen 1991). While many states consciously sought to become 'developmental' in orientation, usually through the adoption of a state-led modernization project, it

[1] Arguably Singapore, as one of the fastest growing developing countries in the world, should be included in this list, though its democratic credentials are open to question.

was only a handful of 'rational' or 'embedded' authoritarian states in North and East Asia (China, South Korea, and Taiwan) that could claim to have succeeded in promoting growth and a rapid increase in living standards (White 1988, Wade 1990, Evans 1996). Third, a worldwide trend towards democracy from the early 1970s—the so-called 'Third Wave'—beginning with a series of democratic transitions in southern Europe, shifted the parameters of the debate. The ending of the Cold War combined with far-reaching political upheavals in Eastern Europe and the former Soviet Union, and the rise of popular movements pressing for democratic reforms in many parts of the developing world, meant that authoritarian rule was no longer a reality, or indeed a future prospect, for many developing countries by the late 1990s (Huntington 1991, Luckham and White 1996).

These transitions to democracy were welcomed by liberal and social democrats, as well as by some radical socialists, who considered it to be an advance on various forms of authoritarian rule which had hitherto prevailed in many developing countries. These political developments also gave empirical and ideological succour to a new orthodoxy which surfaced in the late 1980s, the most forceful proponents of which were neo-liberal economists and policy-makers in governments and international aid agencies. In a complete reversal of the previous consensus, this new orthodoxy holds that democracy and development are not only compatible, but mutually reinforcing. Democracy, in its liberal democratic variant, is founded on respect for civil liberties and political rights, and is perceived to be conducive to the economic freedom and competition which lie at the heart of a functioning market economy. Market competition, in turn, is treated as the critical ingredient of economic growth and successful development. Economic well-being creates the material and social foundations for a healthy and durable democratic society. State institutions are perceived to be inherently oppressive and inimical to economic freedom.

Powerful evidence can be mobilized in support of the contention that there is a strong correlation between democracy and wealth; both the historical record and statistical evidence demonstrate conclusively that most established democracies are founded on material prosperity (Moore 1996). However, there can be less certainty about the case for an inherent compatibility between democracy and socio-economic development. The empirical evidence for such a relationship is at best inconclusive, but at the same time questions the assumption of a positive correlation between development and authoritarian government (Sirowy and Inkeles 1990, Healey and Robinson 1992).

The case for the compatibility between democracy and development has also been questioned on analytical grounds, and the developmental achievements of new democracies are open to question. Leftwich (1996), for example, argues that successful developmental performance is not generally an attribute of democratic states; rather the historical record offers evidence of 'some deep structural incompatibility between at least some phases of development and democracy' (ibid.: 19). Aside from its questionable empirical foundations, the compatibility argument, at least in its cruder variants, is premissed on restricted notions of both democracy and development. Democracy is usually defined in a limited, procedural sense, in which the essence of democratic politics is held to lie in competition for political office through political parties contesting elections based on universal franchise. In established democracies, political equality is supported by a healthy respect for civil liberties. Participatory notions of democracy, which are premissed on the ability of citizens to take a full and active role in decision-making, take second place to the dominant, representative form of democracy (Pateman 1970, Luckham in this volume).

In the current orthodoxy, moreover, 'development' is also narrowly defined; it is usually equated with economic growth and material well-being.[2] Since successful development, in this conception, is predicated on free markets and competition, it is essentially commensurate with capitalism. Hence the case for compatibility rests on the assumption, implicitly or explicitly, that developmental democracy means capitalist democracy. In this respect, there is a systemic relationship between economic markets (capitalism) and political markets (procedural democracy), with similar institutional foundations and structural characteristics.

The narrow premises on which much of the contemporary debate is founded are frequently divorced from empirical reality. Many new democracies lack constitutional provisions to sustain democratic norms and procedures, while civil liberties are often highly circumscribed. Such regimes, which have been typified as 'low-intensity' democracies (Gills et al. 1993), are common in countries which have experienced transitions from authoritarian rule but without developing the institutional trappings of liberal democracy, manifest in the rule of law, the separation of powers, and protection of basic freedoms. A preoccupation with free and fair elections as the litmus test of democratic legitimacy obscures the restricted nature of new democracies, many of which have weak institutional foundations and a substantial degree of 'illiberalism' (Zakaria 1997).

---

[2] This is not to deny that many of the adherents of this approach would justifiably claim to be concerned with poverty reduction and social well-being. Their argument is that such considerations are central to development but that the principal means to achieving such objectives is market-led growth. See, for example, World Bank (1990).

The tendency to equate development with capitalism is also questionable. The developmental limitations of capitalism are well known, in particular its tendency to enrich propertied classes and privileged groups at the expense of the poor and socially marginalized, especially in its early phases when it can assume a harsh and exploitative form. The trickle-down approach has experienced an intellectual renaissance in recent years, founded on the renewed expectation that markets are the engine of economic growth and that the fruits of development will percolate down to the poor through an increase in employment opportunities. In this conception safety-nets are advocated as a short-term palliative to transitory problems of poverty (World Bank 1990).

But many post-authoritarian regimes lack the institutional foundations of advanced capitalist economies, in the form of an effective regulatory environment, a progressive and broad-based system of taxation, and legal provisions to enforce individual property rights. Measures to protect poor and vulnerable groups are ad hoc, under-funded, and limited in their reach. Self-interested elites utilize pre-existing patronage networks to capture economic power and protect their gains through force and subterfuge. Capital accumulation by means of corrupt and illegal practices is commonly a source of private enrichment for a small group of individuals to the detriment of the vast majority of the population. The 'gangster capitalism' that has emerged in Russia since the transition from communism is a particularly extreme manifestation of this phenomenon though it does also characterize other states which have experienced a rapid shift away from state socialism and authoritarian rule. This form of accumulation runs counter to the emergence of a healthy capitalist economy, and has the effect of undermining democratic norms and political institutions. Weak and illiberal democracies encourage the spread of corruption and illegal economic activity (Johnston 1998).

Hence, the reality of many post-authoritarian states in Eastern Europe, Latin America, and sub-Saharan Africa is far from the liberal ideal of capitalist democracy. Many new democracies are illiberal, corrupt, lacking in popular participation, and characterized by enormous inequalities. They are the antithesis of the type of regime envisaged by proponents of an inherent compatibility between democracy and development. Developmental democracy is not an assured outcome of a simultaneous process of economic and political liberalization. But nor is it an illusory ideal. Experience in industrialized societies suggests that there is scope for constructing regimes which fulfil the twin desiderata of broad-based and sustainable development on the one hand, and a legitimate and inclusive democracy on the other. The political and institutional basis for such regimes lies in a new form of developmental state, one which can simultaneously carry forward a development project founded on growth and equality, and which rests on democratic political foundations. This is our conception of the democratic developmental state.

The core argument of this book revolves around the proposition that there are two critical ingredients in constructing successful democratic developmental states.[3] For democracy and development to be made compatible we argue that there is a need for an effective developmental state. This requires a particular mix of politics and institutions which can create, maintain, and deepen democratic structures and shape developmental outcomes in both productive and equitable ways. While political conditions are not easily amenable to manipulation, we argue that there is scope for conscious political intervention in the design of democratic institutions which shape the context for state-led development interventions and the broader policy environment. The scope for such intervention, by policy elites, social actors, and external agents, is heavily influenced by the political dynamics of new democracies, notably the ability of organized interests to influence decision-making and policy choice, the balance of domestic political forces, and their susceptibility to external economic and political influence. Our argument also rests on a broader conception of processes of democracy (more pervasive and participatory) and development (more redistributive and inclusive) which can be mutually reinforcing. In other words, greater mass participation and popular pressure, and increased political representation by women and other disadvantaged groups, can help to make democratic regimes more sensitive to issues of poverty, social welfare, and forms of discrimination based on gender, ethnicity, and the like and impel them to take appropriate remedial action through policy commitments.

We concur with Sklar (1996) that the developmental significance of democracies lies in the way in which particular democratic practices—as 'parts' or 'fragments' of democracy, rather than holistic democratic systems—help to cement the political and institutional foundations of democratic developmental states.[4] Certain democratic institutions have the potential for exerting considerable influence over development outcomes, while others do not have such a discernible

---

[3] For an elaboration of this argument see White (1995) and in this volume.

[4] Sklar (1996: 40), for example, lists the following factors: 'freedom of the press and the autonomy of professional organizations as well as judicial independence; guaranteed health services and welfare benefits . . . elements of industrial democracy as well as electoral democracy.'

or direct effect. Of particular significance in this respect are broad legislative and constitutional arrangements (federal versus unitary systems, presidentialism versus parliamentarism, etc.) on the one hand, and mechanisms designed to achieve more instrumental and narrowly defined developmental objectives on the other, such as local councils and public consultation mechanisms (corporatist devices, deliberation councils, etc.). Drawing on this approach, various chapters in the book (especially those by Goetz, Jenkins, Nattrass and Seekings, Robinson, and White) examine particular types of institutions at different levels of the political system from the vantage point of their developmental significance and the scope for conscious intervention by means of institutional crafting and design.

Implicit in this argument is the premiss that the precise form of the democratic developmental state will vary according to the way in which the developmental project is construed. If the developmental state is to be genuinely democratic, it should be representative of the views of a wide cross-section of its citizens and reflect their needs and aspirations. In most developing societies, where the majority of citizens are poor and disadvantaged in a variety of ways, they lack the power to make their priorities heard. Democratic developmental states should, by definition, cater to their poor citizens and produce policies which address their needs, rather than merely the exigencies of economic growth. Such a perspective is in marked contrast to earlier thinking about developmental states where strong states guided by a clear vision of development were invariably governed by authoritarian regimes which were repressive and unaccountable to the majority of their citizens, even if they laid particular stress (as, for example, in the Chinese case) on poverty reduction and meeting basic needs. It also differs from the perspective offered by Leftwich (1996), who argues that non-democratic systems may be preferable as a means of generating sustained economic development in the absence of a set of political conditions which can sustain a stable democratic system. Clearly political factors are fundamental to creating the conditions necessary for the creation of democratic developmental states, rooted in the basic contours of civil and political society, the nature of state institutions and elites, and the parameters set by the international environment (White in this volume, Leftwich 1996).

In an extension of this argument, the developmental potential of new democracies should be judged in terms of their ability to promote a form of economic growth and development that prioritizes the needs of poor and marginalized social groups. Contrary to the new orthodoxy, which holds that the creation of the democratic developmental state is synonymous with capitalist democracy, the notion of the democratic developmental state has affinities with the basic tenets of social democracy, in which equitable and sustained development outcomes are achievable through the creation of durable and inclusive political institutions. It is currently fashionable to regard the notion of 'social democracy' as defunct. We would contest this on both empirical and ethical grounds. In empirical terms, the 'death' of social democracy has been greatly exaggerated, usually for ideological reasons. Not only are the basic institutions and commitments of social democracy still largely intact in their historical heartland, Western Europe, but there are also substantial aspirations in other regions—Eastern Europe, Latin America, and East Asia—to replicate the achievements of social democracy. In ethical terms, a strong argument can be made that the well-being of the vast majority of the populations of developing societies can better be achieved under the aegis of social democracy which seeks to combine economic growth with social justice than under a cramped and etiolated notion of liberal democracy which tolerates widespread exploitation and allows inequalities to grow. It is our contention that, if a 'model' of democracy is needed to guide the political evolution of developing societies, it should be social rather than liberal democracy.

In the chapters that follow we explore various aspects of the democratic developmental state from a number of different angles, combining empirical studies of specific democratic institutions and their development significance with critical analysis of the concept of developmental democracy. This collection builds on earlier work on the nature of democratization in developing countries (Luckham and White 1996) which arrived at a cautious assessment of the extent to which new democracies can develop enduring institutional foundations and generate sustained developmental benefits.

In this volume we explore the development potential of new democratic states, as well as the performance of more established democracies, in the context of an interplay between political processes, social forces, and democratic institutions. In the first part we are principally concerned with conceptual and analytical issues. The opening chapter by Gordon White considers the feasibility of constructing a democratic developmental state in an era in which democratic political systems are commonplace, but face enormous developmental challenges which they have to overcome if they are to address the material needs and political expectations of their citizens. While there may be some room for manœuvre in designing political institutions for developmental ends, such crafting may only be possible under a political leadership that is committed to a broader vision of societal development rather than narrow, self-interested goals. White concludes that the goal of constructing a developmental democracy that can achieve dynamic and equitable development through an accountable and inclusive political process may only be attained in the context of specific configurations of institutions, political forces, and socio-economic structures which are characteristic of a relatively small number of developing countries.

Adrian Leftwich approaches the question of feasibility by exploring the developmental performance of established democratic states in the developing world. In view of the patent inability of many democratic states to generate sustained and equitable growth (among them Costa Rica, India, Jamaica, and Venezuela), he sets out to identify the conditions that enable democratic states to succeed developmentally. For Leftwich the key explanatory factor is the primary role of politics in shaping the character and capability of states, which is in turn a function of the democratization process and deeper socio-economic factors. Inherent in the process of constructing such a state is a contradiction between the tendency of formal democracies towards an incrementalist style of policy-making on the one hand, and a set of developmental goals that often require fundamental changes in policy direction, and the prevailing distribution of socio-economic and political power on the other. Through a comparative analysis of new and existing Third World democracies Leftwich persuasively argues that the prospects for the creation of democratic developmental states ultimately depend on the successful resolution of this contradictory dynamic.

Mick Moore addresses the possible tensions that arise between democracy and development by exploring the linkages between the various sources of income accruing to the state and political accountability. At the core of his argument is the proposition that a high level of financial dependence on sources of 'unearned' income—i.e. where the state places minimal effort on raising revenue via direct forms of taxation involving political interactions with domestic populations, as compared to foreign aid or various forms of economic rent—undermines the scope for effective democratic governance. To substantiate this line of reasoning Moore draws both on historical evidence on the fiscal foundations of representative government in Western Europe and on contemporary empirical evidence on sources of government income in developing states. An important conclusion he derives from this analysis is not that high levels of aid necessarily undermine democracy but that rebuilding local revenue systems with the support of aid donors may be key to constructing states that are both accountable to their citizens and developmentally effective.

The contributions in the second part of the book examine the interplay between social forces and political institutions (ranging from local government through to federal political arrangements) in shaping the developmental potential of new and established democracies in countries as varied as Bolivia, India, and South Africa. While none of the country cases examined here constitute democratic developmental states in any comprehensive sense, they do provide support for the argument developed in earlier chapters about the need to analyse democracy 'in parts', in this case through particular forms of democratic institutions and their developmental significance, mediated through political contestation and choice.

James Manor builds on the analysis developed by White in the introductory chapter by arguing that the simultaneous task of democratization and the construction of a new kind of developmental state rests on the attainment of some degree of balance between a series of political dichotomies—between order and conflict, between self-interested politics and institutionalization, between formal and informal politics, between 'top-down' and 'bottom-up' initiatives, between continuity and innovation, and between confidentiality and transparency. According to Manor successful democratic developmental states are founded on the existence of healthy partnerships between state and society, and the recognition that reform initiatives are best pursued through incremental policy change in order to avoid undermining the delicate balance between efforts to establish democracy and to build effective developmental states.

A number of contemporary efforts to foster partnerships between states and their citizens as a cornerstone for effective democratic governance are founded on increased levels of participation on the part of ordinary citizens in the formulation and implementation of public policy. Mark Robinson surveys the means by which participation has been institutionalized through reforms in local government to provide poor and marginalized people with greater influence over development decisions. Drawing on comparative evidence from Bolivia and India he finds that official attempts to design institutions to promote participation in policy deliberation are of limited efficacy in the absence of a political agency which can both shape the scope and intensity of political participation and influence policy outcomes to the benefit of the poor majority of citizens.

Rob Jenkins focuses more specifically on the ways in which federal institutions affect the political processes that shape developmental outcomes, in particular efficiency and equity outcomes in the context of market reforms in India. While federalism has been economically suboptimal in some respects, Jenkins argues that the political dynamics emanating from the organization of state power at multiple levels of the political system help overcome the opposition of powerful interests to economic reform, thereby promoting efficiency objectives. Rather than seeking to evaluate the impact of federalism (as one particular institutional variant of democracy) on economic performance, he is concerned to demonstrate how federalism combines with economic reform to produce a form of political contestation that influences developmental performance in terms of both equity and efficiency outcomes.

In their contribution Nicoli Nattrass and Jeremy Seekings investigate the linkages between democratic political institutions and developmental outcomes in the context of post-apartheid South Africa. In particular they examine four institutional challenges facing the new South African state in its attempt to promote development —government policy co-ordination, parliamentary versus corporatist modes of representation, fiscal federalism, and problems of service delivery. As with previous chapters their principal concern is with the problems encountered by democratic political institutions in seeking to reconcile growth and equity objectives. From their analysis of the South African situation Nattrass and Seekings conclude that to be effective, a democratic developmental state has to combine meaningful participation in development through local democratic institutions with strong central direction.

The final part of the book is concerned with the process of democratic deepening, in the sense of moving beyond representative, procedural forms of democracy towards more inclusive forms which are geared towards the attainment of developmental objectives that are meaningful to traditionally disenfranchised communities, especially women and the rural poor. Anne Marie Goetz tackles this issue through a comparative analysis of the developmental consequences of women's political participation in Uganda and South Africa. While political liberalization has enhanced women's participation in politics in some democratizing states, this does not necessarily translate into increased representation of their interests in development policy-making. To address this issue Goetz examines three processes of political and institutional change in South Africa and Uganda—ways in which the interests of women are expressed through women's associations, changes in electoral rules designed to promote increased participation by women, and changes in state bureaucracies to accommodate women's interests. She finds that while formal political liberties and liberal constitutionalism have created the institutional conditions through which the representation of women's political interests can be enhanced, socially entrenched gender inequalities can only be redressed effectively by a state committed to policies aimed at combating these, supported by feminist social movements and politicians who have acquired a legitimate mandate to pursue a reformist agenda.

Susanna Davies examines the consequences of democratization in sub-Saharan Africa from the perspective of the developmental needs of the rural poor. She argues that the process of democratization has been limited on two counts: its failure to empower the poor rural majority, and its association with a form of development that emphasizes growth to the neglect of poverty and vulnerability. Hence the central concern in her chapter is the inappropriateness of democratization to the livelihoods of the rural poor.

To redress this problem Davies calls for a broader conceptualization of democracy to accommodate the notion of 'livelihood democracy', both through the inclusion of informal rural political systems as a means of strengthening the representation of poor people's interests, and through strategies by means of which procedures for determining livelihood decisions which are already inclusive and participatory can be recognized and accommodated.

The final chapter of the book, by Robin Luckham, compares and contrasts the experiences of two states that consciously sought to pursue a very different agenda from the now dominant orthodoxy of the twin merits of liberal democracy and capitalist development. Nicaragua and Tanzania provide us with two examples of regimes that were committed to redistributive economic policies and the construction of political institutions that provided alternatives to traditional representative forms, in the interests of the poor majority of their citizens. While Luckham's review of these popular democratic experiments does not give grounds for optimism on either count, it does highlight the potential conflicts that can arise between popular participation and the formal rules and procedures through which participation is organized, and the problems of harmonizing participatory development with the growth imperatives of a modern developmental state. Arguably, part of the reason for the failure of these experiments lay not in an excess of political participation, but their failure to achieve a workable balance between these competing priorities. The result was the imposition of a centralized model of development from above through political structures which dominated rather than accommodated grass-roots mobilization and popular participation.

Clearly there are a number of common themes which flow through the various chapters of the book. First, there are a number of considerations bound up with the nature and form of the democratic developmental state: the concern with the limitations of formal democracy and the development benefits that accrue from more inclusive forms; the recognition that development has to be conceived in broader terms than economic growth alone; and that participatory forms of democracy and broad-based development can be mutually reinforcing under the right political and institutional circumstances. Secondly, the question of balance is a common refrain: between developmental objectives and the pace of democratic reform; between incremental policy reform and political stability; and between centralized and localized forms of democracy and developmental strategy. Thirdly, our focus on the scope for institutional crafting mediated through conscious political intervention highlights the political and institutional dynamics that lie at the heart of the construction of states that are both democratic and developmentally successful.

REFERENCES

Evans, P. (1996), *Embedded Autonomy*, Princeton: Princeton University Press.

Gills, B., Rocamora, J., and Wilson, R. (eds.) (1993), *Low Intensity Democracy: Political Power in the New World Order*, London: Pluto Press.

Healey, J., and Robinson, M. (1992), *Governance, Democracy and Economic Policy: Sub-Saharan Africa in Comparative Perspective*, London: Overseas Development Institute.

Huntington, S. P. (1991), *The Third Wave: Democratization in the Late Twentieth Century*, London: University of Oklahoma Press.

Johnston, M. (1998), 'Fighting Systemic Corruption: Social Foundations for Institutional Reform', *European Journal of Development Research*, 10/1.

Leftwich, A. (1996), 'On the Primacy of Politics in Development', in A. Leftwich (ed.), *Democracy and Development: Theory and Practice*, Cambridge: Polity Press.

Luckham, R., and White, G. (eds.) (1996), *Democratisation in the South: The Jagged Wave*, Manchester: Manchester University Press.

Moore, M. P. (1996), 'Is Democracy Rooted in Material Prosperity?', in Luckham and White (1996).

Pateman, C. (1970), *Participation and Democratic Theory*, Cambridge: Cambridge University Press.

Sirowy, L., and Inkeles, A. (1990), 'Effect of Democracy on Economic Growth and Inequality: A Review', *Studies in Comparative International Development*, 25/1: 126–57.

Sklar, R. L. (1996), 'Towards a Theory of Developmental Democracy', in A. Leftwich (ed.), *Democracy and Development: Theory and Practice*, Cambridge: Polity Press.

Sørenson, G. (1993), *Democracy, Dictatorship and Development: Economic Development in Selected Regions of the Third World*, Basingstoke: Macmillan.

Wade, R. (1990), *Governing the Market: Economic Theory and the Role of Government in East Asian Industrialization*, Princeton: Princeton University Press.

White, G. (ed.) (1988), *Developmental States in East Asia*, Basingstoke: Macmillan.

—— (1995), 'Towards a Democratic Developmental State', *IDS Bulletin*, 26/2: 27–36.

World Bank (1990), *World Development Report 1990: Poverty*, Oxford: Oxford University Press.

Zakaria, F. (1997), 'The Rise of Illiberal Democracy', *Foreign Affairs*, 76/6: 22–43.

PART I

The Democratic Developmental State

Constructing a Democratic
Developmental State

GORDON WHITE

1. Introduction

If the 1980s saw the rise of a new orthodoxy about the developmental role of states in Third World societies, the early 1990s saw the rise of a new orthodoxy about the developmental role of political regimes. Buttressed by neo-classical economic theory, the former criticized the developmental states of the post-colonial era for excessive economic intervention, advocating a reduction in their role and a freeing up of markets and private enterprise along neo-liberal lines. The latter extended this to a critique of political dirigisme, emphasizing the economic as well as political costs of authoritarian regimes and advocating a transition to democracy along conventional liberal lines. The two critiques combined to advance the thesis that socio-economic development can best be promoted through a 'market-friendly' state presiding over a capitalist economy operating within the political 'shell' of a liberal democratic polity. The combination of democracy and markets became the core element of a comprehensive strategic vision of developmental success, equally valid for all types of societies whether they be poor, emergent, transitional, or industrialized.

The economic and political components of this vision are logically interconnected: markets and private enterprise provide the basis for political pluralism, and the institutionalized limits which the liberal polity imposes on the concentration of political power serve to curb any tendency towards economic dirigisme. The parameters of 'sound' developmental action are thus transformed and narrowed: in economic terms, the interventionist developmental state common to many Third World countries in the 1960s and 1970s became an anachronism to be replaced by a state whose functions are primarily concerned with providing a regulatory framework for the operation of efficient markets. In political terms, regime options are reduced to a model of liberal democracy defined primarily in conventional procedural terms. In this approach, systemic alternatives, political or economic, are not only inadvisable but also unfeasible, not the least because liberal politics and economics at the national level are embedded within, and reinforced by, a global system in which markets increasingly reign supreme and the political atmosphere favours the extension and perpetuation of democratic regimes.

In the triumphalist political atmosphere of the years immediately following the defeat of communism, this vision of the relationship between politics and economics became a model of developmental correctness, presented in overly optimistic ideological terms and rooted in largely unexamined stereotypes of both 'markets' and 'democracy'. It structured the perceptions of those involved in the international business of 'development', particularly those in the governments of the industrialized countries and international agencies who are involved in guiding developing societies along lines which they deem politically and economically acceptable. However, it was also widely shared by politicians and citizens in countries which were emerging from long periods of economic stagnation and political repression, notably in Eastern Europe and the former Soviet Union, sub-Saharan Africa, and Latin America.

But as the practical implications of the new model became increasingly apparent during the 1990s, sobriety set in. Faith in market solutions was dented by the disastrous socio-economic consequences of liberalization in many of the post-communist transitional countries and the uneven impact of structural adjustment programmes in sub-Saharan Africa. It was also obvious that programmes of marketization which were not accompanied by a maintenance or extension of state capacities were likely to run into the sand. Democratization, where it has survived with any substance, has often been accompanied by spreading corruption, a decline in public order, and an erosion of the administrative capacity and authority of the state. The nagging memory of successful industrialization through statist methods under authoritarian regimes in East Asia refused to go away and was given new impetus by the equally impressive success of other authoritarian or semi-authoritarian regimes in the region, such as China, Vietnam, Malaysia, and Indonesia. More fundamentally, a growing awareness of the onset of the processes labelled 'globalization' led to even deeper worries about the viability of market economics and democratic politics. The increasing velocity and volatility of international financial flows brought the danger of macro-economic unpredictability and crisis, witnessed first in Mexico in 1994 then in Thailand, Indonesia, Malaysia, and Hong Kong in 1997, and the dynamics of unregulated international markets threatened to intensify inequalities between countries and create new patterns of insecurity and exclusion within countries. The processes of globalization also threaten to undermine the viability of political systems of any kind—democratic or otherwise—through the challenge they pose to the sovereignty of nation-states and the autonomy of governments.[1]

These trends have led to a widespread rethinking of the markets-plus-democracy model of societal progress: earlier emphasis on re-stricting and reducing the socio-economic role of states has yielded to a recognition that effective states—democratic or not—are essential underpinnings for socio-economic progress organized along market lines,[2] and growing scepticism that a political regime organized along liberal democratic lines, *tout court*, can tackle the massive problems facing many poor and transitional societies. The arch-triumphalist of the early post-Cold War era, Francis Fukuyama (1996), emphasized the need for 'trust' as a key resource needed to restrain the atomizing effects of competitive markets and provide the moral cement for a civilized social order; and there has been a broader realization of the crucial significance of 'social capital' embedded in a 'vibrant civil society' for similar reasons.[3] A prominent figure in the effort to undermine state socialism, financier George Soros (1997), has warned that free markets threaten the basis of open, democratic societies and must be restrained through notions of common interests and sophisticated regulatory systems.

This chapter seeks to make a contribution to this process of intellectual revision by investigating the feasibility of a *democratic developmental state* in an era in which democratic political systems are far more numerous than ever before, but in which newly democratic regimes face formidable developmental tasks which require coherent and strategic action to tackle them. The analysis starts out from certain basic assumptions about both democracy and development. First let us define our terms. This analysis accepts the currently conventional definition of *democracy* in terms of a set of institutional procedures to guarantee basic civil and political rights and allow political competition between political forces, usually organized through

[1] For discussion of the relationship between globalization and democracy, for example, see Held (1991) and Falk (1993).

[2] The World Bank, for example, expanded its earlier narrow conception of the developmental role of the state in its *World Development Report 1997* (World Bank 1997).

[3] The *locus classicus* for the idea of 'social capital' is Putnam (1993); there is a copious literature on 'civil society' and I have tried to make sense of the bewildering array of uses to which the term has been put in White (1994).

parties.[4] Unlike an earlier era, characterized by 'developmental democracies' such as the one-party regimes in Tanzania and Zambia or
'socialist democracies' in the former Soviet bloc, this is the dominant
form of democracy today and is likely to remain so. Our definition of
development reflects the fact that the tidal wave of democratization
over the past decade or more has brought liberal democratic institutions to numerous countries which, to varying degrees, have still to
make a decisive economic transition of the kind experienced by their
industrialized predecessors and their newly industrialized erstwhile
counterparts, notably in East and South-east Asia.[5] For these societies,
development includes a process of economic change involving the
construction of more complex and productive economies capable of
generating higher material standards of living. This requires extensive
involvement—both direct and regulatory—on the part of states. It is
also widely recognized that economic growth should be complemented
to the extent feasible by the pursuit of certain social objectives: the
alleviation of absolute and relative poverty; the correction of glaring
inequalities of social condition (between genders, classes, regions, and
ethnic groups); provision for personal safety and security; and the
tackling of looming threats such as environmental degradation. These
are predominantly societal or public goods which require the decisive
involvement of states. Overall, to the extent that democratic polities
are instrumental in organizing socio-economic progress along these lines,
they can be described as developmentally successful; to a considerable
extent, their success depends on the existence and efficacy of a democratic developmental state.

This chapter sets out to map out some of the main issues surrounding
the longer-term compatibility of democracy and socio-economic development. We are preoccupied with the potential for choice and agency
in the creation of a democratic developmental state; in other words,
going beyond a mere theoretical analysis of compatibility issues to
identify areas of policy and action in which there is potential room for
manœuvre for the 'design' of democratic and developmental institutions which can enhance the synergy between them. The underlying

---

[4] Huntington (1991: 7) uses the procedural notion when he argues that a polity is
democratic 'to the extent that its most powerful collective decision makers are selected
through fair, honest, and periodic elections in which candidates freely compete for votes
and in which virtually all the adult population is eligible to vote'. Dahl (1971: 3) extends
the range of requirements to eight, including freedom of association and expression,
eligibility for public office, alternative sources of information, and institutions for making governments accountable to voters' wishes.

[5] Following normal area demarcations, I am using 'East Asia' to denote the societies
of Japan, Korea, Taiwan, Hong Kong, and China and 'South-east Asia' to denote the
mainland societies of Burma through Singapore and the island nations of Indonesia,
Philippines, and Papua New Guinea.

model of synergistic progress, admittedly an optimistic one, is of a 'virtuous spiral' between socio-economic development on the one hand and political development on the other. By 'political development' here we mean both the construction of efficient and accountable public institutions and the spread of real as opposed to titular democratic citizenship through an increasingly pervasive process of social empowerment. Underlying our distinction between democracy and (socio-economic) development, therefore, lies a broader notion of 'development' which includes political as well as socio-economic dimensions.

The underlying argument is that all is not determined—by globalization or whatever—and choices can be made to make this positive dynamic more likely and alternative, more pessimistic, scenarios of a democratic future less likely. These latter may embody economic progress with political stagnation, mutually reinforcing political and economic stagnation, or a downward 'vicious spiral' of political instability and economic decline. This chapter includes the following: first, a critical assessment of different perspectives on the relationship between democracy and socio-economic development; second, an outline of a normative and positive approach to understanding the nature and feasibility of a democratic developmental state; third, an identification of areas of potential choice in 'designing' a democratic developmental state; and, fourth, a concluding section which assesses the feasibility of the 'virtuous spiral' as opposed to other, more depressing scenarios.

2. Democracy and Development: Some Variant Views

While it is still common to find Western politicians and pundits talking confidently about the hypothetically positive socio-economic consequences of democratization, there is by no means a consensus on the issue among development professionals and analysts. First, there is an *optimistic view*, common until recently among aid circles (particularly in Western national aid agencies and international institutions), that liberal democracy is a powerful stimulus to societal progress, basically because it provides a more conducive institutional environment for market-led economic development and because it carries the potential for more efficient, open, and accountable government. Though this view is most commonly found among liberals and neoliberals, it is also shared, albeit in a different form and for different reasons, by people across a much wider political spectrum, including democratic socialists and advocates of 'participatory development' who see democratization as opening spaces for socio-economically positive forms of popular mobilization.

Particularly in societies with recent histories of autocratic, incompetent, or corrupt authoritarian regimes, this view has obvious attractions. As a general proposition, however, the case is somewhat shaky. First, while it may be true that there is a long-term statistical correlation between democracy and prosperity, the statistical evidence about their causal relationships in the short and medium terms is ambiguous (Moore 1996). Particularly in journalistic accounts, the empirical evidence used to support the case is often flimsy and unconvincing; indeed there has been a tendency to use empirical data like the proverbial drunk uses the lamp-post—for support rather than illumination.[6] Second, even if it were true, as *The Economist* claims,[7] that 'far from inhibiting growth, democracy promotes it', there is still the question of what kind of growth and what sort of implications it has for a broader conception of development. The maintenance of minimal democratic institutional forms is compatible with a pattern of elite-dominated growth which is socially unequalizing and exclusionary and politically disempowering. It is this form of growth which led an earlier generation of development theorists, such as Dudley Seers, Gunnar Myrdal, and Hans Singer, to emphasize the need for a distributional perspective on economic growth. It also lies behind the concerns of those who talk of the dangers of 'low-intensity democracy' in elite-dominated societies in Latin America and East Asia.[8] Third, there is a tendency to praise the potential benefits of an idealized conception of a democratic polity rather than base analysis on the ways in which democracies actually do operate in poor societies—they are often far from the ideal type and characterized by huge disparities in political access and widespread clientelism and corruption (for vivid evidence on this, see O'Donnell 1993 on Latin America and Nicro 1993 on Thailand).

Second, there is a *pessimistic view* which regards democracy as a valuable long-term goal but a potential impediment to the earlier stages of socio-economic development. In other words, democracy is a luxury which poor societies can ill afford. This view is more popular among Third World officials who would agree with Singapore's Lee Kuan Yew when he states that 'I believe that what a country needs to develop is

[6] For example, the reader is invited to see whether he or she is convinced by the evidence for the putative ability of democratic regimes to carry out sweeping programmes of economic reforms reported in the article in *The Economist* cited in n. 7, or the evidence adduced to support the judgement that 'democratization promotes economic development' by Shin (1994 156–7).

[7] 'Democracy and Growth: Why Voting is Good for you', *The Economist*, 27 Aug. 1994: 17–19.

[8] For this literature, see the comparative analysis by Gills et al. (1993) and the analysis of South Korea by Kong (1995).

discipline more than democracy. The exuberance of democracy leads to indiscipline and disorderly conduct which are inimical to development.'[9] The view receives more detached support from social scientists: for example, Leftwich (1993: 13) argues that 'if the primary developmental objective is the defeat of poverty and misery, then liberal or pluralist democracy may also not be what many Third World or Eastern European countries need or can sustain in their present conditions'. This pessimism is also shared to some extent by supporters of democracy who do not expect much from procedural democracy at the national level and therefore concentrate on a 'bottom-up' microstrategy based on the democratizing and developmental potential of grass-roots and community organizations. For example, Landell-Mills (1992: 10) argues that liberal democracy will not necessarily lead to economic growth, or alleviation of poverty, or protection of the weak, or efficient government. In his view, a strong civil society must be developed to achieve more accountable government; but even then, it is 'perhaps not wise government'.

Pessimists tend to list a number of seemingly insuperable post-transitional obstacles to effective democratic governance which Huntington (1991: 209–10) conveniently groups into two categories, contextual and systemic. The former stem from the nature of the particular society and the developmental problems it faces; the latter from the characteristic ways in which liberal democratic polities operate. Contextual problems tend to smother the political system with excessive demands resulting from a 'tide of rising expectations' and undermine its capacity to process these demands. Systemic problems derive from the institutionalized uncertainty, instability, short-termism, and conflict inherent in democratic politics.[10] Both these sets of problems can lead to political fluctuation, paralysis, or disorder which weaken the capacity of democratic governments to shoulder the developmental burden, whether this is defined in narrower regulative or broader interventionist and redistributive terms. By contrast, the experience of the 'rational authoritarianism' of the 'four tigers' of East Asia is cited as evidence of a developmentally desirable and politically appropriate kind of strategic alternative.

However, even four swallows do not make a spring and the dismal deficiencies of most forms of authoritarianism outside East Asia weaken any general case for authoritarianism *per se* as a political recipe for socio-economic success. Authoritarian polities have their own

[9] This is cited in *The Economist*, 27 Aug. 1994: 17.

[10] For instance, Huntington (1991: 210) lists problems which 'tend to be peculiarly characteristic of democratic systems: stalemate, the inability to reach decisions, susceptibility to demagoguery, domination by vested economic interests'.

systemic problems as developmental agents, such as rigidity, corruption, and rent-seeking, rooted in an excessive concentration of political and economic power, in addition to the human costs they impose through repression or denial of civil rights. Indeed, in many countries the impetus towards democratization has been fuelled by the demonstrated developmental failure of authoritarian regimes. In this context, the pragmatic case for 'trying out' the democratic alternative is compelling and is apparently widely accepted among broad sections of the affected populations. Perhaps the most we can grant to the 'rational authoritarian' argument is that, where a non-liberal democratic regime demonstrates a clear capacity to govern effectively and bring about real improvements in the lives of its citizens and is not engaged in gross violations of their civil rights and personal security, it should not be pushed willy-nilly into a wholesale and immediate adoption of a liberal-democratic polity.

A third view on the relationship between democracy and socio-economic development is what one might call the *'don't expect anything'* school. Huntington, for example, argues that the sustainability of a stable democracy depends on 'disillusionment and lowered expectations' on the part of the general population. Furthermore, 'Democracies become consolidated when people learn that democracy is a solution to the problem of tyranny, but not necessarily to anything else' (1991: 263). This kind of view is buttressed by the argument that democratic regimes are not legitimized by their performance but by their procedures,[11] whereas it is one of the inherent weaknesses of authoritarian regimes that they have to derive their legitimacy from their performance and are thus vulnerable to economic downturns. Thus, for example, inflation over 20 per cent p.a. might shake the foundations of the entire Communist regime in China, whereas in a democratic context this might only threaten the government of the day, but not the regime itself.[12]

This kind of argument might make some sense in countries which have already achieved a relatively high level of economic development and still retain a growth momentum. But it is not compelling in the context of countries faced by a combination of extreme poverty and massive inequalities on the one hand and accelerating popular expectations fuelled by the international demonstration effect on the other. As Huntington himself (1991: 258) points out, new democracies face a catch-22 situation because 'lacking legitimacy, they cannot become effective; lacking effectiveness, they cannot develop legitimacy'.

[11] For example, Linz and Stepan (1989) make this argument in the South American context.

[12] This comparison does not deny that democratic regimes may be threatened by economic failure, as was the case in Latin America in the 1960s and 1970s.

A good deal of the political impetus behind democratic transition in a country such as Zambia, for example, was the result of popular disillusionment with the growth performance of the previous regime, not merely its political character (White 1996). In such circumstances, it is probably unrealistic to assume that populations will lower their expectations of the political system and be content with the specific gains, important though they may be, which derive from democratic guarantees and rights. We should add, moreover, that the argument that the legitimacy of democratic regimes rests on their procedures rather than their performance applies primarily to *consolidated* democracies—indeed it is one of the hallmarks of democratic maturity. As Diamond (1992a: 35) points out, 'democracy becomes truly stable only when people come to value it widely not solely for its economic and social performance but intrinsically for its political attributes'. As such, the argument has limited relevance to countries where democracies are still struggling to consolidate themselves in highly inimical socio-economic contexts.

A fourth position on the relationship between democracy and development is that *the nature of the political regime is not the central issue*; rather it is good governance and state capacity, qualities which can be developed under different types of regime. In the context of sub-Saharan Africa, for example, Jeffries argues that 'the current moves towards multiparty democracy are, relatively speaking, an irrelevance' (1993: 30) and the first priority should not be regime change but 'improving the capacity, commitment and quality of government administration, of developing an effective developmental state' (ibid.: 28) He cites the regimes of Rawlings in Ghana and Museveni in Uganda as examples of 'relatively non-corrupt, economically responsible and effectively reforming authoritarian regimes' and questions whether they should have been put under pressure to convert to multi-party democracies. In essence, the argument here is for the primacy of constructing an effective developmental state, whether by authoritarian or democratic means.

This argument is open to question on several counts. Cases of authoritarian regimes capable of 'good governance' are relatively few. But even in their cases, the issue of political regime is not irrelevant. 'Rational' authoritarian regimes have costs in terms of their autocratic behaviour, denial of civil rights, and repression of dissent. Moreover, one can argue that it is exactly this kind of politically and administratively successful regime that is most ripe and ready for democratization, even if we accept Jeffries's point that the transition should not be brought about through a pressured and precipitate transition to multi-partyism. Casting our net more widely, however, most

authoritarian regimes in Africa and elsewhere may have laid claim to
the title of being 'developmental states', but have been singularly unsuccessful in establishing a capacity for good governance and socio-
economic improvement. In such cases, a change in political regime may
be highly relevant as an alternative way of achieving an 'effective developmental state'. Moreover, it is important to listen to our optimists who
argue that certain central features of liberal democracies—selection
of political leaders through popular elections, open and unfettered competition for political office, and the pressures exerted by a free press
and public opinion—are essential mechanisms for creating a state which
is responsive, efficient, and accountable. In situations where authoritarian regimes have failed (as in much of sub-Saharan Africa) or been
superseded (as in much of East Asia and Latin America), the question of the relationship between democracy and development should be
put in more positive terms: to what extent and in what ways can the
parallel priorities of a democratic political system and an effective developmental state be achieved *in tandem?*

To a considerable extent, these debates about the comparative
developmental virtues of democracy and its alternatives have been over-
taken by events. First, in the foreseeable future at least, a combination of domestic and international pressures is likely to maintain many
of the new democratic regimes in at least nominal operation. This
makes arguments about the hypothetical developmental advantages
of authoritarianism versus democracy irrelevant in those societies
where an authoritarian alternative is not on the cards. The authoritarian alternatives of an earlier era—whether of the socialist, Latin
American, or East Asian varieties—have collapsed or been superseded
and international political pressures are, currently at least, hostile to
their resurrection. It is much more likely for continuing or resurgent
authoritarianism to be combined with some limited elements of democracy, as in the cases of Indonesia, Singapore, or Peru. Second, there
is now a much wider acceptance of the inherent virtues of democracy,
even in its limited procedural form. By contrast, even the most 'rational' forms of authoritarianism have not been valued for themselves,
but regarded as undesirable means towards desirable developmental
ends which could be dispensed with when their unpleasant, but historically essential, task was completed. In this light, any arguments
couched merely in terms of the relative virtues of authoritarianism
versus democracy as alternative *means* for achieving development are
miscast. In ideological terms, the last decade has brought a widening
consensus about the intrinsic values of liberal democracy, extending
to include parts of the political spectrum which were previously hostile or sceptical. The idea has gained much greater currency among

the radical left, for example, partly because the Leninist alternative has collapsed and partly because it never delivered much in the way of democracy in any case. Democratic socialists of course seek to extend the notion of democracy outside the polity into the society and economy, but they are now much more willing to recognize the inherent virtues of the standard model of liberal democracy.[13] In political terms, the idea of democracy has also gained ground because it has greater popular appeal among ordinary citizens as a means of protecting civil liberties and political rights.

Third, comparison between systemic alternatives such as 'democracy' and 'authoritarianism' obscures the ambiguities and diversity of real-world political regimes. Just as elements of democratic freedom have existed in many authoritarian regimes, so elements of authoritarianism persist in formally democratic regimes and, as in the case of regimes such as those of Singapore and Malaysia, are rationalized as a distinctive form of democracy consonant with 'Asian values'.[14] This point is made most forcefully by those who have a 'bits and pieces' view of democracy, notably Richard Sklar who argues that comparative analyses of political systems based on whole-system categories are inadequate because they ignore some of the most fundamental relationships of power in society and obscure the fact that democracy is 'being forged in a multitude of political workshops throughout the world, but in pieces and parts, not in its entirety' (1996: 36; cf. Luckham in this volume). The differences between democracy and authoritarianism are therefore best seen as points on a political continuum, rather than as decisively different systems. Moreover, as we shall see below, there are important institutional differences even among well-established and well-functioning liberal democratic systems and these variations may well influence, for good or ill, the capacity of democratic governments to tackle the challenges of socio-economic development in poor societies.

3. Constructing a Democratic Developmental State: Approaching the Issue

Our investigation into the compatibility between democracy and development should take us beyond most current analytical treatments

---

[13] For an early 'socialist-revisionist' discussion of these issues in the African context, see Sandbrook (1988).

[14] For a comparative analysis of the 'semi-democracies' of Singapore, Malaysia, and Thailand, see Case (1993, 1996).

of the relationship. Until very recently, these have mostly focused either on relatively short-term processes—such as the nature of transitions to democracy or the compatibility between democratic politics and programmes of structural adjustment and economic reform. Longer-term analyses have in turn tended to focus on the conditions for consolidating democratic politics in socially and economically unpropitious circumstances.[15] Our analysis seeks to go further by discussing longer-term issues concerning the relationship between democracy and development.

First, while there is substantial disagreement about the extent to which democracy fosters socio-economic growth in the short and medium term, in spite of much statistical effort, there is wide consensus on the idea that the growth of democratic procedures and values depends over the long term on progress in social and economic development. For nascent democratic regimes in poor countries, therefore, long-term democratization in any substantive sense depends heavily on their capacity to preside over a sustained process of socio-economic improvement. Their task is similar to that of the Soviet leaders in the 1920s who talked about the need to establish 'the preconditions for socialism' along with 'the construction of socialism' itself.[16]

Second, democratic citizenship is undermined if there is too great a contradiction between the egalitarian norms of a democratic polity and the inequalities of individuals and groups in civil society. Glaring inequalities undermine democracy in two basic ways: first, by fuelling social discontent and political instability and, second, through the persistence of poverty, by excluding more or less extensive sections of the population from access to the political process and its fruits. This suggests the need for some form of equitable economic development as opposed to economic growth as such, which might be and in fact often is highly inegalitarian and therefore hostile to substantive as opposed to formal citizenship.[17]

Third, unlike an earlier era of 'guided development' in which authoritarian elites of various kinds defined the nature of development trajectories and, where successful at least, heavily influenced the choice of which developmental goods to deliver, to whom, and on what

[15] There are some notable exceptions where longer-term issues of the compatibility of democracy and development have been discussed on a broad canvas: for one useful analysis, see Haggard and Kaufman (1994).

[16] The importance of a long-term relationship between developmental efficacy and democratic consolidation has been stressed by one of the classic writers in the field, Seymour Martin Lipset (1994).

[17] Burnell (1995) argues this case strongly in the context of Zambia, citing Huntington (1991) and Diamond (1992b) in support.

terms, democratization carries the potential for a political reversal whereby a much wider proportion of the population can press its demands on the polity and require satisfaction. This creates a dynamic of demand to which democratic politicians may be pressured to respond, even though their responses may take the form of various forms of 'populism' or 'welfarism' which conflict with an economic logic of 'sound' economic growth. Managing the tensions between the political and economic logic of development thus poses a major challenge to democratic regimes.

It is our thesis that the capacity of democratic regimes to secure sustained and equitable socio-economic development depends heavily on the extent to which they can construct effective developmental states. As Przeworski and his colleagues (1995: 12) argue in their study of the prospects for 'sustainable democracy' in Eastern Europe and South America: 'If democracy is to be sustained, the state must guarantee territorial integrity and physical security, it must maintain the conditions necessary for an effective exercise of citizenship, it must mobilise public savings, coordinate resource allocation, and correct income distribution.' Eatwell and his colleagues, in their study on the politico-economic transformation of Central and Eastern Europe, make a similar argument (1995: 2): '[There is a] need to re-establish public responsibility, i.e. to build the institutions of a democratic developmental state . . . [If] there is to be an effective transition to modern capitalist economies competitive with the economies of OECD and the rest of the world, the developmental state must contribute to the provision of the resources needed for the high quality investment, human and material, that transformation requires.'

Any democratic developmental state will need sufficient political authority and administrative capacity to maintain public order by managing the social and political conflicts arising from structural divisions in society and from the tensions inherent in a successful growth process. It will also need to assume three basic socio-economic functions: regulative, infrastructural, and redistributive. By regulative functions, we refer to the role of the state not only in ongoing macroeconomic management, but also in constructing the institutional framework necessary for the functioning of complex market economies. By infrastructural functions we refer to the process of creating both physical and social infrastructure, the latter pursued through growth-enhancing social policy and welfare provision. By redistributive functions we refer to the need to tackle absolute poverty and ameliorate morally repugnant and social destructive forms of social inequality based on factors such as class, gender, and ethnicity.

There has been a good deal of analysis of what constitutes the basic elements of a successful 'developmental state', in particular drawing on the experience of East Asia.[18] This literature has emphasized the key importance of both *autonomy*—of state institutions and political elites—which allows them to define and implement strategic developmental imperatives, and of specific forms of social *embeddedness* whereby states are part of broader alliances with key social groups which are themselves a stimulus to socio-economic change. While these elements could be identified in the former authoritarian regimes of East Asia, however, to what extent are they compatible with the political and institutional framework of democracy? In the authoritarian cases, to varying degrees between countries and over time within a country, the autonomy of the ruling elite is imposed by that elite, which also sets the terms of 'embeddedness' with other social groups. Since a democratic polity is more porous and malleable to social pressures, state autonomy in this sense would be more difficult to maintain.[19]

However, despite the fact that the authority of the democratic state is rooted in principles of consent and accountability, the developmental imperative would seem to require a substantial degree of *consensual autonomy*, in two senses: first, the capacity of institutionally accountable political elites to define and implement programmes of strategic socio-economic improvement and, second, the autonomy of administrative agencies charged with carrying out these programmes in accordance with institutionalized procedures and subject to political supervision. As Jeffries (1993: 21) points out, 'In the absence of the establishment of relatively autonomous government institutions committed to a national "public interest", democratic politics is likely to exacerbate rather than reduce problems of corruption, wastefulness and short-sighted economic policy formulation.' Autonomous state capacity itself depends heavily on the presence of substantial *institutional coherence* in the constitutional arrangements for the distribution and use of political power, in the relations between different sections of the bureaucratic apparatus, and in the nature of party systems in political society. It is also rooted in what might be called *authoritative penetration* whereby state institutions are able to extend their regulative and extractive capacities on a consensual basis (for example,

---

[18] While this analysis draws on the voluminous literature on developmental states which has emerged since the mid-1980s, it pays particular attention to the work of Peter Evans (1996).

[19] As often remarked, however, some degree of autonomy can be created by technocratic insulation, especially in poor societies where the media are weakly developed and the organizational power of interest groups is not well established.

by elaborating sophisticated and enforceable systems of economic regulation and expanding the base of tax revenue). Finally, for equitable development to be feasible, democratic regimes would need to be characterized by *inclusive embeddedness*, implying that the social basis and range of accountability of democratic politicians goes beyond a narrow band of elites to embrace broader sections of society.

This distinctive political and institutional model of a democratic developmental state should be seen as merely one alternative among a wide range of political economies of democracy with differing levels of state autonomy, institutional coherence, and authoritative penetration and varying ranges of accountability and embeddedness. These different systemic outcomes are shaped by an interplay of certain central structural and institutional features which are configured distinctively in each society. The key features are as follows:

- *socio-economic system*: the general level of socio-economic development of a given society and the nature of its social structure in terms of class, gender, ethnicity, culture, and religion;
- *civil society*: the associational structure of society in terms of the nature and extent of organized socio-political activity on the part of citizens both as individuals and as members of groups;
- *political society*: the character of the institutions created as channels of political participation, particularly the structure and social base of party systems;
- *state institutions*: the institutional structure of the state in terms of the distribution of political and administrative authority between segments and levels, and the rules governing access by citizens and the exercise of authority by officials;
- *international environment*: the nature of external political and economic pressures which impinge upon a society in general and its political life in particular.

To what extent does this constellation of factors allow the exercise of choice in the design of political institutions in the direction of a democratic developmental state? If we focus on politics within individual national states, political actors are constrained by deeply rooted structural features of their country's socio-economic system and by the impact of an international environment largely beyond their control. But institutions, both political and social, can make a crucial difference and there are areas of institutional design which, to varying degrees, are subject to political contestation and choice and which may well make a difference in influencing the emergence of a democratic developmental state. It is to this issue that we turn in the next section.

4. Developmental Democracy by Design?
Potential Arenas of Action

In exploring the possibilities for 'designing' a state which is both democratic and developmental, it is useful to see 'democratization' not merely
as a relatively sudden political rupture caused by regime transition,
but also as a process of institutional accumulation, built up gradually
like layers of coral. We draw here on Richard Sklar's notion of 'developmental democracy'. In his view, '[d]emocracy comes to every country in fragments or parts; each fragment becomes an incentive for the
addition of another' and he stresses the need for 'political invention
and improved design' of democratic institutions to confront the problems of development (1987: 714).

This process of institutional accumulation reflects the operation of
both broad structural conditions and political choice.[20] To the extent
that the latter takes place, democratic institutions can be 'designed'
and a contemporary developmental democrat can be seen as a modern
Machiavelli who is constantly seeking to reconcile the democratic and
developmental imperatives through conscious, incremental institutional innovation. The emergence of these elements of a democratic
developmental state and its relations with society should be seen
as the potential outcome of political bargains and accommodations
negotiated over time. Each national form of democracy takes on its
particular institutional character in response to the specific socio-
economic structure of the society in which it emerges and successive
sets of political choices by political actors over time. Democracy
should thus be seen as a broad paradigm allowing a wide range of
internal institutional variations rather than a precise institutional
model.

In our search for the kind of choices which might contribute to the
building of an effective and accountable democratic developmental state,
we can identify three political terrains as potential arenas for institutional design or 'crafting': state institutions, political society, and civil
society.[21] In each area we can raise some initial questions about the
extent to which particular sets of institutional arrangements influence

---

[20] There exists a long tradition in political sociology of structural analyses of the
emergence of democracy, the most illustrious of which being Barrington Moore's
pathbreaking comparative study of the class bases of different political systems (1966).
For a relatively recent piece of analysis in this tradition, which seeks to explain the
different historical antecedents of liberal and social democracy, see Joseph (1994). For
a useful overview of structural and political analyses of the evolution of democratic
institutions, see Geddes (1996: 16–23).

[21] For a discussion of the ideas of 'political society' and 'civil society', see White (1994).

the key elements of the democratic developmental state which we identified earlier. Let us discuss each in turn.

(i) *The institutional design of the state.* The increase in the number of democracies and growing evidence of their diversity has led to growing intellectual interest in the potentially crucial role to be played by political institutions in shaping processes of democratic politics and influencing policy outcomes, drawing on the 'new institutionalist' current in political science.[22] In O'Donnell's words (1996: 98), 'in the functioning of contemporary, complex societies, democratic political institutions provide a crucial level of mediation and aggregation between, on one side, structural factors and, on the other, not only individuals but also the diverse groupings under which society organizes its multiple interests and identities'. There is a range of institutional alternatives in designing political and governmental arrangements which may, by their impact on the internal structure of the regime and its relationships with political and civil societies, affect its capacity for effective, authoritative governance and inclusive, accountable decision-making.

Institutional design involves broad areas of traditional political engineering such as electoral systems, division of powers (notably differences between presidential and parliamentary systems), administrative decentralization, and devolution of government.[23] A complex and so far inconclusive debate has developed over recent years over the impact of different constitutional arrangements for the stability and coherence of new democracies. Drawing on Lijphart's classic earlier work (1984) on institutional variations among twenty-one long-established democracies, for example, Lijphart and Waisman have conducted a comparative assessment of the political and economic consequences of institutional choices in the recently democratized polities of Eastern Europe and Latin America, emphasizing the key significance of electoral systems and executive–legislative relations in determining political and policy outcomes. Debate has particularly focused on the respective merits of parliamentary and presidential forms of government in promoting coherent and authoritative governance. Advocates of parliamentarism have argued that, by combining executive and legislative powers, this offers an institutional matrix which can encourage more coherent, stable, and inclusive politics; advocates of presidentialism have argued by contrast that parliamentarism can lead to fragmented or stalemated governance, particularly in the context

---

[22] For a basic exposition of this approach, see March and Olsen (1996).
[23] The role of legislative politics and federation are discussed in this volume by Goetz and Jenkins respectively.

of a fragmented party system, and that a strong executive presidency offers the possibility for building popular mandates for wide-ranging and long-term policy programmes through the exercise of strong centralized leadership.

The battle still rages—in both academic and practical political circles—and neither side has yet to establish a clearly cogent position. For example, Haggard and Kaufman (1994: 14) have highlighted the pitfalls of parliamentarism in terms of its frequent failures in organizing consensus and producing clear lines of accountability, while O'Donnell (1993, 1996) has emphasized the drawbacks of presidentialism in contexts such as Latin America and the Philippines as a form of 'delegative democracy' which, by concentrating political authority in one powerful individual, appears to offer the possibility for strong and coherent governance but in reality impedes the basic processes of representation and institution-building which are central to the evolution of a mature democratic polity. For O'Donnell, these latter processes embody the principle of 'representative democracy' which involves multiple processes of accountability which run both vertically—between elected officials and citizens or organized interests—and horizontally between different institutional sectors with some degree of autonomy, the traditional separation of powers between executive, legislative, and judiciary. While delegative democracies may seem appealing because of their very ability to transcend these institutional constraints and therefore take bolder policy initiatives, they are inherently unstable and can only deliver in the short term. While representative democracies may be slower and more incremental, they are more effective in the longer term because they are able to organize consensus, avoid mistakes, absorb opposition, and give policies a stronger and more sustainable institutional imprimatur than the personal stamp of an individual president. In the Latin American context, these differences are visible in the relatively unsuccessful 'delegative' experiences of Collor in Brazil, Alfonsín in Argentina, and García in Peru as opposed to the more 'representative' experiences of Aylwin's Chile and Sanguinetti's Uruguay where earlier democratic institutions have been revived and strengthened. These conclusions are supported by Stepan and Skach who draw on a wide variety of comparative data to argue the case that parliamentarism provides an institutional framework more conducive to democratic consolidation because, for example, it embodies a greater propensity for governments to have majorities to implement their programmes and a 'greater tendency to provide long party-government careers, which add loyalty and experience to political society' (1993: 22).[24]

---

[24] For a discussion of the parliamentary vs. presidential issue in the context of Eastern Europe, see Baylis (1996).

How do these debates over institutional alternatives relate to the possibility of constructing democratic developmental states? One can ask a series of questions about the hypothetical impact of a given institutional option. For example, would a first-past-the-post voting system increase the chances of producing more integrative political parties capable of providing programmatic alternatives and credible government? Alternatively, would a system of proportional representation contribute to the formation of broad policy programmes by generating the broad range of consensus they require? Will a presidential or a parliamentary system better enable democratic polities to grasp fundamental issues of developmental policy such as poverty alleviation or environmental degradation? Does a federal system allow more credible and accountable governance by tailoring political institutions to socio-economic diversity and avoiding the transaction costs of over-centralization?

At this stage of our knowledge, answers to these and other questions are elusive and ambiguous. This is partly because, as Lijphart and Waisman emphasize (1996: 238), institutional choices are usually defined in terms of dichotomies—for example, the distinction between the majoritarian and proportional principles in electoral systems and between parliamentary and presidential systems in executive–legislative relations—which may be analytically helpful as ideal types, but do not reflect the institutional complexities of actual political systems which often embody shifting combinations of both principles. This is partly because relations between cause and effect depend on a broader nexus of other factors—the main categories of which we outlined above—and because these factors are distinctively configured in specific societies. For example, majoritarian systems may sit more easily in societies which are relatively homogeneous or are only riven by cleavages largely based on class, whereas societies riven by stubborn ethnic, religious, or regional differences may require a more 'consociational' system of representation.[25] This is also partly because the real dynamics of power may vary within similar frameworks of formal institutions. For example, a strong presidential system may contain significant elements of 'representational democracy', in O'Donnell's terms, if the president has strong party ties or puts an emphasis on engineering consensus among competing political forces and social interests. Hahm and Plein (1995) make this point in the context of

---

[25] Wilson (1994: 197 ff.), for example, demonstrates how the traditional Westminster model has proven inadequate in coping with societies with serious ethnic and cultural divisions since it tends to generate 'zero-sum' political solutions with clear winners and losers which tend to exacerbate existing conflicts. Conversely, Lijphart (1996) argues the case that Indian democracy has survived because it embodies key elements of the power-sharing principles of consociational democracy.

South Korea where the President is a commanding figure in formal terms, but has increasingly been forced to act as broker and coalition-builder between competing interests in his effort to sustain long-term economic policies.

The relationship between institutional option and political outcome is also systematically ambiguous not merely because of contextual contingencies, but also because each apparent institutional 'solution' may resolve one set of problems while exacerbating another. 'Good' institutions do not necessarily produce 'good' developmental outcomes since this linkage depends on the quality of policies and other intervening variables. Larry Diamond (1996) highlights these contradictions in terms of three sets of 'paradoxes': between conflict and consensus, representativeness and governability, and consent and effectiveness. As we suggested earlier, effective democratic governance would seem to rely on the ability to establish balances between these conflicting principles through a process of incremental institutional accumulation rooted in political contest and accommodation and guided by skilled leadership. Central to these processes are the nature of political and civil societies, to which we now turn.

(ii) *The character of political society.* As used here, political society refers primarily to the nature of political parties which function as crucial links between citizens/civil society and state institutions in structuring representation and enforcing accountability.[26] The nature of parties and party systems also has an important impact on strategic policy outcomes, as numerous studies of Western societies have demonstrated.[27] They can thus act as key determinants of the kinds of attributes we have indicated as central elements of developmental democracy: the capacity to provide a stable and authoritative regulatory environment; to include large sections of the population and channel the views of diverse constituents; to implement programmes of social welfare and redistribution; to take the longer-term strategic

[26] Alfred Stepan (1988: 4) has provided the classic definition of 'political society' which is, however, broader than that used here since it includes institutional arrangements—such as electoral rules and legislatures—which we include under the previous category of state institutions.

[27] One example of the longer-term relationships between parties and policy outcomes is provide by Huber and Stephens (1993) in their quantitative analysis of the relationship between the governmental impact of political parties and welfare programmes, specifically public pensions. Their data, covering the period 1958 to 1986, suggest that the party composition of gvernments has a substantial impact on welfare policy: both Christian democratic and social democratic incumbency are associated positively with pension expenditure, while only the latter is associated with lower levels of inequality and poverty among the elderly. Chhibber (1995) has also argued that the emergence of electoral competition to the Congress Party has significantly influenced the level and direction of government expenditures in India.

perspectives necessary to tackle deep-going developmental problems; and to organize accountability through both intra-party processes and inter-party competition. If democracy needs political parties, developmental democracy needs them even more.

The salience of parties as forces of political intermediation is commonly identified as an important contributor to stable and effective governance. In part, this reflects a positive assessment of the specific character of political intermediation through parties as opposed to other agencies, notably individuals and cliques. Cansino (1995), for example, has noted the lack of party influence on policy-making (relative to Western Europe) in many Latin American countries where the dominant principle of politics is presidential and clientelist and programmatic policy outcomes are likely to be fragile and evanescent. Political parties are thus unable to play certain key roles which are essential to the functioning of a democratic polity, notably in terms of establishing links between state and society, determining the formation of governments, and guaranteeing some degree of universalism in the representation of social interests.[28] This point is reinforced by other writers on Latin America who argue that economic elites have strong incentives and opportunities to pursue non-party clientelist strategies to secure their interests at the expense of the poor and excluded.[29]

The potential effectiveness of political parties from this perspective depends on a wide range of attributes. One factor of importance is the nature of individual parties—the extent to which they are capable of including and organizing relatively broad coalitions of social interests, as opposed to having narrow social bases which accentuate rather than alleviate social conflict; or the extent to which they can represent programmatic alternatives as opposed to clientelistic or personalistic interests. At a broader level, we must consider variations in the structure and dynamics of national party systems—their degree of stability, cohesion, and inclusiveness. The conventional notion of liberal democracy includes a 'multi-party system' as a central defining element. However, a consistent strand in thinking about the relationship between democracy and governance in the industrialized world, at least in Anglo-America, has been that 'multi' should ideally denote no more than two, since a two-party system can combine the advantages of both political competition and stable governance, as opposed to multi-party

[28] Similar views of the positive functions of stable and influential party systems in relation to the emergence of effective democratic governance underlie the analyses of Morlino (1995) in relation to southern Europe and McAllister and White (1995) in relation to Russia.

[29] This literature is surveyed by Bartlett and Hunter (1997: 90–1).

systems which have to survive through shifting and often unstable coalitions which make the definition and implementation of long-term policies more difficult. Similarly, in a study of six new democracies in Africa, Sandbrook argues that '[most] propitious for durable and effective governance is a two-party system or stable coalition of parties organised on a left–right basis' as opposed to an 'unstable factional model' composed of numerous parties which are 'poorly organised, shallowly rooted, personalistic vehicles engaged in clientelistic and/or communal appeals' (1996: 76). From his point of view, only one of the six party systems reviewed—Ghana—seemed to be developing a stable two-party system, in contrast to those emerging in Zambia, Niger, Mali, Madagascar, and Tanzania.[30]

Moreover, several of the relatively few successful developmental democracies over recent decades have been one-party-dominant systems, notably Japan and Botswana and, more contentiously, India (since less successful developmentally) and Singapore (since less democratic).[31] There may be a case that, *ceteris paribus*, for poor countries faced with formidable developmental challenges, the best potential underpinning for a developmentally effective democratic polity is a one-party dominant system, which, to varying degrees, may combine the best of both developmental and democratic worlds. In these societies, the dominant party was subject to regular democratic tests at the ballot box and constantly subject to the pressures of an active civil society, while at the same time maintaining the coherence, authority, and capacity for long-term decision-making.[32] In the case of Botswana, for example, as Holm points out (1996: 111), the presence of elections and political rights did not prevent a developmental elite from dominating the policy process and organizing economic growth with a high degree of autonomy. The post-authoritarian political elite in South Korea—with the Japanese precedent very much in their minds—have sought to forge just such a dominant-party system through the amalgamation of the former ruling party and part of the opposition parties, in an attempt to retain the previous developmental capacity

[30] This view of Ghana might well be contested, given the apparently high degree of factionalism among the Ghanaian opposition. In the African context, however, the number of parties is less important than the fact that most of them are based on personalism, ethnicity, or region, rather than strategic policy alternatives of a left–right kind.

[31] For a systematic analysis of existing 'developmental democracies', see Leftwich (1996 and in this volume).

[32] For a comparison of 'one-party dominant regimes', see Pempel (1990); for a study of one-party dominance in Botswana, see Molutsi and Holm (1990) and Holm (1996). Di Palma (1990) discusses the difficulties involved in establishing such systems and Ferdinand (1994) argues that the global dynamics of the post-Cold War era are undermining these systems. The recent experience of the Mexican PRI regime may be good evidence for his argument.

of the state in the new democratic context. However, countries such as Singapore and Botswana are very special cases and political conditions in most societies in Latin America and sub-Saharan Africa are not conducive to a dominant-party scenario.

Current experience would suggest that certain regions, and certain countries within regions, are more likely to develop the kind of party systems—relatively stable, programmatic, and inclusive—which could be conducive to effective developmental democracy: for example, in societies such as Latin America or East Asia where social cleavages are more likely to be based on class rather than ethnic or religious rivalries; or in countries whose political histories and experience of democratic transition have contributed to the evolution of relatively mature party systems—for example, Chile, Uruguay, Costa Rica, and perhaps Brazil in Latin America, Hungary and the Czech Republic in Eastern Europe, and Taiwan in East Asia.[33] However, even where political conditions are conducive, the requirements of developmental democracy embody certain fundamental political contradictions which find expression in party systems. Where attempts are being made to consolidate a ruling party, as in South Korea for example, this may well embody the dominance of key elite groups, notably state officials and big business—and the restriction of the organized power of labour (Kong 1995, Kim 1993).

Moreover, the seemingly unexceptionable principle of political inclusiveness carries implications of serious political conflict and instability. As Fatton (1995) has pointed out in the African context and Rueschemeyer et al. (1992) in the Latin American context, there is a fundamental contradiction between, on the one hand, the desire of established elites to secure and protect their position and, on the other hand, the desire of newly enfranchised mass publics to press their own claims on the polity. Political parties are at the heart of this process and maintaining a balance can be a tortuous struggle; as Fatton (1995: 90) points out, '[the] consolidation of democracy is ... a delicate and contradictory process requiring simultaneously a balance of power between dominant and subordinate classes, and yet the political over-representation of ruling class interests through the relative de-activation or fragmentation of radical mass parties'.

(iii) *The character and role of civil society.* The nature and impact of democratic political institutions are heavily influenced by the character and behaviour of organized groups in 'civil society'. However, a good deal of well-intentioned nonsense has been written over recent

---

[33] For an analysis of the evolving party systems in Eastern Europe, see Waller (1995), and for Taiwan, see Tien and Chu (1996).

years about the allegedly positive relationship between civil society and democracy. The link has often been achieved by defining civil society in intrinsically democratic terms with predictably tautological conclusions. To make the term useful for empirical political analysis, one needs an operational definition which seeks to avoid any normative loading, as follows: civil society denotes an intermediate associational realm between state and family populated by organizations which are separate, from the state, enjoy autonomy in relations to the state, and are formed voluntarily by members of society to protect or extend their interests or values.[34] Using this kind of definition, one discovers that 'actually existing' civil societies are politically ambiguous and problematic: while some associational forces have indeed acted as a powerful impetus for the establishment and consolidation of democratic polities, others can act to pick apart, overwhelm, or overthrow democratic institutions.[35]

Civil society can thus be seen as a highly variable form of intermediate organizational linkage with highly diverse political consequences. Its role in strengthening or subverting a democratic developmental state in any particular society depends on two key sets of concrete relationships: with the socio-economic structure on the one side and with the political society/state on the other. On the first relationship, two points are important. First, if the socio-economic structure of a given society is riven by multiple divisions and a substantial proportion of its component groups are either indifferent or hostile to democracy, as is the case in certain North African societies, civil society may serve to impede or subvert democracy of any kind, developmental or otherwise. Second, civil society is an associational map of a society's basic groupings, but the nature of the matching may vary from group to group. There is a well-known phenomenon of 'associational slippage' whereby some groups are able to organize themselves more effectively in the political arena: for example, relatively small elite groups are able to exert far greater influence by means of their concentrated organizational resources than relatively large groups such as poor people, women, or indigenous peoples whose capacity to organize is impeded by physical separation and lack of resources. To this extent, 'civil society' may serve to intensify inequalities of political access rather than correct them. If we are to achieve the redistributive objectives of developmental democracy, therefore, there is a strong case for a strategy

---

[34] This definition is defended and used for empirical purposes in White (1994). Since many intermediate organizations in the real world do not fully embody all these characteristics, this definition should be seen as an ideal-type.

[35] These points are made vividly by Fatton (1995) in his study of civil societies in Africa.

of associational mobilization of politically marginalized groups, along the lines advocated by David Korten (1990) and Pierre Landell-Mills (1992). The problem with such 'participatory' approaches, however, is that, if they really do succeed in making a difference in terms of increasing political access or redistributing socio-economic resources, they may lead to political conflict and instability.

On the second relationship, the key elements for our purposes are the mode and pattern of articulation between civil society and political parties/state institutions. The key axis of difference in modes of articulation is between clientelistic (corrupt or otherwise) and institutionalized access (through parties and other organized channels). Developmental democracy would seem to require the latter. We have already discussed the potential importance of broadly based and programmatically oriented political parties. There is another realm of articulation which Brian Crisp (1994: 1501) calls the 'consultative arena', a network of decision-making bodies linked to specific areas of policy which bring together state officials and representatives of key groups in civil society. As Crisp shows in the context of Venezuela, this system of political co-ordination tends to lead to a 'mobilization of bias' in societies in which the distribution of socio-economic resources is highly unequal, since it provides opportunities for powerful elites to interact with their political and governmental counterparts to influence the policy process in their favour. The consultative arena is likely to be an important component of developmental democracy since it can contribute to political access and organize co-ordinated action on key developmental issues. But if we are interested in extending political access and influence to a wider range of social groups, attention needs to be given to the inclusiveness and internal accountability of consultative processes to prevent their capture by elites (for an extended discussion of these issues, see Robinson in this volume).

One well-established paradigm for organizing the consultative arena is corporatism, commonly presented as an effective way of establishing stable links between state, political society, and civil society so as to create the political consensus, stability, and capacity needed for longer-term developmental decision-making (for example, Cheng and Krause 1992 advocate an explicitly corporatist model for a democratic South Korea). However, corporatist systems are notoriously difficult to establish and maintain (Bianchi 1986), particularly so in more heterogeneous and schismatic societies. Moreover, where a form of developmental corporatism has operated, as in Japan and South Korea, it has taken an exclusive form, involving a pact of domination based on an alliance between state officials, a dominant political party, and a hegemonic section of civil society (big business).

Such solutions may improve the developmental capacity of the polity, but may have problematic distributive consequences. The range of corporatist concertation would need to be more inclusive, along Western European and Scandinavian lines, involving coalitions between disparate sections of civil society and brokered by broadly based political parties. As numerous commentators have pointed out, however, these coalitions are hard to build and maintain, an issue to which we will return in the concluding section.

5. Concluding Remarks

Given the particular characteristics of the democratic developmental state that we have outlined, it would be reasonable to be sceptical about their feasibility. Democratic developmental states may turn out to be the exception rather than the rule. First, there are more than enough reasons for pessimism. There are *historical* reasons. Economic historians tell us that many of the early wave of successful developers, such as Japan, Germany, and Russia, did so under political circumstances that could hardly be called democratic; that in the great forerunner, the United Kingdom, the developmental breakthrough preceded democratization; and, more recently, that the exceptional developmental successes of East Asia and South-east Asia were all achieved under the auspices of authoritarian or authoritarian forms of democratic regimes. Moreover, recent cases of successful developmental transition under democratic regimes are hardly legion. Second, there are *contextual* reasons for pessimism. For example, while it is evident that many of the authoritarian developmental states of the post-colonial era have been egregiously unsuccessful, this is not in itself evidence that a change of regime would make a positive difference. While it is common to attribute their lack of success to predatory elites, the latter can also be found in democratic polities. Moreover, they were also undermined by the deeper dynamics of the societies in which they were embedded and weakened by overwhelming political and economic constraints, both domestic and international, which remain to confront their democratic successors. Any desire to 'design' developmentally effective democratic institutions in such contexts may reasonably be seen as utopian. Third, there are *systemic* reasons for pessimism. To the extent that democracy is a form of regularized conflict between political forces which reflect sectional interests competing in a 'political market' and policy outcomes are the result of competing pressures, it is ill equipped to generate the kind of broader forms of public interest necessary to provide basic collective goods such as a regulative

superstructure, a social and economic infrastructure, and environmental protection. Moreover, to the extent that the societies in which
democratic polities are located are characterized by various forms of
inequality—of power, status, income, and wealth—one would expect
these to be roughly reflected in levels of political voice and access to
the policy process, making programmes of social redistribution and
poverty alleviation politically unfeasible.

One can also be pessimistic about the potential for human agency
to move events in the direction of the democratic developmental state.
To a considerable extent institutions rest on and are moulded by
profound structural factors—the specific character of the social and
economic system, the dominant systems of cultural thought and
behaviour, the specific impact of the state-based and international
constellations of power, and the constitution of civil and political
societies—which set, and often radically reduce, the room for political manœuvre. Much of the analysis of the process of 'democratization'
in the sense of regime transition has emphasized the importance of
human, particularly elite, agency in 'crafting' transitions at this crucial genetic phase of democratic polities.[36] In such fluid and malleable
situations, the parameters for institutional design and creativity may
be relatively flexible. However, if we understand 'democratization' in
the longer-term sense of the consolidation and deepening of democratic
institutions and predispositions, there is a 'settling in' process, like
ships in the mud, whereby evolving institutions become increasingly
embedded in the deeper structures of power and interest in society
and become harder to change in consequence.

Even assuming room for manœuvre in institutional design, however,
there are also concerns about the nature of political agency. Studies
of institutional design in new democracies have suggested that decisions about basic democratic institutions at points of transition tend
to be taken by political forces motivated by their own interests and
not some larger commitment to democracy (Geddes 1996). As Lijphart
and Waisman conclude on the basis of their collection of studies on
Latin America and Eastern Europe, 'political-self-interest, that of
both politicians and their parties, is the dominant motivation behind
the choice of institutional designs. And these politicians are not just

---

[36] For a review of this literature, see Shin (1994: 38–41). To the extent that the
institutional arrangements which emerge from these elite-defined transitions reflect
the interests of these very elites, one of the most urgent, and developmentally crucial,
elements of democratic consolidation is to improve the political access of wider sections
of society and involve them in the process of institutional 'crafting'. In the history of
Western societies, for example, the role of labour parties based on an organized working
class played an important role in providing the political impetus for and designing the
central features of their 'welfare states'.

self-interested thinkers but also short-term thinkers . . . the institutions that are adopted are mainly expedient bargains' (1996: 244). While it is reasonable to expect that the formation of institutions must reflect a struggle between competing interests, it cannot be confidently assumed that the resulting institutions will contribute either to the long-term strength of democratic institutions or to the kinds of capacities required for strategic developmental action. Political leadership of a broader, more visionary kind would seem to be essential to achieve these longer-term aims.

A democratic developmental state of the kind we have outlined may thus be a rare bird on the developmental scene in the future, as it has been in the past. This is partly because it is defined in terms which are potentially contradictory and difficult to achieve: autonomy *and* accountability; growth *and* redistribution; consensus *and* inclusiveness. As we have seen, these pairs of desirabilia embody fundamental contradictions which are difficult to resolve in the real world of politics. This model is essentially one of a kind of developmental social democracy akin to the advanced social democracies of northern and Western Europe rather than the liberal democracies of Anglo-America. It is just one possible scenario for the evolution of those polities that do succeed in remaining democratic, in procedural terms at least. Huber et al. in their study of new democracies in Latin America, conclude (1997: 338) that 'in the current conjuncture the balance of class power is unfavorable for advancing towards participatory democracy and pursuing social democratic policy but mildly favorable for the survival of formal democracy, albeit of a deficient variety'. Whitehead (1992: 151) goes further and points to a range of systemic possibilities in Latin America: 'impotent, bankrupt and socially explosive democracies; "unstable populism"; neo-liberal "depoliticized democracies"; and internationally dependent or insecure democracies'. Prognostications of the African and Eastern European future also tend to be pessimistic, particularly in the former case where the possibilities for 'façade', corrupt, or unstable forms of democracy are likely. Views of South Asia vary according to country (more optimistic about India and less so about Pakistan or Bangladesh), or across sub-units within countries (for example, greater optimism about the states of West Bengal or Kerala).

However, though many countries may not succeed either in consolidating democratic institutions or in achieving socio-economic development, there are prospects for forms of 'developmental democracy' which differ from the one specified in this chapter. Two types of potentially successful developmental regimes stand out: first, authoritarian 'semi-democracies' along East and South-east Asian lines which restrict the operation of democratic politics, are dominated by elite coalitions, but which emphasize social cohesion and the restriction of socio-economic differentials; and, second, elitist democracies along Latin American lines which are dominated by a relatively narrow coalition of social interests and manage to sustain economic growth but at a cost of widening socio-economic differentials.

Does all this make the search for a developmental social democracy merely a chimera? Most of the hypothetical alternatives, democratic or otherwise, would seem to be inferior, both politically and developmentally, and a strong case can be made that this kind of regime can best achieve effective and equitable development in the interests of the broad masses of the population in poor, developing, and transitional countries. To repeat a point made earlier, effective developmental performance is crucially important for the political future of the new democracies of the erstwhile Second and Third Worlds. While conditions over recent years have favoured their emergence, one should not be complacent about their future. If they are developmentally ineffective, a vicious downward spiral of mutually reinforcing economic and political decline may well set in. Moreover, if they continue to rest on vast inequalities and remain as oligarchic 'semi-democracies' operating largely in the interests of dominant elites, their role as agents of both democratization and development will be severely circumscribed. If they are not successful in 'producing the goods', they will be prey to authoritarian reversals based on ideologies which thrive on the ideas that democratic polities are inherently corrupt, divisive, unstable, or ineffectual.

It is therefore worth trying to think systematically about the ways in which this model of developmental democracy can be achieved and in what circumstances. For example, it is possible to specify the conditions under which this alternative might be more likely to emerge. *Ceteris paribus*, democratic developmental states may be more feasible in the following circumstances:

- *socio-economic system*: in societies at a higher level of socio-economic development,[37] with a relatively homogeneous population, a relatively strong sense of national identity, a relatively cohesive social structure, and a lack of gross inequalities of condition.
- *civil society*: not just whether or not civil societies are 'vibrant', but also the extent to which the forces of civil society can forge broad developmental coalitions to strengthen the strategic capacity of the state and tackle problems of poverty and insecurity. The

[37] This does not just reflect a relationship based on quantitative levels of development, but on structural changes in the class system, as Huber et al. (1993) argue.

nature and impact of political coalitions is a crucial determinant
of the trajectories of different forms of democratic governance.[38]

- *political society*: where party systems are relatively well developed,
  concentrated rather than fragmented, broadly based, and organized along programmatic rather than personalistic or narrowly
  sectional lines.

- *state institutions*: in societies where political power is organized
  to allow a concentration of executive authority, whether this be
  within the institutional integument of a presidential, parliamentary, or hybrid system, and where the state apparatus is staffed
  by professional civil servants.

- *international environment*: in societies where the autonomy of
  national elites is not so undermined by external political or economic dependence as to reduce significantly their capacity to rule
  and the principle of democratic accountability.

Particlar configurations of institutions and socio-economic structures
differ widely across societies and only a minority will have the conditions and potential necessary to achieve anything like this. Assessments vary and each case is contestable. A hypothetical list might
include South Africa and possibly Ghana in Africa; Chile, Costa Rica,
and Venezuela in Latin America; Poland, Hungary, and the Czech Republic in Eastern Europe; certain states within India in South Asia;
and Taiwan in East Asia. Even where basic conditions are favourable,
however, the evolution of a democratic developmental state requires a
prolonged process of political and institutional *tâtonnement* or 'groping'
which involves trial and error, reversals and advances. As Sklar and
others have argued, moreover, democratic developmental states are only
likely to emerge in pieces, rather than as a systemic whole. In short,
in most countries, developmental democracy will only come in parts.

This initial enquiry into the nature and feasibility of the democratic
developmental state should be situated within a much larger intellectual
endeavour which faces political scientists in the aftermath of the
'third wave' of democratization. The post-Cold War era has generated
a profusion of different types of 'democratic' society. Just as the long-
established democracies of the industrialized world differ in terms of
their institutional systems and political dynamics, one must expect a
far greater range of variation as the new democracies consolidate and

---

[38] This factor is stressed by many analysts. For example, Haggard and Kaufman
(1994: 11) stress the need for 'encompassing coalitions' to counter poverty; Bartlett
and Hunter (1997: 100 ff.) discuss the differential political implications of different class
coalitions in the context of Latin America and Eastern Europe; and Holm (1996: 111)
cites the Botswana case as one which 'demonstrates that the primary need is to form
a political coalition of elites committed to development'.

evolve. A sophisticated consideration of institutional variations needs to be complemented by an equally comprehensive understanding of the underlying political dynamics of the new democracies: the ways and extent to which different groups and interests gain access to political power and the resulting consequences for developmental outcomes; the political coalitions which influence the shaping of formal institutions; the relative roles of 'electoral' and 'consultative' arenas of state–society interaction; and the relationship between real as opposed to formal 'citizenship'. It is hoped that the studies in this book make a useful initial contribution to this enquiry.

REFERENCES

Bartlett, David, and Hunter, Wendy (1997), 'Market Structures, Political Institutions and Democratization: The Latin American and East European Experiences', *Review of International Political Economy*, 4/1 (Spring): 87–126.

Baylis, Thomas A. (1996), 'Presidents versus Prime Ministers: Shaping Executive Authority in Eastern Europe', *World Politics*, 48 (Apr.): 297–323.

Bianchi, Robert (1986), 'Interest Group Politics in the Third World', *Third World Quarterly*, 8/2 (Apr.): 507–39.

Budge, Ian, and McKay, David (eds.) (1994), *Developing Democracy: Comparative Research in Honour of J. F. P. Blondel*, London: Sage.

Burnell, Peter (1995), 'The Politics of Poverty and the Poverty of Politics in Zambia's Third Republic', *Third World Quarterly*, 16/4: 675–90.

Cansino, César (1995), 'Party Government in Latin America: Theoretical Guidelines for an Empirical Analysis', *International Political Science Review*, 16/2: 169–82.

Case, William F. (1993), 'Semi-democracy in Malaysia: Withstanding the Pressures for Regime Change', *Pacific Affairs*, 66/2 (Summer): 183–205.

—— (1996), 'Can the "Halfway House" Stand? Semidemocracy and Elite Theory in Three Southeast Asian Countries', *Comparative Politics*, 28/4 (July): 437–64.

Cheng Tun-jen and Krause, L. B. (1992), 'Democracy and Development: With Special Attention to Korea', *Journal of Northeast Asian Studies* (Summer): 3–25.

Chhibber, Pradeep (1995), 'Political Parties, Electoral Competition, Government Expenditures and Economic Reform in India', *Journal of Development Studies*, 32/1 (Oct.): 74–96.

Crisp, Brian (1994), 'Limitations to Democracy in Developing Capitalist Societies: The Case of Venezuela', *World Development*, 22/10: 1495–509.

Dahl, Robert A. (1971), *Polyarchy: Participation and Opposition*, New Haven: Yale University Press.

Diamond, Larry (1992*a*), 'Introduction to Political Culture and Democracy in Developing Countries', manuscript, cited in Shin (1994).

—— (1992*b*), 'Economic Development and Democracy Reconsidered', *American Behavioral Scientist*, 35/4–5: 450–94.

—— (1996), 'Three Paradoxes of Democracy', in Diamond and Plattner (1996).

—— and Plattner, Marc F. (eds.) (1996), *The Global Resurgence of Democracy*, 2nd edn., London: Johns Hopkins University Press.

Di Palma, Giuseppe (1990), *To Craft Democracies*, London: University of California Press.

Eatwell, John, et al. (1995), *Transformation and Integration: Shaping the Future of Central and Eastern Europe*, London: Institute for Public Policy Research.

Evans, P. (1996), *Embedded Autonomy*, Princeton: Princeton University Press.

Falk, Richard (1993), 'Democratising, Internationalising, and Globalising: A Collage of Blurred Images', *Third World Quarterly*, 13/4: 627–40.

Fatton, Robert, Jr. (1995), 'Africa in the Age of Democratization: The Civic Limitations of Civil Society', *African Studies Review*, 38/2 (Sept.): 67–99.

Ferdinand, Peter (1994), 'The Party's Over: Market Liberalisation and the Challenges for One-Party and One-Party Dominant Regimes: The Cases of Taiwan and Mexico, Italy and Japan', *Democratization*, 1/1 (Spring): 133–50.

Fukuyama, Francis (1996), *Trust: The Social Virtues and the Creation of Prosperity*, London: Penguin Books.

Geddes, Barbara (1996), 'Initiation of New Democratic Institutions in Eastern Europe and Latin America', in Lijphart and Waisman (1996).

Gills, Barry, Rocamora, Joel, and Wilson, Richard (eds.) (1993), *Low Intensity Democracy: Political Power in the New World Order*, London: Pluto Press.

Haggard, Stephan, and Kaufman, Robert R. (1994), 'The Challenges of Consolidation', *Journal of Democracy*, 5/4 (Oct.): 5–16.

Hahm Sung Deuk and Plein, L. Christopher (1995), 'Institutions and Technological Development in Korea: The Role of the Presidency', *Comparative Politics*, 28/1, 55–76.

Held, David (1991), 'Democracy, the Nation-State and the Global System', *Economy and Society*, 20/2 (May): 138–72.

Holm, John D. (1996), 'Development, Democracy and Civil Society in Botswana', in Leftwich (1996).

Huber, Evelyne, and Stephens, John D. (1993), 'Political Parties and Public Pensions: A Quantitative Analysis', *Acta Sociologica*, 36/4: 309–25.

—— Rueschemeyer, Dietrich, and Stephens, John D. (1993), 'The Impact of Economic Development on Democracy', *Journal of Economic Perspectives*, 7/3 (Summer): 71–85.

—— —— —— (1997), 'The Paradoxes of Contemporary Democracy: Formal, Participatory, and Social Democracy', *Comparative Politics*, 29/3 (Apr.): 323–42.

Huntington, Samuel P. (1991), *The Third Wave: Democratization in the Late Twentieth Century*, London: University of Oklahoma Press.

Jeffries, Richard (1993), 'The State, Structural Adjustment and Good Govern-ment in Africa', *Journal of Commonwealth and Comparative Politics*, 31/1 (Mar.): 20–35.

Joseph, Antoine (1994), 'Pathways to Capitalist Democracy: What Prevents Social Democracy?', *British Journal of Sociology*, 45/2 (June): 211–34.

Kim, Eun Mee (1993), 'Contradictions and Limits of a Developmental State: With Illustrations for the South Korea Case', *Social Problems*, 40/2 (May): 228–49.

Kong, David C. (1995), 'From Relative Autonomy to Consensual Develop-ment: The Case of South Korea', *Political Studies*, 43: 630–44.

Korten, David C. (1990), *Getting to the 21st. Century: Voluntary Action and the Global Agenda*, West Hartford, Conn: Kumarian.

Landell-Mills, Pierre (1992), 'Governance, Civil Society and Empowerment in Sub-Saharan Africa: Building the Institutional Basis for Sustainable Dvelopment', Washington: World Bank, Africa Technical Department (10 June).

Leftwich, Adrian (1993), 'Voting can Damage your Wealth', *The Times Higher Education Supplement*, 13 Aug.: 11–13.

—— (ed.) (1996), *Democracy and Development: Theory and Practice*, Cam-bridge: Polity Press.

Lijphart, Arend (1968), 'Consociational Democracy', *World Politics*, 21/1 (Jan.): 207–25.

—— (1984), *Democracies: Patterns of Majoritarian and Consensus Govern-ment in Twenty-One Countries*, London: Yale University Press.

—— (1996), 'The Puzzle of Indian Democracy: A Consociational Interpreta-tion', *American Political Science Review*, 90/2 (June): 258–68.

—— and Waisman, Carlos H. (eds.) (1996), *Institutional Design in New Democracies*, Oxford: Westview Press.

Linz, Juan, and Stepan, Alfred (1989), 'Political Crafting of Democratic Consolidation of Destruction: European and South American Comparisons', in R. A. Pastor (ed.), *Democracy in the Americas*, New York: Holmes & Meier.

Lipset, Seymour Martin (1994), 'The Social Requisites of Democracy Re-visited', *American Sociological Review*, 59/1: 1–22.

Luckham, Robin, and White, Gordon (eds.) (1996), *Democratisation in the South: The Jagged Wave*, Manchester: Manchester University Press.

McAllister, I., and White, S. (1995), 'Democracy, Political Parties and Party Formation in Post-Communist Russia', *Party Politics*, 1/1: 49–72.

March, James G., and Olsen, Johan P. (1996), 'Institutional Perspectives on Political Institutions', *Governance: An International Journal of Policy and Administration*, 9/3 (July): 247–64.

Molutsi, Patrick, P., and Holm, John, D. (1990), 'Developing Democracy when Civil Society is Weak: The Case of Botswana', *African Affairs*, 89/356: 323–40.

Moore, Barrington (1966), *The Social Origins of Dictatorship and Democracy*, Boston: Beacon Press.

Moore, Mick (1996), 'Is Democracy Rooted in Material Prosperity?', in Luckham and White (1996).

Morlino, L. (1995), 'Consolidation and Party Government in Southern Europe', *International Political Science Review*, 16/2: 145–67.

Nicro, Somrudee (1993), 'Thailand's NIC Democracy: Studying from General Elections', *Pacific Affairs*, 66/2 (Summer): 167–82.

O'Donnell, Guillermo (1993), 'On the State, Democratization and Some Conceptual Problems: A Latin American View with Glances at Some Post-Communist Countries', *World Development*, 21/8 (Aug.): 1355–70.

—— (1996), 'Delegative Democracy', in Diamond and Plattner (1996).

Pempel, T. J. (ed.) (1990), *Uncommon Democracies: The One-Party Dominant Regimes*, London: Cornell University Press.

Przeworski, Adam, et al. (1995), *Sustainable Democracy*, Cambridge: Cambridge University Press.

Putnam, Robert (1993), *Making Democracy Work: Civic Traditions in Modern Italy*, Princeton: Princeton University Press.

Robinson, M. (1996), 'Economic Reform and the Transition to Democracy', in Luckham and White (1996).

Rueschemeyer, Dietrich, Stephens, Evelyne Huber, and Stephens, John (1992), *Capitalist Development and Democracy*, Chicago: University of Chicago Press.

Sandbrook, Richard L. (1988), 'Liberal Democracy in Africa: A Socialist-Revisionist Perspective', *Canadian Journal of African Studies*, 22/2: 240–67.

—— (1996), 'Transitions without Consolidation: Democratization in Six African Countries', *Third World Quarterly*, 17/1: 69–87.

Shin Doh Chull (1994), 'On the Third Wave of Democratization: A Synthesis and Evaluation of Recent Theory', *World Politics*, 47/1 (Oct.): 135–70.

Sklar, Richard L. (1987), 'Developmental Democracy', *Comparative Studies in Society and History*, 29/4 (Oct.): 686–714.

—— (1996), 'Towards a Theory of Developmental Democracy', in Leftwich (1996).

Soros, George (1997), 'The Capitalist Threat', *Atlantic Monthly*, Feb.: 45–58.

Stepan, Alfred (1988), *Rethinking Military Politics*, Princeton: Princeton University Press.

—— and Skach, Cindy (1993), 'Constitutional Frameworks and Democratic Consolidation: Parliamentarism versus Presidentialism', *World Politics*, 46 (Oct.): 1–22.

Tien Hung-mao and Chu Yun-han (1996), 'Building Democracy in Taiwan', *China Quarterly*, 148 (Dec.), 1141–70.

Waller, Michael (1995), 'Adaptation of the Former Communist Parties of East-Central Europe: A Case of Social-Democratization?', *Party Politics*, 1/4: 473–90.

White, Gordon (1994), 'Civil Society, Democratization and Development (I): Clearing the Analytical Ground', *Democratization*, 1/3 (Autumn): 375–90.

—— (1995), 'Towards a Democratic Developmental State', *IDS Bulletin*, 26/2 (Apr.): 27–36.

—— (1996), 'Civil Society, Democratization and Development', in Luckham and White (1996).

Whitehead, Laurence (1992), 'The Alternatives to "Liberal Democracy": A Latin American Perspective', *Political Studies*, 40 (special issue): 146–59.

Wilson, Graham (1994), 'The Westminster Model in Comparative Perspective', in Budge and McKay (1994).

World Bank (1997), *World Development Report 1997: The State in a Changing World*, Oxford: Oxford University Press.

2

Forms of the Democratic Developmental State
Democratic Practices and Development Capacity

ADRIAN LEFTWICH

1. Introduction

Few states in the developing world have been able to sustain even the most basic elements of democracy. Those which have been able to do so include Venezuela, Costa Rica, Jamaica, Botswana, Mauritius, Malaysia, Singapore, and India. Even so, many analysts balk at calling Singapore and Malaysia 'democratic' (Ahmad, 1989) and hence refer to them as only 'partially democratic' states (Potter 1997: 38). But, that aside, only a few states from this broad democratic or quasi-democratic category have been able to generate high annual average rates of growth in their GNP per capita over the last thirty years or to lift the bulk of their people out of poverty, hardship, and vulnerability: they include Botswana, Singapore, Malaysia, and Mauritius. Though each is very different with respect to key variables such as physical size, population, history, resource endowments, cultural and class structures, they have each generated political elites and state structures with the determination and capacity to preside over economic growth and welfare. For present purposes these will qualify as examples of *developmental democratic states*[1] or 'developmental democracies' (Sklar 1996)

I am grateful to my colleague Professor T. V. Sathyamurthy for some helpful observations on an initial draft of this chapter and to Mark Robinson and Gordon White for supplying the fruits of a literature search and for eagle-eyed comment and suggestions. Responsibility for what is written here remains mine alone.

[1] Instead of describing these as democratic developmental states I refer to them, I think more accurately, as developmental democratic states. This is partly to make the distinction with non-developmental democratic states more semantically and

in that they meet *both* democratic and developmental criteria. For present purposes I differentiate these from the other democracies named above (Costa Rica, Venezuela, Jamaica, and India) whose states have not been able to manage comparable levels of growth and where, by contrast, sluggish or even negative annual average rates of growth in GNP per capita have prevailed (at least until fairly recently). I refer to these as *non-developmental democratic states* in that while they satisfy democratic criteria, they do not perform nearly as well in terms of developmental criteria.

This distinction between developmental and non-developmental democracies is in some respects misleading. For instance, although Botswana and Mauritius have had faster growth rates than both Venezuela and Costa Rica, the latter score better on the human development index (HDI) (UNDP 1996). And while Jamaica and India have performed weakly in respect of *both* growth and the HDI, they score better in terms of income distribution than Venezuela, Costa Rica, or Botswana (World Bank 1992, 1996; Good 1993). And although I shall use these developmental and non-developmental democracies categories to highlight important distinctions, it may be useful to think of all these democratic states as being ranked as 'high' or 'low' developers along a variety of related but not identical continua, with some performing better on the growth continuum and others performing better on the human development and distributional continua. None the less, growth is such a crucial precondition for other developmental goods that it must remain a critical indicator of developmental performance and promise. See Table 2.1.

Now while there are many good explanatory accounts of why some *non-democratic* political systems such as South Korea, Taiwan, and Indonesia have been able to manage rapid and sustained economic growth over time (Rueschemeyer and Evans 1985, Diamond 1992, Leftwich 1995, Weiss and Hobson 1995), it is much less clear why some *democratic* states have also been able to do so. More crucially for this chapter, what explains the difference between developmental and non-developmental democratic states? In short, what conditions enable a democratic state to generate the capabilities which transform it into a successful *developmental* democratic state? The 'third wave' of democratization (Huntington 1991, Potter et al. 1997) has added a very considerable number of states to the current list of full or partial democracies and, by 1995, had confined authoritarian rule to about 26 per cent of states in the modern world (Potter 1997: 1–10). But few,

substantively sharp, but equally to stress that what differentiates this broad group of states is not so much their democratic credentials or practices (though these differ) but their developmental capacities.

TABLE 2.1. *The Human Development Index*

Countries	GNP p.c. 1994 ($)	Av. annual growth of GNP p.c. 1965–90	Av. annual growth of GNP p.c. 1985–94	Life expectancy 1994	Literacy (%) 1995	Human rights record 1991 (%)[a]	Human development rank 1996[b]
Botswana	2,800	8.4	6.6	68	70	79	0.741 (71)
Singapore	22,500	6.5	6.1	75	91	60	0.881 (34)
Malaysia	3,480	4.0	5.6	71	83	61	0.826 (53)
Mauritius	3,150	3.2	5.8	70	83	n/a	0.825 (54)
India	320	1.9	2.9	62	52	54	0.436 (135)
Costa Rica	2,400	1.4	2.8	77	95	90	0.884 (23)
Jamaica	1,540	−1.3	3.9	74	85	72	0.702 (86)
Venezuela	2,760	−1.0	0.7	71	91	75	0.826 (53)

Note: The Human Development Index (HDI) is a composite index incorporating three main dimensions: long and healthy life expectancy, knowledge (education), and standard of living (UNDP 1996: 28). Life expectancy, educational attainment, and income are the quantified variables chosen to represent these qualities of life.

[a] The world average in % terms is 62%.

[b] Countries ranked by the UNDP from best at 1.0 to worst at 0.0 are 1 (best, Canada) to 174 (worst, Niger) (UNDP 1996).

Sources: Humana (1992), UNDP (1996), and World Bank (1992 and 1996).

if any, of the new democracies in the developing world may *yet* be called effective developmental democratic states. Given this and contemporary official concerns to treat or promote democracy as a condition of development, it is an important question to resolve.

The point of course is that developmental democratic states cannot be had to order. 'Institutional development' alone will not deliver (or sustain) developmental democracies if their politics do not support it, as widespread historic and contemporary democratic reversals, in Huntington's phrase, clearly show. Thus while the transition to democracy is clearly a necessary condition for the emergence of developmental democratic states, it is not a sufficient condition. Furthermore, democratic states come in a variety of types, each of which embodies a different form of democratic politics which in turn influences developmental capacity.

The main contribution of this chapter will be to suggest that the explanation for the different developmental capacities and records of these Third World democracies turns crucially on the primary role of *politics* in shaping the character and capability of their *states*. This originates in the course of their transitions to democracy and in the politics of its subsequent consolidation. The central thesis here, therefore, is that the developmental capacities of democratic states in managing development, or 'governing the market' (Wade 1990), need to be understood primarily as a function of their politics which in turn reflects far more complex legacies in their economic, social, class, and ethnic structures.

2. Theory and Argument

Developmental democratic states must satisfy two sets of independent criteria to qualify as being *both* developmental and democratic. The primary developmental criterion which I use here is an annual average rate of growth in GNP per capita of at least 4 per cent over the last twenty-five to thirty years. And for present purposes I use the term 'democracy' in its minimalist Schumpeterian sense to refer to a national political system in which people, political parties, and groups are free to pursue their interests according to peaceful, rule-based competition, negotiation, and co-operation within an 'institutional arrangement for arriving at political decisions in which individuals acquire the power to decide by means of a competitive struggle for the people's vote' (Schumpeter 1965: 269). In practice this means free and regular elections, plus peaceful succession where governments change; low barriers to political participation; and the protection of civil and political liberties (Diamond et al. 1989: p. xvi). 'Partial' democracy (Potter 1997: 5) is a somewhat weaker version of this where, despite regular and open elections, civil and political rights are curtailed.

At the heart of the argument here are two propositions which, when taken together, define the central structural contradiction which makes developmental democratic states so difficult to establish and sustain and which constitute the starting point for explaining their diverse types and capacities.

The first proposition is that *democracy*, once consolidated and stabilized, especially in its minimal representative form, is a conservative system of power. I shall elaborate on this shortly, but for the present I mean that both the decision-making processes and policy output in consolidated democracies are generally 'conservative' in that they normally involve inter-elite accommodation, compromise, consensus, and incrementalism, and seldom entail much popular participation (as Schumpeter recognized). For many that is the virtue of democracy; for others, it is its vice. The second proposition is that *development* is both by definition and in practice a radical and commonly turbulent process which is concerned with often far-reaching and rapid change in the use and distribution of resources, and which—if successful —must transform the fundamental structures of economic and social life, thereby generating new political interests and challenging established ones. For, as Hugh Stretton observed, 'People can't change the way they use resources without changing their relations with one another' (Stretton 1976: 3). For many, too, that is the virtue of development; for others, that is its vice. The problem, of course, is that the perceived vices and virtues of democracy and development rarely coincide. This is not to say that democratic politics cannot be turbulent, but that where the fundamental basis of consensual and accommodational politics breaks down, or is put under severe stress, democracy itself may be overturned or be put under threat (as occurred in Chile and Jamaica in the early and mid-1970s).

In having to fulfil both democratic and developmental objectives, the contradiction which democratic developmental states have therefore to contain and resolve is that, under most circumstances, the *rules* and hence practices of stable democratic politics will tend to restrict policy to incremental and accommodationist (hence conservative) options. On the other hand, developmental requirements (whether liberal or radical) will be likely to pull policy in the direction of quite sharp changes affecting the economic and social structure of the society and hence important interests within it. It is this structural contradiction between the conservative requirements of stable democratic survival and the transformative logic of economic growth which new or old democracies must survive and ultimately transcend if they are to become effective developmental democracies. This is especially so if they are to avoid the 'vicious cycle' of economic and political decline discussed by Gordon White in Chapter 1 of this volume. For it is not only the case that poor developmental performance can undermine the consolidation of democracy (as the Venezuela case, later, will show), but also that unconsolidated and unstable democracy has a high probability of restraining or undermining economic growth.

In what follows I first explore some key conditions for democratic consolidation in order to show why modern democratization needs to be understood, paradoxically, as both a radical and conservative process. I then define the developmental state and offer a preliminary classification of the various types of developmental and non-developmental democratic state. The central point here will be that each of these types represents the particular political resolution of the fundamental contradiction referred to above, and that each form broadly defines the possibilities and limits of its developmental capacities. Throughout, I draw comparatively on the practices of the democratic and partially democratic states mentioned above, but for reasons of space focus mainly on Mauritius, Jamaica, and Venezuela. I shall also refer more speculatively to South Africa as a 'proto' democratic developmental state, to Cuba as a conceivably 'nascent' democratic developmental state, and to China as a non-democratic 'socialist' development state (White 1984, 1985) which is experiencing strong non-socialist economic transformations and democratic pressures. In linking discussions of democratization and developmental states, I hope too that this will help to bring the discipline of political science more directly to the core of development theory and practice, for no topic lends itself better to this task than that of the developmental democratic state.

3. Democratic Transitions, Democratic Consolidation, and the Democratic Developmental State

The question of the origin and endurance of developmental and non-developmental democratic states is inseparable from the question of democratization itself. However, it is important to distinguish between two phases of democratization: the transition to democracy and the consolidation of democracy (Mainwaring et al. 1992: 3, Rueschemeyer et al. 1992: 76). The former does not guarantee the latter. But, clearly, since *only consolidated democracies can become developmental democratic states*, the conditions of consolidation are crucial in shaping the democratic developmental state.

The routes by which different societies have reached democracy have varied greatly. The accumulated comparative evidence, worldwide (Potter et al. 1997), makes clear that the major forces and agents of modern democratization have sometimes been mainly *internal* (Costa Rica, Venezuela, Korea, Taiwan) and sometimes mainly *external* (Japan after 1945 and sub-Saharan Africa in the 1990s) (Chalker 1994, Holmquist and Ford 1994, Wiseman 1997). Commonly, however, a varying mixture of both internal and external forces has been involved, as in Central and Eastern Europe in the 1980s and 1990s (Lewis 1997). Internal pressures for democracy have sometimes come mainly from below (as in the Philippines, and Central and Eastern Europe); in others, top-level negotiations between elites, sometimes in secret to start with (Karl 1986: 79), have been far more salient than either popular action or external pressure, as some of the Latin American transitions in the 1980s illustrate (Little 1997). The case of South Africa, however, is a remarkable demonstration of the combination of internal popular pressures, external influences, and inter-elite negotiation in the transition to democracy (Sparks 1995). But whatever the route to democracy and whatever the combination of forces and agents, the transition to democracy requires subsequent consolidation if it is to survive. This is essentially an internal matter and it is in this context that the question of the developmental democratic state comes decisively into the picture.

But what is to count as consolidation? The simplest single defining feature is that 'all major political actors take for granted the fact that democratic processes dictate government renewal' (Mainwaring et al. 1992: 3). How is this to be achieved and what conditions favour consolidation around such an agreement? I have suggested elsewhere (Leftwich 1997) three essential political conditions for democratic consolidation and two factors which both hinder consolidation and limit the developmental capability of democratic states (Leftwich 1997). I summarize these here.

(a) Legitimacy

Although notoriously difficult to define and measure (Held 1996: ch. 5), a central characteristic of legitimacy is some degree of acceptability. There are three primary dimensions of this. They are *geographical, constitutional, and political* legitimacy and involve: (i) acceptance by the people of the territorial definition of the state and their place in it; (ii) acceptance of the rules for the organization and distribution of political power; and (iii) acceptance that the government has achieved power by fair electoral play. Without these, the potential for violent secessionist, irredentist, or civil conflict is considerable, as we have seen so widely in the developing world and more recently in former Yugoslavia and Chechnya. Weakened democracies therefore inevitably and fatally weaken the prospects for developmental democratic states.

(b) Consensus and constitutionalism

Democratic consolidation requires agreement about the rules of the political game by the major parties and groups, preferably built into constitutional provisions, as occurred in the 1961 Venezuelan constitution (Kornblith 1991) and as has also been illustrated in the political processes which led up to the new South African constitution (Sparks 1995; Republic of South Africa 1996).

This means that while losers in electoral contests must accept the outcome, they know that they will be able to try again in four or five years. Regular military forces, whether allies of the winners or losers, must return to, and remain in, their barracks or, as in the remarkable Costa Rican case, be disbanded. In return, guerrilla forces must commit themselves to demobilization or absorption into the regular forces, as in Zimbabwe, Nicaragua, and South Africa. Generally, the military must also agree to uphold the rules of the game and defend the outcome (often in return for amnesty for past excesses).

(c) Policy restraint by winners

Third and crucially, however, no party, functional group, or sectoral interest (such as the army, private capital, or labour) is likely to accept the rules of the new democratic political game if it fears that electoral outcomes would mean that it, or the interests it represents, would lose too much, or that its losses would not be compensated. Indeed the less such parties or groups stand to lose, the more committed they will become to the democratic political process and the narrower will be the range of politically feasible policy options. What this means is that while *losers* must accept the outcome of the electoral process, *winners* must accept that there are significant limits to what they can do with their newly acquired power and, indeed, that they may have to share some of that power with the losers. That is to say, democratic consolidation is most likely where the elected governments do not pursue highly contentious or controversial policies too far or too fast, *especially* where such policies might seriously threaten or undermine other interests or those on the losing side.

Two factors make it especially difficult to meet these three conditions. The first is pervasive poverty associated with profound inequality, so common in developing countries. The main reason why serious poverty and inequality restrain democratic consolidation is that in such countries the struggle for scarce resources, and the enormous advantages which permanent control of the state may bring to a party or faction (and hence its clients), make acceptance of the rules of democracy unlikely. Incumbents holding state power will be reluctant to engage in compromise and will be very unwilling to lose control (Bayart 1993; Young 1994). Suspending democracy is a good way of staying in power.

Second, sharp ethnic, cultural, or religious cleavages (especially where these overlap with material inequalities between the groups) also make the transition to democracy and its consolidation very difficult. Such obstacles can be overcome by carefully crafted constitutions, elaborate inter-elite arrangements, and pacts or painstakingly constructed coalitions. But these are very difficult to achieve and maintain where deep and *principled* cultural and especially religious differences prevail.

It is apparent that in meeting these conditions for democracy (and especially consensus and policy restraint), new or born-again democratic states may often have problems in meeting the developmental criteria. Adam Przeworski has theorized democratization as 'a process of institutionalising uncertainty, of subjecting all interests to uncertainty' (Przeworski 1986: 58, 1988). Theoretically, he is right, but in practice, democracies are unlikely to consolidate unless the scope of uncertainty is systematically *reduced*. Indeed that is precisely what those elite groups which prioritize democracy usually seek to do. Where they are successful in doing so, the net effect is the emergence of consensus about (at least) the limits of reform and hence a reduction in the range of policy choices available.

It should now be more clear why democracy may be thought of as being simultaneously a radical and conservative system of power and why developmental democratic states embody serious structural contradictions. It is of course true that democracies can be considered radical in that no other political systems have promoted and protected *individual political rights and civil liberties* to the same extent (Freedom House 1992; Humana 1992), though *not* a broader set of social and economic rights (what the Chinese have called 'subsistence rights'). But democracies may also be considered 'conservative' from a developmental point of view given the difficulties they face in taking rapid and far-reaching steps which may be necessary to promote growth. For although new democratic governments (like the ANC in South Africa) or older ones (as in India or Costa Rica) may be committed to growth, to poverty reduction, and to the promotion of the welfare of the masses, it is often the case that radical and essentially *non-consensual* steps are necessary for this, as they are for states seeking to promote policies of liberalization. The difficulty is that such steps could easily breach the formal or informal 'pacts' or coalitions, constitutional provisions, or agreed restraints on policy which may have helped to bring about democratization in the first place and the observance of which helps to keep democracy intact.

Land reform is a good example, since it is widely recognized that this can be an important condition for rural development which in turn contributes to political stability, as in South Korea in the 1950s (Lee 1979). But landowners in general do not favour land reform! And democratic Third World governments have seldom been effective in overcoming such vested rural interests to achieve the restructuring of rural wealth and power which land reform is designed to bring about as the cases of both India and Pakistan (even in one of its partially democratic phases under Bhutto) show so well (Lipton 1974, Bardhan 1984: 46 and ch. 6, Herring 1979).

4. Defining Developmental States

The developmental state remains both insecurely defined and weakly theorized and generally gets no mention in standard texts of political science (Dunleavy and O'Leary 1987, Held 1996). For present purposes I define the developmental state in the following preliminary way.

(i) The developmental state is a transitional form of the modern state which has emerged in late-developing societies, from the nineteenth century to the present. It is a state whose political and bureaucratic elites have generally achieved relative autonomy from socio-political forces in the society and use this in order to promote a programme of rapid economic growth with more or less rigour and ruthlessness.

(ii) The developmental state is typically driven by an urgent need to promote economic growth and to industrialize, in order to 'catch up' or to protect or promote itself, either economically or militarily or both, in a world or regional context of threat or competition, and to win legitimacy by delivering steady improvement in the material and social well-being of its citizens.

Developmental states are thus commonly associated with a high degree of both economic and political nationalism.

(iii) Though the Soviet and Chinese states represented the socialist version of non-democratic developmental states, most and the most successful developmental states have been those which have thrived in mixed capitalist economies, since one of the key characteristics of this state type is its determination and ability to stimulate, direct, shape, and co-operate with the domestic private sector and arrange or supervise mutually acceptable deals with foreign interests. However, in both China and Cuba at the present (1998) we are seeing profound changes occurring in developmental state–society relations as economic liberalization promotes a greater role for the private sector, while state power in, and influence over, the economy remains.

(iv) Developmental states are constituted by particular political forces and processes which are not found, nor can they be easily replicated, in all developing societies. These politics have given rise to two broad types of developmental states: non-democratic and democratic ones; and our interest is here with the latter. As mentioned above, for present purposes I define *developmental* democratic states as those which have been able to sustain formal processes of democracy (defined above) while generating an average annual rate of growth in GNP per capita of 4 per cent, at least, over the last twenty-five to thirty years (see Table 2.1), and *non-developmental* democratic states are those whose rates of growth fall below this.

(v) Finally, developmental states are not static. They are transitional forms of the modern state in that their success in promoting economic growth has often had the effect of creating interests and organizations in an increasingly complex economy and civil society which then successfully challenge the power, authority, and autonomy of the state, and hence produce further political change. Thus most developmental states, whether democratic or not, go through a lifespan which commences with origins, progresses through consolidation, and continues with metamorphosis as other state forms emerge.

I have suggested elsewhere (Leftwich 1995: 405) some central defining features of developmental states which, in their more extreme manifestations, have been most clearly expressed in non-democratic developmental states (both capitalist and socialist), but milder versions may be found in the structure and politics of various democratic developmental states. These features include (i) a dedicated developmental elite; (ii) relative autonomy for the state apparatus; (iii) a competent and insulated economic bureaucracy; (iv) a weak and subordinated civil society; (v) the capacity to manage effectively local and foreign economic interests; and (vi) a varying balance of repression, legitimacy, and performance which appears to succeed by offering a trade-off between such repression as may exist and the delivery of regular improvements in material circumstances.

It is worth summarizing the central argument so far. The conditions which promote the consolidation of democracy are likely to impose various structural constraints on the developmental capacity of new or born-again democratic states. But the problem, as Gordon White argues in Chapter 1, is not whether democracy is good or bad for development. Rather, the problem is to recognize that the kinds of informal or formal pacts and agreements which underpin the different forms of democratic politics will have very different implications for the developmental autonomy, capacity, and performance of the state.

5. Forms of the Democratic Developmental State: A Preliminary Classification

The central political and institutional features of Third World democratic states do not come in a standard form. I therefore suggest a preliminary classification of four broad types of democratic state in descending order of developmental capacity. They are of course only ideal types since there are no pure examples in practice. Each concrete instance represents only a major tendency in one direction. Yet what each example typically reveals is the way in which political factors shape the relationship between democratic practices and developmental capabilities. In the classification below the countries in brackets fit only partially into one or more of the categories.

1. Developmental democratic states:

    (i) Dominant-party developmental democratic states: Botswana Singapore (Malaysia);
    (ii) Coalitional developmental democratic states: Mauritius, Malaysia (India);

2. Non-developmental democratic states:

    (iii) Class-compromise non-developmental democratic states: Venezuela, South Africa;
    (iv) Party-alternation developmental democratic states: Jamaica, Costa Rica (India).

Adrian Leftwich

(a) *Dominant-party developmental democratic states*

This type in some respects approximates most closely to the non-democratic state in many of its features since the unity, authority, and relatively unchallenged central power of a single and overwhelmingly dominant party distinguishes it decisively from the other types and goes a long way to explain its autonomy and developmental success. The paradigm case here was of course Japan where the Liberal Democratic Party (the LDP) held power without break from 1955 to 1993 which ensured policy continuity buttressed by the strength and influence of the bureaucracy (Johnson 1982). But these central characteristics have also been found in Singapore and Botswana, two of the most remarkable of the developmental democratic states although their resource endowments and associated economic strategies and trajectories could not be more different.

In Singapore, the People's Action Party (PAP) has dominated politics, economy, and society from before independence in 1965, as has the Botswana Democratic Party (BDP) since independence in 1966. The strength of these dominant parties originates in the pre- and early-independence period of democratization when they and the rules of the political game in the new states were established. In the case of Singapore, leftist groups were effectively eliminated (Bradley 1965, Bellows 1970) and much of the local political talent was co-opted into the party with its power base built on labour unions and worker constituencies (Chan 1978, Sours 1997), making it a dominant multi-class party from the start. Moreover, and in contrast with both Venezuela and South Africa at the time of their transitions to democracy (1958 and 1992–4), Singapore and Botswana inherited no legacy of established parties representing old and powerful interests. Nor was there a proliferation of new parties or splits in old ones (as in Mauritius). In short, socio-economic structures in Singapore and Botswana (though very different) generated little serious or lasting contestation over the distribution of power, the rules of the game, the shape of new constitutions, or the broad direction of development strategy. Moreover, social and demographic structures in both societies (and tough political action by party and government in the case of Singapore) meant that no major regional, ideological, class, or ethnic cleavages existed, or were allowed to exist, as poles around which powerful contending parties could have mobilized (as in Fiji and Nigeria). Civil society was clearly weak, or weakened, from the start (and kept that way in Singapore). Where (as in the case of Botswana) new and independent organizations (farmers, parent-teaches, co-operatives) came into existence in the post-independence years, they were quickly absorbed by the BDP or financed by the state (Molutsi and Holm 1990).

Furthermore, again unlike Venezuela or South Africa, the structure of the Singaporean and Botswanan economies during democratic consolidation meant that no significant institutionalized economic interests had become established prior to these parties consolidating their power in the democratic state structures. Thus the playing field was not so much level as open and the dominant feature within it was the more-or-less unopposed but formally democratic party-controlled state. Moreover, unlike those societies where authoritarian regimes have long been the norm (typically, in Latin America), the military apparatus was not only new but had no historical association with older established classes or ethnic groups (as in South Africa) and hence was far less of a threat.

Taken together, therefore, the combination of a relatively undeveloped economy, few organized interests and a weakly differentiated class structure, relative socio-cultural homogeneity, and no long-standing military apparatus which had to be controlled or conciliated enabled dominant parties to emerge and to have a relatively clear run. These circumstances enabled power to be concentrated at the political centre and enhanced the relative but 'embedded' autonomy of the state (Evans 1989: 575–81). This provided the conditions under which determined leaderships were able to enhance state developmental capacity. They did so, especially, by creating and promoting key economic developmental bureaucracies, and were able to protect them from politicians and from the clamour of other special interests and to keep a sharp eye on the development of the economic and political institutions of civil society. In Singapore this was the powerful Economic Development Board (Haggard 1990, Low et al. 1993, Huff 1995), and in Botswana it was the Ministry of Finance and Development Planning (MFDP) (Raphaeli et al. 1984, Holm 1988, Charlton 1991). Using these institutions, the PAP and the BDP (as dominant developmental parties) have been able to pursue consistent, coherent, and continuous developmental policies without fearing seriously that the allegedly 'uncertain' outcomes of democratic electoral politics would derail their strategies or that losers in repeated electoral contests could or would threaten the stability of the polity. They have helped to generate powerful private sector interests, but have been able to work with them in pursuing developmental goals. The formal procedures of democratic electoral politics have imposed few restraints on developmental policies and programmes: on the contrary, they have repeatedly legitimized them. In short, and paradoxical as it may seem, democracy has been dependent on the unchallenged hegemony of these parties. And while satisfying formal democratic criteria, the hegemony of those parties has bestowed a degree of relative autonomy on the state which has led both to be independently described as 'administrative states' (Picard 1987: 13, Crouch 1984: 11).

Given these politics, the contradiction between the restraining and consensual logic of democratic bargaining and the logic of transformative developmentalism in these dominant-party developmental democratic states has been resolved in favour of the latter. And while their growth performances have been remarkable, they raise very uneasy implications for both the theory and practice of liberal (or social) democracy and the protection of civil rights, as the Singaporean case graphically illustrates. Rates of raw economic growth have been high in Singapore. And while this has also gone along with relatively uneven patterns of income distribution, by comparison with other high-income economies (World Bank 1996: table 5), it has none the less enabled the Singaporean state to maintain low unemployment and fund far-reaching social welfare programmes which have in turn sustained the hegemony of the party and the legitimacy of the state. Similarly, in Botswana, while capital accumulation and economic growth have been rapid, social inequalities have sharpened and environmental decline has occurred (Good 1993, Yeager 1993).

(b) Coalitional or consociational developmental democratic states

The political resolution of the contradiction of developmental democracy is very different in societies where no single party has emerged to dominate and hence where the developmental autonomy of the state is accordingly relatively reduced. If democracy is to survive under these circumstances then the solution lies in political coalitions. And if developmental momentum is to be established and maintained, a broad agreement needs to be negotiated between all major participating parties about the direction, shape, and pace of development strategy, so that whatever may be the composition of the coalition of the day, the strategy is kept on course (or altered or renewed by agreement).

In coalitional (or consociational) developmental democracies, the two prime political conditions for democratic consolidation (agreement about the rules of the game and, commonly, about the distribution of the spoils of power, and about the limits of policy) are much more important than in the first model, and *need to be* if democracy is to consolidate and if developmental continuity is to be ensured. Under these circumstances, moreover, the political vision and skills of elites play a much more important role than is sometimes allowed to human agency in the more deterministic theories of democratization, whether of the modernization or structuralist schools (Levine 1988: 378, Potter 1997). The origin, structure, and role of coalitions is not a new theme in mainstream political science where theories of consensual or consociational democratic forms are well established (Lijphart 1974, 1984; Lane and Ersson 1994). But what is important here is to see the connections between the insights of political science and these developmental issues.

Societies still characterized predominantly by sharp and primary vertical cleavages in ethnicity, culture, or religion—even where this is compounded by regional foci or horizontal cleavages in class—are the most obvious candidates for the emergence of coalitional developmental democracy. Class-compromise developmental democracies (see Venezuela below) are inappropriate since class formation in such plural societies is usually rudimentary and unconsolidated. The party-alternation model is also inappropriate for two reasons: first, because it requires clear (and changing) majorities which individual parties in these societies cannot muster (as in Mauritius); and, second, because even if they can muster such majorities (as with UMNO in Malaysia), the suspicion and unease with which significant excluded minorities would view their stranglehold on power could easily provoke violence and would deprive the ruling party of precisely the co-operation it needs for developmental effectiveness. This is especially the case where a community holding the majority of *political* resources needs the co-operation of a community controlling a majority or major part of *economic* resources (as in Malaysia and, also, South Africa).

Coalitional developmental democracies do not arise easily or quickly. However, they are likely to be the product of economic or political crises which lead at least one major party (or all) to recognize the political and economic virtues of settling down to forge (and perhaps formalize) the new rules of the political game and a workable policy consensus about development.[2] The case of Mauritius fits very closely the parameters of the model.

An intricately plural society, Mauritius has produced what has been described as an almost 'seamless web of consolidation and fragmentation' amongst the political parties (Bowman 1991: 68). This is hardly surprising given the heterogeneous complexity of the society drawn from Indian, French, African, Chinese, and British antecedents, of which the Indo-Mauritians constitute nearly 70 per cent. But these

---

[2] The role of external agencies in using a mixture of conditionality and mediation in such pre-coalition situations is, as yet, weakly theorized and little developed in practice. But the idea is important and some recent contractualist justifications for intervention are worthy of careful consideration (Hawthorn and Seabright 1996).

ethno-cultural groups are further divided by religion: some 51 per cent of the population is Hindu, 30 per cent Christian, and 17 per cent Muslim (Bowman 1991: 44 and Derbyshire and Derbyshire 1996: 382). Further linguistic subdivisions have complicated the picture further, as have caste and class divisions within and across communal boundaries.

From the time of its independence in 1968, the history of Mauritian politics has been characterized by a kaleidoscopic pattern of coalitional fusion and fission both within and between parties. But the first fifteen years or so were also accompanied by much deeper economic and political crises, stemming from the structural legacies of the colonial plantation economy and its associated social structure (Bowman 1991, Pandit 1995). Described as 'the perfect worst case', Mauritius in the 1960s was a poor, sugar-dependent economy with limited land, high rates of population growth and unemployment, coupled with the pluralism described above (Beckford 1972, Lempert 1987, Wils and Prinz 1996: 220). It is hardly surprising that by the late 1960s these circumstances had given rise to a sharp ideological cleavage with the rise of the Mouvement Militant Mauricien (MMM) which challenged the hitherto communal bases of coalition politics in Mauritius with a class analysis and appeal. This led to widespread industrial disturbance, political instability, and the suspension of democracy and emergency rule from 1972 to 1975.

Escalating economic crises from the mid-1970s (declining sugar prices, negative balance of payments and trade deficits, mounting debt, and swelling unemployment), compelled the major parties on left and right to realize that their welfare objectives (such as unemployment benefits), not to mention job creation and wage increases, were simply unattainable without rapid economic growth. By the early 1980s, with a series of IMF and World Bank austerity and structural adjustment programmes in place, the economy began to boom. New economic policies involved the modernization of the sugar sector, diversification of agriculture, tourism, and especially the promotion of exports through a major extension of the Export Processing Zone, originally established in the early 1970s (Minogue 1987, Bowman 1991, Pandit 1995).

But crucially underpinning all this was an emerging policy consensus about development strategy which the multiple economic and political crises of the 1970s and early 1980s had precipitated, cemented by a commitment both to toleration in communal, religious, and linguistic matters and to the democratic process. This has distinguished Mauritius sharply from what has occurred in the not entirely dissimilar plural society of Fiji where native Fijian claims to exclusive and dominant status in the political domain have undermined democracy (Carroll 1994).

Thus while fusion and fission of alliances have remained the central feature of Mauritian politics, the underlying stability of this fluid coalitional democracy since the early 1980s has rested on two key pillars: first, on a fundamental policy consensus about a national development strategy which has successfully generated an annual average growth of GNP per capita between 1985 and 1994 of almost 6 per cent (World Bank 1996); and, second, on respect for the constituents of its pluralist social structure.

Although Malaysia has certain features of the dominant-party type, it is better thought of as a further example of the kind of plural society which has successfully generated a coalitional developmental democratic state. Some 58 per cent of the population is Malay (and primarily rural), 32 per cent is Chinese (and primarily urban), and 9 per cent originated in the Indian subcontinent; 54 per cent of the population is Muslim, 19 per cent Buddhist, 12 per cent Confucian/Daoist, and 7 per cent Christian (Derbyshire and Derbyshire 1996: 167–8). It is certainly the case that although the offices of head of state and prime minister are open only to Malays, and although the United Malays National Organization (UMNO) has been the dominant political party, its power and authority have been mediated and refracted through a complex ruling coalition (now called the Barisan Nasional) and a federal structure against a background of historically sensitive and often tense cultural pluralism. This places Malaysia in the coalitional category discussed here.

The tensions between (primarily) the Malay and Chinese communities exploded in 1969 and brought about the suspension of democracy. But this in turn led to a new consensus, embodied in the dominant coalition, the Barisan Nasional, which pursued a broadly agreed development strategy (based on the New Economic Policy) through a constitution and political deal which has concentrated considerable power and developmental direction at the centre. This in turn has invested the politico-bureaucratic elite with relative developmental autonomy to develop or amend strategy and the role of the state in it (Ahmad 1989, Bowie 1991, Ravenhill 1995). Malaysia has generated a remarkable record of growth which has yielded an average annual rate of growth in GNP per capita since the mid-1980s of 5.6 per cent (World Bank 1996).

Thus while coalitional democracies clearly satisfy the formal democratic criteria, their political resolution of the structural contradiction of developmental democracy involves agreement and compromise about a common denominator of development policy which is likely to be lower than some would hope for and higher than others would want. And while the relative autonomy of the state appears less than that found in the dominant-party model, the democratic consolidation which such a political agreement can achieve produces stability which naked majoritarian politics of the dominant-party model would simply not allow in these contexts.

(c) *Class-compromise non-developmental democracies*

Though it is not altogether inaccurate, there is something inappropriate about referring to this type (and the party-alternation type) as 'non-developmental'. But the term is used here, first, to exaggerate the differences between the dynamic growth achievements of dominant-party and coalitional democracies in the first two categories and the relatively sluggish (or sometimes negative) rates of growth of those in the latter two categories; and, second, to highlight the policy and developmental implications of different patterns of democratic politics, something which is graphically illustrated in these democratic class-compromise states, a notion admirably pioneered in political science by Przeworski and Wallerstein (1982) and applied to Venezuela by Jennifer McCoy (1988).

The class-compromise democratic state is most likely to be the best (or only) *democratic* political resolution attainable in those societies where (i) class is the dominant cleavage, though not the only one; where (ii) the major political forces and interests ranged on either side of the central class rift have come to recognize that while successful revolution (the seizure of state power) is impossible, continued repression has profound economic costs and is thus counter-productive; and where (iii), even if one party can gain a large enough majority to push through its policies, radical and sectarian changes (however necessary they may be from a developmental point of view, or however desirable from a social justice point of view) will threaten other interests (internal and external) so fundamentally that those interests are likely to adopt non-democratic means to protect themselves, thereby destroying democracy (as occurred in Chile). Furthermore, formal or informal coalitions (as in Venezuela and in the initial phase of South African democratization) within or between parties are a likely means of institutionalizing and monitoring the fundamental agreement that underpins this type of class-compromise democratic state.

However, although there are some elements in common, two major factors differentiate the class-compromise type from the coalitional type. First, the fundamental assumption underlying democratization in these class-compromise states has been that the practices of democratic politics should not be used to undermine the essential principles of capitalist economic life, even where the state is allotted a significant role. Second, there have been clear (and, so far as possible, constitutional) agreements on the limits of policy. There is no better illustration of this type of non-developmental democratic state than that provided by the case of Venezuela.

The political history of Venezuela from the nineteenth century to the mid-twentieth century may be summarized crudely as a history of uprisings, revolts, regional *caudillos*, and dictatorial military regimes, most notably and recently those of General Gómez between 1909 and 1935 and General Marcos Pérez Jiménez between 1948 and 1958 (Levine 1989, Kornblith 1991). The relatively stagnant agrarian economy at the time of independence in 1830 was given some stimulus by the emergence of the coffee export economy in the mid-nineteenth century. But it was the growth of the oil industry from the 1920s that transformed Venezuelan society by 'destroying agriculture; spurring massive internal migration; and funding an active state' (Levine 1989: 250). These developments stimulated profound political and civil change which frightened the economic and social elites and which the military sought to repress. In particular, it spurred the growth of powerful trade unions (though heavily repressed) and other organizations in civil society. Some liberalization under the Medina government from 1943 allowed the emergence of the Acción Democrática (AD) party which, with the help of young military officers, overthrew the regime and established democracy, but it was only to last for three years, the so-called *trienio*.

During the *trienio* the AD was largely unassailable politically, at least in formal democratic terms, and hence (unadvisedly, as it turned out) ruled without consultation or conciliation as a dominant party, attacking established interests head-on. Its pro-peasant, pro-worker, and anti-Church educational reform policies threatened both materially and symbolically many established interests (rural landowners, oil, business, and Church) (Karl 1986: 72–6). This brought into being a conservative opposition, notably the Comité de Organización Política Electoral Independiente (COPEI) and in November 1948 finally provoked a military coup which instituted a further decade of brutal military rule under General Marcos Pérez Jiménez which proceeded to reverse the major policy reforms of the *trienio*. However, over the next decade, despite severe suppression by the security apparatus, there was again a build-up of opposition, including the Catholic Church. This led to popular protests and demonstrations which ultimately brought down the military regime in January 1958 and initiated the democratic system which has lasted until now.

What is crucial to note here, however, is that the AD and other major parties had learned from the experience of the *trienio* that if democracy was to survive, politics would have to be based on 'conciliation, compromise and prudence', and *serious reform would have to be postponed* (Levine 1989: 257, 265). The 'political class' had learned that in the context of sharp class and ideological cleavages, Venezuelan democracy could only survive on the basis of elite pacts and coalitions, a *limited* programme of reform, controlled and channelled participation in politics, and the exclusion of the revolutionary left (ibid.: 257); in short, a very 'conservative' programme.

To this end, a set of negotiated compromises was embodied in a series of remarkable pacts which aimed to 'establish political rules of the game for competition among elites . . . institutionalize the economic boundaries between public and the private sectors, provide guarantees for private capital and *fix the parameters of future socio-economic reform*' (Karl 1986: 66, my emphasis). These pacts, concluded in 1958, were the Pact de Punto Fijo, a Worker–Owner Accord, and the Declaration of Principles and Minimum Programme of Government which set down the common economic and political programme to be followed by all parties and which was later incorporated in the constitution (McCoy 1988). What did they amount to?

Politically, it was agreed by the three major parties that they would keep the communists out and that each party was guaranteed a share of government posts and patronage, irrespective of which party won the presidential election (McCoy 1988: 88, Przeworski 1992: 124)— a practice quite different from that operating in the *communes* of Côte d'Ivoire, as described by James Manor in this volume. Moreover, the military received amnesty for earlier abuses and the promise of improved salaries and new equipment (Levine 1989: 258). Economically, they agreed to a national development strategy involving a significant role for the state but which was none the less 'based on local and foreign capital, subsidies to the private sector, principles of compensation for any land reform, and a generally cautious approach to economic and social reform' (ibid.).

What is important here—and illustrates the thesis about one aspect of the conservatism of democracy outlined earlier—is that these pacts and accords meant in practice that 'capitalists accepted democratic institutions as a means for workers to make effective claims to improve their material conditions, while workers accepted private appropriation of profit by capitalists as an institution in expectation of further gains from production' or, in short, that 'workers accepted capitalism and capitalists accepted democracy, *each forgoing a more militant alternative*' (McCoy 1988: 86).

Three factors made this particular resolution of the contradiction of developmental democracy both possible and workable. First, so long as the flow of oil revenues continued, especially in the boom years of the 1970s when the price of oil rocketed from $2 to $14 per barrel, the state was able to fund this deal and the state bureaucracy expanded to provide basic services (health, housing, education, welfare) to a wider section of the population, thereby consolidating the legitimacy of the pact settlement (McCoy and Smith 1995: 122). However, during this time the state proved developmentally ineffective in 'sowing the oil', that is in using the oil revenues to promote diversification, productivity, employment, and wages in the non-oil sector of the economy (ibid.: 127). Second, although federal, Venezuela had always been a highly centralized federation (for instance, until recently state governors and city mayors were appointed from the centre). This enabled the dominant political elites to extend and maintain control nationally, from the centre (unlike India). Third, while the power, autonomy, and developmental effectiveness of the state were clearly limited by the class-compromise pacts and coalitions, this was compensated by co-operation between the two highly centralized and elite-run political parties (AD and COPEI) which achieved institutional expression in the wide use of relatively autonomous policy-making commissions. These commissions were largely appointed and used by the executive to hammer out developmental policies (within the terms of the agreed principles of the Minimum Programme). Moreover, they were effectively insulated from popular participation and legislative control, thereby serving to institutionalize inter-elite compromises and deals while restricting participation (Crisp 1994).

It is clear that these politics in Venezuela were initially far better at protecting and consolidating democracy than either stimulating growth outside the oil sector or promoting greater socio-economic equality and opportunity. Thus the relative decline of its oil revenues in the 1980s and escalating external public debt severely limited the Venezuelan state's ability to continue to fund the fundamental compromise implicit in the pacts and the legitimacy of the political system itself went into decline. This was hastened by the effects of austerity programmes of the IMF to which Venezuela had to turn in the late 1980s and which exaggerated already sharp inequalities and deepened poverty: the number in poverty jumping from 32 per cent in 1981 to 53 per cent in 1989 (McCoy and Smith 1995: 124–5). Unsurprisingly, this led to massive protests (*caracazo*) and two attempted coups in 1992. Although the Punto Fijo consensus held the line against a descent into military rule, it would appear that until and unless Venezuelan democracy is able to 're-equilibrate' its politics (ibid.: 156) around a new set of political, economic, and social agreements which, unlike the circumstances of the 1970s, would have to take account of the significantly reduced oil revenues, both its democratic and developmental prospects will remain strained.

The situation in South Africa suggests parallels and places that country in the same category of non-developmental democracy. For although it is too early to predict the outcome, the problems of achieving successful developmental democracy in South Africa are not entirely dissimilar to those of Venezuela (Lodge 1996). The ending of apartheid clearly involved a class compromise, profoundly complicated by ethnic legacies (unlike Venezuela). The new democratic state has three major tasks to achieve. It has to correct the gross inequalities of the past by undertaking redistribution. But in order to do so, it must also promote rapid economic growth of the private sector, attracting foreign investment and aid. Finally, it must maintain democratic political stability. Whether these tasks can be achieved simultaneously, and whether such essentially centrifugal objectives can be held together, not only poses the central problem for democratic development in polities constituted by democratic class compromises but also defines the multiple form which the contradiction takes in such democracies.

These problems also illustrate why, *ceteris paribus*, class-compromise democratic states are likely to have slow growth rates and why the agreements which compose these democracies tend to be so conservative in practice. For while civil and political liberties are protected in both Venezuela and post-apartheid South Africa, developmental state autonomy is necessarily limited by the pacts and agreements which underwrite the democratic process.

(d) Party-alternation non-developmental democratic states

The remaining party-alternating democratic state type is likely to occur where there is no single dominant party (as in Botswana, Singapore, or even Malaysia); where ethnic, cultural or religious pluralism is not central to politics (as it is in Mauritius); and where the class-compromise solution, at least initially, has been excluded because the main contending parties themselves are cross-class parties, each based on the incorporation of working- and middle-class elements, each (when in power) dispensing clientelist patronage to its followers and supporters, and each differentiated from the other mainly by a combination of historical association, personal loyalties, anticipation of patronage prospects, and—at times—ideological-policy orientations (Stone 1980, Stephens and Stephens 1986, Edie 1991).

The party-alternating type can only secure democratic stability where the major multi-class parties have reached a broad consensus about development policy—and Costa Rica is a good example of this. There, in a unitary state where there was no legacy of typical Latin American rural inequality or a powerful class of landholders (Cammack 1997: 170–1), and where the standing army was abolished, two dominant and multi-class parties, the National Liberation Party (PNP) and the (now) Christian Socialist Unity party (PUSC), have alternated in power since 1949. Both have adopted a strongly anti-communist line (as in Venezuela) and both have also been committed to a mixed economy, the extension of public welfare, and the reduction of inequality based on the belief that 'unfettered capitalist development causes undesirable and destabilizing socioeconomic dislocations and inequalities' (Booth 1989: 404). Costa Rican democracy has survived under these conditions, though it has presided over low rates of growth and only slight reductions in the considerable social inequalities.

But when a major ideological divide opens up between such parties, leading to sharp shifts in policy (both internal development policy and external relations), democratic stability has come under intense pressure which has in turn had negative implications for growth and development as has been the case in Jamaica. The island's colonial history, dominated by its plantation economy (Beckford 1972), had produced little industrialization by independence in 1962 and had given rise to high levels of unemployment and sharp income inequality: even in the early 1990s the top 20 per cent took 47 per cent of income and the bottom 20 per cent took less than 6 per cent (World Bank 1996). The two main parties, the Jamaica Labour Party (JLP) and the People's National Party (PNP), have dominated Jamaican politics since its largely peaceful 'constitutional decolonization' (Munroe 1972). Both parties have been multi-class parties and both have been committed to a mixed economy. However, the PNP has historically been more left of centre, while the JLP has always adopted a more centrist position, being more sympathetic to private (especially foreign) capital and emphasizing co-operation with the USA.

Until the early 1970s, under the first JLP government, these differences remained relatively subdued, though inequality was sharp and unemployment high (23 per cent in 1972) and political violence, especially around election times, became common (Stephens and Stephens 1986: 42–4). In the 1972 election, the PNP won power after a decade of JLP government, and embarked on a more radical programme, aiming to reduce economic dependence, increase the role of the state (including nationalization of utilities and greater control of the bauxite

industry), promote more equal distribution, achieve political independence from the West, and establish better relations with Cuba
(Stephens and Stephens 1986: 101, Huber and Stephens 1992: 63–5).
The net effect was to shatter whatever tacit accord had existed between the state and the private sector, thereby making it difficult to
make the mixed economy work and provoking capital flight. Political
and civic instability mounted and violence escalated, leading to a State
of Emergency in 1976 and in 1980 the threat of a military takeover
(Stephens and Stephens 1986: 231). As the PNP ran into even more
difficulties with an increasingly hostile USA and a severe balance of
payments crisis, it was compelled to turn to the IMF. When it failed
to meet the IMF terms, the PNP was ejected from government in the
election called in 1980 and Edward Seaga's Jamaica Labour Party took
office again.

Another shift in policy now occurred as the JLP shelved the PNP's
democratic socialist objectives in favour of policies which were more
in line with IMF thinking and the conventional battery of structural
adjustment programmes. But these, in turn, though helping to promote growth by the late 1980s, were unpopular, and the PNP again
won power in 1989. This time there was greater continuity in policy
for the PNP 'has essentially followed the JLP's model of the 1980s'
involving 'liberalization, privatization, austerity policies and export
promotion' (Huber and Stephens 1992: 79). Clientelism and patronage
remain central to the inner dynamics of Jamaican politics (Stone 1980,
Edie 1991). But it appears that Jamaica is, for the moment, moving
closer to the more stable Costa Rican version of the alternating-party
democratic state around a broadly common (*if reluctant*) development
consensus, from which there appears no escape. The parties are
becoming essentially competing management teams, with relatively
minor differences in emphasis and style, while still allowing the government of the day to reward its followers and supporters with the
accepted prizes of patronage and perks.

Both the Jamaican and Costa Rican examples illustrate very
clearly a central point in the earlier argument that the consolidation
of democratic politics can only be achieved in these alternating-party
democracies where a broad consensus and continuity in development
policy has been achieved, often (as is increasingly the case) when internal economic circumstances and external conditionality shape its
dominant features.

Before concluding it is worth adding that I have excluded any
detailed discussion of India from this account, largely because its
size and daunting complexity (like that of China) suggest a need for
a theory of Indian exceptionalism which is beyond this chapter. But

India does not fall easily into any one of these categories. None the less its political history is instructive. For Indian democracy started life as a short-lived dominant-party type. But unlike dominant parties elsewhere, this quickly dissolved and the consolidation of Indian democracy in the first two decades was won at the price of the developmental ineffectiveness of the Indian state (Nayar 1976) brought about by factionalism, patronage politics, and the attempt to incorporate, reconcile, and placate contradictory interests and expectations in and around the party, all of which led to 'incoherence at the level of policy formulation and implementation and . . . intraparty dissidence' (Mitra 1996: 709, Kaviraj 1996). The three decades since then have seen the dissolution of Congressional dominance and the emergence of coalition politics in the context of increasing regional, religious, and class conflicts. Holding such coalitions together in the face of such multiple pulls will become increasingly difficult, raising further doubts about the capacity of the central state to manage the urgency and immensity of India's developmental needs.

6. Conclusions

Democratic developmental states cannot be had to order. Where they exist, their provenance is intimately bound up with the processes of democratization which establish them and especially with the critical stage of consolidation. These are political processes and it has been one of my aims here to emphasize the *primacy* of politics in shaping both the forms of democracy and the developmental possibilities of the state. However, I am not arguing for the *autonomy* of politics. For it is clear that in each instance the political possibilities are a function of structural legacies in the history, economy, and social structure of the society in question. That being said, it is also clear that, given such structural legacies, the internal role of inter-elite political leadership, skill, and vision can be decisive. Externally, the multiple impacts of globalization constitute another set of factors (McGrew 1977), but this only underlines the need for effective developmental democratic states to manage and mediate their effects. I do not underestimate these, but my point here has been to emphasize the centrality of politics, that is the domestic macro-political context, in shaping the forms and relations of both democratic and developmental practice.

As the comparative evidence suggests, the minimal conditions for democratic consolidation are also and simultaneously the conditions which can and do constrain developmental autonomy, strategy, and capacity. The extent of such constraints is a direct function of the *politics* of these societies and, in particular, the pacts, agreements, and understandings which underwrite the politics of democratization and the ensuing democratic institutions and practices. Yet those very limitations on developmental capacity may also be seen as vindicating virtues of democracy since they have been crucial in preventing these democracies from descending into the dark night of military rule. By contrast some dominant-party and dominant-coalitional developmental states which have been successful in promoting growth have been less constrained politically, but are also characterized by limited popular sovereignty, low participation, and questionable human rights records—akin to what has been called 'low intensity democracy' (Gills and Rocamora 1992). In short, 'regulated' and consolidated democracies appear to have been more successful developmentally than those where greater political equality and participation have been the norm.

It is clear therefore that the gross concept of the democratic developmental state needs to be disaggregated and its forms and possibilities classified. For just as the main Third World democracies discussed here may be ranked as 'high' or 'low' developers along a series of developmental continua, they may also be ranked as 'high' or 'low' in terms of their democratic characteristics. The preliminary classification offered here requires refining, elaborating, and applying over time to the new wave of democracies and partial democracies that have now arisen. But only the simple-minded can now believe that 'democracy' is a sufficient condition for development or that 'development' is incompatible with democracy. The middle ground, represented by a variety of democratic developmental states, is wide open.

REFERENCES

Ahmad, Z. H. (1989), 'Malaysia: Quasi Democracy in a Divided Society', in L. Diamond et al. (eds.), *Democracy in Developing Countries*, iii: *Asia*, Boulder, Colo.: Lynne Rienner.

Bardhan, P. (1984), *The Political Economy of Development in India*, Oxford: Basil Blackwell.

Bayart, J.-F. (1993), *The State in Africa: The Politics of the Belly*, London: Longmans.

Beckford, G. L. (1972), *Persistent Poverty*, New York: Oxford University Press.

Bellows, T. (1970), *The People's Action Party: The Emergence of a Dominant Party System*, Southeast Asia Studies Monograph 14, New Haven: Yale University Press.

Booth, John A. (1989), 'Costa Rica: The Roots of Democratic Stability', in Diamond et al. (1989).

Bowie, A. (1991), *Crossing the Industrial Divide*, New York: Columbia University Press.

Bowman, L. (1991), *Mauritius. Democracy and Development in the Indian Ocean*, London: Dartmouth.

Bradley, C. P. (1965), 'Leftist Fissures in Singapore Politics', *Western Political Quarterly*, 18/2: 292–308.

Cammack, P. (1997), 'Democracy and Dictatorship in Latin America, 1930–1980', in Potter et al. (1997).

Carroll, T. (1994), 'Owners, Immigrants and Ethnic Conflict in Fiji and Mauritius', *Ethnic and Racial Studies*, 17/2: 301–24.

Chalker, L. (1994), *Good Government: Putting Policy into Practice*, London: Overseas Development Administration.

Chan, Heng Chee (1978), *The Dynamics of One Party Dominance: The PAP at the Grass Roots*, Singapore: Singapore University Press.

Charlton, R. (1991), 'Bureaucrats and Politicians in Botswana's Policy-Making Process: A Re-interpretation', *Journal of Commonwealth and Comparative Politics*, 29/3: 265–82.

Crisp, B. (1994), 'Limitations to Democracy in Developing Capitalist Societies: The Case of Venezuela', *World Development*, 22/10: 1491–509.

Crouch, H. (1984), *Domestic Political Structures and Regional Cooperation*, Singapore: Institute of Southeast Asian Studies.

Derbyshire, J., and Derbyshire, I. (1996), *Political Systems of the World*, Edinburgh: Chambers.

Diamond, L. (1992), 'Economic Development and Democracy Reconsidered', *American Behavioral Scientist*, 35: 450–94.

—— Linz, Juan J., and Lipset, S. M. (eds.) (1989), *Democracy in Developing Countries*, iv: *Latin America*, Boulder, Colo.: Lynne Rienner.

Dunleavy, P., and O'Leary, B. (1987), *Theories of the State*, London: Macmillan.

Edie, C. J. (1991), *Democracy by Default: Dependency and Clientelism in Jamaica*, London: Lynne Rienner.

Evans, P. B. (1989), 'Predatory, Developmental and Other Apparatuses: A Comparative Political Economy Perspective on the Third World State', *Sociological Forum*, 4/4: 561–87.

Freedom House Survey Team (1992), *Freedom in the World: Political Rights and Civil Liberties, 1991–1992*, New York: Freedom House.

Gills, B., and Rocamora, J. (1992), 'Low Intensity Democracy', *Third World Quarterly*, 13/3: 501–23.

Good, K. (1993), 'At the Ends of the Ladder: Radical Inequalities in Botswana', *Journal of Modern African Studies*, 31/2: 203–30.

Haggard, S. (1990), *Pathways from the Periphery: The Politics of Growth in Newly Industrializing Countries*, Ithaca, NY: Cornell University Press.

Hawthorn, G., and Seabright, P. (1996), 'Governance, Democracy and Development: A Contractualist View', in Adrian Leftwich (ed.), *Democracy and Development*, Cambridge: Polity Press.

Held, D. (1996), *Models of Democracy*, 2nd edn., Cambridge: Polity Press.

Herring, R. (1979), 'Zulfiqar Ali Bhuto and the "Eradication of Feudalism" in Pakistan', *Comparative Studies in Society and History*, 21/4: 519–57.

Holm, J. D. (1988), 'Botswana: A Paternalistic Democracy', in L. Diamond et al. (eds.), *Democracy in Developing Countries*, iii: *Asia*, Boulder, Colo.: Lynne Rienner.

Holmquist, F., and Ford, M. (1994), 'Kenya: State and Civil Society. The First Year after the Election', *Africa Today*, 4th Quarter: 5–25.

Huber, E., and Stephens, J. D. (1992), 'Changing Development Models in Small Economies: The Case of Jamaica from the 1950s to the 1990s', *Studies in Comparative International Development*, 27/2: 57–92.

Huff, W. G. (1995), 'The Developmental State, Government and Singapore's Economic Development since 1960', *World Development*, 23/8: 1421–38.

Humana, G. (1992), *World Human Rights Guide*, New York: Oxford University Press.

Huntington, S. P. (1991), *The Third Wave: Democratization in the Late Twentieth Century*, Norman: University of Oklahoma Press.

Johnson, C. (1982), *MITI and the Japanese Miracle*, Stanford, Calif.: Stanford University Press.

Karl, T. L. (1986), 'Petroleum and Political Pacts: The Transition to Democracy in Venezuela', *Latin American Research Review*, 22/1: 63–94.

Kaviraj, S. (1996), 'Dilemmas of Democratic Development in India', in Adrian Leftwich (ed.), *Democracy and Development*, Cambridge: Polity Press.

Kornblith, M. (1991), 'The Politics of Constitution-Making: Constitutions and Democracy in Venezuela', *Journal of Latin American Studies*, 23: 61–89.

Lane, J.-E., and Ersson, S. (1994), *Comparative Politics*, Cambridge: Polity.

Lee, E. (1979), 'Egalitarian Farming and Rural Development: The Case of South Korea', *World Development*, 7: 493–517.

Leftwich, A. (1995), 'Bringing Politics back in: Towards a Model of the Developmental State', *Journal of Development Studies*, 31/3: 400–27.

—— (1997), 'From Democratization to Democratic Consolidation', in Potter et al. (1997).

Lempert, D. (1987), 'A Demographic-Economic Explanation of Political Stability: Mauritius in a Microcosm', *Eastern Africa Economic Review*, 3/1: 77–90.

Levine, D. H. (1988), 'Paradigm Lost: Dependence to Democracy', *World Politics*, 40: 377–94.

—— (1989), 'Venezuela: The Nature, Sources and Prospects of Democracy', in Diamond et al. (1989).

Lewis, P. (1997), 'Democratization in Eastern Europe', in Potter et al. (1997).

Lijphart, A. (1974), 'Consociational Democracy', in K. McRae (ed.), *Consociational Democracy: Political Accommodation in Segmented Societies*, Toronto: McLelland & Stewart.

—— (1984), *Democracies*, New Haven: Yale University Press.

Lipton, M. (1974), 'Toward a Theory of Land Reform', in D. Lehmann (ed.), *Peasants, Landlords and Governments*, New York: Holmes & Meier.

Little, W. (1997), 'Democratization in Latin America, 1980–1995', in Potter et al. (1997).

Lodge, T. (1996), 'South Africa: Democracy and Development in a Post-apartheid Society', in Adrian Leftwich (ed.), *Democracy and Development*, Cambridge: Polity Press.

Low, L., et al. (1993), *Challenge and Response: Thirty Years of the Economic Development Board*, Singapore: Times Academic Press.

McCoy, J. (1988), 'The State and the Democratic Compromise in Venezuela', *Journal of Developing Societies*, 4: 85–133.

—— and Smith, W. C. (1995), 'Democratic Disequilibrium in Venezuela', *Journal of Inter-American Studies and World Affairs*, 37/2: 113–79.

McGrew, T. (ed.) (1997), *The Transformation of Democracy? Globalization and the Post-Westphalian World Order*, Cambridge: Polity Press.

Mainwaring, S., O'Donnell, G., and Valenzuela, J. (1992), 'Introduction', in S. Mainwaring, G. O'Donnell, and J. Valenzuela (eds.), *Issues in Democratic Consolidation: The New South American Democracies in Comparative Perspective*, Notre Dame, Ind.: University of Notre Dame Press.

Minogue, M. (1987), 'Mauritius', in Colin Clarke and Tony Payne (eds.), *Politics, Security and Development in Small States*, London: Allen & Unwin.

Mitra, S. K. (1996), 'Politics in India', in G. A. Almond and G. B. Powell (eds.), *Comparative Politics Today*, New York: Harper Collins.

Molutsi, P., and Holm, J. D. (1990), 'Developing Democracy when Civil Society is Weak: The Case of Botswana', *African Affairs*, 89/356: 323–40.

Munroe, T. (1972), *The Politics of Constitutional Decolonization: Jamaica, 1944–1962*, Kingston: Institute of Social and Economic Research, University of the West Indies.

Nayar, B. R. (1976), 'Political Mobilization in a Market Polity: Goals, Capabilities and Performance in India', in R. I. Crane (ed.), *Aspects of Political Mobilization in South Asia*, Foreign and Comparative Studies, South Asia Series, 1, Syracuse, NY: University of Syracuse.

Pandit, K. (1995), 'Labour and Employment under the "NIC" Model of Development: Recent Evidence from Mauritius', *Singapore Journal of Tropical Geography*, 16/2: 158–80.

Picard, L. (1987), *The Politics of Development in Botswana: A Model for Success*, Boulder, Colo.: Lynne Rienner.

Potter, D. (1997), 'Explaining Democratization', in Potter et al. (1997).

—— Goldblatt, D., Kiloh, M., and Lewis, P. (eds.) (1997), *Democratization*, Cambridge: Polity Press.

Przeworski, A. (1986), 'Some Problems in the Study of the Transition to Democracy', in F. O'Donnell et al. (eds.), *Transitions from Authoritarian Rule: Comparative Perspectives*, Baltimore: Johns Hopkins Press.

—— (1988), 'Democracy as a Contingent Outcome of Conflicts', in J. Elster and R. Slagstad (eds.), *Constitutionalism and Democracy*, Cambridge: Cambridge University Press.

—— (1992), 'The Games of Transition', in S. Mainwaring, G. O'Donnell, and J. Valenzuela (eds.), *Issues in Democratic Consolidation: The New South*

American Democracies in Comparative Perspective, Notre Dame, Ind.: University of Notre Dame Press.

Przeworski, A., and Wallerstein, M. (1982), 'The Structures of Class Conflict in Democratic Capitalist Societies', *American Political Science Review*, 76: 215–38.

Raphaeli, N., et al. (1984), *Public Sector Management in Botswana*, World Bank Staff Working Paper 709, Washington: World Bank.

Ravenhill, J. (ed.) (1995), *The Political Economy of East Asia: Singapore, Indonesia, Malaysia, the Philippines and Thailand*, vol. i, Aldershot: Edward Elgar publishing.

Republic of South Africa (1996), *Constitution of the Republic of South Africa, 1996*, Cape Town: Constitutional Assembly, 8 May.

Rueschemeyer, D., and Evans, P. B. (1985), 'The State and Economic Transformation: Toward an Analysis of the Conditions Underlying Effective Intervention', in Peter B. Evans, Dietrich Rueschemeyer, and Theda Skocpol (eds.), *Bringing the State back in*, New York: Cambridge University Press.

—— Stephens, E. H., and Stephens, J. D. (1992), *Capitalist Development and Democracy*, Cambridge: Polity Press.

Schumpeter, J. A. (1965), *Capitalism, Socialism and Democracy*, London: Unwin.

Sklar, R. (1996), 'Towards a Theory of Developmental Democracy', in Adrian Leftwich (ed.), *Democracy and Development*, Cambridge: Polity Press.

Sours, M. H. (1997), 'Comparative Development Strategies in Asian Authoritarian National Regimes', unpublished paper delivered to the International Studies Association Annual Convention, Panel C-3, Toronto, 20 Mar.

Sparks, A. (1995), *Tomorrow is Another Country: The Inside Story of South Africa's Negotiated Revolution*, London: Heinemann.

Stephens, E. H., and Stephens, J. D. (1986), *Democratic Socialism in Jamaica*, London: Macmillan.

Stone, C. (1980), *Democracy and Clientelism in Jamaica*, New Brunswick, NJ: Transaction.

Stretton, H. (1976), *Capitalism, Socialism and the Environment*, Cambridge: Cambridge University Press.

UNDP (United Nations Development Programme) (1996), *Human Development Report*, New York: Oxford University Press.

Wade, R. (1990), *Governing the Market: Economic Theory and the Role of Government in East Asian Industrialization*, Princeton: Princeton University Press.

Weiss, L., and Hobson, J. M. (1995), *States and Economic Development*, Cambridge: Polity Press.

White, G. (1984), 'Developmental States and Socialist Industrialization in the Third World', *Journal of Development Studies*, 21/1: 97–120.

—— (1985) 'The Role of the State in China's Industrialization', in G. White and R. Wade (eds.), *Developmental States in East Asia*, IDS Research Report 16, Brighton: Institute of Development Studies.

Wils, A., and Prinz, C. (1996), 'Living in a Small Crowded Room: Scenarios for the Future of Mauritius', *Population and Environment*, 17/3: 217–42.

Wiseman, J. A. (1997), 'The Rise and Fall and Rise (and Fall?) of Democracy in Sub-Saharan Africa', in Potter et al. (1997).

World Bank (1992), *World Development Report 1992*, New York: Oxford University Press.

—— (1996), *World Development Report 1996*, New York: Oxford University Press.

Yeager, R. (1993), 'Governance and Environment in Botswana: The Ecological Price of Stability', in S. J. Stedman (ed.), *Botswana: Political Economy of Democratic Development*, Boulder: Lynne Rienner.

Young, C. (1994), *The African Colonial State in Comparative Perspective*, New Haven: Yale University Press.

Death without Taxes
Democracy, State Capacity, and Aid Dependence in the Fourth World

MICK MOORE

1. Introduction

The title of this volume assumes tensions between 'democracy' and 'development'. What are they? Which state institutions and the government practices are development-friendly but democracy-averse? There is a long list of familiar claimants to a place on this list. For example: the need for governments to take some key, difficult economic policy decisions both secretly and independently of the influence of economic pressure groups; the requirement that trade unions be controlled and that environmental standards be held low for fear of discouraging (foreign) investment; incentives for government to enter into corporatist-type arrangements, with business, labour, and other economic interests, that privilege these interests and the organizations that represent them in relation to the rest of the population; the temptation to give priority to 'continuity', 'predictability', and 'government credibility' over the uncertainty inherent in democratic elections; and the pressure for states in fiscal trouble to enter into (secret) economic policy agreements with (foreign) creditors at the expense of transparency or democratic accountability.

This chapter deals with a development–democracy tension that is far less familiar: in fact, so unfamiliar that any shorthand summary —e.g. 'the tension between democratic governance and the financial

For useful comments on earlier drafts of this chapter, I am indebted to Keith Bezanson, Deborah Brautigam, Susanna Davies, Gus Edgren, Emmanuel de Kadt, Anuradha Joshi, Robin Luckham, James Manor, Robert Neild, Jean-François Médard, Mark Robinson, Mark Schacter, Ken Sigrist, Mike Stevens, Judith Tendler, and Gordon White. Gordon was especially helpful with ideas and relevant literature. The argument has been sharpened in presentations at the Institute of Development Studies, Yale University, and the Department for International Development, London.

dependence of governments on "unearned income" '—will leave readers in the dark. It is therefore especially important that the outlines of the argument be summarized clearly at this point. There are five main components:

(i) State incomes can be located conceptually on a continuum according to the degree to which they are earned. The extent of 'earnedness' depends on (*a*) the bureaucratic and organizational effort put into revenue-raising by the state and (*b*) the degree to which there is effective reciprocity between citizens and state, i.e. real services in return for tax contributions.

(ii) The greater the dependence of the state on earned income, the more likely are state–society relations to be characterized by account-ability, responsiveness, and democracy.

(iii) In recent years, the governments of many of the poorest coun-tries (the 'Fourth World') have become heavily dependent on un-earned income. They tend anyway, for logistic and historical reasons, to derive a high proportion of their revenues from unearned sources. This dependence has been magnified over the last two decades by a large relative shift of foreign aid to poor, small countries. Aid alone now accounts for almost half the income of the typical government of a low-income country. Two decades ago, the typical figure was about one-quarter.

(iv) The anti-democratic effect of this high level of dependence on (unearned) aid income is exacerbated by the fact that aid is disbursed within each recipient country by a multiplicity of (official) donors who are effectively in competition with one another for activities to fund. This competition, and the variety of procedures and policies adopted by individual donors, make it impossible for the recipient governments to engage in effective central budgeting, and thus for their citizens and legislatures to exercise effective democratic control over the ways in which these states raise and spend money.

(v) The exercise of citizen influence over state revenue and expend-iture lies at the heart of effective democracy. By the means they use to promote development in the poorest countries, official aid donors are undermining the values of democracy and good governance that they are otherwise trying to promote through general 'political condi-tionality' and specific aid interventions.

The argument here is only mildly heretical. But even casual heretics need to protect themselves against the possibility of the scholarly *fatwa*. I hope to achieve that, and provide the reader with some useful orienta-tion, by making three general points about my thesis at this stage:

(i) Throughout this chapter I use the term 'democracy' in a particu-lar sense, which is shared by the editors of this volume, but differs from much popular usage. There are two main, related dimensions to my definition. First, I adopt a substantive rather than a procedural conception of the term. A 'polity is democratic to the extent that there exist institutionalized mechanisms through which the mass of the population exercise control over the political elite in an organized fashion' (Moore 1996: 40). I would be happy to add in some reference to 'political equality' as part of the definition, but that would not change anything I argue here. For present purposes, I reject procedural definitions—those that equate democracy with the vitality of contested elections, associational freedom, or other procedures and institutions employed to enable the mass of the population to exercise control over the political elite. To adopt procedural definitions is to confuse ends with means. Second, I see democracy as a continuous or relative rather than an absolute concept: one can, and should, talk of degrees of democracy, rather than of countries being simply democratic or not. There is some element of democracy in almost all polities, for few regimes can afford entirely to ignore mass pressures. The extent and character of those democratic elements however vary widely, as do the other, competing power elements that bear on national political elites: e.g. other states; organized private interests with direct access to decision-making; the state apparatus itself; or the structural power of the controllers of capital[1] (Moore 1996: 40). These apparently scholastic definitional issues have practical implications. Some people will claim that there is democracy in Camgola and Haitistan because there are elections and parliaments that meet international standards. I want to be free to say that, all the time that the Camgolan and Haitistani legislatures have only nominal influence over the ways in which governments raise and spend money, there is little substance in their democracy: the state elites will be largely free to do as they wish. I conceive democracy as a subspecies of a broader concept: the accountability of state to society. I have in most cases used the term 'accountability' here.

(ii) I am not suggesting here that development aid always, or even generally, undermines democracy or accountability. It certainly has that potential, but in the same way that carrots have the potential to inflict carotene poisoning on the human body: eat large quantities of carrots in a diet that contains little else, and you will be in trouble. In normal circumstances, carrots are a very good thing. So too is development aid.[2] Context is all important. My contention here is that the dependence of states on unearned income is a special problem in the contemporary Fourth World (a) because the absolute levels of aid

---

[1] This concept is explained in Winters (1996: ch. 1).

[2] See Burnside and Dollar (1997) for some recent powerful evidence that, when combined with appropriate economic policies, aid does indeed boost economic growth.

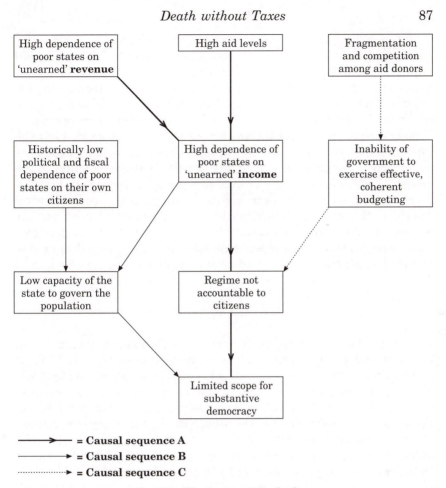

FIG 3.1: *The Argument in Outline*

dependence have become unusually high and (*b*) because this dependence interacts in a malign fashion with other features of contemporary Fourth World states and their relation to the international state
system.

(iii) While much less complex that the processes out there in the
real world that it attempts to capture, my argument here has more
components and causal linkages than one would wish. To simplify by
omitting elements would make it positively misleading. To help the
reader, I have overcome an aversion to bubble charts, and summarized the three main causal sequences—A, B, and C—in Fig. 3.1.

Section 2 of this chapter provides some empirical grounding for the
abstract arguments summarized in Fig. 3.1: a brief introduction to
the 'Fourth World' and a summary of the statistics on the growing

extent of aid dependence of the governments of Fourth World countries over the past two decades. Sections 3 and 4 jointly deal with causal
sequence A from Fig. 3.1. Section 3 comprises the conceptual core of
the chapter: the linkages between state income sources and accountability. The corresponding empirical material—variations among
countries in the sources of state income—is presented in Section 4.
Section 5 deals with causal sequence B: the ways in which both the
international state system and the high dependence of governments
on unearned income tend to generate or perpetuate weak states in the
Fourth World, and thus undermine prospects for democracy through
a second, indirect channel. Section 6 covers causal sequence C: the ways
in which the prevalent mechanisms for aid disbursement further
undermine the scope for accountable governance by making impossible effective, coherent budgeting on the part of heavily aided governments. The concluding comments are presented in Section 7.

2. The Fourth World of Underdevelopment

The Third World is dead. In so far as it still respects international
frontiers, underdevelopment is now concentrated in a new Fourth World
of countries defined by three main sets of characteristics. The first and
most obvious set are low incomes and poor economic performance,
including in some cases falls in average real income per head during
the 1970s and 1980s. The second set are weak state capacity—limited
ability to control populations, exercise authority, provide law and
order, or raise taxes—and political systems that operate mainly
through personal connections and patrimonial principles rather than
through distinct, enduring political institutions. Although the reach
of state power is limited, it is exercised in relatively arbitrary and coercive ways. The accountability of the state apparatus to society is low,
and democracy is both rare and, where it does appear, more formal
than substantive, in the sense that it does not enable the mass of the
population to exercise much institutionalized influence over political
elites. The third set of characteristics uniting the Fourth World is the
high degree of dependence of their economies and governments on international aid.

The boundaries of the Fourth World are fuzzy. Most countries that
are indisputably within it are located in sub-Saharan Africa. Others
are scattered from South-east Asia (e.g. Cambodia) across to the
Caribbean (e.g. Haiti). A few of the new Asian states that emerged
from the break-up of the Soviet Union may be eligible for membership. India clearly does not belong in the Fourth World because it is

largely independent of aid and the state is relatively strong and institutionalized. The Bangladeshi and Pakistani states are intermediate
cases: weaker, less institutionalized, and more aid dependent than India,
but not heavily aid dependent by the standards of many smaller but
equally poor countries. Much of the empirical material and many of
the ideas used in this chapter derive from sub-Saharan Africa. However, it is not a chapter about sub-Saharan Africa. There are dimin-
ishing returns to debating sub-Saharan Africa's development problems
as if they were generic and unique to the region. An Africa focus
generates insufficient comparative perspective, and excessive scope
for suspicions about implicit racism. We may be able to think more
clearly and creatively if we look instead (a) at regional and national
differences within sub-Saharan Africa (Lewis 1996: 128–9) and (b), as
I have done here, at a broader category of states defined by political
and economic characteristics rather than regional location.

The Fourth World is economically underdeveloped, politically
underdeveloped, and highly aid dependent. Why do these three characteristics tend to occur together? There can be little doubt that economic and political underdevelopment are found together in part
because they are mutually reinforcing. Why are these same countries
also the most aid dependent? One reason is tangible and self-evident:
aid donors recently have concentrated their assistance on the countries that seem most in need. The other reasons, which I deal with in
this chapter—the causal linkages from aid dependence to economic and
political underdevelopment—are less tangible and more contestable.
They are explored in later sections. My purpose at this point is to
summarize the main facts about this relative shift of aid to the
Fourth World over the past two decades. The details and the discussions of the weaknesses and treatment of the statistical data are in
Appendix 3.1. For present purposes the Fourth World is defined as
those countries categorized as 'low income' by the World Bank. Excluding those with a population of less than one million, there are about
fifty such countries at present. The main conclusions of the analysis
of trends in aid are:

(i) The typical government of a Fourth World country currently obtains
almost half its income from aid. Two decades ago, aid accounted for
only about a quarter of income.[3]

(ii) Levels of aid dependence increased steeply in the 1970s and 1980s
because aid funds were increasingly concentrated on the poorest
economies, which were growing only slowly or shrinking. The countries

---

[3] There is more uncertainty about the accuracy of that figure than about the figure of
one-half for the present time. It is imputed from the statistics in Tables A3.3 and A3.4.

of the Former Third World that have enjoyed faster economic growth
have become less aid dependent.

(iii) The increasing aid dependence of the governments of Fourth
World countries is not in any major part due to faltering in their own
revenue-raising efforts. In so far as their own revenues have stagnated
or declined, this is mainly due to falls in the world market prices for
the primary commodity exports that have historically been their main
single revenue source. The factor that has changed most is the level
of aid inflows.[4]

What are the effects of high aid dependence on state–society relations?
Can governments that obtain most of their income from overseas ever
be accountable or responsive to their own citizens? What levels of aid
dependence might begin to undermine such accountability? To answer
those questions we need to go back to conceptual basics: the connections
between the sources of state income and the nature of state–society
relations.

3. Public Finance and State–Society Relations

Political economy has its origins as a distinct discipline in concerns
about taxation and public finance. These same topics are among the
staples of contemporary economics and political science. Yet we have
available no general theoretical or conceptual framework about the
connections between state income sources and state–society relations
that could be used to begin to tackle the questions set out above.[5] We
have to construct our own framework. Fortunately, we do not have to
construct it from scratch. For a number of groups of scholars have
recently been working on these issues in specific geographical and
historical contexts, often with reference to contemporary developing
countries.[6] They offer a number of generalizations and hints that can
be combined to create a framework—some concepts and some causal

---

[4] Opponents of aid sometimes argue that it acts as a substitute for the revenue-
raising efforts of the recipient government. Attempts to test that proposition with
econometrics have been inconclusive (White 1992: 163–240).

[5] The existing jargon of taxation specialists does not even provide the basic tools for
this purpose. Tax specialists are mainly concerned with operational, economic values
of simplicity, efficiency, and equity, while my focus is on broader and more abstract
issues of the place of taxation in the shaping of state–society relations. My emphases
and biases, especially the notion that in some circumstances the existence of active
revenue-raising bureaucracies has an intrinsic political value almost independent of
the revenue actually raised (see Section 5), run counter to some of the core assumptions of taxation specialists.

[6] As Bachman (1987: 119) explains, political scientists working on developing countries have only recently shown much interest in issues of revenue and taxation.

propositions—that enables us to talk in general terms about these issues and reach some plausible conclusions.

I draw in particular on a rich seam of political science research on the contemporary Middle East centred around the concept of 'rentier states'.[7] The proposition driving this work is that the unusually authoritarian nature of twentieth-century Middle Eastern regimes[8] stems not from cultural legacies (Ottoman, Arab, or Islamic), but from the fact that most Middle Eastern governments have been 'rentiers' in a fiscal sense: dependent on foreign grants (and military support), revenues from the export of natural resources (oil and phosphates), and income from 'location-specific physical infrastructure' (canals, oil transmission lines, military bases); and largely independent fiscally of their own citizens. Another major source of inspiration is comparative historical work on the evolution of constitutional and representative government in Europe that identifies as a key factor the emergence of 'bargaining' between state executives and controllers of capital over levels and modalities of taxation.[9] The counter-insurgency intellectuals, employed to help deal with the problems of some of the Western nations' Third World allies during the Cold War, developed some useful insights into the local political consequences of states' fiscal independence of their citizens (Odon 1992: 219). Finally, and in midstream, Jean-François Medard, a specialist on African politics, explained to me how well the ideas presented here fitted his own conception of a significant categorical divide among African states, between the 'mineral-based' states where patrimonial, personal rule flourishes (e.g. Angola, Gabon, Nigeria, Sierra Leone, Congo), and the 'agricultural' states, of which Côte d'Ivoire is the extreme case, where political authority has generally been more institutionalized.

From the ideas contained in these various bodies of literature, one can build up a general argument about the connection between

[7] Mahdavy (1970) is generally cited as the originator of the concept. His work was substantially economistic. I have relied more on recent scholars who have developed the political dimensions of the concept: (Anderson 1994, 1995; Chaudhry 1989; Shambayati 1994). Mahdavy (1970: 428) defined the rentier state in terms of dependence on *external* rents, but classified oil revenues as 'external' on grounds that are difficult to accept. Later discussion of the precise definition of 'rentier state' and of alternative concepts such as 'exoteric' (versus 'esoteric') and 'allocation' (versus 'production') states (e.g. Beblawi and Luciani 1987: esp. 1–21) do not appear to have advanced us very far.

[8] In cross-national comparisons, countries of the Middle East consistently score lower in terms of democracy, civil liberties, etc. than other countries at similar income levels.

[9] There is a large literature on this topic. The key references are Bates and Lien (1985) for the formalization of the argument and Tilly (1992) for historical comparisons of the different state trajectories.

sources of government finance and state–society relations. I do that in Proposition 6 below, but precede that with four preliminary ideas (Propositions 1 to 4), and with a new language for classifying government income sources (Proposition 5).

(a) *Proposition 1. Income-seeking is an important determinant of the behaviour of states*

States are not commercial organizations, and are therefore responsive to a wider range of concerns than finance alone. One of the more useful frameworks for understanding states is to view them as responding, in different degrees according to circumstances, to five sets of imperatives: hegemony, autonomy, legitimacy, accumulation, and revenue (Young 1994: ch. 2). However, revenue concerns tend to be relatively pressing for modern states: without money in the treasury, it is difficult to pursue other objectives, and things fall apart.[10] The capacity to raise taxes is increasingly used by political scientists as a key indicator of state capacity (Wang 1995: 88–9, Weiss and Hobson 1995: ch. 1).

(b) *Proposition 2. States broadly, and in the long term, act rationally in the pursuit of income*

States are not monolithic. However, the longer the time scale of our analysis, the more it is acceptable to assume that states act rationally in accordance with accurate perceptions of their own interests.[11]

(c) *Proposition 3. States' income-seeking behaviour reflects their strategic interaction with income providers*

Crudely, the ways in which a state will seek income will depend on the perceptions and experience of its controllers about what is to be obtained from potential income sources, and how the policy of the state itself will affect the behaviour of the controllers of those sources. How far are these relationships potentially zero-sum, and to what extent do they provide scope for co-operation and joint gains? Is it better to

---

[10] In attempting to interpret the behaviour of governments as if they were revenue maximizers, Levi (1988) helped to right the balance in political science, at the cost of overstating the centrality of revenue concerns.

[11] Little purpose would be served in exploring here the notion of rationality of an institutional actor. And it does not matter for present purposes whether rational behaviour is interpreted (*a*) as the purposive outcome of processes of data collection and processing, and evaluation of options, or (*b*) as a more experiential process of learning what does and does not work.

try to tax directly every peasant farmer or to strike long-term bargains with local landlords, warlords, or governors, ceding them direct taxation powers in return for fixed annual payments? Will the removal of controls on capital movements lead to capital flight or to a net capital inflow as a result of enhanced 'business confidence'? In deciding on which strategies to pursue, states will consider, *inter alia*, relative logistical costs, risks, and the range of choices open to the other actors.

(d) Proposition 4. Governments will be especially responsive to (i) major individual income providers and (ii) those providers who have an 'exit' option

The term 'income providers' refers to individual agents; it is to be distinguished from 'income sources'. Business turnover tax could be a major source of government income, but in virtually all cases comes from a large number of relatively small-scale providers, i.e. businesses. Typical major individual government income providers are: public or private monopolies (and near-monopolies) in the provision of basic consumer goods—salt, tobacco, alcohol, foodstuffs, etc.—at low levels of national income;[12] oil and other mineral exports; location-specific physical infrastructure (canals, oil transmission lines, military facilities for other states, airports, harbours); and foreign aid of various kinds. The ownership, management, and taxation arrangements for enterprises and activities that generate high revenues for the state may vary widely. Similarly, the extent to which non-state actors have an 'exit' option will vary widely according to circumstances. For example, a transnationally owned tobacco company may bear a great deal of 'squeezing' if high import tariffs and brand promotion provide it with an effective monopoly in the domestic consumer market. If the company faces real competition, high tobacco taxes might lead it (to threaten) to pull out of the country. In general, governments will tend to be more accommodating to the concerns of major income providers[13] and those who could plausibly go elsewhere.

---

[12] Market dominance rather than a strict monopoly status may be adequate. For example, in 1995 the San Miguel brewery enterprise, which faces considerable market competition, paid 6.8% of the Philippines' government revenues (*Financial Times*, London, 11 June 1996). The Ceylon Tobacco Company, a subsidiary of British American Tobacco, which faced little market competition within Sri Lanka, provided 10% of government revenue in 1988 (Central Bank of Ceylon 1991: table 54, Ceylon Tobacco Company Ltd. 1989: 13).

[13] A recent example is the laxness of the British government in enforcing environmental regulations on its major income provider, the North Sea oil and natural gas extraction industry.

(e) Proposition 5. Government income sources can usefully be classified on a continuum between 'earned' and 'unearned'

Regular public finance jargon—for example, direct versus indirect and progressive versus regressive taxes, the buoyancy and elasticity of tax revenues—is of little use for the purposes of this chapter. We need some concepts that refer to the broad political and institutional dimensions of state income and state–society relations. The language of 'earned' versus 'unearned' income, familiar to British income tax-payers, can be pressed into service here. What do I mean here by 'earned' income? The term is not used normatively. It refers to the notion of 'working for' something, i.e. putting purposive effort into attaining it.[14] More precisely, I use it here to refer only to the state in relation to the mass of its citizens (or subjects). State income is 'earned' to the extent that the state apparatus has to put in effort in working with citizens in order to get its money. There are two criteria we can use to judge how far state income is earned:

(i) Organizational effort: how large, elaborate, differentiated, and efficient is the bureaucratic apparatus that the state deploys to collect its income? A state that has a number of distinct and effective services to assess and collect, for example, income, property, customs, and turnover taxes, is working much harder for its income than is a state that receives a large annual cash subvention from an oil-rich neighbour and collects the remainder through a flat rate import duty.

(ii) Reciprocity: how far are citizens obtaining some reciprocal services in return for their tax contributions? 'Reciprocal services' range from (a) what we may term 'rudimentary' (a state apparatus that does not coercively and arbitrarily exploit citizens when collecting taxes or otherwise interacting with them); through (b) a 'minimal contractual relationship' (the provision of law, order, justice, and security); to (c) 'extended reciprocity' (e.g. the services associated with 'welfare' and 'developmental' states).

States earn their income to the extent that they both (a) deploy an extensive organization to collect it and (b) provide reciprocal services to citizens—even if those services are intended solely to increase citizens' future taxable capacity. Note that the operations of the state 'in relation to the mass of its citizens' are part of my definition of earned income. It follows that the deployment of a relatively elaborate bureaucratic apparatus to nurture, monitor, and tax a concentrated, major income source—for example, a large phosphate deposit—would lead

---

[14] The use of the concept of 'earned income' is in fact a logical extension from the term 'rentier': rentier income is 'unearned' in the language of classical political economy.

to a lower ranking on the 'earnedness' scale than would a similar effort that was more widely dispersed. The same would apply to the efforts of a state to establish a good relationship with a major aid donor. One indicator of the extent to which state income is earned is the proportion of potential income providers who are brought into the revenue net.

(f) Proposition 6. The more government income is 'earned', the more likely are state–society relations to be characterized by accountability, responsiveness, and democracy

This proposition, the keystone to the argument of this chapter, is deeply rooted in the recent research literatures listed above. I go beyond those literatures here in the sense that I try to make explicit arguments that are left implicit there, and are in some respects more problematic than they first appear.

Two Africa specialists have recently drawn our attention to the connections between state income sources and the relative weakness and non-accountable nature of contemporary Fourth World states (Brautigam 1991, 1996; Guyer 1992). To make their case they have used a mixture of historical and intuitive arguments, both with a strong deductive element. Let us take first the historical arguments.

The most direct historical evidence relates to the origins of representative government in Western Europe, especially in England and France (Bates and Lien 1985). Representative government originated in political struggles between rulers and private owners of capital about the linkage between taxation and representation. A deal was struck and, over time, institutionalized and extended: owners of capital, in the form of members of legislatures elected on very narrow franchises explicitly to represent 'interests' (i.e. property), obtained influence— and eventually control—over levels of government spending, the composition of revenue, and rates of tax. The predictability and stability of taxes that could result from a negotiation process was to the advantage of both sides. Rulers could borrow more easily and cheaply on the strength of expected revenues; property owners could accurately estimate their future tax obligations; and both sides could gain from a less contested and arbitrary process of tax collection. The owners of capital had necessarily to be represented corporately for such bargaining to be effective.

However, such representative negotiating institutions did not take root everywhere. While cultural context was no doubt important, a major factor affecting their presence and vitality was the extent to which capital was mobile (i.e. in the form of financial and trading assets) rather than fixed (especially landed property). For there was particularly wide scope for shared gains from co-operation between rulers and owners of mobile capital involved in (international) trading and financial operations. Owners of mobile capital had two particular interests in such a deal. One was protection against the arbitrary and exploitative taxation practices—e.g. sudden changes in tax rates or introduction of new taxes—to which they, more than landowners, were especially vulnerable because such a high proportion of their assets were in goods that could easily be confiscated by political authorities. The other was direct, legitimate influence over the military and diplomatic policies and apparatuses of the state, which could be used against competing trading nations.[15] In granting domestic political influence to owners of mobile capital, rulers could reasonably hope (*a*) to reduce the incidence of tax evasion, (*b*) to retain within their jurisdiction existing capital owners and their business, and thus benefit from the taxes they paid and the loans they might advance to the crown, and (*c*) to attract other capital owners from other political jurisdictions where they had less political influence and less personal and economic security. There was inter-state competition for the allegiance of owners of mobile capital that did not operate in the case of owners of real estate.

The evidence on the causal link between representative government and states' fiscal dependence on citizens is in the English and French cases direct and graphic: the debates and disputes surrounding the emergence of parliamentary power were framed, at least by supporters, in terms of an exchange or contract between state and citizens that was later succinctly summarized as 'no taxation without representation'. Other historical evidence is based on a similar understanding of the logic of co-operation between states and capital but has a more inductive basis: Charles Tilly's (1992) long-term comparison of the development since AD 990 of European states located in different economic zones. In a book that has received great acclaim from historians, Tilly uses the idea of a continuum of patterns of state formation, from 'coercion intensive' to 'capital intensive'. 'Coercion-intensive' states relied heavily on simple physical coercion to obtain the resources they needed from their subjects and to ensure compliance. By contrast, the 'capital-intensive' relationship was more one of state–citizen than state–subject. States obtained their revenues through regularized taxes on economic activities or wealth, permitted those who paid the taxes some say in their imposition, purchased goods and services through the market more than they 'commanded'

---

[15] Crudely, overseas trade was heavily backed by state military power. Landowners did not have the same interest in the use of state military power outside national borders.

them, and permitted a substantial devolution of power to municipal governments controlled by the wealthy. In the more extreme cases of the Mediterranean and north European city states—Venice, Milan, Genoa, the early Dutch Republic, the Hanseatic League—municipality and state were virtually merged, and both controlled by coalitions of trading oligarchs. The 'capital-intensive' strategy was more common in wealthier areas with substantial trade, and the 'coercion-intensive' strategy the norm in the poorer, agricultural areas. This makes sense in terms of the logic of co-operation set out above. Where there was little mobile capital and little prospect of attracting any, rulers' object-ives were more likely to be achieved through coercive taxation (and appropriation) and an (often unstable) alliance with landowners who were permitted wide discretionary power over the populations under their control. The state income obtained by such means ranks low in the 'earnedness' scale: there was no elaborate, dedicated taxation apparatus and little reciprocity in the state–citizen relationship.

There is then considerable historical evidence for the proposition that the emergence of (*a*) representative government, in form and substance, and (*b*), more diffusely, interdependence and mutual accountability between states and citizens is more likely in situations where states face incentives to increase income through bargaining with citizens. How plausibly can we argue by historical analogy in the contem-porary world? Is it convincing to say that, because representative government emerged historically in a context of bargaining between states and citizens over fiscal issues, a similar kind of bargaining—and thus a fiscal dependence of states on citizens—is essential to the health of democracy in contemporary poor countries? At least in its strong form, such an argument is suspect. The mechanisms through which institutions originate and those through which they are maintained and replicated may be significantly different. Once an institution (say, representative democracy) exists, it may (*a*) provide a model that people consciously attempt to reproduce in very different circumstances; and (*b*) become a crusading force in its own right. Both processes are evident in the spread of modern democracy. We cannot therefore assume that there is some inevitable causal linkage between (*a*) fiscal dependence of states on citizens and (*b*) represent-ative government, democracy, or mutual state–society accountability. We can however establish a strong prima facie case for such a link in the modern world on deductive grounds.

These deductive arguments implicitly take the general form: 'How can you expect a state to be responsive to the needs of citizens and to consult them or be accountable to them when those who control the state apparatus obtain their money basically by virtue of that control over the state, and can continue in power provided that they keep the oil flowing, keep the Saudis happy, etc.' (for example, Shambayati 1994: 308–10). The mechanisms likely to be at work are largely self-evident. Suppose that a government derives a large fraction of its income from oil royalties or aid. It will have privileged information about those income sources—the exact amounts, the conditions attached, the advantages and disadvantages of alternative ways of trying to increase income, etc.—that it will not wish to share with the ordinary members of the legislature or the public. It can use this privileged relationship to control the policy and administrative agenda: to claim that certain things have to be done in certain ways because of the 'needs' of the major income source. Members of the legislature and the public have little opportunity to acquire or develop knowledge about public finance because so many decisions are taken in closed, privileged arenas where leading representatives of the state negotiate with major income providers. People excluded from such arenas therefore have limited scope to develop and present alternative policy agendas. And, where government income sources are few and concentrated, there are especially strong incentives for holders of state power and those who control the income sources (if different sets of people) to deal with one another to maintain the political status quo. The controllers of the income source provide material resources or other assistance to keep the existing regime in power. They receive in return security and predictability.[16]

We have some strong suspicions about the possible linkages between state income sources and patterns of state–society relations. Let us connect them to the real world by examining how contemporary states make a living.

4. The Livelihoods of Contemporary States

How would we in practice classify the main sources of state incomes on an 'earnedness scale'? The following represents my first attempt to answer that question at an abstract level, without looking at particular cases:

(i) Sources of government income that are generally 'earned' to a relatively high degree: business turnover taxes; income taxes; property taxes; head taxes; contributory social security funds; profits from state ownership of productive enterprise, especially activities that are

---

[16] The controllers of major sources of state income may of course choose to try to install an alternative government if they feel that to be in their interests.

organizationally and technically demanding and non-monopolistic; and commercial borrowing.

(ii) Sources of government income that are generally 'earned' to an intermediate degree: commodity export taxes; control of location-specific physical infrastructure (canals, oil transmission lines, military facilities for other states, airports, harbours); and monopoly state activities that are relatively low technology but require active 'husbandry' (commercial forestry with protection and replanting; liquor sales monopolies).

(iii) Sources of government income that are generally 'unearned': direct grants and the concessional element in soft loans; profits from maintaining fixed, overvalued exchange rates; royalties, fees, and taxes from authorizing the extraction of natural resources—oil, timber, minerals, etc.

It would be a major undertaking to use this framework to produce comparable data for a large sample of countries. For one would have to investigate individual countries in some detail, and then make judgements on the basis of economic analysis specific to each case. What is the monopoly income element in state ownership of ports and airports in Camgola? How do we trace and value the benefits to the Haitistani state of maintaining an overvalued exchange rate? It certainly inflates the value of foreign aid receipts, but has other consequences depending on, for example, the import intensity of state expenditures. If we are to use available statistical series to sketch a global picture of how states make a living, we need to adopt more rough and ready standards. Above all, we need to limit our observations to a formal concept of 'state income': that income that appears in accounts as either 'foreign aid' or 'government revenue'.[17]

There are cross-national statistical series that (*a*) provide figures on these aggregates, (*b*) disaggregate 'government revenue' into tax revenue and non-tax revenue, and (*c*) provide a breakdown of the composition of tax revenue among various categories of taxes. We have to use some judgement to allocate various types of state income on the 'earnedness scale'. In interpreting the figures that result, we need to bear in mind that the extent to which a particular category of state income is earned may vary according to context. Take, for example, commodity export taxes. It requires relatively little continuing effort to tax the export of a bulk product like tea, grown mainly on large corporately owned estates, and compulsorily marketed through tea

---

[17] Commercial borrowing is, arguably, a 'source of income' in the broad sense in which the term is used here. Since my main focus is on poor Fourth World states that have little effective access to commercial borrowing, I prefer not to complicate the chapter further by discussing it.

Mick Moore

TABLE 3.1. *Sources of state revenue, 1988*

	Low-income countries	Lower-middle-income countries	Upper-middle-income countries	High-income countries
No. of countries for which there are data	21	26	8	18
% of government income from:				
A. Aid	43	12	2	neg.
B. Taxes on international trade and transactions	17	18	13	2
C. Non-tax revenue	9	16	11	10
D. Domestic taxes on goods and services	16	25	32	27
E. Other taxes	2	4	4	3
F. Taxes on income, profit, and capital gains	13	21	24	34
G. Social security contributions	1	4	14	24
Total	100	100	100	100
(Current revenue as a % of GNP)	(17)	(23)	(27)	(37)
% of government income from sources classified by degree of 'earnedness':				
Very low (=A)	43	12	2	neg.
Low (=B+C)	26	34	24	12
Average (=D+E)	18	29	36	30
High (=F+G)	14	25	38	58
Total	100	100	100	100

Notes: Excludes all centrally planned economies, except Yugoslavia. Country classifications are as of 1988. Singapore and Kuwait are excluded from the 'high-income' category because their very high dependence on non-tax revenue—54% and 97% respectively—would grossly distort the average for the group.

Source: World Bank (1990: tables 12, 20).

auctions, from an island with only a small number of ports. In extreme contrast, much more effort would be required to tax the export of a high value-to-bulk commodity such as the ginseng root, grown mainly by smallholders, from a country with land borders open for trade. In the first case, government can rely for information and enforcement of taxation on sources and agents located in the ports and the tea auctions, supplemented by the accounts of the corporations owning estates. In the second case, government would probably need to identify and record production at source in the villages.

The figures in Table 3.1 are unweighted averages for countries within country groups. The country groups—low, lower-middle, upper-middle, and high income—are those used by the World Bank. The figures are based on the data available for 1988 (see Appendix 3.1 for details). In the first rows of the table, state income is classified into seven main, formal sources.[18] In some respects the group averages hide as much as they reveal. In particular, governments that rely very heavily on oil revenues are scattered among all four income groups. Were the countries to be grouped in the table by region, the extent of the dependence of Middle Eastern governments on oil revenues would be clearer. However, the main conclusions are clear enough. Aid dependence has already been emphasized earlier in this chapter. Leaving aid aside, poor countries are relatively dependent on taxes on international trade, which are relatively easy and cheap to collect (Bleaney et al. 1995: 888). These taxes accounted for 30 per cent of state revenue in low-income countries in 1988, as opposed to 2 per cent for high-income countries. Richer countries rely more on a wider range of taxes whose collection requires sophisticated apparatuses, notably social security contributions and direct taxes on incomes, profits, and capital gains. 'Domestic taxes on goods and services' are important in all categories of countries. The wealthier the country, the more likely they are to take the form of complex-to-administer value added taxes, rather than simple excise, turnover, or sales taxes.[19] Both low- and middle-income countries depend relatively heavily on non-tax revenues. These cover a variety of income sources. Royalties and other income from oil and other mineral exports are important for many middle-income countries in particular; it is often only the income from exploiting these natural resources that puts otherwise poor countries into the middle-income category in the first place. Other governments obtain a high proportion of their income from non-tax revenues because they control 'location-specific physical infrastructure' such as major canals (Panama), or because (in 1988) they practised pervasive ownership and control of the economy (Ethiopia, Myanmar).

In the lower rows of Table 3.1, these formal income sources are classified into four degrees of 'earnedness'. Bearing in mind all the reservations above about the basis on which this classification is made, the figures are striking: sources in the categories of 'very low' and 'low earnedness' in 1988 provided an average of 69 per cent of state income in low-income countries, and 12 per cent in high-income

---

[18] Zee (1996) provides a more detailed cross-national comparison of government revenue sources.

[19] In developing countries, 'turnover', 'sales', or other taxes that appear to require a substantial state organizational effort to collect, including the fast-spreading value-added tax, are often in practice levied mainly on a small number of large enterprises and/or at the point of import or export (Patel et al. 1997: 3–6). They are in practice 'earned' to a lesser degree than is implied in the categorizations used here.

countries. The typical governments of low-income countries are so dependent on unearned incomes that one must take seriously the thesis in Section 3 about the link between state income and patterns of state–society relations.

5. Weak States and the International System

However, it is not only the high dependence of states on unearned income that generates low accountability. Other dimensions of the relation of poor countries to the international state system also help generate and reproduce low levels of accountability of states to citizens. In brief, the international system tends to support states that are internally both weak and 'disconnected' from their citizens. This is causal sequence B from Fig. 3.1. The easiest way to convey the distinctive features of that relation for contemporary poor countries is to draw a contrast with the history of state formation in Europe.

The core processes underlying the creation of effective states in Europe (over the past millennium) have been military competition between states, the search for reliable sources of state revenue to support the military, and the strategic interaction between states and various socio-economic groups in relation to revenue-raising. Reference has already been made in Section 3 to the consequences of that strategic interaction for political representation. We are here interested in the implications for the state bureaucracy. They are best presented in the words of the premier interpretative historian of this process, Charles Tilly:[20]

the central paradox of European state formation: that the pursuit of war and military capacity, after having created national states as a sort of by-product, led to a civilianization of government and domestic politics. That happened . . . for five main reasons: because the effort to build and sustain military forces led agents of states to build bulky extractive apparatuses staffed by civilians, and those extractive apparatuses came to contain and constrain the military forces; because agents of states bargained with civilian groups that controlled the resources required for effective warmaking, and in bargaining gave the civilian groups enforceable claims on the state that further constrained the military; because the expansion of state capacity in wartime gave those states that had not suffered great losses in war expanded capacity at the ends of wars, and agents of those states took advantage of the situation by taking on

[20] This section derives above all from the recent work on European state formation of Charles Tilly (1992). His work in turn both reflects and is reflected in a wide range of other historical scholarship. It represents a particularly incisive synthesis of a large body of research, not an isolated intuition. A very useful conceptual summary of the relevance of this work to the study of contemporary states is to be found in Weiss and Hobson (1995: ch. 1).

new activities, or continuing activities they had started as emergency measures; because participants in the war effort, including military personnel, acquired claims on the state that they deferred during the war in response to repression or mutual consent but which they reactivated at demobilization; and finally because wartime borrowing led to great increases in national debts, which in turn generated service bureaucracies and encouraged greater state intervention in national economies. (Tilly 1992: 206)

The business of successful state-making in Europe comprised two main components: a Darwinian process of inter-state military competition; and an intra-state process of resource mobilization for war that stimulated the creation of state–society linkages, markets, bureaucracies, taxation systems, and all the paraphernalia of a modern civilianized state. In the process, the nature of 'powerful' states underwent a change. States generally lost 'despotic power', i.e. direct, arbitrary control over individual citizens. But they gained enormously in 'infrastructural power', i.e. the capacity to penetrate society, to extract resources from it, and to co-operate with social classes and groups in achieving collective goals (Weiss and Hobson 1995: ch. 1). The history of the emergence of contemporary Third World states, diverse though it is, generally has been different from that of European states in three important respects.

First, simple, brutal (colonial) conquest has played a greater role in the creation of Third World states than in Europe. This is especially true of sub-Saharan Africa, where colonial conquest was relatively recent and swift, and took place in a context where the differences between conquerors and victims in military and organizational technology were unusually large, where the process of redrawing the borders of pre-colonial polities was especially radical, and where there was relatively little co-option of local elites into the system of colonial rule (Young 1994). Colonial and post-colonial states were often rooted more in the arid soil of coercion and conquest than in the rich compost of history, tradition, co-operation, and consent.

Second, the former European colonies in Africa, Asia, the Pacific, and the Caribbean became independent after the operative rules of the international state system had effectively been rewritten with the creation of the United Nations. The previous rule—the product of the competitive basis of European state formation—was that effective control of territory and populations—the demonstrated capacity to resist internal and external political rivals—was the main condition for recognition of statehood by other states. After 1945 in particular, effective control of territory and populations ceased to be the de facto condition for recognition by other states. To be the legitimate successor of colonial rule was itself adequate to guarantee the recognition and the more substantial material resources, including international aid, that accrue to those holding governmental power. And in most of the ex-colonial world, but most strikingly in sub-Saharan Africa, Darwinian processes of inter-state competition were not only discouraged, but positively ruled out by the new international and regional state systems. Governments that lost effective control of the populations and territories over which they nominally ruled did not as a matter of course fear wholesale predation on the part of their neighbours. There was conflict aplenty, but almost all internal (Tilly 1992: 201). The incentives for states to maintain control of their territories and populations—to rule as well as to reign—have thus diminished in favour of incentives to nourish connections to the international state system (Jackson 1990).

Third, during the Cold War in particular, many Third World governments were able to profit from a bargaining position in relation to great power rivalry that had earlier in the century been confined mainly to some puppet and quasi-puppet regimes in the Middle East. Exploitation of these rivalries could generate valuable support from abroad, including cash and the military equipment and, sometimes, the active military back-up that might reduce internal political support to an optional extra rather than a basic necessity for effective rule (Luckham 1996, Tilly 1992: ch. 7).[21]

There is great variation in the history and the current character of states in poor countries. However, it is generally the case—more so in Africa and the Middle East than in Asia and Latin America, more so for small than for big countries, and more so for countries with valuable natural resources than for others—that they are relatively dependent on external sources of legitimacy and political support, and relatively independent of their own citizens. This general 'independence-of-states-from-citizens' interacts with the more specific fiscal 'independence-of-states-from-citizens' (Sections 3 and 4) in malign ways that can best be approached by answering the question: 'What happens in countries where the government is almost entirely dependent on a few major income providers—oil, other minerals, aid, etc.—and has scarcely any apparatus to tax even the local business, trading, and property-owning classes?' In the short run, their citizens might rejoice, and libertarians elsewhere might express approval. However, many historians and political scientists would predict trouble. Why? What is likely to go wrong when states refrain from extracting any significant resources from even the 'taxable classes'?

---

[21] 'To the extent that their states generated revenues by selling commodities on the international market, bought arms overseas, and received military aid from great powers, . . . the armed forces enjoyed insulation from reliance on taxation and conscription authorised by civilian governments' (Tilly 1992: 200–1).

Answers to that question depend very much on context. One set of concerns arises if state incomes are so high that states compound the absence of significant taxation by engaging in lavish welfare spending on their citizens. This has been an issue in relation to many Middle Eastern states.[22] However, our concerns here are with poor cash-strapped states. In that context, the absence of a significant income-raising apparatus can have three malign effects on the polity:[23]

(i) A taxation system is simultaneously a mechanism for political control. It comprises two main elements: (*a*) sets of information on citizens—names, addresses, occupations, incomes, business turnover, wealth—that states might not otherwise collect and maintain; and (*b*) a network of public tax collection agents who use this information, collect a great deal more in an informal way, and become repositories of knowledge about what is going on in the far-flung parts of polities where state elites may have little direct knowledge or influence. In the eyes of some political scientists, the capacity to create such a taxation system is the defining feature of effective, stable modern states. For, in the absence of such bureaucracies or functional equivalents like effective mass political parties, states are vulnerable to the organizational challenge of competitors—guerrillas, private armies based on the narcotics trade, and non-state movements of various kinds, including, in contemporary sub-Saharan Africa, autonomous Christian and Islamic movements (Ellis 1996: 11–12). The revenue itself may not be the most valuable product of tax-raising activity. The key insight, shared *inter alia* by counter-insurgency specialists, is that active revenue-raising may be an important means of keeping the state machinery alive and active at the grass roots. If the revenue-raising function is permitted to decay, weak states leave themselves vulnerable to more committed and organized predators:

In the course of an internal war, economic assistance tends to become an alternative source of revenue for the local regime, allowing it to neglect its domestic tax base and thus leave it to the insurgents to exploit. This is not to suggest that regimes facing an internal war ought to tax their populations more heavily, but it is to say that, in order to tax the countryside and the urban sectors, they have to rule those sectors. If they rule them, the insurgents do not. (Odon 1992: 219)

---

[22] Anderson (1994) and Shambayati (1994), for example, argue that 'soft budget constraints' in the Middle East have been conducive to the suppression of independent associational life through 'state purchase', and to the emergence of highly oppositional illegal associations and strong identity politics.

[23] This argument draws to a large degree on Anderson (1994, 1995), Chaudhry (1989), and Shambayati (1994). See also Madhavy (1970).

(ii) To be effective, an extractive bureaucratic apparatus requires the core virtues of a classic, 'Weberian' bureaucracy—technical competence, hierarchical accountability, impersonal procedures, and distance from societal interests—to a greater extent than does a redistributive apparatus. States that earn their income face stronger incentives to reduce the influence of patrimonial principles and personal linkages when recruiting and managing the public service. All else being equal, these will be more effective states.

(iii) States dependent on a small number of income providers are vulnerable to the sudden disruption of those sources. When foreign aid suddenly dries up (Somalia in 1990–1), or oil revenues shrink drastically (Iraq after the Gulf War), states that have little capacity in place to raise alternative revenues through taxing their citizens have several options: even more direct dependence on some alternative foreign source; a drastic shrinkage of the state apparatus itself, with all the resultant risks of political unrest; or the imposition of coercive taxation without the time to negotiate, establish data bases and procedures, or otherwise make taxation acceptable. None of those options is in general conducive to political stability or to any kind of state–citizen accountability. The more elaborate the existing taxation infrastructure —with officers, understood procedures, current information on the names, addresses, occupations, incomes, business turnover, wealth, etc. of potential taxpayers—the more likely is it that a state can substitute in a non-coercive fashion for sudden shortfalls in major income sources.

The high dependence of Fourth World states on unearned income thus helps undermine accountability and democracy both indirectly, through causal sequence B, as well as directly, through sequence A. The weak incentives for heavily aided states to establish effective extractive bureaucracies exacerbate an existing situation of low dependence on citizens, and of corresponding political fragility and instability. Political stability is almost by definition a precondition for effective accountability or democracy. Democracy is impossible in a polity that does not operate according to a core of stable rules. In the circumstances of the contemporary Fourth World, the route to increasing state capacity is the same road that leads to the increasing accountability of state to society and thus, in the longer term, towards democracy.

6. Aiding and Budgeting

One very important practical step towards increasing both the developmental effectiveness and the accountability of states in much of the Fourth World would be the (re)introduction of comprehensive, effective state budgetary systems, such that the government, its citizens, its critics, and the state bureaucracy would be able accurately to discover how much it had spent on what in the previous year, and how much it was likely to spend in the coming year. The absence of effective central budgeting in part reflects the general political and institutional weakness of Fourth World states. However, it also reflects the ways in which the high aid inflows discussed above are actually controlled and disbursed.

'Aid' is an abstract concept. Development aid appears in many forms. Two features of the (official) aid received by Fourth World states are of special interest to us. One is that it is now given largely in the form of grants or very concessional loans. Bilateral donors in particular mainly give grants. In consequence, the individual donor agencies tend to have a strong voice in how 'their' money is used. The second relevant feature of the aid system is the multiplicity of (official) aid donors who give support to, and maintain offices in, individual Fourth World countries. It is not unusual for recipient governments to have to deal with a dozen significant official aid donors.[24] These numerous aid donors each have their own agendas, priorities. targets, and procedures. Contrary to some concerns about the dominance of the 'Washington consensus' among aid donors, donors collectively do not target their assistance closely toward countries that adopt 'Washington consensus' policies (Burnside and Dollar 1997). Aid agencies remain individualistic, largely because they are ultimately responsible to legislatures back home that have little knowledge of, or concern with, the indirect impact of their aid programmes. To a large degree, aid agencies within individual recipient countries are competitors for the local resources that will help validate their activities: good projects to fund; the assistance of influential politicians and bureaucrats in expediting their programmes; and the secondment of the best local public servants to manage their projects (Wilson 1993).

People with a conventional view of the potential 'dependency' problems of aid recipients tend to welcome the individualism and competitiveness of aid agencies as a safeguard against collective 'aid imperialism' on the part of donors. In fact, these patterns of donor behaviour directly perpetuate the weakness of the recipient states, and undermine the prospects for effective state accountability. For 'sovereignty', in the form of centralized information about, and control over, public expenditure, has been lost. Such sovereignty would

---

[24] And with an equal number of small-scale official donors and dozens of international non-government organizations with individual programmes in each country that impinge on government in some way or another.

anyway tend to weaken in the face of a multiplicity of competitive aid donors funding a significant proportion of public expenditure on a grant basis. It has weakened even further in many Fourth World states because of the way in which government budgeting procedures have evolved in the face of growing aid dependence. Let us tell the typical story in summary terms, starting in the 1960s, a period of recent independence and relative economic prosperity for most countries of the Fourth World.

In these early years, developing countries typically practised a dual budget system.[25] The local (i.e. recipient) government financed the recurrent budget from local revenues. It made a 'local contribution' to the capital (or investment) budget, which was funded largely by aid donors, with the recent colonial power typically playing a significant role. The capital budget was prepared within the framework of a national development plan. The 1970s and after were marked by economic and fiscal crisis, increased aid inflows, and growth in the number of (official) aid donors. Major changes in budgeting practices resulted. With recipient governments unable to meet 'local contributions', aid projects became 100 per cent donor funded. They began to be omitted from the formal government budgeting process because they did not require public funds. As public sector salaries declined, donors increasingly, through a range of 'allowances', paid the salaries of the government staff formally seconded to their projects, or working in closely related activities. Donor influence over the deployment of local public servants followed inevitably. As local government recurrent expenditure was reduced further, donors began informally to assume wider financing responsibilities in sectors that appeared high priority to them, such as health.[26] Aid 'projects' began to fund a mix of investment, rehabilitation, and recurrent activities. Local government funding was concentrated on urgent local priorities, which often included the military. On the one hand the donors, locked into situations where they cannot permit their projects openly to fail, appear to be behaving in a more intrusive fashion. On the other hand, their aid is to a large degree fungible: knowing that donors are committed to keeping health and education services on their feet, recipient governments can concentrate their limited funds on the military and other activities that they regard as priority. And the fact that the budgeting process no longer has much substance makes this easier. It has become increasingly

---

[25] I owe this paragraph almost entirely to Mike Stevens. See also Cohen (1991) and Wilson (1993). The issues are discussed briefly in World Bank (1997: 84–5).

[26] 'For example, vehicles provided for the project became vehicles for the ministry; drugs for a particular programme get used all over the country, etc.' (Mike Stevens, personal communication).

difficult for anyone to know what money is being spent on what by government, or by aid donors in the name of government. There is little accountability of any kind.

These problems have long been discussed in development aid circles, although the implications for democracy and accountability appear not to have been much considered. The currently fashionable attempt to remedy the situation is the Sectoral Investment Programme (SIP), in which a number of donors agree to pool their funds to support sector-wide activities (e.g. in agriculture or health) in return for commitments from the recipient government about policy toward the sector in the medium term (World Bank 1997: 85). This is a step in the right direction, although ideally aid funds should be pooled at national rather than sectoral level. These are however tentative experiments, which have not yet had any significant impact on the fragmenting effects on national sovereignty of the competitive individualism of the aid donor community.

7. Concluding Comments

The core argument in this chapter is the political science equivalent of the economists' 'Dutch disease' or 'resource curse' thesis: the generic case that the excessive inflow into an economy of a free or cheap resource—American gold into Spain in the seventeenth century, North Sea oil in 1980s Britain, aid to Tanzania in the 1990s—will bring economic ruin.[27] Like Dutch disease arguments, it is vulnerable to abuse by doctrinaire economists who believe in looking in the mouths of all gift horses in all circumstances, i.e. rejecting all aid, or all oil royalties, as harmful because they 'distort' the recipient economy. That is not my view. The argument here is much more situation specific. Aid does not necessarily undermine democracy.[28] It has become a problem in some countries because of a conjunction of circumstances: high

[27] The founding father of the theory of rentier states, Mahdavy (1970), was indeed an economist developing a 'Dutch disease' argument, in relation to oil revenues in Iran.

[28] Critics will note, among other things, (a) that all kinds of pro-democracy influences also ride on the back of much contemporary development aid, and (b) that there are some poor countries that stand out as conspicuous exceptions to the general argument of this chapter. In contemporary Africa, Botswana and Eritrea appear to be the great exceptions. Although very wealthy from minerals (especially diamonds), the state in Botswana has conspicuously failed to lapse into personal rule or experience a drastic decline in state capacity. Since explaining Botswana exceptionalism is a small academic industry in its own right, I do not want to enter that debate here. The Eritrean case is less puzzling. The current Eritrean government is autonomous and capable to a much higher degree than one would expect given its high aid dependence. The enduring consequences of a long period of war mobilization clearly play a major role here.

levels of aid dependence of governments (causal sequence A); an inheritance of weak states relatively independent of their citizens for political and fiscal support (causal sequence B); and modes of dispersing aid that fragment fiscal sovereignty and undermine budgetary accountability (causal sequence C). At the opposite extreme, high aid levels appear to have played a very positive role in Taiwan and South Korea in the 1950s and 1960s, in a very different context: high commitment to economic development of state elites in front-line geopolitical and ideological competition with Communist China and North Korea respectively; and a single dominant aid donor, the United States, that shared the geo-political, ideological, and economic objectives of the recipient regimes.[29]

What should be done about the adverse consequences of high aid dependence in Fourth World countries? To some extent, the situation is beginning to be resolved, albeit in a way that will leave many people unhappy: aid levels are now declining worldwide. That might in turn stimulate Fourth World governments to look more seriously at the prospects for increasing their own revenues. That does not necessarily mean that poor people will become poorer at the expense of governments. In many Fourth World countries, poor people pay all kinds of illegal levies to agents of the state at road blocks and in government offices (Mamdani 1996: 58–9). These flows could and should be rechannelled into public accounts. Aid donors may be able to give more help in reconstituting local revenue systems. However, their biggest potential contribution has already been signalled in Section 6: stop playing the game of competitive individualism; cease funding projects because they conform to American (or British, Canadian, Danish, Dutch, European, French, German, Japanese, Norwegian, Swedish, UN) aid policies; and pool aid funds into budgetary support for those Fourth World governments that make and keep credible commitments to pursue policies that meet common-sense standards of developmental effectiveness.

APPENDIX 3.1: STATISTICS ON THE NEW INTERNATIONAL AID DEPENDENCE

There is at first sight a clear paradox: the aid lobbies have long been complaining about declining volumes of aid to developing countries, and I am here warning about the dangers of increasing aid dependence. The paradox dissolves when one appreciates that the problem is specific to certain countries

[29] See, for example, Haggard (1990: chs. 3–4), Ho (1978: 111–20), and Jacoby (1996).

and regions of the Former Third World. We are interested in that category of countries defined in the main text as the Fourth World. The boundaries of that category are however fuzzy. My operational definition is those countries defined by the World Bank as 'low income' (see below).[30]

Let us begin with changes in real incomes. From 1965 to 1980, most people in the world (85 per cent) lived in countries where average real incomes per head were growing at an average annual rate of between zero and 5 per cent. Since 1980, the performance of national economies has been more diverse. Between 1980 and 1993, more than a quarter of the world's population lived in high-performing economies, mainly located in East Asia, where average incomes per head increased at more than 5 per cent annually. At the same time, a fifth of the global population lived in countries where average incomes declined. These were mainly Latin Americans, who have seen something of an economic upturn in the 1990s, and Africans, who have not yet been so fortunate (UNDP 1996: 12).

Suppose that aid donors had maintained into the 1990s exactly the same pattern of aid giving as in the 1970s—the same amounts, in real terms, to the same countries. There would nevertheless have been substantial changes within the category of aid recipients in the ratios of aid to GNP. The ratio would have declined for the fast-growing economies and increased for those economies that had themselves shrunk in real terms.[31] The pattern of aid giving was not however stable. There was a relative shift to the low-income economies that had been performing poorly, and especially to those with smaller populations, i.e. not to Nigeria in Africa, and not to the low-income Asian population giants—Bangladesh, India, Indonesia, Pakistan, and the Philippines. It does not require a radical shift in the global distribution of aid for poor, small countries to experience a substantial increase in the ratio of aid to GNP, especially if those GNPs are also declining.

The ratios of aid to GNP have increased for the poorest countries. This is documented below. We are however interested here in the aid dependence not of economies but of governments, and therefore in the ratio of aid to government revenue (or expenditure). The governments of the poorest countries have probably become aid dependent at an even faster rate than the economies over which they preside, because their own revenue sources appear to have shrunk. I say 'appear' because the data required to prove that point conclusively are not available. In order to provide evidence on this and the other points

---

[30] The World Bank's list of 'low-income' economies includes a few countries that are clearly not part of the Fourth World as I have defined it: India, Indonesia, China, and Vietnam. There are however so few reliable statistics available on China and Vietnam that only India and Indonesia feature in the tables below.

[31] Let us take as an illustrative example two countries, A and B, that had the same per capita GNP in 1970 and the same ratio of aid to per capita GNP—4%. Suppose that over the next twenty years (*a*) per capita GNP grew at an average annual rate of 4% in country A and declined by 1% in country B, (*b*) population growth rates were the same in both countries, and (*c*) real aid inflows per capita in 1990 were the same for both countries as in 1970. In 1990, aid would amount to 2% of GNP in country A and 5% in country B.

made above, we are obliged to peer into the murky waters of national income data availability for poor countries.

The only way to obtain a broad picture of trends in the ratios between aid, GNP, and government revenue for the developing world is to use the few standard data bases that exist and are generally recognized to be credible. There is a fair degree of consistency in these standard sources that would not exist if one were to attempt to fill in their gaps in an ad hoc way, using data originating from a variety of national sources. I have used two standard sets of data here:

(i) The first set, which will be termed 'the 1970s–1990s data set', was constructed by combining OECD Development Assistance Committee figures on aid volumes and IMF-World Bank figures on GNP and government revenue.[32] Data were assembled for each year between 1972 and 1993 for every country for which there was a significant amount of information. There are however many gaps, especially in the earliest and the latest years. I have used these data to illustrate long-term trends from the early or mid-1970s to the early 1990s. The exact choice of base, intervening, and terminal years for particular tables reflects an effort to obtain the widest possible coverage of countries over the longest possible time periods.

(ii) The second set, which will be termed 'the 1980–94 data set', comprises comparative figures for the years 1980 and 1994 in the ratios of aid and government revenue to GNP. The data from which these ratios are calculated are conveniently provided in two tables of the World Bank's *World Development Report 1996* (World Bank 1996). This embraces a shorter time period than the first data set but covers more countries.[33]

I have used the World Bank's classification of countries into 'low-income', 'lower-middle-income', 'upper-middle-income', and 'high-income' categories, focusing mainly on the first two. The World Bank statisticians occasionally move countries from one category to another as relative income levels change or new data result in revised national income estimates. For all the analysis reported in this chapter, countries are placed in the categories in which they appear in the *World Development Report 1996* (*WDR* 96).

The main tables in *WDR* 96 cover 51 low-income countries (with per capita incomes up to $750 in 1994), ranging from Rwanda and Mozambique at the bottom end of the income scale up to Lesotho; and 40 lower-middle-income economies (incomes $750–$2,900), ranging from Bolivia up to Estonia. These tables exclude countries with populations of less than one million. This is a common convention in compiling and using cross-national statistics.[34] I have followed it here. Still, these *WDR* 96 listings do not adequately define our

---

[32] I am grateful to David O'Brien and Jason Ward for doing the routine work of constructing this data set, and to the OECD-Development Assistance Committee Secretariat for providing the data on aid disbursements.

[33] The original sources are essentially the same as those for the first data set; in a few cases, '1994' figures actually relate to an earlier year.

[34] The main reasons are the scarcity of national income figures and the relative insignificance of these micro countries in population terms.

statistical populations of low- and lower-middle-income countries, i.e. the categories of countries about which we wish to draw general conclusions. We need first to take a few countries out of these lists and bring a few others in:

(i) We need to exclude a number of new countries that emerged very recently from the break-up of the Soviet Union, Czechoslovakia, and Yugoslavia.

(ii) We need to bring into the list a number of countries that do not feature in the main tables of *WDR* 96 because few recent reliable national income statistics of any kind are available. These are mainly countries gripped by internal conflict.[35] These form part of the population of countries in which we are in principle interested.

Once these adjustments have been made, we have a total 'statistical population' of 53 low-income and 35 lower-middle-income economies. These are the countries that existed as separate entities in the early 1970s and had a population of more than a million people in 1994. They constitute the population on which we would like to obtain comprehensive or statistically representative data. That objective cannot always be met. As the figures in Tables A3.1 to A3.6 demonstrate, there are many gaps in the two data sets used here. The coverage is in some respects patterned rather than random. First, data on total government revenue are more sparse than estimates of GNP and of aid, and figures on the sources of that revenue even more rare. Second, the availability of reliable data of any kind is correlated with income levels: we have the fewest usable numbers on the poorest (and smallest) economies. These data problems are not so severe that we cannot draw useful conclusions. They are severe enough to prevent us from refining many of these conclusions, or from even beginning to examine some more detailed questions relevant to this chapter, notably the changing patterns of dependence of governments of poor countries on different categories of tax revenue.

The figures in Table A3.1 cover about half our statistical population of low-income countries and two-thirds of lower-middle-income countries. They tell a clear story: between 1972 and 1993, the ratio of aid to GNP increased greatly in low-income countries, and remained about the same in the lower-middle-income countries. One could have put in figures for intermediate years, or chosen slightly different initial and terminal years, without changing the conclusions: there was a steady trend increase in aid dependence for the low-income economies and stability for the lower-middle-income economies. The medians are the most useful measures: for low-income economies, the median ratio of aid to GNP more than trebled, from 4 per cent to 13 per cent, over two decades. The figures in Table A3.2, which cover a shorter time period (1980–94) but a larger number of countries, tell the same story. At first sight, they appear to indicate much higher absolute levels of aid dependence among low income countries than do the figures in Table A3.1. This difference is however a by-product of differences in sample coverage: the poorest low-income

---

[35] There are seven low-income countries in this category: Afghanistan, Bosnia-Hercegovina, Eritrea, Liberia, Somalia, Sudan, and Congo.

TABLE A3.1. *The ratio of aid (official development assistance) receipts to GNP: all low- and lower-middle-income countries for which data are available for both 1972 and 1993* (number of countries, grouped according to ratio of aid to GNP)

Ratio of aid receipts to GNP (%)	Low-income countries		Lower-middle-income countries	
	1972	1993	1972	1993
25+	0	5	0	0
15.0–24.9	0	7	2	0
10.0–14.9	3	7	1	1
5.0–9.9	9	8	3	7
2.0–4.9	12	0	6	4
Less than 2	7	4[a]	14	14
Total number of countries	31	31	26	26
Median ratio of aid to GNP (%)	4.0	13.2	1.8	1.9

[a] These four countries are India, Indonesia, Nigeria, and Pakistan.

Source: '1970s–1990s' data series; see text.

TABLE A3.2. *The ratio of aid receipts to GNP: all low- and lower-middle-income countries for which data are available for both 1980 and 1994* (number of countries, grouped according to ratio of aid to GNP)

Ratio of aid receipts to GNP (%)	Low-income countries		Lower-middle-income countries	
	1980	1994	1980	1994
50+	1	3	0	0
25–49.9	1	9	0	0
15.0–24.9	1	13	0	0
10.0–14.9	9	6	2	1
5.0–9.9	18	4	2	2
2.0–4.9	7	2	3	5
Less than 2	4	4	19	18
Total number of countries	41	41	26	26
Median ratio of aid to GNP (%)	8.3	18.3	1.8	1.9

Source: World Bank (1996: table 3).

countries, which also tend to be the more aid dependent (see below), are much less well represented in Table A3.1 than in Table A3.2.

The heavily aid-dependent economies are nearly all in sub-Saharan Africa: of the thirty-two countries in Table A3.2 where aid exceeded 10 per cent of GNP in 1994, only five—Bolivia, Haiti, Mongolia, Nepal, and Nicaragua—were

TABLE A3.3. *The ratio of aid receipts to government revenue: all low- and lower-middle-income countries for which data are available for both 1975 and 1991* (number of countries, grouped according to ratio of aid to government revenue)

Ratio of aid receipts to government revenue (%)	Low-income countries		Middle-income countries	
	1975	1991	1975	1991
200+	1	2	0	0
150–199	0	3	0	0
100–149	4	3	1	1
50–99	5	3	5	5
20–49	4	3	6	8
Less than 20	0	0	5	3
Total number of countries	14	14	17	17
Median ratio of aid to government revenue (%)	29	46	7	11

Source: '1970s–1990s' data series; see text.

not African. This largely reflects the low levels of income in sub-Saharan Africa. The country-size factor also comes into play: large, poor countries receive little aid per head of the population. This category includes Nigeria in Africa and the countries that contain most of Asia's poor: Bangladesh, India, Indonesia, Pakistan, and the Philippines.

Tables A3.1 and A3.2 leave us in no doubt about the increasing aid dependence of the poorest economies. However, to repeat, we are more interested in the aid dependence of governments, and therefore in the ratio of aid to government revenue. Let us first clarify that 'government revenue' does not include aid, and comprises both tax and non-tax revenue. We may for present purposes consider government revenue and aid jointly to constitute 'government income'.

The relevant figures available from our two data series are summarized in Tables A3.3 and A3.4. Considerably fewer countries are included than in Tables A3.1 and A3.2 because of the relative scarcity of reliable figures even on total government revenue. The coverage is however sufficient to indicate clearly (*a*) that the governments of the low-income countries have become much more dependent on aid for their income over recent decades, and (*b*) that the aggregate picture in relation to the governments of lower-middle-income countries is again stable over time—although there are big changes for some individual countries. Once again, the dependence story is mainly a story about sub-Saharan Africa. Of the sixteen low income countries in Table A3.4, the ratio of aid to government revenue fell between 1980 and 1994 in only five countries. Only one of these countries, the Gambia, is in Africa. The others are Asian: India, Myanmar, Pakistan, and Sri Lanka. Nine of the eleven countries where the ratio of aid to revenue increased are in sub-Saharan Africa.

TABLE A3.4. *The ratio of aid receipts to government revenue: all low- and lower-middle-income countries for which data are available for both 1980 and 1994* (number of countries, grouped according to ratio of aid to government revenue)

Ratio of aid receipts to government revenue (%)	Low-income countries		Middle-income countries	
	1980	1994	1980	1994
200+	0	2	0	0
150–199	0	4	0	0
100–149	2	1	0	0
50–99	3	3	1	0
20–49	9	2	3	3
Less than 20	2	4	15	16
Total number of countries	16	16	19	19
Median ratio of aid to government revenue (%)	39	78	8	4

Source: World Bank (1996: tables 3, 14).

The discussion so far has been about trends. What about absolutes? What is the extent of the aid dependence of governments at present? It is clear that high dependence is confined almost exclusively to governments of low-income countries. Do the figures relating to 1994 in Table A3.4—a median ratio of aid to revenue of 78 per cent, and an average of 88 per cent—provide us with a picture that is representative of low-income countries? We cannot be confident of that. For those figures relate only to 16 out of our population of 53 low-income countries. We could add in two more countries that do not appear in Table A3.4 because of the absence of data for 1980, but for which there are relevant data for 1994. That leaves us with data on 18 countries, a third of our total statistical population. Since these are the only data we have, we will use them to estimate a representative figure of current aid dependence for the governments of low-income countries. We do however have to estimate rather than simply project, for it is clear that the levels of aid dependence indicated for 1994 in Table A3.4 are underestimates of the average picture.

The reason that aid dependence is underestimated is that the larger low-income countries are very much over-represented among the 18 on which we have data.[36] And the 'country-size effect' in aid distribution that was mentioned

[36] I classified the statistical population of 53 low-income countries according to (*a*) whether we have 1994 data on the aid–revenue ratio, (*b*) population size, and (*c*) regional location. The availability of 1994 data was unaffected by regional location, but very much influenced by country population size. Data on the aid–revenue ratio were available for 4 out of 7 countries with a population of more than 50 millions (57%), 7 out of 18 with a population of 10 to 50 millions (39%), and only 7 out of 28 with a population of 1 to 10 millions (25%).

above is in operation here: the governments of the larger low-income countries are less aid dependent than the governments of the smaller countries.[37] I produced a new estimate of the average aid–revenue ratio for all low-income countries (for 1994) that corrects for this bias in the sample.[38] This re-estimate suggests both an average and a median aid–revenue ratio of about 100 per cent, indicating that the typical government of a low-income country is, as of 1994, as dependent financially on income from aid as on the tax and non-tax revenues that it raises itself. One could argue that this figure exaggerates aid dependence. It is based on the ratio of aid to government revenue. To the extent that governments run a fiscal deficit after aid is counted in—i.e. their total income (revenue plus aid) is less than their total spending—they 'command' resources in addition to those indicated by these income measures. That issue however takes us into difficult conceptual territory where we do not need to tread at the moment. We have a conclusion that is adequate for present purposes: the government of a typical low-income country is now dependent on aid funds for about half its income.

Before examining the implications for democracy of this growing aid dependence of governments, it is useful to look in more detail at the causes. We know that it reflects largely the redirection of aid to poorer, smaller countries where national incomes have been often stagnant or declining. But how far does it reflect changes in the capacities of the governments of those countries themselves to raise revenues, either through taxation or from non-tax sources? The relevant data are sparse, but they do provide us with some insight. Table A3.5 indicates that, for all the talk in recent years of the 'fiscal crisis of the state'—normally argued, in the advanced countries, to reflect the growing 'middle-class' resistance to taxation and/or the declining capacity of states to tax capital that is internationally ever more mobile—the crisis has yet to materialize on a global scale. In 1994, most governments were appropriating a higher proportion of national income than they had in 1980. However, both the pattern itself and the adequacy of the statistical coverage vary widely and consistently according to levels of national income. In so far as there is a contemporary 'fiscal crisis of the state', it is taking place in the low-income countries. In Table A3.5 there are figures for almost all high-income economies: the ratio of government revenue to GNP increased between 1980 and 1994 in

---

[37] I classified the eighteen countries for which 1994 data are available into a two-by-two matrix according to whether they were above or below the median figure in respect of (*a*) population size and (*b*) the ratio of aid to revenue. There were seven countries in each of the following two cells in the matrix: 'above median population and below median aid–revenue ratio' and 'below median population and above median aid–revenue ratio'; and two countries in each of the two remaining cells.

[38] I divided low-income countries into three population size groups (see n. 37 above) and calculated an average aid–revenue ratio for the countries within each group, using the data we have. I then assumed that the same average would hold within each group for the countries on which we do not have data. I used two measures of group averages—the arithmetic mean and the median—but they produced a virtually identical overall result: aid–revenue ratios of 1.03 and 0.98 respectively. I did not include the aid–revenue ratio for Rwanda in calculating the arithmetic average because the figure was so high in 1994—935%—that it would grossly have distorted the results.

Mick Moore

TABLE A3.5. *Changes in the ratio of government revenue to GNP,
1980 and 1994*

	No. of countries in the category (with a population of more than 1 million)[a]	No. for which there are figures on the ratio of government revenues to GNP for 1980 and 1994	No. of countries where the ratio of government revenues to GNP increased 1980–94
Low-income countries	53	16	5
Lower-middle-income countries	35	20	13
Upper-middle-income countries	17	9	6
High-income countries	24	21	18
All countries	129	66	42

[a] Excludes new countries that did not exist as independent entities in 1980.

Source: World Bank (1996: table 14).

TABLE A3.6. *Changes in the ratio of government revenue to GNP,
1973–1975 to 1990–1992*

	Average ratio of government revenue to GNP[a] (%)		
	1973–5	1980–2	1990–2
16 low-income countries	16.5	18.8	18.7
17 lower-middle-income countries	19.4	19.5	21.0

[a] In a few cases, data were not available for each year of the 3-year subperiods;
such figures as were available were used, i.e. for one or two years.

Source: '1970s–1990s' data series'; see main text.

almost all cases. At the other end of the scale, the statistical coverage for low-income economies is very poor, but the figures that are available indicate that declines in the government revenue–GNP ratio were twice as common as increases. The figures in Table A3.6 are broadly consistent with those in Table A3.5, and in particular help to confirm that the experiences of the low-income and the lower-middle-income economies have been different. Average revenue–GNP ratios have increased in the lower-middle-income economies, especially in the 1980s, while in the low-income economies the increase took place in the 1970s.

The experiences of the low-income and lower-middle-income countries appear to have diverged largely as a result of relative price changes for goods and services in international markets. Most governments of low-income countries depend substantially for revenue on the taxation of primary commodity exports—coffee, tea, cocoa, etc. (Section 4). The substantial increase in the revenue–GNP ratio that they achieved during 1973–80 coincided with good world market prices for these exports. During 1973–80, the terms of trade for low-income countries improved at an average annual rate of 4.1 per cent. By contrast, the terms of trade for middle-income countries improved by 1.9 per cent annually over that period. After 1980, the terms of trade moved against both categories of countries, but most strongly in the case of the low-income countries (World Bank 1990: table A.8). More middle-income countries had or have developed turnover taxes that provide fiscal cushioning against fluctuations in the prices of commodity exports. Turnover taxes are, for reasons to do with the costs of tax collection and scarce organizational capacity, less significant in the low-income countries. Their governments have been struggling with the shrinking of one of their main tax bases, the taxation of primary commodity exports.

In conclusion:

(i) Since about 1980, the governments of low-income countries, unlike other governments, have experienced significant difficulties in maintaining revenue–GNP ratios at their previous levels. In many cases they have been unable to do so.

(ii) The main reason is reductions in world market prices for the commodity exports on which they rely relatively heavily for tax revenues.

(iii) Reductions in revenue–GNP ratios have at most played a marginal role in bringing about the increasing aid dependence of the governments of low-income countries; the shift in the direction of aid to the relatively small low-income countries is the major reason.

REFERENCES

Anderson, L. (1994), 'Liberalism, Islam, and the Arab State', *Dissent*, Fall: 439–44.

—— (1995), 'The Traditions of Imperialism: The Colonial Antecedents of the Authoritarian Welfare State in the Arab World', paper prepared for the Annual Meeting of the American Political Science Association, Chicago, Aug. mimeo.

Bachman, D. (1987), 'Implementing Chinese Tax Policy', in D. M. Lampton (ed.), *Policy Implementation in Post-Mao China*, Berkeley and Los Angeles: University of California Press.

Bates, R. H., and Lien, D.-H. D. (1985), 'A Note on Taxation, Development, and Representative Government', *Politics and Society*, 14/1: 53–70.

Beblawi, H., and Luciani, G. (1987), *The Rentier State*, London: Croom Helm.

Bleaney, M., Gemmell, N., and Greenaway, D. (1995), 'Tax Revenue Instability, with Particular Reference to Sub-Saharan Africa', *Journal of Development Studies*, 31/6: 883–902.

Brautigam, D. (1991), *Governance and Economy: A Review*, Policy Research Working Papers, WPS 815, Washington: World Bank.

—— (1996), 'State Capacity and Effective Governance', in B. Ndulu and N. van de Walle (eds.), *Agenda for Africa's Economic Renewal*, Washington: Overseas Development Council.

Burnside, C., and Dollar, D. (1997), 'Aid, Policies and Growth', Policy Research Working Paper 1777, Washington: World Bank.

Central Bank of Ceylon (1991), *Annual Report 1990*, Colombo.

Ceylon Tobacco Company Ltd. (1989), *Annual Report and Accounts 1988*, Colombo.

Chaudhry, K. A. (1989), 'The Price of Wealth: Business and State in Labor Remittance and Oil Economies', *International Organization*, 43/1: 101–45.

Cohen, J. (1991), 'Foreign Advisors and Capacity Building: The Case of Kenya', *Public Administration and Development*, 12: 493–510.

Ellis, S. (1996), 'Africa after the Cold War: New Patterns of Government and Politics', *Development and Change*, 27/1: 1–28.

Guyer, J. I. (1992), 'Representation without Taxation: An Essay on Democracy in Rural Nigeria, 1952–1990', *African Studies Review*, 35/1: 41–80.

Haggard, S. (1990), *Pathways from the Periphery: The Politics of Growth in Newly Industrializing Countries*, Ithaca, NY: Cornell University Press.

Ho, S. P. S. (1978), *Economic Development of Taiwan, 1860–1970*, New Haven: Yale University Press.

Jackson, R. H. (1990), *Quasi-States: Sovereignty, International Relations and the Third World*, Cambridge: Cambridge University Press.

Jacoby, N. H. (1966), *U. S. Aid to Taiwan: A Study of Foreign Aid, Self-Help, and Development*, New York: Praeger.

Levi, M. (1988), *Of Rule and Revenue*, Berkeley and Los Angeles: University of California Press.

Lewis, P. M. (1996), 'Economic Reform and Political Transition in Africa', *World Politics*, 49/1: 92–129.

Luckham, R. (1996), 'Democracy and the Military: An Epitaph for Frankenstein's Monster?', *Democratization*, 3/2: 1–16.

Mahdavy, H. (1970), 'The Patterns and Problems of Economic Development in Rentier States: The Case of Iran', in M. A. Cook (ed.), *Studies in the Economic History of the Middle East from the Rise of Islam to the Present Day*, London: Oxford University Press.

Mamdani, M. (1996), *Citizen and Subject: Contemporary Africa and the Legacy of Late Colonialism*, Princeton: Princeton University Press.

Moore, M. (1996), 'Is Democracy Rooted in Material Prosperity?', in R. Luckham and G. White (eds.), *Democratization in the South: The Jagged Wave*, Manchester: Manchester University Press.

Odon, W. E. (1992), *On Internal War: American and Soviet Approaches to Third World Clients and Insurgents*, Durham, NC: Duke University Press.

Patel, C. K., Toh, S., and Brownridge, M. (1997), 'Overview', in C. K. Patel (ed.), *Fiscal Reforms in the Least Developed Countries*, Cheltenham: Edward Elgar.

Shambayati, H. (1994), 'The Rentier State, Interest Groups, and the Paradox of Autonomy: State and Business in Turkey and Iran', *Comparative Politics*, 26/3: 307–32.

Tilly, C. (1992), *Coercion, Capital and European States, AD 990–1992*, Cambridge: Mass.: Blackwell.

UNDP (1996), *Human Development Report 1996*, New York: Oxford University Press.

Wang, S. (1995), 'The Rise of the Regions: Fiscal Reform and the Decline of Central State Capacity in China', in A. G. Walder (ed.), *The Waning of the Communist State: Economic Origins of Political Decline in China and Hungary*, Berkeley and Los Angeles: University of California Press.

Weiss, L., and Hobson, J. M. (1995), *States and Economic Development: A Comparative Historical Analysis*, Cambridge: Polity Press.

White, H. (1992), 'The Macroeconomic Impact of Development Aid: A Critical Survey', *Journal of Development Studies*, 28/2: 163–240.

Wilson, L. (1993), 'Kenyanization and African Capacity "Shuffling" ', *Public Administration and Development*, 13: 489–99.

Winters, J. A. (1996), *Power in Motion: Capital and the Indonesian State*, Ithaca, NY: Cornell University Press.

World Bank (1990), *World Development Report 1990*, New York: Oxford University Press.

—— (1996), *World Development Report 1996*, New York: Oxford University Press.

—— (1997), *World Development Report 1997: The State in a Changing World*, New York: Oxford University Press.

Young, C. (1994), *The African Colonial State in Comparative Perspective*, New Haven: Yale University Press.

Zee, H. H. (1996), 'Empirics of Crosscountry Tax Revenue Comparisons', *World Development*, 24/10: 1659–72.

PART II

Political Institutions and Social Forces

·················
4
·················

Democratization and the
Developmental State
The Search for Balance

JAMES MANOR

1. Introduction

In his initial chapter, Gordon White reminded us of three sets of political dichotomies which Larry Diamond (1996) has noted—between
conflict and consensus, between representativeness and governability,
and between consent and effectiveness. In White's view, 'effective
democratic governance would seem to rely on the ability to establish
balances between these conflicting principles through a process of incremental institutional accumulation rooted in political contest and
accommodation and guided by skilled leadership'. The present chapter calls attention to six other dualities, between which some sort of
balance must be achieved if democratization and a new kind of developmental state—the two main concerns of this book—are to make much
headway. We deal here with the need for balance:

(a) between order and conflict;
(b) between self-interested, personalized politics and institutional-
    ization;
(c) between informal and formal politics/institutions;
(d) between 'top-down' and 'bottom-up' initiatives;
(e) between continuity and innovation; and
(f) between confidentiality and transparency.

The first three of these sets of dualities have rather more to do with
the process of democratization than with the fostering of a new developmental state. The last three have more obvious developmental implications. But as we shall see, particularly in the concluding section

of this chapter, democratization and a new kind of developmental state
are closely bound up with one another and tend to be mutually reinforcing. The emphasis here, when the developmental state is discussed,
is on healthy partnerships between state and society—the kinds of links
which lend themselves to what Peter Evans calls 'synergy' (Evans 1996).

This chapter stresses the dissonances within these six dualities
because some observers—mainly in some bilateral and international
development agencies rather than in the scholarly community—are not
entirely aware of them. They sometimes fail to see either the need to
achieve a degree of balance between them or the sad fact that the search
for balance may require restraint in the pursuit of some other aims
which reformers rightly cherish.

It is understandable, for example, that reformers who are mightily
tired of excessive commandism by governments should wish to make
every effort to maximize 'bottom-up' approaches to development. But
in the real world, this could provoke a commandist reaction from
top-level politicans and bureaucrats who are only gradually opening
their minds to initiatives from below. It is also understandable that
reformers who are exasperated with senior leaders' long-standing persistence with outmoded policies should regard 'continuity' as a synonym
for stagnation, and want to move ahead with innovation as rapidly as
possible. But to do so sometimes asks too much of government agencies
and triggers disasters.

In such circumstances, the unattainable 'best' can be the enemy
of the realizable 'good'. The search for balance—which this chapter
argues is a necessity—requires realism and restraint in the pursuit
of reform which are often painful to admirably principled champions
of change. In some of the sections which follow, we will also see that
some of the things with which reformers are understandably impa-
tient, because governments have pursued them with excessive zeal, have
value in their own right—but only provided that they are pursued in
a more restrained manner.

2. Seeking Balance

(a) Between order and conflict

Order and conflict should not be seen as polar opposites. The opposite
of order is not conflict, but disorder. There can be plenty of social and
political conflict without disorder. Indeed, democracy and the kind of
'development' which this book is seeking to define require a considerable degree of *both* order and conflict (or, if you prefer, competition).

Democracy and development can only flourish if a balance can be struck between these two things.

At the risk of some banality, let us pursue this a little further. A modicum of order is required if politicians are to undertake the kinds of reforms discussed in this book. Without it, they will lack the confidence to initiate change. But 'order' need not mean 'control' of events and social forces by the state. Political leaders who seek to exercise 'control' tend towards the commandist abuses that created the problems which the process of democratization is addressing. But the state and power-holders within in it can quite legitimately aspire to exercise considerable *influence* over events and social forces. However, their influence is, paradoxically, likely to be greater if they do not seek thoroughgoing control—if they restrain their coercive tendencies in favour of accommodations with social forces.

We are talking here about political accommodations which lend themselves to democratization, but they also have developmental implications. They make it more likely that government agencies and institutions will become more responsive to the felt needs of grass-roots communities, and more capable of perceiving, understanding, and incorporating 'local knowledge' about the management of resources and the conduct of society's business. They make it more likely that policy innovations will be realistic, and *seem* realistic and creative to ordinary people. They tend to increase the flow of information between state and society, in both directions. They enhance the chances that popular cynicism about any government initiative will be broken down. They make it more likely that groups at the local level will develop a sense of ownership about development projects, so that such projects become more sustainable because such groups make efforts to sustain them.

Since such accommodations entail a somewhat permissive attitude towards competition and conflict between political parties and organized interests, they tend to produce rather untidy politics. But such untidiness usually earns the political system greater legitimacy and makes it more stable than systems that are organized around attempts to coerce and control. It is more stable because a balance has been achieved between order and conflict. Conflict which might otherwise yield disorder is restrained by the informal understandings that arise from political accommodation.

We need to recognize, however, that it is legitimate and even essential that the state retain some coercive power. The state needs it to cope with criminality and with severe social conflict, neither of which advances the cause of democracy or development. The difficulty is to find ways of preventing political leaders from abusing their coercive powers—hence the need for balance.

Those seeking, through political reform, to promote a balance between order and conflict need to consider the extent to which the political system abets the diffusion and moderation of conflict by providing, for example, a multiplicity of arenas within which competition and conflict can occur. Political parties and interest groups in some countries compete for prizes in a large number of arenas—in a national parliament, sometimes in regional legislatures or assemblies, and/or in elected councils at one or more lower levels, and even (informally) in arenas at the peripheries of the political system, such as co-operative societies.

Such cases stand in stark contrast to countries where the only meaningful political prizes are those at the apex of the system. Sometimes, there is only one important prize, the post of supreme leader. In some countries (for example, in parts of francophone Africa), parties compete at elections organized around a 'list' system in which each party nominates a number of candidates equal to the total number of seats at stake—and the party receiving the largest number of votes wins *all* of the seats. Such winner-take-all systems inspire a sense of exclusion and bitterness among unsuccessful groups which threatens moderate politics and the legitimacy of political institutions.

If a multiplicity of prizes are available in a number of different arenas, it gives losers in any one contest good reasons to remain engaged with the political system and to moderate their actions. They can look forward to further opportunities to compete for prizes in other arenas. Their eagerness to do so can be enhanced if elections are held frequently and regularly and, of course, fairly (Jenkins 1997). In such systems, the way in which the political system is structured and operates helps to maintain the diffusion and moderation of social conflict. This makes it easier to achieve a balance between order and conflict. And that lends itself to democratization and the emergence of what we see as a new sort of 'developmental state'.

(b) *Between the pursuit of self-interested, personalized politics and institutionalization*

Those who seek to foster democratization and the redefinition of the developmental state should not expect to change human nature and deflect politicians, entrepreneurs in the private sector, or members of other social groups from engaging in conflict in pursuit of their individual and collective interests. Nor should they expect personalized politics to give way entirely to institutions.

Two interrelated issues are especially important here. First, some policy-makers in international development agencies tend to the view that if politicians in less developed countries display statesmanlike generosity in their dealings with civil society and the private sector, then people in the latter two categories will respond in kind, and a new era of altruism and harmony will dawn.[1] Second, we see analysts in powerful development agencies—including the World Bank (for example, Husain 1994)—setting out a sanitized notion of politics which implies naive expectations about how politicians actually behave when reforms are being implemented. These analysts sometimes urge leaders who are introducing reforms to abandon manipulative behaviour in favour of unfailingly transparent actions—on the dubious assumption that this will produce success.[2] These two misperceptions deserve critical attention.

In considering the first notion, we should not be surprised or even dismayed when we find politicians and elites who initiate political and/or economic reforms doing so because they believe that they can manage—or, indeed, manipulate—change in ways that benefit them. They would hardly seek reform if they thought otherwise. It is also important that they continue in this belief as reforms evolve, because if they see things going against them, they may abandon the process.

We should also recognize that reforms—such as democratization, democratic decentralization, a more permissive posture towards civil society or towards the private sector—do not quell political conflict and the active pursuit of self-interest. They encourage these things. They seek and tend to render these things more restrained and constructive by drawing them into the rule-bound relationships that develop in democracies and into partnerships between state and society. But they do not discourage them. Nor do they inspire the emergence of altruism or, except in rare cases, harmonious consensus.

If civil society is allowed greater freedom and space, if democratization occurs, or if the market is freed up, rivalries between interest groups often become more, not less, competitive and even antagonistic as a result. When leaders of competing social groups are given the chance to stand for election to public office, they often magnify the differences between their groups and others. Those who get elected often use power and distribute spoils in ways that produce the same outcome. When civil society is given greater freedom and allowed greater

---

[1] Some readers may find it hard to believe that such views actually exist, but this writer heard them passionately expressed by several senior figures—not least from within the United Nations Development Programme—in a discussion of democratic decentralization at the OECD in Paris, June 1996.

[2] I am grateful to Rob Jenkins for calling attention to this.

access to resources and decision-making, competition between interest groups tends to quicken. When entrepreneurs are permitted greater freedom, they pursue profits and their self-interest in vigorous competition. These things make it more, not less, difficult to promote cooperative, community-wide efforts favoured by those who seek to foster 'community participation in development'.

That does not mean that such reforms cannot bear fruit. There is no necessary contradiction between such self-interested behaviour and successful experiments with reform. Such behaviour will sometimes impede reforms, but if it is drawn into institutionalized relationships which moderate and contain conflict within limits—and that is one purpose of such reforms—it can also advance it. What is crucial is that architects of reform devise their strategies on the assumption that self-interest will preoccupy most actors. If their plans depend on altruism or acts of self-denial, they will fail.

In considering the second notion noted above, we must recognize that furtive, manipulative, Machiavellian actions by politicians are often necessary to introduce and consolidate the kinds of reforms discussed here. Such actions must be taken with restraint since utterly cynical behaviour by leaders will wreck reform, but they have their uses. This is especially true, as Rob Jenkins has shown (1997), when governments are opening up space for market forces. But it also applies to democratization and to efforts to foster more extensive, constructive interactions between states and civil society.

When reforms occur, it is crucial that the politicians who implement them possess the skills to set those who gain and lose from the change against one another. They also need the skills to conceal and at times even to misrepresent the scale and direction of planned changes. (In this connection, see Section 2 (*f*) below.) If they lack these skills, opposition from important interests can thwart the changes. That is as true of elites who might resist democratization because they have prospered from autocracy as it is of groups which gain less than their rivals (or which lose outright) when economic liberalization takes place.

Skills are not the only important thing here. It also helps if, in Blanca Heredia's words, there has been a 'long history of particularistic negotiations', of political bargaining, between the state apparatus and organized interests (Heredia 1993: 274). If (as Jenkins has shown) this long history has previously involved governments in improvisation, it can create an expectation among organized interests that even if they lose out in one round of competition for benefits from a particular reform, they may gain something at a later stage, since improvising politicians may later turn things to their advantage.

It also helps (as we saw in Section 2 (*a*) above) if the political system within which reforms are attempted offers losers in a particular round of competition some compensation for defeats, and some hope of influence despite defeats. Jenkins has noted the benefits which flow from the existence in India of a multiplicity of arenas (noted above) within which competition occurs. This helps to persuade interest groups that may lose on one occasion to remain engaged with the democratic process, since they may win at the next opportunity (Jenkins 1997). The creation and the empowerment of such a diversity of arenas are constructive policy options which can help to establish institutional environments in which the inevitable pursuit of self-interest can be moderated. The pursuit of self-interest can help promote greater communication and consultation between state and society, as individuals and organized interests assert themselves in a self-interested manner. Such assertiveness creates pressure on state agents and institutions to become more responsive to social groups and to actors in the private sector. So such empowerment (which is one form of democratization) can help to foster a new kind of developmental state. Such options can also help to establish a balance between self-interest and institutionalization, because actors seeking to advance their interests gain access to the most attractive opportunities by operating within institutional rules.

Further insights into the achievement of this balance emerge from analyses of patronage systems—that is, networks through which goods, services, and funds controlled by the state are distributed by politicians to social groups in order to gain partisan advantage. Such systems exist to some degree in virtually every polity, but the proportions of government resources which are distributed in this way vary (often greatly) from country to country. They are worth considering here because in many less developed countries, they have been an important (and often the principal) means by which those in government have sought to build a relationship with organized interests in society.

Patronage systems operate according to informal sets of rules and understandings which almost always entail a mixture of institutional and personal elements. The precise mixtures vary from place to place and time to time. This reference to 'institutional elements' in patronage systems may seem surprising, since such systems are often seen as entirely personalized. This is sometimes true, but not always. When, for example, a patronage system is largely controlled by a political party which possesses corporate substance, it can impose institutional rules on the operations of the system. It can compel individuals (through disciplinary mechanisms) and/or persuade them (by inspiring loyalty) to subordinate their personal interests to the collective interests of the party, an informal institution.[3] By these means, a party can curtail acts of individual indiscipline—for example, the theft of funds or goods from the patronage system, or the allocation of such resources to cronies rather than to interest groups which the party seeks to cultivate. Personal elements loom large when parties lack strength (or, obviously, when patronage systems exist in the absence of an institutional presence). If individuals at any level within the system face little pressure to subordinate their interests to some collective or institutional good, they tend to behave ineffectively and to skim off personal profits. That undermines the effiency of the patronage system.

Patronage systems in which institutional elements predominate often play a positive role in sustaining the democratic process. They can also help to foster a developmental state by ensuring that government resources are distributed to social groups which are building partnerships with government—partnerships which enable them to meet felt needs, to bring local knowledge and influence to bear on development policy, and to ensure the implementation of development projects which they prefer.

More institutionalized patronage systems tend to be less prone than personalized systems to serve narrow, particularistic purposes—that is, they can facilitate the implementation of broader policies which are aimed at benefiting wider social coalitions. They can render governments more responsive than when a ruling party does not distribute patronage. Politicians who forswear these practices may appear more principled, but they can also cause organized interests to become exasperated at inadequate responses. Interest groups which have given or promised politicians their support expect something in return, and institutionalized patronage systems can be an effective means of meeting those obligations.

So patronage systems in which institutional elements have strong influence do not invariably inspire popular cynicism towards the state, as personalized systems do. There is not an inescapable connection between all patronage systems and a decline in regime legitimacy.[4]

Patronage systems are usually (and often rightly) seen as wasteful and corrupt, especially where more personalized systems are concerned—and there are plenty of them. Not surprisingly, then, many analysts have looked for alternative ways of linking state and society.

---

[3] When we say that parties are informal institutions, we mean that they are almost never (except in a few cases like China) official, formal institutions of state. (For more on this, see Section 2 (c).) But they are institutions none the less.

[4] For more on patronage systems—especially their damaging impact—see Eisenstadt and Lemarchand (1981) and Eisenstadt and Roniger (1984).

But even when alternatives can be found, patronage distribution will persist. Politicians everywhere will continue to channel resources to social groups whose support they have or seek. So while we look for alternatives, we also need to search for ways of reforming patronage systems, to make them less personalized and more capable of fostering healthy partnerships between state and society. If this can be done, it will contribute to a more satisfactory balance between self-interest and institutionalization, and even to the emergence of a new developmental state.

To consider the utility of both alternatives to and the reform of patronage systems, let us examine an episode from Côte d'Ivoire in which some headway was made on both fronts. The outcome was attended by glaring imperfections, but things still improved. Yves A. Faure has argued that for the first ten years after independence from France in 1960, Côte d'Ivoire was governed in part through a patronage system 'of a neatly pyramidical type, tightly run and controlled from the top' by President Houphouet-Boigny. During that decade, as export earnings and foreign loans injected huge amounts of money into the country and the patronage system, it changed from a 'pyramidical' to a 'segmentary structure, [with] each agent who controlled a network and each holder of a resource in the universe of patronage claiming a growing autonomy' (Faure 1989: 70).

When the economy overheated, inflation took off, and export prices then declined, an economic and a political crisis ensued. The regime had initially sought—with considerable success—to arrange things so that 'the whole of society is well and truly framed in a vertical manner by the structure . . . of clientelism' (Faure 1989: 68–9). The crisis consisted in part of the loss of central control over the patronage system and, through it, over much of society. (Readers who understandably applaud that as a sign of progress are asked to bear with us.) 'Other "bosses" had emerged (at lower levels) who controlled powerful networks and reigned over fortunes that allowed them also to accumulate resources and followers' (Faure 1989: 71).

Houphouet-Boigny and his circle responded to this between 1977 and the mid-1980s with a series of formal and informal political changes. These consisted in part of an attempt to 'revive presidential control . . . of the patrimonial regime' via a 'recentralisation of power within it'. But they also entailed several changes in formal political institutions which made the polity more open and rule bound. That is, they sought both to change the patronage system and to generate alternatives to it. Those alternatives both hemmed it in and made it somewhat less personalized and more institutionalized—more subject to predictable, impersonal rules.

Electoral reform, beginning in 1980, ended one-party rule and created what Faure calls 'a semi-competitive regime'. From 1985 onward, the regime embarked on a serious experiment with democratic decentralization by permitting elections to newly empowered *communes* near the local level. In making these democratizing reforms, the President cleverly chose 'to let the electors do some of the "dirty work"; by entrusting them with the task of ousting the extravagant prebend-alists of the political class' (Faure 1989: 70–1).

This had the effect of strengthening his hand in relation to these prebendalists. But these reforms also weakened both the domination which 'the political class' (including the President) could exercise over society, and the power of the office of the President within the formal institutions of state—that is, those which are established in law, in contrast to *in*formal institutions such as parties (see Section 2 (*c*) below). These reforms achieved this by creating formal institutions—elected *commune* councils—which were often beyond his control and which opposition parties could, and sometimes did, capture.

These political reforms occurred at the same time as a structural adjustment programme shrank and reorganized the public sector in ways which undermined the importance of the patronage system that had now moved back under the President's control. Jean-Francois Bayart (1993: 225–6) has shown that other structural adjustment programmes, for example in Senegal and Congo-Brazzaville, produced similar results. Structural adjustment in Côte d'Ivoire caused great hardship among ordinary people and produced a 'sharp deterioration of the [financial] resources of the dominated layers of Abidjan society' (Faure 1989: 72–3).[5] There was clear dissonance between this and the provision of greater *political* resources to individuals and organized interests. It also created bitterness among the people which under-mined the promise of political reform for a more genuine partnership between state and society. So the combined effect of the post-1977 changes was ambiguous.

Despite the centralization of power within the patronage system, the overall importance of patronage within the political system was reduced. The patronage networks were hedged about with new formal institutions such as *commune* councils, and more open electoral pro-cesses, which made the political system more democratic, rule bound, and responsive. And because the ruling party was now forced to com-pete with opposition parties for popular support, strong incentives emerged to manage its patronage system in the party's collective inter-ests, so that it could compete effectively.

[5] For more detail, see Faure and Contamin (1990: esp. ch. 6).

The outcome in Côte d'Ivoire, despite many painful imperfections, indicates that patronage systems—which cannot be expected to disappear—are reformable and adaptable amid other political reforms. When both kinds of changes occur, they can make the state more open, accountable, and responsive, and can give civil society greater space, freedom, and influence. This tends to foster a more predictable and trustworthy partnership between state and civil society which in turn fosters both democratization and sustainable development. Ordinary people—individually and collectively—find predictable, reliable political institutions easier to comprehend, anticipate, and trust; more capable of comprehending and responding to local preferences, pressure, and complaints; more capable of mounting locally desirable development projects which inspire local efforts at maintenance. Such institutions are worth engaging with. They also help in striking a balance between self-interest and personalized politics on the one hand, and institutionalization on the other.

(c) Between informal and formal politics and institutions

In every political system, there is a formal sphere and an informal sphere. Every system consists in part of formal state institutions, which are designated in constitutions and laws: legislatures, courts, executive agencies, etc. But political systems are also made up of informal institutions or entities. Political parties loom large here,[6] but this category also includes factions within parties, organized interests, and structures like patronage networks, plus non-official bodies (which are both players in the political game and arenas within which groups contend for influence) such as non-governmental organizations (NGOs) and co-operative societies.

Informal entities play a role in linking society and the formal institutions of state. Some (like NGOs and organized interests) mainly originate within society. Others (like patronage networks presided over by politicians) tend to derive mainly from the state. Still others (notably, political parties) vary in their origins and orientation according to circumstance. They may derive their existence largely from the state, or they may emerge from society.

Given the huge powers that formal institutions have wielded and sometimes abused in recent years, many people are understandably and legitimately preoccupied with reforms that will check them. But many of these abuses have occurred because informal forces—parties, cliques, families, etc.—have achieved excessive power within formal

---

[6] See n. 3.

structures. So while the overweening power of state institutions needs to be curbed, it is often necessary—*at the same time*—to rebuild and reform them.

Reformed formal institutions offer two advantages to those who seek more predictable, rule-bound governance that conforms to agreed norms. Rules tend to be more fully elaborated and more explicitly set down within formal institutions than within informal institutions. It is therefore usually easier in the formal sphere to achieve adherence to rules. Second, formal institutions tend to be populated by professionals (bureaucrats) who have a greater commitment to the observance of established rules and procedures than do informal institutions. Reform is often needed to prevent bureaucrats from manipulating such rules in ways that thwart the goals of democratizers and advocates of a new type of developmental state. But if that occurs, formal institutions can play valuable roles.

The goal should be formal institutions which are strong enough to resist domination by informal forces, but which are restrained from destructive action by laws, by widely accepted rules (formal and informal), and by the ability of informal forces that originate from within society to check such actions. The goal, in other words, should be a balance between the formal and the informal.

The importance of this can be illustrated by contrasting two cases—the Philippines and the Indian state of West Bengal. When the Americans took control of the Philippines at the beginning of this century, they organized elections almost immediately for mayoral posts in localities throughout the archipelago, even before bureaucratic structures had been put in place. By contrast, British rulers—in Bengal and all across their Afro-Asian empire—delayed elections and the empowerment of elected bodies until long after strong bureaucratic agencies were in place. This caused understandable frustration among nationalists, but it had certain long-term advantages.

The mayors who were so swiftly elected in the Philippines were able to pack the bureaucracies which were then created with their cronies—an option which was not open to Bengali politicians when the British finally gave them the chance to fight and win elections. In the Philippines, this meant that bureaucracies had next to no institutional autonomy. They became the personal tools of elected politicians who abused them by, among other things, grabbing huge landholdings. This enabled the politicians to transform themselves into local bosses who could exercise crass political and economic dominance over local and regional arenas. These bosses found their way into national legislatures where they have remained formidable ever since. Not surprisingly, their power has made it exceedingly difficult for Filipino governments to institute land reforms. The result has been a nation plagued by gross inequality and brutal politics that have impeded development.[7]

In West Bengal, the tradition of a strong, more professionalized, and relatively crony-free bureaucracy persisted after Indian independence. One feature of that professionalism was a commitment to implementing the policies of elected governments, policies which changed as ruling parties changed (Potter 1989). So in West Bengal, unlike the Philippines, a reasonable balance had been achieved between a formal institution (the bureaucracy) and informal forces (ruling parties representing different social coalitions). So when a Communist government took power in 1977 (for a period of rule that extends to the present), that professionalized bureaucracy proved an effective agency for the implementation of a meaningful land reform programme—even though some civil servants were unenthusiastic about the policy.

This suggests that the American enthusiasm for rapid democratization in the Philippines was not enlightened but dangerously naive—because it made it impossible for a balance to be achieved between formal institutions and the bosses' pernicious networks which were informal structures. This is worth noting amid the current enthusiasm for democratization. It is essentially a healthy thing, but if it is pursued incautiously and without an awareness of the need for this and other types of balance, it can produce unintended and unwelcome results.

When informal structures gain excessive influence within governments and abuse it, one impracticable 'solution' is sometimes proposed. This is the notion—which emerges from crude thinking by specialists (often practitioners) in public administration—that formal laws and elaborate formal rules governing the actions of informal forces can somehow minimize their influence within state institutions.

Formal provisions can help a little here, but not much. Informal forces will inevitably find ways of making a major impact. The answer to what is essentially a political problem is not administrative but political. Two related lines of action need to be pursued. The first is to foster responsive, accountable, rule-bound formal structures (which is usually to say, democratic structures) that can serve both as arenas within which informal forces contend for influence and as counterweights to informal forces. The second is for politicians to encourage less personalized and more institutionalized (that is, more rule-bound) processes within informal structures, on the grounds that this change is in the politicians' longer-term interests.

[7] I am grateful to John Sidel for these insights.

(d) Between 'top-down' and 'bottom-up' initiatives

Discussions both of democratization and of redefining the developmental state often and rightly stress the need to de-emphasize 'top-down' approaches and to create opportunities for 'bottom-up' inputs into political institutions and development processes. The desire to give people at and near the local level greater voice is apparent from, *inter alia*, recent experiments in scores of countries with varied forms of democratic decentralization.

This trend is, generally speaking, healthy and promising. But its promise is in jeopardy from some of its most ardent admirers—people with unrealistically high expectations about what can be achieved at and near the local level. Those expectations will inevitably produce disappointment that may cause the abandonment of reforms which still offer plenty of promise in other ways. So in order to protect such reforms from these enthusiasts, we need to understand what is usually not possible in most local-level contexts.

It makes sense to consider two distinct bundles of expectations. Let us first take six ideas—which are often espoused by people in international development agencies who are steeped in public administration —that groups and democratic institutions at or near the local level can:

(i)   play an effective, formal role in planning from below;
(ii) effectively monitor and formally evaluate development projects;
(iii) devise, or at least understand and implement, complex development projects;
(iv) mobilize local resources beyond the reach of central governments;
(v)   reduce absenteeism by government employees who work at the local level; and
(vi) reduce the overall level of corruption in government institutions.

All of these expectations are unrealistic in most contexts.[8]

'Planning from below' has been often been taken very seriously. This is unfortunate, because the available empirical evidence (Manor 1998, Crook and Manor 1998) clearly indicates that two formidable sets of problems afflict it. The problem at lower levels is that elected leaders are disinclined to 'plan' seriously, partly because they tend to operate with a short-term time horizon, and partly because plans would limit their freedom to improvise. Lower-level bodies also often lack the administrative capacity to prepare genuine plans. The problem at higher levels of government is that despite pious pledges of seriousness,

---

[8] Throughout this section, I am drawing on my research for the World Bank on experiments with decentralization throughout Asia, Africa, Latin America, and Eastern Europe, set out in Manor (1998).

powerful actors there often disregard the plans which come up to them when they allocate resources to lower levels.

Experiments with democratic decentralization, drafted by public administration specialists, often include requirements that authorities at lower levels engage in formal monitoring and evaluation of development projects. This seldom happens very effectively in any formal way. These authorities often lack the capacity to do so—indeed, they are usually at full stretch just implementing projects. That rightly seems to them to be more important than monitoring and evaluation. So most formal reports (if any get written) to central governments on monitoring and evaluation are—like most plans from below—largely fictional. But since development projects in decentralized systems are implemented by local people, in or near local arenas, informal monitoring and evaluation by ordinary folk often happens. They can see what is happening so close to home, and they register their 'reports' at the next available election.

Decentralized democratic authorities worldwide have exhibited a preference for small, uncomplicated development projects—usually involving the construction of some small facilities. They tend to avoid complex projects for a number of reasons, including (in most cases) an inability to comprehend and implement, let alone devise, such projects.

Decentralized bodies are often, and unjustly, expected to mobilize substantial local resources in tax revenues. They tend to fail partly because they often face deep popular cynicism towards all government institutions which makes people unwilling to pay taxes. That might be broken down, given time and improved governance, but other problems would still remain. In very poor countries, there are limits on the amount of mobilizable resources. More crucially, elected members of decentralized bodies are reluctant to impose new taxes since it makes them unpopular. And they know that much of the tax burden will fall on elite groups—from which they usually come, and upon whom they usually depend for re-election.

In one or two countries that have decentralized in recent years (India and possibly the Philippines), we have evidence that it can reduce absenteeism by government schoolteachers and health workers at the local level, and (only in India) that it can reduce the overall amount of money lost to corruption. Elsewhere, key contextual elements which we find in India and (to a lesser degree) the Philippines are missing. These are a free press, a lively multi-party system, and, most crucially, a substantial army of activists at lower levels in the system who possess political skills needed to achieve these things. Elected politicians' skills at developing links with ordinary people (which enable them to learn of absenteeism or acts of corruption), and at lobbying other elected politicians and bureaucrats (to press for action against such abuses) are especially important. But in nearly all of the places where decentralization has been tried, not enough of these things are available to prevent reductions in absenteeism and corruption (Manor 1998).

The second bundle of expectations relate to the capability of local groups and democratic institutions to:

(i) devise, or at least implement, poverty alleviation programmes; and

(ii) devise and fund, or at least implement, social welfare programmes for disadvantaged groups.

Evidence from a wide range of countries indicates that these things— especially the first—are difficult to achieve. Funding is sometimes a constraint, but the crucial problem is the unwillingness of prosperous people who usually dominate local communities and political institutions to channel resources to the poor. In many, though not all, political systems, leaders at higher levels have greater interest in assisting the poor than those at the grass roots where hierarchical attitudes are stronger and more uncompromisingly pursued. In such systems, it makes sense to leave programmes to aid the poor in the hands of higher-level actors.

The nature of the local context here is hugely important. This becomes apparent if we consider the one region of the world which offers numerous exceptions to the generalizations in the previous paragraph. In many Latin American countries, we find poorer groups at the local level who are (i) well organized for the promotion of their collective interests and (ii) inclined to engage co-operatively with state institutions and agencies in pursuit of those interests.[9] Given that context, decisions to entrust local institutions with programmes to help poorer groups often have a realistic chance of success.

This discussion of things which we cannot expect of democratic decentralization and of people at lower levels is not intended to suggest that we should abandon efforts to promote 'bottom-up' inputs into the political and policy processes. Decentralized authorities and grass-roots communities are capable of many other, very important contributions both to the deepening of democracy (one aspect of democratization) and to the emergence of a new kind of developmental state (Manor 1998*b*). They nearly always trigger greater associational activity and political participation. They tend strongly to make government more responsive to grass-roots communities—by enhancing the speed, quantity, and quality of responses (when 'quality' is measured

---

[9] I am grateful to Jonathan Fox and James Dunkerley for stressing this point.

by the conformity of responses to popular preferences). They usually act as a counterweight to urban bias. They greatly increase the flow of information between government and the local level, in both directions.

This last trend has great political value, and it makes vital developmental contributions—indeed, it saves lives. It does so by providing early warnings of potential disasters in remote areas, such as outbreaks of disease and droughts. And since elected representatives can explain the utility of government programmes for inoculations, antenatal care, etc. in terms that ordinary folk can understand, it enhances the uptake on such programmes and prevents needless illness and even death. Since ordinary people have greater influence (through local democratic institutions) over development projects, they become more committed to the maintenance of such projects and that helps to make development more sustainable.

These and several other benefits which tend to follow from democratic decentralization and other devices to promote 'bottom-up' inputs greatly advance both democratization and the growth of a developmental state (Crook and Manor 1998, Manor 1998). But since decentralized authorities usually have difficulty performing certain other important tasks—like much needed but complex development initiatives, or poverty alleviation—there remains a role for 'top-down' efforts. There is, in other words, a need to find a balance between these two types of approaches.

(e) *Between continuity and innovation*

There is a danger that in their understandable enthusiasm to reorient government agencies in ways that will facilitate partnerships between the state and groups at the grass roots, policy-makers may attempt reforms that are too radical. One example was the Indian government's introduction of a joint forest management programme.

The aims of this scheme could not have been more admirable. The bureaucratic agency that administered forest lands, the Indian Forest Service, was asked to develop mechanisms for consultation and collaborative decision-making with rural communities living in forested zones. The aims of the reform were more open, responsive government and—since villagers would acquire a meaningful voice in forest management—more appropriate and sustainable development of resources.

The great difficulty was the character of the Indian Forest Service. Since the British period, its task had been to police forest reserves, to play a role akin to that of gamekeepers. Its mission was to detect, arrest, and prosecute villagers who came onto forest lands in search of firewood and fodder for livestock. Not surprisingly, it had developed a deeply antagonistic relationship with rural dwellers over the decades. Mutual distrust and distaste ran deep on both sides of the chasm that separated the Forest Service from villagers.

The joint forest management programme asked the Service to adopt, all of a sudden, a diametrically opposite approach to that which it had always pursued. If such collaborative policies were urged upon government schoolteachers or primary health care workers, the change would have been far less radical and there would have been a reasonable chance of success. But the wildly unrealistic demands placed on the Forest Service led, predictably, to severe problems (Saxena 1996).

There are plenty of other examples of reformers' unwarranted beliefs that radical transitions are possible. In countries where civil society has long been energetically repressed, it is unwise to expect it to join, swiftly and formidably, in partnerships with government. Where NGOs are understandably suspicious of all government institutions and initiatives, after years of bitter disappointments, it is unrealistic to expect them to respond quickly to new official programmes—even if these come from elected local councils. Where citizens view government cynically, as a result of consistently wretched performance by state agencies, they can hardly be expected—all at once—to become compliant payers of taxes and user charges. When central governments offload onerous tasks onto local communities and/or decentralized authorities without providing the funds or the administrative resources to perform them, it is silly to expect them to shoulder these responsibilities effectively.

The implications are plain. Reforms which are aimed at fostering a new kind of 'developmental state' must be undertaken cautiously, on the basis of a realistic understanding of the recent experiences of key actors. There is a need for balance between innovation and continuity.

(f) Between confidentiality and transparency

Transparency is, for the most part, a goal worth pursuing. It is an important part of any effort at democratization. Access to information helps to empower citizens and organized interests, enhances their bargining power and their capacity to influence the making and implementation of policy, facilitates greater political accountability, etc. For these and other reasons, it also helps to foster a new kind of developmental state. It increases the chances that local knowledge and preferences can be incorporated into government initiatives. That makes it more likely that ordinary folk will feel some sense of ownership of development projects, so that they assist in sustaining them, etc.

But we need to recognize that it makes less sense to seek thoroughly transparent government than to strive for a balance between confidentiality and transparency. Given the conditions that prevail in most less developed countries, a marked enhancement of transparency will be required for anything like a balance to develop. But to say that is not the same thing as advocating an end to confidentiality.

Advocating that is unwise for four reasons. It is wildly unrealistic. It could alienate politicians and bureaucrats who might otherwise undertake reforms which would promote democratization and the new developmental state. The maintenance of a degree of confidentiality can facilitate the implementation of reform—including, ironically, moves towards greater transparency. And we need to recognize that greater transparency is a mixed blessing which can produce certain results that may undermine reform.

The last two of these points need a little explaining. First, furtive actions by leaders implementing reforms are sometimes crucial to their success. If their full intentions are revealed at the start, powerful interests who are sceptical of, say, democratization, or changes to make government more responsive to grass-roots communities, might offer stout resistance that could scuttle reform. It may even be necessary to conceal a government's full reformist agenda, to offer potential opponents false reassurance until the reform process begins to develop a constituency for change. Selective obfuscation is often quite creative. Hence the need for a balance between confidentiality and transparency (Jenkins 1997).

Second, greater transparency can produce results which, ironically, undermine popular confidence in reforms. For example, in one Indian state, the creation of powerful elected councils quite near the local level radically increased the amount of information available to villagers about government development programmes. Before decentralization, only about four or five politicians and bureaucrats at the subdistrict level (higher up in the system) knew how much money the state government had allocated for development. Their monopoly on this information enabled them, routinely, to pocket sizeable proportions of these funds without being found out. After decentralization, the amounts provided for development were known to hundreds of local councillors across each subdistrict, and to the press and many citizens. This made the previous kind of grand theft from programmes for education, health care, housing, etc. no longer possible.

However, because the system had become so transparent, citizens were much more able to see the many, petty acts of malfeasance which then took place. This led them to conclude that corruption had increased as a result of decentralization, even though the overall amount of money then being stolen was smaller than before. Their misperception inspired not an appreciation of decentralized institutions which the facts warranted, but exasperation and some cynicism. Fortunately, these were tempered by a popular recognition of other benefits that decentralization had delivered (Crook and Manor 1998).

This indicates that dangers attend transitions to greater transparency, that there remains a place for a degree of confidentiality—and for a balance between it and transparency.

3. *Conclusion*

(a) *The enhanced likelihood of achieving such balances*

It is easy to say that a degree of balance is needed between the sets of alternatives discussed above. Achieving it is another, more difficult matter. But all across the world, a striking change in the temper of the times has made it more likely that such balances can be struck. The late 1970s and early 1980s witnessed a loss of confidence in centralized, commandist governance—after a phase following the Second World War when such confidence had reached unprecedented heights. Crawford Young has described it as an era in which we saw 'hubris resonating throughout the world' (Young 1994: 3).

Commandists and centralizers in that earlier period had only limited interest in seeking such balances. More recent efforts to establish and deepen democracy, and to foster developmental states which are more responsive, open, and enabling, positively require that such balances be sought. The very purposes which now preoccupy many policy-makers enhance the chances that headway can be made on these fronts.

One notion that animated governments in the heyday of commandism was the belief that centralized, state-led approaches could yield spectacular results—huge development projects (large dams and other public works, major hospitals and the like) or massive experiments with social engineering. In a discussion of early post-independence attempts of this kind in sub-Saharan Africa, David Apter and Carl Rosberg (1993: 39) have noted that 'massive developmental change is extremely difficult to realize under acceptable political conditions, and such circumstances predispose one to reconstitute power by authoritarian and coercive means'.

The loss of confidence in centralized approaches is helpful in that it has made policy-makers much less inclined to seek 'massive developmental change'. They are more open to strategies which seek incremental change and which stress smaller-scale development projects, often in consultation with communities (or at least elites) at the local level. This kind of development depends less on coercive methods—indeed, it can happen only if those methods are de-emphasized. So even though some analysts still worry that democratization and development may not be achievable simultaneously, it makes much more sense to pursue them concurrently now that 'development' is being redefined in more incremental terms.

It is possible that this loss of confidence will make no difference in the pursuit of balance in one of the six areas noted above. In their impatience with old ways, policy-makers today are arguably as likely as the centralizers and commandists to seek to innovate incautiously, without due regard for the need to sustain some continuity. (Although even here, their abandonment of the huge aspirations of the centralizers and commandists may curb their excesses somewhat.) But in the other five areas, they appear more likely to seek and achieve balances. Such leaders seldom share commandists' intense preoccupation with the need for order, or their occasional tendency to provoke severe conflicts to force their will upon others. They are more likely to welcome a degree of conflict, and to seek to ensure that it is drawn into a process of political bargaining to prevent it from wrecking democratization and new developmental approaches.

They are less likely to promote personalized politics, or to undermine institutions in pursuit of personal rule as many commandists formerly did. They tend more often to recognize the need for balance between formal and informal institutions, and to permit the institutionalization of processes within informal structures. They are usually far more inclined to encourage 'bottom-up' input into decision-making, and somewhat more inclined to make government more transparent.

(b) The interrelationship between democratization and the new developmental state

We noted earlier that the first three sets of dualities analysed above had rather more to do with democratization than with the emergence of a new kind of developmental state, while developmental issues were more apparent in assessments of the last three. We also saw, however, in the discussions of the six sets of dualities, that all of them had implications for both democratization and development.

These two processes—our central preoccupations in this book—are closely bound up with one another and tend to be mutually reinforcing. However, we need to recognize that this benign relationship is true only within certain limits, lest unrealistic expectations arise. Consider three examples.

First, we will encounter—at least over the short term—some dissonance between democratization (either at the national level or through decentralization) and greater partnerships between state institutions and indigenous NGOs and voluntary associations. Such partnerships are a key element of the new developmental state. Research on experiments with democratic decentralization indicates that NGOs/voluntary associations remain nearly as suspicious of new democratic bodies at lower levels as of central government in early, more commandist times. And elected members of decentralized bodies tend to regard NGOs with suspicion—as unelected, unaccountable entities. We are just beginning to see signs of a thaw in this relationship in a few places, but it will take time for more robust partnerships to blossom (Manor 1998).

Second, there is some dissonance between greater freedom for the private sector—with which the new developmental state ought to develop an enabling relationship—and democratization. The dissonance is not total. A reduction in state controls over the economy can undercut certain kinds of corruption, facilitate the emergence of organized interests, and make civil society more vigorous, more capable of avoiding co-optation or dominance by government. But greater freedom for market forces often tends to produce greater inequalities. This can make it more difficult for civil society as a whole—the entire array of organized interests—to play a more energetic role, because it sometimes damages the capacity of less prosperous groups to do so. And since the pursuit of greater social justice is one goal of the new developmental state, greater inequalities are, in themselves, an impediment to its emergence.

Third, we noted in Section 2 (f) that greater transparency (one result of democratization) sometimes inspires, ironically, greater popular mistrust of government—at least at first. This can make it more difficult to foster partnerships between state and society—a goal both of the new developmental state and of democratization itself.

A fourth problem might be added here, although it actually deserves to be dismissed from this discussion. We saw in Section 2 (b) how the more lively competition between interests, which democratization and the lifting of state controls foster, tends to undermine the prospects at the grass roots for community-wide harmony and participation in development. If 'community participation in development' were crucial to the emergence of a new developmental state, this would qualify as a serious difficulty. But in this writer's view, it is more in the nature of a utopian dream—and an unhelpful dream at that, since it stands in the way of the freer, more lively competition within societies which democratization and the new developmental state should and can encourage.

In most respects, however, democratization and the emergence of this new kind of developmental state tend to resonate with one another.

Many of the things that we associate with the new developmental state tend to enhance popular enthusiasm and pressure for democratization. Democratization can provide people with some compensation for the pain which attends economic reform which regimes often feel forced to undertake. Governments which liberalize their economies in the interests of growth and—in the process—dilute or abandon pre-existing social welfare systems place their legitimacy and popularity at risk. Fresh opportunities for democratic participation can ease the resentments which follow from these changes. Such opportunities may be seized by organized interests to restructure welfare systems and other government initiatives in ways that take greater account of local particularities and preferences. That may win governments some grudging appreciation which buys time for growth to provide other sorts of compensation.

Social groups which find governments more open to their views and influence develop appetites for greater democratization. If governments respond to these, a virtuous circle can develop—with increased pressure for power-sharing producing greater democratization which in turn generates further pressure, while individuals on both sides of the state–society divide grow more inclined to develop partnerships and more skilled at making them work.

Democratization also tends, in the main, to help foster the new developmental state. Despite the ironies that sometimes attend increases in transparency and some other aspects of democratization, greater democracy tends to trigger enhanced associational activity within society, enhanced participation, more responsive governance, a culture of political bargaining which moderates conflict even as it quickens, the observance of formal and informal rules and norms, etc. These things tend to bolster the popular legitimacy of government. That has two implications which make it more likely that a new developmental state will emerge. It inclines actors in civil society to engage more energetically and positively with the state. And it eases the anxieties of politicians who, in the more relaxed mood which follows, tend to operate in less commandist ways.

If democratization and the new developmental state are fostered cautiously, realistically, and (crucially) with an awareness of the need for the types of balance examined here, some of the unhelpful ironies that attend both processes can be minimized. So can dissonances between the two processes. That can make the simultaneous pursuit of these two goals more likely to meet with some success.

REFERENCES

Apter, D. E., and Rosberg, C. G. (1993), 'Changing African Perspectives', in D. E. Apter and C. G. Rosberg (eds.), *Political Development and the New Realism in Sub-Saharan Africa*, Charlottesville: University of Virginia Press.

Bayart, J.-F. (1993), *The State in Africa: The Politics of the Belly*, Harlow: Longmans.

Crook, R., and Manor, J. (1998), *Democracy and Decentralisation: Local Government in South Asia and West Africa*, Cambridge: Cambridge University Press.

Diamond., L. (1996), 'Three Paradoxes of Democracy', in L. Diamond and M. F. Plattner (eds.), *The Global Resurgence of Democracy*, 2nd edn., Baltimore: Johns Hopkins University Press.

Eisenstadt, S. N., and Lemarchand R. (eds.) (1981), *Political Clientelism, Patronage and Development*, Beverly Hills, Calif.: Sage.

—— and Roniger, L. (1984), *Patrons, Clients and Friends*, Cambridge: Cambridge University Press.

Evans, P. (1996), 'Introduction: Development Strategies across the Public–Private Sector Divide', *World Development*, June: 1033–38.

Faure, Y. A. (1989), 'Côte d'Ivoire: Analysing the Crisis', in D. B. Cruise O'Brien, J. Dunn, and R. Rathbone (eds.), *Contemporary West African States*, Cambridge: Cambridge University Press.

—— and Contamin, B. (1990), *La Bataille des entreprises publiques en Côte d'Ivoire*, Paris: Karthala.

Heredia, B. (1993), 'Making Economic Reforms Politically Viable: The Mexican Experience', in W. C. Smith, C. H. Acuna, and E. A. Gamarra (eds.), *Democracy, Markets and Structural Reform in Latin America: Argentina, Bolivia, Brazil, Chile and Mexico*, New Brunswick, NJ: Transaction Publishers/North–South Center, University of Miami.

Husain, I. (1994), 'Why Do Some Economies Adjust More Successfully than Others? Lessons from Seven African Countries', Policy Research Working Paper no. 1364, World Bank: Africa Regional Office, Oct.

Jenkins, R. (1997), 'Democratic Adjustment: Explaining the Political Sustainability of Economic Reform in India', University of Sussex D.Phil. thesis.

Manor, J. (1998), *The Political Economy of Democratic Decentralization*, Washington: World Bank.

Potter, D. (1989), *India's Political Administrators*, New Delhi: Oxford University Press.

Saxena, N. C. (1996), 'Policies, Realities and the Ability to Change: The Indian Forest Service: A Case Study', and 'A Review of Forestry Programmes in India', in Indo-Swedish Cooperation Programme, *Sharing Challenges*, Stockholm: SIDA.

Young, C. (1994), *The African Colonial State in Comparative Perspective*, New Haven: Yale University Press.

Democracy, Participation, and Public Policy
The Politics of Institutional Design

MARK ROBINSON

1. Introduction

The reinvigoration of democracy in many parts of the developing world has created new opportunities for political participation on the part of organized groups in civil society which have been excluded from the formal political arena and the formulation of public policy. This increase in political participation is evident in the flourishing of independent organizations such as trade unions, farmers' organizations, and business associations, whose ability to influence policy under authoritarian regimes was extremely limited. The expectation is that democratic politics provides space for groups and individuals to organize themselves politically, to freely express divergent opinions, and to become involved in a more open and inclusive policy-making process. Hence, political participation is considered to be desirable as a means of both deepening democracy and enhancing the effectiveness of public policy.

In the procedural or minimalist conception of democracy, the primary vehicle for political participation is competitive party-based elections in which voters are free to choose between the alternative policy agendas of political elites. In this scheme, political parties aggregate public preferences and compete for political power. Governments secure an electoral mandate for a stated set of policy commitments

The assistance of Edward Anderson in preparing a bibliography and collecting background materials is gratefully acknowledged.

and can be held to account for their actions by the legislature. Public involvement in the policy process is restricted to periodic ratification (or rejection) of the policy agenda of the ruling party.[1]

In contrast, participatory conceptions of democracy emphasize the deliberative nature of public policy, in which the formulation and implementation of public policy is subject to debate and contestation among key stakeholders (Barber 1984, Pateman 1970). Pluralist theorists consider a high level of public involvement in decision-making to be an intrinsic feature of an established democracy, in which contending interest groups seek to influence public policy in the best interests of their members and constituents. This perspective is criticized by proponents of a sharp distinction between the private and public realms, who argue that the principles of interest-group representation are incompatible with the procedural norms of liberal democracy, and that structured interaction between organized interests and the state in policy-making undermines the legitimacy of democratic institutions (Anderson 1977).

These approaches are principally concerned with democracy as a process, and most established democracies incorporate features of both. However, the relationship between democracy and public policy is also construed in more instrumentalist terms, in which the latter encapsulates both the technical design of policy measures and the design of institutions through which decisions are taken (ibid.: 130). This is founded on the premiss that the involvement of key stakeholders in deliberations over the scope and content of public policy initiatives will enhance their viability and the prospects for successful implementation. In other words, greater participation is conducive to better policy outcomes. A variant of this argument infuses contemporary debates about the appropriate political and institutional conditions for the effective implementation of development policy, both at the level of macro-economic reform and social policy, and in the context of discrete development projects. In the former, political participation is a means of mobilizing constituencies in favour of policy reforms in a democratic political environment, the successful implementation of which is considered crucial for the attainment of long-term development objectives. The active involvement of key stakeholders in the process of reform by means of participation in decision-making is seen as key to this (Landell-Mills 1992, Gordon 1996). This is in sharp contrast to the view which prevailed in the early 1980s, which held that authoritarian and technocratic government was required for

---

[1] For a critique see Nordlinger (1981) and Pateman (1970).

the successful implementation of economic reforms. Far from being a positive force for reform, organized interest groups were considered to be an impediment to successful reform efforts.[2]

The instrumentalist case for greater participation in macro-economic policy is also manifest at the level of public services and development projects. Here the argument centres on the expected developmental dividends of involving the intended beneficiaries in project design and implementation. As in the case of macro-economic policy, the case for increased participation hinges in part on the enhanced legitimacy of the decision-making process, and in part on the expectation that projects will be more effective and sustainable if they secure the interest and involvement of those which they are seeking to assist (Chambers 1983, Bhatnagar and Williams 1992, Nelson and Wright 1995, World Bank 1997).[3]

To a considerable extent the scope for increasing opportunities for political participation depends on the existence of a democratic political environment. However, this is subject to two limiting factors. First, many of the new democratic regimes that have emerged since the late 1970s have not established deep roots and remain unconsolidated. They also lack political legitimacy and accountability, due to curbs on opposition political activities, periodic abuses of civil and political rights, weaknesses in the judicial system, and the persistence of authoritarian practices (Beetham 1993, Luckham and White 1996). Such regimes, which have been characterized as 'low-intensity' or 'illiberal' democracies (Gills et al. 1993, Zakaria 1997), are prevalent among the new governments that have come to power through competitive elections in Africa, Asia, and Latin America since the early 1980s. Aside from their illiberal features, they tend to discourage active citizen participation. Second, socio-economic factors compound deficiencies in the formal political sphere, and further militate against a rapid increase in opportunities for political participation in many developing countries. These include mass poverty, low levels of education, limited technical capacity, poor communications, and cultural barriers, all of which limit an expansion in political participation, and, by extension, the deepening of democracy.[4]

---

[2] For a discussion see Toye (1992) and Robinson (1996).

[3] For instance, the *World Development Report 1997* argues that increased opportunities for voice and participation improve state capability by increasing the credibility of policy decisions, reducing information problems and transaction costs, and exerting pressure on government to improve the quality and delivery of public services. It is stated that 'There is compelling evidence that arrangements that promote participation by stakeholders in the design and implementation of public services or programs can improve both the rate of return and the sustainability of these activities' (World Bank 1997: 117).

[4] For a classic rendition of this argument see Lipset (1959) and Huntington (1965).

For these reasons, one should not succumb to misplaced optimism about the developmental consequences of increased opportunities for participation in poor countries embarking on a gradual and uneven process of democratization. Such caution is especially warranted in the case of poor and disadvantaged people who have historically been subject to political and social exclusion. Yet despite such limitations, there may well exist considerable scope for institutional innovations within the confines of unconsolidated democracies, which are conducive to increased participation with the prospect of generating better development outcomes.[5] Such innovations can assume a wide variety of institutional forms, depending on the level and policy domain in which opportunities for increased participation present themselves. The electoral process remains the dominant sphere through which political participation takes place, and variations in election procedures can shape the form and extent of participation and its impact on public policy. In the context of social and economic policies, more direct forms of participation take the form of pressure and influence exerted by organized interest groups representing *inter alia* business and labour, and formal consultative mechanisms can be created to channel such influence, in the form of deliberation councils and other corporatist devices. A variety of institutional mechanisms can be employed to involve the poor in decision-making at the level of individual projects, often through intermediary organizations (such as non-governmental organizations) which represent their interests (Riddell and Robinson 1995). And yet most of these devices are imperfect means of promoting political participation on the part of poor and excluded groups. Macro-economic policy often remains the prerogative of elite groups representing special interests, to the exclusion of most ordinary citizens. Participation at the level of individual projects can be construed as an attempt to legitimize predetermined decisions in the absence of popular control over resource allocations and programme design (Goulet 1989, Craig and Mayo 1995a, Rahman 1995).

Some of the most innovative attempts to broaden political participation beyond voting in periodic elections or occasional consultation over projects have centred on institutionalized participation, often in the context of efforts to decentralize political power to local government. In such instances the intention has been to maximize the opportunities for poor and socially marginalized groups to exert influence over policy choice, resource allocation, and programme design, by creating

---

[5] In adopting this approach it is important to acknowledge Schönwalder's (1997) cautionary remark about the 'institutional fetishism' inherent in approaches to popular participation that stress the virtues of institutional design in the absence of more fundamental changes in the underlying structures of economic and political power.

institutional space for structured interactions with policy-makers, through the medium of intermediary organizations such as community groups, voluntary organizations, and social movements. Hence, in keeping with our concern with citizens who have historically been denied access to the public policy realm, institutional innovations designed to broaden the scope and intensity of political participation will constitute the principal focus of this chapter.

Such considerations raise a series of questions about the scope and intensity of political participation and the forms it assumes in new democratic states. To what extent has democratization been accompanied by increased political participation? What forms does political participation assume in new democracies? Which groups actively participate in decision-making processes, under what circumstances, and in relation to what policies? What is the developmental significance of increased participation in terms of policy choice and policy outcomes? The remainder of this chapter sets out to examine these questions in the light of the theoretical literature on political participation, and contrasting experiences of institutionalized participation in selected developing countries.

Before embarking on the analysis, there are two methodological caveats which need to be taken into consideration. First, while the evidence is not sufficiently robust to permit one to attribute development policy outcomes to differential rates of political participation with any degree of precision (not least because of the influence of other intervening variables), the analysis will nevertheless attempt to assess the extent to which the expected benefits of participation are realized in the form of changes in policy choice and resource allocations. Second, while the chapter consciously adopts an instrumentalist approach by focusing on the outputs of decision-making, it is also concerned with the process of political participation in the context of democratic politics. Implicit is the recognition that the developmental significance of participation lies not only in the extent to which it can generate better socio-economic development outcomes (in the form of economic growth, reduced poverty, and higher levels of human development), but also in reshaping the political process through institutional innovation.

The chapter adopts a limited focus in keeping with its primary concern with the developmental significance of participation for poor and socially marginalized groups. Hence, it will attempt to identify the conditions under which institutional mechanisms can be crafted to enhance the participation of a broad range of societal actors, and not just an elite grouping of key stakeholders who stand to gain most from privileged access to the public policy sphere. In this respect the findings of the chapter feed into a central concern of this book, namely the potential in democratizing societies for designing political institutions which are conducive to developmentally efficacious policy outcomes from the perspective of the material concerns of socially excluded groups.

The analysis is predicated on the following hypotheses. First, democratization is conducive to greater political participation by broadening access to the formal political arena and the public policy process. Second, effective participation in policy-making in developing societies is limited in terms of scope and inclusiveness, and favours groups with access to wealth and power. Third, institutions can be crafted to induce greater participation on the part of poor and socially excluded groups.

The next section reviews the theoretical literature on political participation, in order to establish an acceptable definition, and to determine the main factors shaping the form and extent of political participation among different groups of citizens. The third section turns to the nature of the policy process in developing countries, examining the form that it assumes in authoritarian regimes, and the changes that are expected to take place in newly democratizing countries. This is followed by an analysis of concrete examples of participation in the formulation of public policy, focusing in particular on formal mechanisms for promoting consultation and policy dialogue, and the types of actors involved in and excluded from the policy process. The main empirical section considers two contrasting cases of institutionalized participation—the Law of Popular Participation in Bolivia and Panchayati Raj in India—as a means of analysing the developmental significance of institutional innovations designed to enhance the participation of the poor. The chapter ends by considering the scope for active intervention in the crafting of institutional mechanisms designed to promote enhanced participation and policy dialogue in new democracies as a means of generating developmentally efficacious policy outcomes.

2. Democracy and Political Participation

The study of political participation has long been a focal point for political scientists concerned with democracy and democratization. It has given rise to a vast literature and numerous empirical studies, which can assist in the analysis of contemporary manifestations of political participation and policy-making in new democracies in the developing world. Although the study of political participation covers all forms of independent citizen action, the principal concern of this chapter is with collective action designed to influence decision-making and shape policy outcomes. For the purpose of this study, political participation is analysed as instrumental action designed to influence policy choice, and not purely as a form of political behaviour which strengthens democratic legitimacy. Public policy is taken to refer to all aspects of decision-making, from deliberation and agenda-setting through to implementation. As such it embraces both the substance of policy decisions and the process through which decisions are arrived at.

(a) Definitions

Political participation is defined by Nie and Verba (1975: 1) as 'legal activities by private citizens which are more or less directly aimed at influencing the selection of government personnel and/or actions they take'. In their view participation 'is a technique for setting goals, choosing priorities, and deciding what resources to commit to goal attainment' (ibid.: 4). Huntington and Nelson (1976) define participation in broader terms to include all citizen actions which are designed to influence government decision-making. Such actions can be individual or collective, organized or spontaneous, peaceful or violent, legal or illegal. Successful participation is manifested in the number and scope of government decisions that are actually influenced and the degree of influence over the content of decisions.

Such definitions focus attention on instrumental action designed to influence government decision-making, though radical democratic theorists recognize the intrinsic value of political participation as an educational device and as a vehicle for promoting empowerment (Pateman 1970, Friedmann 1992). Liberals emphasize the educative function of participation as a means of enhancing the democratic skills and intellectual capacity of individuals, and on the possibilities it presents for collective action in the public interest, as opposed to preserving narrow self-interests. Modernization theorists consider political participation to be a constitutive element of political development, generally expressed in higher rates of electoral participation. Such behaviour can be conducive to political development by giving people a stake in the political system and inculcating democratic values, but at the same time some proponents of this approach warn of the dangers posed by uncontrolled mobilization for political stability (Huntington and Nelson 1976).

More instrumental interpretations stress the value of participation in enhancing the effectiveness of the public policy process. In this schema, the higher the level of participation, the greater the potential for generating policy choices that reflect the needs and interests of ordinary citizens. Advocates of participation argue that greater stake-holder involvement in the decision-making process enhances the acceptability of policy and the prospects for effective implementation. This argument extends to the efficiency of implementation in that higher levels of participation are expected to generate better policy outcomes.[6]

There is a further distinction which is relevant to our analysis, namely between a functional approach which stresses the instrumental benefits of participation, and a more political approach which takes the empowerment of poor and excluded groups as its starting point (Oakley et al. 1991, Schönwalder 1997). The former tends to equate participation with greater consultation over needs and priorities, and increased involvement in the design and implementation of develop-ment projects, while the latter is concerned with the creation of new institutional channels for popular participation which challenge exist-ing power structures and the established distribution of economic resources. While much of the debate about the benefits of participa-tion is couched in functional terms the wider political significance of the process also requires due consideration.

Political participation assumes a wide variety of forms in different political and socio-economic settings, though it is possible to discern some broad patterns. Parry and Moyser (1994) identify five principal modes of political participation: voting, contacting, campaigning, group action, and protest. Voting in periodic elections is the most widespread form of political participation in terms of the numbers of people involved, but it conveys little information about policy prefer-ences, since a range of factors determine voting behaviour and polit-ical parties are imperfect channels for articulating voice, especially in countries lacking established democratic traditions (ibid.: 48–50). Contacting refers to individual efforts to influence officials and policy-makers. This form of political participation is usually confined to personal issues or particularistic concerns, and does not involve group activity, even though it may indirectly influence public policy. Organized activity to influence government actions in the form of lobbying is a direct form of participation which is geared towards the attainment of collective outcomes. Party campaigning channels participation into forms of activity designed to strengthen organiza-tional structures and the resource base of political parties with a view to achieving success in elections. Political protest (in the form of strikes, petitions, and demonstrations) is a fifth form of participation

[6] Evidence is drawn from the industrial sphere as well as from development pro-jects to substantiate this claim. See, for example, Pateman (1970) and Bhatnagar and Williams (1992).

that does not receive much attention from political theorists, but is one that can be significant for groups excluded from decision-making fora and in situations where organized channels for citizen influence are limited.

Collective efforts to influence decision-making, which are the principal focus of this chapter, may be self-generated or influenced by intermediaries. In this respect Huntington and Nelson (1976: 7–10) make a useful distinction between autonomous and mobilized participation. Autonomous participation refers to self-initiated activity by organized interest groups which is designed to exert influence over decision-making. In the case of mobilized participation, political activity is a response to coercion, persuasion, or material inducements on the part of other interested parties, where influence over decision-making may not be the explicit intention of those taking part in such activity. This is most obviously manifested in the case of voting, where politicians try to secure votes through a variety of means, and many examples of mobilized participation exist in developing countries where free and fair elections are not firmly established. In practice most political systems display a mix of both these forms of participation.

As a means of extending the analysis, a third category of political participation can be employed, which might be termed mediated participation. The notion of mediation refers to the role played by intermediaries in galvanizing groups of people to participate in political affairs, as well as acting as their representatives in decision-making fora. It might plausibly be argued that this mediated form of participation is more likely to feature in societies where groups lack the power, capacity, and resources to influence policy-makers directly. These intermediaries can be political parties, grass-roots organizations, or voluntary associations. It is our contention that autonomous forms of participation will tend to be the prerogative of interest groups who have direct access to politicians and policy-makers by virtue of their wealth, power, and influence.

One further dimension of participation which is pertinent here lies in the distinction made by Huntington and Nelson (1976) between the scope and intensity of participation. The scope of participation refers to the proportion of people engaged in a particular form of political activity, while intensity is the scale, duration, and importance of a particular activity. Huntington and Nelson argue that the scope and intensity of participation tend to be inversely related, in that small numbers of people engage in a highly intense fashion with policy-makers, by virtue of the nature of the lobbying process, whereas voting entails large numbers of people engaged in a periodic activity which is low intensity (ibid.: 11–12).

These dimensions of participation are also likely to vary according to the policy issue in question, the complexity of the implementation process, and the nature of the group involved in a particular activity. For example, one would expect to see differences in the scope and intensity of participation in relation to different types of macro-economic policies. The technical complexity and speed of decision-making, and generalized effects of a decision to devalue the exchange rate, entail a more intense process of participation involving a limited number of people, whereas privatization is a more protracted and less intensive process where larger numbers of people have a definable stake in the outcome and the effects of a policy decision are more concentrated. Hence, while the scope and intensity of participation are inversely related in the context of efforts to influence public policy, variations in this relationship according to the policy in question will shape the potential involvement of different groups of people.

(b) Participation and social exclusion

Despite putative claims to political equality, it would be naïve to assume that citizens in a democratic society possess equal opportunities for political participation. While this might be potentially true of free and fair elections, it is much less plausible in the case of lobbying and organized efforts to influence public policy, where differentials of wealth, power, and education shape people's ability and willingness to participate and influence policy outcomes. In developing societies characterized by enormous wealth differentials, socio-economic factors are likely to be critical determinants of participation.

Modernization theorists argue that political participation increases with socio-economic development. In other words, the level of political participation is likely to be higher in wealthy societies. Factors conducive to participation include increased income, high levels of education, urbanization, and the existence of mass media. Highly urbanized societies offer increased opportunities for participation since they are generally characterized by high rates of interaction and social activity, well-developed communications networks, and proximity to decision-makers and the locus of political power (Nie and Verba 1975). Participation is also fostered by what Nie and Verba term 'a syndrome of supportive civic attitudes' associated with modernization, namely a sense of political efficacy (that participation can make a difference), access to information about politics, and a sense of obligation to participate (ibid.: 32). According to Huntington and Nelson (1976) socio-economic development increases organizational involvement and heightens group consciousness which feed into higher levels of participation. This would suggest conversely that predominantly rural societies with low levels of socio-economic development and poor communications will be characterized by more limited opportunities for participation.

However, the contextual and behavioural factors emphasized by modernization theorists are not the sole determinants of political participation. Three further sets of factors condition people's propensity to participate in political activity. First, material factors such as differential access to power and resources, as well as the overall level of socio-economic development, are conditioning variables which shape the scope and intensity of participation by different social groups. Second, variations in the organizational capacity of interest groups are a determinant of their ability to exert influence over public policy, and are a function of skills, resources, and leadership. As noted earlier, intermediary organizations such as political parties and voluntary organizations perform an important mediating function, which can be especially significant when people's capacity for collective action is subject to structural constraints and social exclusion. Third, ideological motivations are also important, irrespective of socio-economic status, in that some poor societies are characterized by high levels of political participation, resulting from historical experience of political engagement (anti-colonial struggles, mass religious activism, etc.) or an ethos of political mobilization consciously promoted by governments or political parties (in the form of mobilized participation characteristic of communist regimes). Such considerations should be taken into account when seeking explanations of the concrete forms that political participation assumes in established Third World democracies.

Although behavioural interpretations fail to offer an adequate explanation of low propensity to participate among low-status groups, the experience of established Western democracies demonstrates that there is a tendency for disadvantaged groups to 'under-participate'. Despite an expansion in opportunities to participate, various empirical studies have demonstrated that only a small minority of citizens are active beyond the periodic act of voting and there is a tendency towards concentration of political activity among a relatively small group of citizens (Nie and Verba 1975, Parry and Moyser 1994).

This form of political exclusion has both class and gender dimensions, which are likely to be magnified in poor societies (Held 1987, Phillips 1991). Poor and disadvantaged groups may be disinclined to participate by virtue of their inferior economic status, low levels of educational attainment, and a cultural environment which prevents women and low-status groups from assuming a visible public role. Moreover, poor people's participation is constrained by the time needed to meet overriding consumption requirements for daily survival (Chambers 1983). They also lack the material resources and technical skills to organize effectively for collective action, especially when the focus of such efforts is government policy. The poor are also divided by race, religion, or language which renders collective action more difficult to attain. In rural areas poor communications and dispersed settlement patterns are inimical to effective organization. The poor have a low sense of political efficacy which emanates from an expectation that their demands will be resisted or ignored.[7] For these reasons, Huntington and Nelson (1976: 119) argue that 'for most of the poor under most conditions, political participation was and is, objectively, a difficult and probably ineffective means of coping with their problems and advancing their interests'.

Some analysts are sanguine about low rates of participation in poor societies. One line of argument is that poor citizens lack the skills to determine the long-term consequences of their actions and may undermine their own interests by short-run and ill-conceived demands (Nie and Verba 1975: 4). An example of this is strike action by government employees to secure short-term gains in wages which might result in cutbacks in public sector employment to the long-run disadvantage of those same employees. A further argument is that citizens with low levels of education and income are not predisposed to participate politically. Elite theorists such as Dahl and Sartori were concerned that people of low socio-economic status would be inclined towards non-democratic forms of government, reflecting non-participatory authority structures in the workplace and the family (Pateman 1970). In a similar vein Huntington and Nelson (1976) argue that an uncontrolled expansion in opportunities for political participation would give free expression to newly mobilized groups with goals which could undermine political stability in new democracies.

While repeated studies point to low rates of participation among low-status groups, there is also evidence of a positive correlation between high socio-economic status and high rates of political participation. According to Nie and Verba (1975: 46), 'The more educated or affluent individual is more likely to be interested in politics, more likely to have a sense of political efficacy, and more likely to have the necessary monetary and other resources to allow him or her to be active politically.' They argue that political activists are not representative of citizens as a whole since they are overwhelmingly drawn from higher-status groups. As political leaders tend to be more responsive to the demands

---

[7] Similarly Bachrach (1967) argues that poor citizens in liberal democracies may not be aware of their best interests and political capabilities since they have been socialized into accepting the limitations of collective action.

of organized citizens, the preferences of citizens from higher-status groups will dominate popular attempts to influence policy choice.

In the absence of conscious efforts to promote greater equality of access and influence, attempts to increase political participation can reinforce inequality as the relatively more advantaged sections of the population find it easier to get their views heard. Increased participation can protect autonomous spheres of action for well-entrenched and well-organized groups with particularistic interests. For this reason, greater citizen involvement in decision-making cannot be equated with increased democracy if it results in the devolution of power and influence to 'unaccountable oligarchies' (Parry and Moyser 1994). Clearly the quality, and not just the extent, of participation is an important determinant of policy outcomes, in that forms of political participation which favour the few are likely to result in policy choices that accord more with narrow self-interests than the general interest of citizens as a whole. In this scenario elite dominance of the policy process can produce policy outcomes that are distinctly undemocratic unless decision-makers are subject to effective citizen oversight and legislative accountability (Anderson 1977). This problem is compounded when the decision-making process is dominated by an approach founded on technocratic rationality which privileges the role of experts at the expense of a more open process of public deliberation (Fischer 1993). Hence, the advent of democracy poses a conundrum for elite theorists who accept the developmental case for higher levels of participation, but who recognize that the increased influence of previously excluded groups threatens the power of middle-class elites who dominate the public policy process.

It was argued earlier that rather than assuming autonomous or mobilized forms, political participation is likely to be mediated by a variety of organizations that seek to aggregate interests and exercise collective influence on policy-makers. Political parties have traditionally performed such roles in established democracies but in developing countries with weak democratic traditions their ability to aggregate opinion and influence policy is limited (Fox 1994). Rather than performing an effective intermediary policy role political parties have often served as a means of satisfying the personal ambitions of individual politicians and securing employment and special privileges for their supporters (Grindle 1980). In new democratic states political parties often lack financial resources, technical skills, and the organizational capacity required to enable them to make an effective input into the policy process. But despite the much-vaunted capacity of organized interests within civil society to intervene in the policy process, interest groups may not be effective in presenting collective demands and exercising voice on the part of their members. Like political parties they are vulnerable to capture by dominant interests or function as pawns of government, and suffer from organizational weaknesses, which limits their scope to intervene effectively in the policy process. According to Grindle (ibid.: 16):

These characteristics mean that frequently there are few organizations in existence that are capable of representing the interests of broad categories of citizens and formulating policies responsive to their particular needs. Those few that are effective in this role tend to be the creatures of wealthy and powerful groups such as bankers, industrialists, and landowners.

In other words, not only are poor and socially marginal groups disinclined to or discouraged from active participation in the policy process, but organizations which are established to aggregate interests and influence public policy play a fairly limited role and exacerbate rather than mitigate exclusion (Fox 1994, Smith 1996).

  The foregoing discussion suggests that the prospects for a sustained increase in political participation in developing countries undergoing a process of democratization are not very encouraging. The socio-economic conditions prevalent in most developing societies are not conducive to high rates of autonomous participation. Educated elites with access to power and resources are more likely to secure preferential access to policy-makers, whereas effective participation on the part of the poor and disadvantaged is constrained by structural and behavioural factors. While mobilized and mediated forms of political participation are more likely to prevail than autonomous participation in poor countries due to a low sense of political efficacy, and wide differentials of wealth and power, political parties and organized interest groups may be constrained in performing an effective intermediary role. This has evident implications for countries embarking on a process of democratization, which often brings with it the expectation that greater opportunities will arise for political participation on the part of poor and socially excluded groups.

3. Politics and Public Policy

Numerous studies have drawn attention to the importance of the character of the political system as a key determinant of the form and character of the public policy process, which refers to the manner in which government policy is deliberated, formulated, and implemented. In this respect Grindle (1980) distinguishes between open and closed political systems, arguing that each is associated with a distinctive public policy process. Closed political systems are more likely to be characterized by a style of policy-making that is centralized, secretive, and unresponsive, whereas open political systems are likely to be associated with a reverse set of characteristics: decentralized, consultative, and responsive. However, these are ideal types and the characteristics associated with closed political systems are not limited to authoritarian regimes but may continue to persist in new democracies in the developing world.

Authoritarian rule in Africa was associated with a highly exclusive, state-centred policy process, where decision-making was largely the prerogative of a small, tightly knit group of technocrats, civil servants, and politicians. Policy formulation was confined to narrow policy circles with limited input from organized interests, and little attempt to build a broad consensus around policy initiatives. Business interests were more interested in securing special favours and exemptions, rather than shaping broad-based policies. In the limited number of instances where consultation took place in rural areas, it was limited to large farmers who benefited from a policy regime which maintained high levels of input subsidies and favourable price levels set by state marketing boards (Bates 1981). Peasant smallholders, industrial workers, and informal sector producers were denied any formal input into policy-making. Elected representatives had a very weak role in relation to national policy-making, and voters were not free to choose between competing policy alternatives or governing elites. Unelected one-party regimes or dictatorships stifled public debate over policy options and alternative prescriptions, though in some countries (notably in Zambia) churches and trade unions were able to articulate an independent perspective (Healey and Robinson 1992, Brinkerhoff and Kulibaba 1996).

A similar pattern of elite dominance and exclusion of marginal groups prevailed in much of East Asia and Latin America under authoritarian rule, but with some important differences. Unlike sub-Saharan Africa, most authoritarian regimes in East Asia were developmental in orientation and action. In Korea and Taiwan such regimes drew in sections of the business elite into a highly selective and corporatist style of policy management, from which small farmers and the industrial working class were largely excluded (Evans 1992, Wade 1990). Many Latin American countries were characterized by highly elitist and centralized forms of politics, in which military leaders formed alliances with modernizing technocrats to constitute a distinctive form of 'bureaucratic-authoritarian' regime. As with the more traditional regimes dominated by landowning oligarchies, policy-making was a distinctively elite-dominated exercise, even in those states which retained democratic political structures (Crisp 1994). Technocrats were given considerable discretion in policy formulation in collusion with domestic business interests, while the voice of the peasantry and the industrial working class was largely excluded (Ames 1987, Collier 1979). Despite their numerical dominance, the indigenous peoples of the Andean region were completely marginalized from the formal political realm and the public policy process (Canoghan 1996).

With the transition to democracy in many developing countries from the early 1980s there was an expectation of a commensurate increase in political participation, resulting from a more open and inclusive electoral process, increased freedom of expression and association, and greater regime legitimacy and accountability (Healey and Robinson 1992: 116–17). There is some evidence from several African countries (to varying degrees, Tanzania, Uganda, and Zambia) which appears to confirm such expectations, but at the same time political participation is subject to strict limitations, especially in the realm of economic policy, which remains largely impervious to popular involvement (van de Walle 1994, Brinkerhoff and Kulibaba 1996, Gordon 1996). Three points can be made in support of this contention, drawing on recent experience in sub-Saharan Africa. First, while voting figures suggest that the electoral process commands some degree of popular legitimacy (though turnouts have often been low in comparison with established Western democracies), elections provide little scope for the citizens to choose between competing policy alternatives. Policy issues do not generally feature prominently in elections and political parties in Africa tend not to assume widely divergent policy positions, especially over macro-economic policy. For example, in Mozambique, Senegal, and Uganda there are political parties which hold strong views on economic policy issues but these are rarely well developed or articulated into a coherent alternative (Harvey and Robinson 1995). Second, popular responses to economic policy reforms sometimes express themselves in the form of demonstrations, street protests, or various forms of noncompliance. Those involved are often students, workers, and civil servants who stand to lose out from reforms, through either reductions in public expenditure (on food subsidies and higher education) or reforms in the public sector with employment implications (privatization and civil service reform). However, even such expressions of popular dissent tend to be the exception rather than the norm and their influence over policy decisions is limited, despite well-documented cases of policy swings following food riots in one or two African countries (Wiseman 1986, Bratton and van de Walle 1992). Third, instances of formal participation in the public policy process are still comparatively rare, and are by and large restricted to elite groups with privileged access to policy-makers.

Hence, contrary to expectations, the pre-existing pattern of selectivity and exclusion in the public policy process does not appear to have changed very significantly with the advent of democratic rule. This tendency is especially marked in relation to macro-economic policy, where the very nature of the policy issue at stake (technical complexity, speed of decision-making, and political sensitivity) appears inimical to enhanced participation and consultation. Substantive participation by organized citizens in economic policy design and formulation is uncommon, although there appears to be more input in the process of implementation (Healey and Robinson 1992, Brinkerhoff and Kulibaba 1996).[8] This pattern of policy-making is not confined to newly emerging democracies in Africa, but is also characteristic of established democracies elsewhere in the developing world. For example, evidence from India demonstrates that, despite the high degree of openness and responsiveness of the political system, decisions concerning the macro-economic reforms in the early 1990s were essentially the responsibility of a small group of technocrats, senior civil servants, and politicians (Shastri 1997).

In view of such trends, is there any evidence of increased consultation and deliberation in the formulation of economic policy in new democracies? South Africa is perhaps unique in the African continent, having developed a distinctive pattern of institutionalized consultation involving government, business, and labour in the transition from apartheid rule (Pretorius 1996, Nattrass and Seekings, in this volume). Aside from this, there are some isolated examples of structured consultation elsewhere in Africa, but access to government policy-making circles is usually restricted to sections of the business elite with political connections and economic resources (Nyang'oro and Shaw 1989).[9] Economic and political liberalization since the 1980s has created a climate which has been conducive to new deliberative mechanisms. In Nigeria, for example, the three main business associations created the Organized Private Sector (OPS) as a forum to represent the views of the business community in its discussions with the government. Similar bodies have been formed by employers' organizations in Ghana, Kenya, and Swaziland for the purpose of institutionalizing a consultative process between the government and the private sector (Etukudo 1991, 1995). The West African Enterprise Network was formed by business persons from eleven countries in the region in 1993 to promote policy dialogue with governments in the region (Orsini et al. 1996).

---

[8] There is an added dimension to this pattern of policy-making in the African context, in that the formulation and design of economic policy are often in the hands of foreign experts who are not directly accountable to domestic political constituencies or susceptible to influence by organized group activity.

[9] For a detailed study of corporatism in Zimbabwe see Skalnes (1995).

While structured consultations between government and business have become more commonplace in countries undergoing a simultaneous process of democratization and economic liberalization, the poor remain marginalized from the policy process due to their 'lack of access to institutionalized channels that service their needs and interests' (Brinkerhoff and Kulibaba 1996). Periodic consultation restricted to government officials and a small but influential set of organized business interests is a very modest expression of enhanced political participation. In many respects this is not surprising as the principal objective of business associations is to lobby government in the hope of exacting concessions over budgetary commitments, taxation policy, access to credit and foreign exchange, and other issues of concern to their members (Moore and Hamalai 1993).[10] Given the limited nature of societal participation in policy-making, it is difficult to estimate the developmental significance of such initiatives, even though adherents of increased participation claim that it will lead to improved policy outcomes (World Bank 1997). The skewed and exclusionary nature of policy-making that continues to prevail in much of Africa gives reason to believe that policy outcomes will reflect the interests and concerns of business elites with privileged access to the policy process, which was previously identified as a source of blockage to effective reform (Healey and Robinson 1992).

In order to regularize interactions between government officials and a wider set of organized interest groups several established democracies have created corporatist mechanisms for structured policy dialogue with peak associations representing business, labour, and professional bodies. These were especially prevalent in northern Europe in the 1960s and 1970s, but fell into disuse with the advent of regimes wedded to neo-liberal economic policies which necessitated a sharp break with these practices.[11] Institutionalized consultation has also been attempted in several established democracies in the developing world, which offers some useful insights from the perspective of political participation and the inclusiveness of this process.[12]

In Venezuela, a series of commissions comprising government officials and representatives of organized interests (principally industrialists,

---

[10] This is beginning to change as younger, more reform-minded entrepreneurs have become better organized and demand changes to the established policy regime founded on patronage politics (Orsini et al. 1996).

[11] See, for example, Lehmbruch and Schmitter (1982), Cawson (1985), Williams (1989).

[12] On South Africa, see Nattrass and Seekings, in this volume. Deliberative mechanisms have not been confined to democratic states. For example, in East Asia tripartite deliberation councils comprising labour unions, industry, and government were used by policy-makers to secure agreement on and strengthen the credibility of economic policy issues (Evans 1992).

labour unions, and professionals) were established by successive governments for policy-making purposes following the restoration of democratic rule in 1958. These commissions have played an instrumental role in deliberating and formulating policy across a whole range of government activity, including planning, regulation, production, and private sector promotion. However, evidence collected by Crisp (1994) indicates that these commissions were not balanced in their composition and that domestic capitalists participated much more extensively than labour or other organized interests. Participation was determined by the government, which selected individuals from lists put forward by peak associations drawn from business and labour, which were not in themselves fully representative of the wider range of interests in these sectors. Not only were these commissions uneven in their representation, but they had the effect of displacing the policy deliberation functions of the legislature and elected representatives. In other words, 'the consultative arena has been key to legitimising the regime for the powerful organized minority interests' (ibid.: 1501).

In Jamaica the public policy process, particularly in the realm of macro-economic decision-making, was largely confined to government and business circles in the 1970s and early 1980s, to the exclusion of most organized interests (Stone 1980). With the re-election of Michael Manley's People's National Party in 1989 the government sought to widen the debate over economic policy by creating a National Planning Council as a consultative mechanism involving senior government ministers along with representatives from the private sector, the trade unions, academia, and professional bodies. In addition the private sector secured representation on the Economic and Production Council and various sectoral councils responsible for tourism, education, industry, and commerce. Despite expectations that structured consultation between government and organized interests would strengthen public–private dialogue, these hopes have not been fulfilled. The government has not recognized the potential of the private sector to contribute substantively to public policy while business interests have been reluctant to concede some measure of independence in return for a more active role in policy-making, with the result that the policy process is adversarial rather than genuinely consultative (Garrity and Picard 1991). As with similar deliberative mechanisms in Venezuela, business associations are the principal focus of efforts to institutionalize consultation, with trade unions and other organized interests consigned to a fairly marginal role.

Botswana is often cited as an example of an African country which has maintained formal democratic rule since independence (Holm 1988). Although one party has dominated the political scene, the government has been careful to consult its citizens over key policy decisions covering areas such as land reform, conservation, and housing. The institutional medium for this process of consultation is the *kgotla* or local council which is convened by the traditional Tswana chiefs (Molutsi and Holm 1990). In some instances government planners have commissioned public opinion surveys to canvass citizens more widely about possible policy options (Holm 1996). While the *kgotla* provide a form of mobilized participation whereby civil servants can elicit the views of rural people on programme priorities (and in some cases revise their original plans), the parameters of debate and the ability of ordinary citizens to influence policy are limited. While technically neutral, the role of the village headman responsible for convening *kgotla* meetings is to ensure that discussion remains non-partisan and within acceptable bounds. In line with Tswana traditions young people and women are not expected to speak in meetings. The restricted mandate and exclusionary nature of the *kgotla* limits political participation and is compounded by other institutional features of the political system. Senior civil servants and government planners exercise considerable autonomy in policy formulation and implementation and are subject to limited accountability. Opposition political parties do not pose a serious challenge to the continued dominance of the ruling party, while interest groups are weak, non-political, and largely disengaged from public policy. Such features of the Botswana political system lead one seasoned observer to conclude, 'Democratic structures, even though they meet conventional Western norms, can serve as a façade for autocratic development processes when civil society and political party competition are restricted in their impact on government policy processes' (Holm 1996: 111).

The examples reviewed yield a number of interim conclusions about the nature of policy-making in poor countries which are either established democracies or are currently embarking on a process of democratization. In line with the expectations of the theoretical literature, it would seem that democracy is not conducive to increased participation by the poor in developing countries. Policy-making remains the preserve of technocratic elites and policy dialogue is generally restricted to organized interests with power and resources, which provides them with privileged access to those responsible for making decisions. Structured consultation mechanisms formalize the process of policy dialogue, but they do not bring about greater inclusiveness. The policy domain remains largely inaccessible to the poor, who lack the organizational capacity, technical skills, and resources to participate meaningfully in policy deliberation. It is therefore difficult to discern any significant increase in substantive participation as a result of democratization, aside from periodic voting in elections. The only options to those excluded from the policy process under such circumstances are resigned acceptance, protest (voice), or exit, i.e. withdrawal from active engagement with the state. The inevitable consequence of such exclusion is development policy that does not conform to the needs and interests of poor and marginalized groups.

These constraints on political participation, together with the acknowledgement that development policy outcomes are sub-optimal when those affected are excluded from the decision-making process, have prompted several governments to introduce legislation designed to institutionalize participation for poor and marginal groups. Clearly such innovations are not free from political self-interest and there are expectations of a political dividend emanating these reforms. Nevertheless, the very creation of new institutional structures has generated the possibility for greater popular involvement in decision-making, and merits close investigation in view of the manifest limitations of existing corporatist arrangements in this regard.

In Bolivia this has taken the form of a Law of Popular Participation effected in 1994, which aims to subject local government expenditure decisions to greater popular control and accountability. While the Law is still relatively new, considerable changes have taken place in local governance which offer insights on Bolivia's attempt to institutionalize participation and its developmental consequences. This can be compared with a parallel government initiative in India, the 73rd Constitutional Amendment Act, which came into effect in April 1993, which was designed to reinvigorate the Panchayati Raj system (local self-government) by creating three tiers of local government institutions at the village, subdistrict, and district levels. The potential for the new legislation to expand opportunities for participation through Panchayati Raj can be examined through a review of the experience of two Indian states—West Bengal and Karnataka—which had sought to strengthen *panchayats* (local councils) through institutional reforms in the 1970s and 1980s.

4. Institutionalized Participation in Bolivia and India

The extent to which decision-making processes have become more participatory under the transition to more democratic forms of government or by means of institutional reforms within an existing democracy can be respectively examined in the light of these two contrasting experiments in Bolivia and India. In both cases the reforms form part of an overall programme of administrative and political decentralization, though the focus of this section is more narrowly concerned with the implications of the reforms for political participation and policy outcomes. Four aspects of participation as a process are singled out for particular attention: scope (the proportion of people engaged in a particular form of activity), inclusiveness (form and extent of involvement), intensity (the scale, duration, and importance of a particular activity), and mediation (the role played by intermediaries). The developmental significance of institutionalized participation can be examined in term of outputs (in terms of development policy choices) and outcomes (long-term development impact). But the outcomes of institutionalized participation are hard to measure since few empirical studies have examined this relationship and there is an inherent methodological problem in seeking to attribute impact to policy choice. Moreover, a relatively short space of time has elapsed since the introduction of the reforms which makes it difficult to ascertain their developmental impact. We therefore restrict our attention to instrumental concerns focused on policy outputs: the logical expectation is that a high and inclusive level of participation should produce commensurate changes in local spending priorities and resource allocations which reflect the needs and priorities of local people.

(a) Context of the initiatives

Although there was provision in Article 40 of the Indian constitution for the creation of Panchayati Raj institutions as organs of local government in rural areas these generally did not assume the powers and responsibility that had originally been envisaged.[13] While the institutional fabric of Panchayati Raj was generally in place, local bodies were either dormant or were dominated by vested interests to the exclusion of the majority of local people (Singh 1994). Even though some states such as Karnataka and West Bengal had made efforts to strengthen local councils prior to this, the legislation passed in early 1993 established a constitutional mandate for the reinvigoration of Panchayati Raj institutions in states which were not receptive to such proposals. The Act was promulgated by the Congress government under Prime Minister Narasimha Rao, which was anxious to capitalize on the potential political legitimacy that it could gain in the process. It provided for the creation of a uniform three-tier system of local

---

[13] The formal three-tier structure of the Panchayati Raj system was put into place following the government's acceptance of the recommendations of the Balwantrai Mehta Committee report in 1959. This entailed the formation of a *gram panchayat* at the village level, the *panchayat samiti* at the block or intermediate level, and the *zilla parishad* at the district level. The intention was that these councils would assume responsibility for undertaking all planning and development work at the local level (Singh 1994).

councils, with elections to each tier. In an effort to ensure adequate representation for poor and marginal groups, seats were reserved for Scheduled Castes and Scheduled Tribes in accordance with their share of population within the *panchayat*, of which one-third were reserved for women from these categories. Women were guaranteed one-third of the seats at all three levels. Leadership positions have also been reserved for women and 'weaker sections'. *Panchayats* are able to collect taxes, duties, and fees, and receive grants-in-aid from state funds. They are also empowered to prepare plans for economic development and poverty reduction using resources from a variety of central and state programmes (Singh 1994, Webster 1995).

The Left Front government which came to power in West Bengal in 1977 had an ideological commitment to decentralizing decision-making to local government institutions. The dominant partner in the Left Front coalition, the Communist Party of India (Marxist), favoured decentralization as a means of consolidating its rural power base and to provide an institutional platform for its land reforms programme. In this latter respect, the *panchayats* were entrusted with rural development, the identification and redistribution of surplus land, and relief work. The CPI(M)-led government revised existing Panchayati Raj legislation enacted by the previous Congress government in 1973, creating a three-tier structure with direct party-based elections at three-year intervals. In a radical departure from top-down administrative traditions, local officials were expected to implement decisions taken by elected *panchayat* members. As noted by Webster (1992: 150), 'Before the new panchayats there was no effective participation for the poor. They relied upon philanthropy and personal appeal to those in power, be they local officials or village leaders or their power brokers.'

A similar approach was adopted by the Janata Party in the south Indian state of Karnataka following victory in the 1983 state assembly elections. As in the case of West Bengal, elected councillors were given extensive influence over the administrative machinery, and local councils at the district and subdistrict levels assumed responsibility for a wide range of development activities. In a further parallel with West Bengal, the Janata government believed that the new system of elected councils at the district level would help to strengthen its party structure in the state. In an effort to promote the representation of low-status groups, 25 per cent of all council seats were reserved for women and 18 per cent for Scheduled Castes and Scheduled Tribes, with further reservations for members of the more advanced but socially marginalized 'Backward Classes' (Crook and Manor 1998: ch. 2).

The Law of Popular Participation (LPP) in Bolivia was promulgated in April 1994 as part of a broader programme of fiscal and administrative decentralization by the government of President Sanchez de Lozada, which entailed the decentralization of the responsibilities of the health and education ministries from the national to the departmental level. There are three main elements to the LPP: decentralization of government expenditure, new opportunities for community involvement in the planning and regulation of local government activities, and legal recognition of the territorial authority of indigenous and popular organizations (Booth et al. 1997). While the Bolivian Law has the first two objectives in common with the Indian Panchayati Raj legislation, the formal status accorded to local organizations in representing poor and marginal groups at the local government level is distinctive and perhaps unique in the developing world.

The entire decentralization programme in Bolivia hinges on the creation of a new tier of elected autonomous municipalities covering urban and rural areas. The fiscal decentralization measure entails the transfer of a 20 per cent share of national taxation revenues distributed in accordance with the share of total population. This core budget can be supplemented by grants and soft loans from government and foreign donors. The second key feature is the legal recognition given to indigenous and popular organizations at the local level. These organizations (termed Organizaciones Territoriales de Base (OTBs) —Territorial Base Organizations) are assigned a range of responsibilities, centring on participation in decisions about municipal expenditure and monitoring its subsequent use. The monitoring function was vested in Vigilance Committees elected by the OTBs which were supposed to scrutinize municipal spending. There was initially considerable resistance to this measure from opposition parties who feared that their power would be undermined and resistance on the part of the trade union movement which was suspicious of government intentions (especially in a political context which was traditionally averse to popular initiative) and critical of the lack of consultation that preceded the implementation of the programme. In spite of this initial resistance, OTBs were established in most of the 311 municipalities within a year of the programme's inception, a process that was accelerated by the release of funds following official registration.

The Bolivian reforms mark a significant break with past political and administrative practices, in that the Bolivian state has historically been highly centralized, exclusionary, and authoritarian, with government and party politics dominated by the Hispanic elite (Gamarra and Malloy 1995, Slater 1995). As with the case of other Andean countries, indigenous groups and other non-Hispanic minorities have traditionally been excluded from the formal political realm and effective citizen participation in public life has been minimal (Canoghan 1996). Policy-making has been the preserve of government with minimal public consultation. Economic policy-making is firmly in the hands of neo-liberal technocrats, a trend established with the economic reform programme initiated by the previous government in the late 1980s, though social policy was open to influence by reform-oriented intellectuals within government (Booth et al. 1997). The fact that the government decided to initiate the reforms is therefore all the more remarkable in this context, though part of the explanation for the decision lies in the scope they offer for expanding the ruling party's political base in the indigenous areas.

(b) *Participation as process*

The LPP and Panchayati Raj are both designed to increase popular participation in decision-making, with an explicit focus on poor and socially marginalized groups, especially women. Even though there were clear expectations of a political dividend in the two cases, both are motivated by the perception that local politics have been dominated by powerful elites and that the public policy process excludes the majority of ordinary citizens. Two main institutional mechanisms have been employed as a means of achieving this objective: widening the representation of poor and marginal groups in elected local authorities, and increasing opportunities for structured participation in public expenditure decisions.

While there is formal provision for increased opportunities for political participation, the process of implementation has been very uneven, both spatially and socially. In line with the expectations of the theoretical literature, evidence from the two countries suggests that the true extent of political participation is determined by the pre-existing distribution of wealth and power, in the absence of a significant mediating force in the form of a well-organized political party or popular organization representing the interests of poor and marginal social groups.

In Bolivia, elections were introduced at the municipal level prior to the enactment of the Law of Popular Participation, but local authorities were traditionally the preserve of the non-indigenous urban elites, who fought elections along traditional party lines. The December 1995 local elections posed a challenge to the existing balance of political power, with a substantial increase in the numbers of councillors of indigenous or peasant origin to just over a quarter of the total.

One survey covering a third of the municipalities in the country found that three-quarters of elected mayors and councillors were from the locality, while 40 per cent claimed not to have any prior political affiliations. Despite some improvement in the representativeness of the municipal councils, levels of political participation are generally very low in areas where indigenous people lack voice and organizational capacity. In such areas institutionalizing participation merely serves to legitimize decisions taken by local elites. In contrast, in areas with strong rural trade union traditions ordinary people were able to challenge vested interests and the established political parties, using the provisions of the Law to exert popular pressure over municipal spending priorities. However, in many cases effective participation continued to be constrained by organizational and technical weaknesses on the part of the designated base organizations (OTBs). The Vigilance Committees, which were intended to perform an oversight function, operated intermittently since they lack the technical expertise required for them to carry out effective monitoring and auditing functions. Geographical distances are often considerable and members of Vigilance Committees lack the time and resources to enable them to attend meetings in the municipal headquarters (Booth et al. 1997).

There is some evidence from Karnataka and West Bengal which points to an increase in political participation on the part of the rural poor when the political and institutional conditions are favourable. Webster's findings from two village-level *gram panchayats* (village councils) in Burdwan district in West Bengal point to a discernible increase in representation from among the poorer and marginal social groups, especially the landless, marginal farmers, scheduled castes, Muslims, and women, who now 'have a presence and involvement in local government and development that they had never previously possessed' (1992: 150). This is directly attributed to the CPI(M)-led implementation of Panchayati Raj in the district, which was a means of strengthening its rural party apparatus and the institutional basis of the land reforms programme. A more extensive survey over four *gram panchayat* areas in four distincts during the 1993 *panchayat* elections indicated high levels of awareness about *panchayat* institutions, accompanied by a widespread understanding of their role and function (Keemar and Ghosh 1996: 21–4).

But despite evident improvement there are still real constraints to effective participation by the poor. For instance a survey conducted by the government of West Bengal after the first *panchayat* elections in 1980 found that the poor were under-represented relative to their overall share of the local population; landless labourers and marginal farmers owning less than 2 acres of land accounted for approximately one-third of total members but two-thirds of total population. Moreover, formal representation on *gram panchayats* did not translate into equality of access in decision-making or an ability to assert a presence at village meetings, which was attributable to prevailing caste practices and social mores (Webster 1992: 152–3).[14]

This is supported by similar evidence from Karnataka, where a representative cross-section of villagers from four sub-districts were asked about their participation in village meetings convened by the sub-district (*mandal*) councils. Only a small proportion of the scheduled caste villagers attended and spoke at the meetings, which were designed to elicit feedback on the work of the councils and to identify those villagers who were most eligible for government assistance. However, there was some degree of consultation on the part of elected councillors with villagers on local development projects, often at the instigation of individual constituents. Seat reservations gave scheduled castes formal representation on district councils, but their ability to translate this into effective participation in decision-making was heavily circumscribed by the prevailing pattern of caste dominance in local politics. This feature of district-level politics was magnified in the *mandal* councils where the landowning castes wielded considerable power, with the result that poor and marginal groups were unable to exercise any influence at all on local policies and resource allocation, in part because these were predetermined to a significant extent by central government (Crook and Manor 1998).

One of the weakest features of both initiatives in terms of the quality of participation is that of gender equity. While women had increased their representation in village *panchayats* in West Bengal, this was a only a 'token presence' which was achieved 'more often by co-option than by election' (Webster 1992: 150). Women's willingness to come forward as candidates was circumscribed by social mores and cultural practices which perpetuated their political exclusion. Women's participation in twice-yearly *panchayat sabhas* (village meetings) was much lower than that recorded for men, while even fewer contributed to discussions.[15] The CPI(M) party machinery did not appear willing to tackle this issue head on, despite its professed commitment to strengthening the representation of other poor and marginal groups.

---

[14] A study of *gram panchayats* established in Haryana, Kerala, Madhya Pradesh, and Uttar Pradesh since 1993 has similarly found that 'participation of members of weaker sections in Gram Panchayat meetings has been rather uneven' (PRIA 1997). Cf. Keemar and Ghosh (1996: 51–67).

[15] Attendance at the *gram sabhas* was high for men with 65% attending and a further 12% attending and speaking, and low for women, with 17% attending and a further 2% attending and speaking (Webster 1992: 154). Similar gender differentials were found in Karnataka (Crook and Manor 1998).

In Karnataka, while women were engaged in various forms of political participation at the local level, they assumed a less active role than men in village meetings and displayed less proclivity to contact officials and elected representatives. Despite having 25 per cent of the seats on local councils reserved for them, women played a marginal role in council affairs. Those elected to office were often related to politically influential men, and few actively represented the interests of female constituents (Crook and Manor 1998).

In Bolivia, despite an explicit commitment to promoting women's empowerment, the LPP contains no special mechanisms to achieve a decisive shift in gender relations. Women's organizations are denied formal recognition as OTBs as they are generally organized along sectoral rather than on territorial lines, with membership reserved exclusively for women. Women's representation in formal political structures has also declined, which is reflected in a decrease in the numbers of municipal seats held by women following the 1995 local elections. Hence women are denied effective representation in both the formal and informal political spheres, leading Booth et al. to conclude that the LPP 'lacks teeth for advancing women's political participation' (1997: 26).

(c) *Policy consequences*

The policy consequences (or outputs) of institutionalized participation should be evident from changes in local expenditure patterns, with spending priorities matching the needs and aspirations of the poor majority, and more generally in the quality of local governance, i.e. improved accountability and legitimacy of local government institutions. Some insights on this issue can be gleaned from existing studies from Bolivia and India but the evidence is limited and it is difficult to draw comparative insights which are both conclusive and robust.

The developmental consequences of the LPP in Bolivia are partially reflected in the significant increase that has taken place in the quantity of locally financed services and investment projects, from 400 in 1993, to 2,500 in 1994, and 9,500 in 1995 (Booth et al. 1997: 25–6). According to official figures, total spending in the municipalities (derived from a higher share of national taxation revenues) was scheduled to increase from $US93 million in 1994 to $US228 million in 1995, of which 80 per cent was for social sector investments (principally for the construction of schools and health centres), though there has been a trend towards productive projects.[16] However, a

---

[16] Ministerio de Desarrollo Humano (1996: 17).

preoccupation with welfarism and service provision permeates the municipal planning process, with the result that many municipalities adopted a standardized approach centred on social sector investments.

It is more difficult to observe changes in public expenditure patterns at the local level in India and attribute these to the influence of Panchayati Raj institutions. While Panchayati Raj is intended to increase popular influence in the district planning process, there is limited scope for influencing public expenditure priorities since a large proportion of the funds handed down to local councils are already earmarked for specific programmes. The local councils are able to exercise discretion over the geographical and social distribution of funds but within the guidelines established by state and national governments. Although Panchayati Raj in Karnataka achieved little by way of improvements in the planning process *mandal* councils were able to bend the rules and utilize the substantial resources passed down to them for their preferred ends. In an apparent vindication of the decentralization process, the evidence indicates that a high proportion of the development projects implemented by district councils conformed to community needs, and that there was a high degree of satisfaction with these projects. As in the case of Bolivia, there was a bias towards investments in infrastructure (roads, school buildings, borewells, etc.) which reflected both pressure from organized citizens and local politicians' desire to reap political capital. But the extent to which decentralized planning produced durable benefits for poor and socially marginal groups in Karnataka is open to question (Crook and Manor 1998). Indeed, there is no clear evidence that decentralized planning has produced clear development benefits for the poor as opposed to local citizens more generally.

A rather different picture emerges from West Bengal. Evidence from two *gram panchayats* in Burdwan district reveals that the development programmes for which they were responsible 'were being implemented both efficiently and according to the purposes for which they were intended' (Webster 1992: 155). Similar findings were reported by Keemar and Ghosh who discovered that 83 per cent of all respondents in four distincts considered *panchayats* to be 'very useful', while 72 per cent believed that the *panchayats* had improved the condition of the poor and broken the domination of landowners and the higher castes (1996: 24–35). The active involvement of the *gram panchayats* (with the political backing of a well-organized and disciplined political party)—which were responsible for identifying potential recipients and implementing the programmes—ensured that benefits were being received by the designated economic and caste groupings (Kohli 1989). More effective programme implementation has contributed to 'a general improvement in the condition of most villagers', but not to the extent that there was a significant reduction in poverty. A notable failure was that women were largely excluded from the direct developmental benefits arising out of these programmes by virtue of structural oppression and low levels of political participation which the ruling party failed to address systematically (Webster 1992: 157).

The incidence of corruption is also a useful indicator of the development impact of institutionalized participation. In Bolivia increased popular control over local expenditure decisions could help to reduce corruption if popular organizations are able to carry out the vigilance functions assigned to them. However, the obverse might also have occurred, resulting from politicization of lower levels of the administrative system, with municipal politicians seeking to exploit opportunities presented by the increased availability of funds at the local level. The scope for corrupt practices can increase when popular oversight over public expenditure decisions is blunted by organizational weaknesses and technical limitations, which prevents local Vigilance Committees from effectively performing their designated role (Booth et al. 1997: 50).

In India, by comparison, it is sometimes argued that fiscal decentralization should lead to reduced scope for corruption at higher levels of the administrative system while local officials should be subject to greater oversight by elected councillors, resulting in more restricted opportunities for corruption at this level. This has resulted in the paradoxical scenario observed by Crook and Manor (1998) in which there was a substantial decrease in the volume of funds sequestered by corrupt officials while the number of officials engaged in corrupt activities has increased markedly, resulting in what might be termed the localization of corruption. Unlike the LPP in Bolivia, there is no provision for community oversight of spending decisions in the Panchayati Raj legislation, and low levels of political participation keep accountability to a minimum. However, in West Bengal development progammes appeared to suffer reduced levels of corruption compared to those characteristic of the period prior to the introduction of the Panchayati Raj legislation. Corrupt acts on the part of bureaucrats or elected officials were dealt with summarily by the CPI(M). Moreover, subjecting the previous year's expenditures and future expenditure proposals to public deliberation in *gram sabha* meetings in which poor and marginal groups are well represented has created an effective accountability mechanism (Webster 1992: 156).

The experiments reviewed here provide many insights on the scope of institutionalized participation to provide for a more inclusive planning process which actively draws in poor and socially marginal groups in the expectation of generating development outcomes that more accurately reflect their needs and priorities. The evidence on the implementation of the Law of Popular Participation in Bolivia and Panchayat Raj legislation in India points to some interesting parallels as well as illuminating contrasts in this respect. In their different ways the two initiatives underline the critical importance of both institutional design and political agency in shaping successful outcomes, which we turn to in the concluding section.

5. Conclusions

The central concern of this chapter is the extent to which democracy creates the conditions for enhanced levels of popular involvement in decision-making, which in turn is expected to become more inclusive and in the process generate better developmental outcomes. It was argued that public policy under authoritarian regimes was centralized, secretive, and exclusive. In such regimes public policy was the preserve of a tightly knit group of politicians, senior policy-makers, and technocrats. Access to the policy process was limited to well-organized elite groups with political connections, who sought special favours and policies which would benefit their members or avoid harming their interests.

The advent of democratic forms of government is expected to increase political participation and widen the scope for public involvement in the public policy process. Much of the literature treats this relationship as axiomatic. But evidence from established democracies in the developing world indicates that such expectations are unlikely to be fulfilled and that one should only expect a modest expansion in political participation in countries undergoing democratization. The socio-economic conditions prevalent in many developing countries limit the extent to which poor and socially marginal groups can play an active role in politics and in shaping public policy. Access to the formal political realm and to the public policy process invariably remains confined to groups with wealth, power, and resources, who are able to represent their members' concerns and engage meaningfully in policy dialogue. Formal consultative mechanisms have generally been highly elitist, with membership confined to government officials in conjunction with representatives from business associations, trade unions, and professional organizations. Policy outcomes, especially in the realm of macro-economic or social policy, rarely conform to the needs and priorities of poor and marginal social groups, who remain largely excluded from the public policy process. Although democratization widens the scope for popular involvement in formal politics, participation is by and large restricted to campaigning and voting in periodic elections, while the public policy domain remains relatively impervious to popular influence.

At the same time, democratic politics can produce regimes which are more sensitive to the needs and priorities of the poor and socially excluded. In some cases, they have sought to increase the scope for such groups to influence public policy decisions by crafting institutional mechanisms designed to widen political participation. But such innovations emanate from genuine ideological commitment only in a minority of cases. The Law of Popular Participation in Bolivia and Panchayati Raj in India ostensibly represent two of the most ambitious attempts by democratic governments in the developing world to effect a shift in the balance of power in favour of poor and marginal groups by creating democratic structures at the local level which enhance their political representation and ability to participate in decision-making processes. In practice the reforms have been motivated by narrowly instrumental considerations, with the intention of strengthening the political legitimacy of the governing party and improving the effectiveness of development policy.

The evidence indicates that attempts to design institutions that promote political participation and policy deliberation are fraught with difficulty. Entrenched inequalities in the rural power structure and scarce educational and organizational resources on the part of poor and marginal groups limit the effectiveness of such reforms. When formal channels of political representation are rendered more accessible to the poor, through seat reservations or by widening the franchise, there is scope for such groups to exert direct influence on policy decisions and resource allocations. However, dominant social groups often continue to exercise considerable leverage over local politics to ensure that local spending decisions conform with their own priorities and interests; this was evident both in the Indian state of Karnataka and in indigenous areas in Bolivia. Despite provision for greater citizen oversight of public expenditure decisions and decentralized planning through *gram sabhas* (village meetings) in India and Vigilance Committees in Bolivia, these functioned imperfectly as mechanisms for bringing about increased transparency and accountability. Public meetings in India were poorly attended and the proceedings dominated by the upper castes. Ordinary villagers rarely had the technical knowledge or educational skills required for them to perform this role effectively, and decisions about resource allocations and programme design continued to be the preserve of government officials and technical staff. As a result spending decisions either failed to correspond to the needs and priorities of the poor majority, or development projects were designed on the basis of a standardized top-down approach with minimal input from the intended beneficiaries.

However, these experiments were not a total failure and there were some notable exceptions to this general rule. Panchayati Raj in West Bengal did succeed to a considerable extent in giving poor people greater voice in determining local spending priorities and programme design and implementation. Greater numbers of landless people and marginal farmers secured representation on local councils, but without any marked change in women's status or political involvement. Clearly the presence of a well-organized and disciplined party committed to social reform contributed to a political environment which was more conducive to success, in marked contrast to Karnataka where the ruling party was dominated by landholding castes. Similarly in Bolivia, the LPP was more effective in achieving its objectives in areas with a tradition of rural trade unionism and strong popular organizations.

Both examples highlight the importance of mediation and political agency in shaping the scope and intensity of political participation and in influencing policy outcomes. Democratic structures can create the institutional space for political parties and popular organizations to function as effective intermediaries on behalf of poor and socially marginal groups, both in challenging the dominance of vested interests and in exacting greater accountability on the part of decision-makers. At the same time, the pervasiveness of structural and organizational constraints on autonomous participation throws into sharp relief the limitations of institutional innovation in the absence of political mediation and more fundamental socio-economic reforms. The lesson is that institutional design from above has to be complemented by conscious political intervention from below for efforts at enhancing political participation on the part of poor and excluded citizens to succeed.

REFERENCES

Ames, B. (1987), *Political Survival: Politicians and Public Policy in Latin America*, Berkeley and Los Angeles: University of California Press.

Anderson, C. W. (1977), 'Political Design and the Representation of Interests', *Comparative Political Studies*, 10/1: 127–52.

Bachrach, P. (1967), *The Theory of Democratic Elitism: A Critique*, London: University of London Press.

Barber, B. (1984), *Strong Democracy: Participatory Politics for a New Age*, Berkeley and Los Angeles: University of California Press.

Bates, R. (1981), *Markets and States in Tropical Africa*, Berkeley and Los Angeles: University of California Press.

Beetham, D. (1993), 'Liberal Democracy and the Limits of Democratization', in D. Held (ed.), *Prospects for Democracy: North, South, East, West*, Cambridge: Polity Press.

Bhatnagar, B., and Williams, A. C. (eds.) (1992), *Participatory Development and the World Bank: Potential Directions for Change*, Washington: World Bank.

Booth, D., Clisby, S., and Widmark, C. (1997), *Popular Participation: Democratising the State in Rural Bolivia*, Stockholm: SIDA.

Bratton, M. and van de Walle, N. (eds.) (1992), *Governance and Politics in Africa*, Boulder, Colo.: Lynne Rienner.

Brinkerhoff, D. W. (1996), 'Process Perspectives on Policy Change: Highlighting Implementation', *World Development*, 29/9: 1395–401.

—— and Kulibaba, N. (1996), 'Perspectives on Participation in Economic Policy Reform in Africa', *Studies in Comparative International Development*, 31/3: 123–51.

Canoghan, C. M. (1996), 'A Deficit of Democratic Authenticity: Political Linkage and the Public in Andean Polities', *Studies in Comparative International Development*, 31/3: 32–55.

Cawson, A. (ed.) (1985), *Organized Interests and the State*, London: Sage.

Chambers, R. (1983), *Rural Development: Putting the Last First*, London: Longman.

Collier, D. (ed.) (1979), *The New Authoritarianism in Latin America*, Princeton: Princeton University Press.

Craig, G., and Mayo, M. (1995*a*), 'Community Participation and Empowerment: The Human Face of Structural Adjustment or Tools for Democratic Transformation?', in Craig and Mayo (1995*b*).

—— —— (eds.) (1995*b*). *Community Empowerment: A Reader in Participation and Development*, London: Zed Press.

Crisp, B. (1994), 'Limitations to Democracy in Developing Capitalist Societies: The Case of Venezuela', *World Development*, 22/10: 1491–509.

Crook, R., and Manor, J. (1995), 'Democratic Decentralisation and Institutional Performance: Four Asian and African Experiences Compared', *Journal of Commonwealth and Comparative Politics*, 33/3: 309–34.

—— —— (1998), *Democracy and Decentralization: Local Government in South Asia and West Africa*, Cambridge: Cambridge University Press.

Crosby, B. L. (1996), 'Policy Implementation: The Organizational Challenge', *World Development*, 24/9: 1403–15.

Etukudo, A. (1991), 'From Scepticism to Confidence: African Employers' Organizations as Partners in Development', *International Labour Review*, 130/1: 113–22.

—— (1995), 'Reflections on the Role of African Employers' Organisations in Tripartism and Social Dialogue', *International Labour Review*, 134/1: 51–64.

Evans, P. (1992), 'The State as Problem and Solution: Predation, Embedded Autonomy, and Structural Change', in S. Haggard and R. R. Kaufman (eds.),

The Politics of Economic Adjustment: International Constraints, Distributive Conflicts, and the State, Princeton: Princeton University Press.

Fischer, F. (1993), 'Citizen Participation and the Democratization of Policy Expertise: From Theoretical Inquiry to Practical Cases', *Policy Sciences*, 26/3: 165–87.

Fox, J. (1994), 'Latin America's Emerging Local Politics', *Journal of Democracy*, 5/2: 105–16.

Friedmann, J. (1992), *Empowerment: The Politics of Alternative Development*, Cambridge, Mass.: Blackwell.

Gamarra, E. A., and Malloy, J. M. (eds.) (1995), 'The Patrimonial Dynamics of Party Politics in Bolivia', in S. Mainwearing and T. R. Scully (eds.), *Building Political Institutions: Party Systems in Latin America*, Stanford, Calif.: Stanford University Press.

Garrity, M., and Picard, L. A. (1991), 'Organized Interests, the State and the Public Policy Process: An Assessment of Jamaican Business Associations', *Journal of Developing Areas*, 25/3: 369–94.

Gills, B., Rocamora, J., and Wilson, R. (eds.) (1993), *Low Intensity Democracy: Political Power in the New World Order*, London: Pluto.

Gordon, D. F. (1996), 'Sustaining Economic Reform under Political Liberalization in Africa: Issues and Implications', *World Development*, 24/9: 1527–37.

Goulet, D. (1989), 'Participation in Development: New Avenues', *World Development*, 17/2: 165–78.

Grindle, M. S. (1980), 'Policy Content and Context in Implementation', in M. S. Grindle (ed.), *Politics and Policy Implementation in the Third World*, Princeton: Princeton University Press.

Harvey, C., and Robinson, M. (1995), 'The Design of Economic Reforms in the Context of Political Liberalization: The Experience of Mozambique, Senegal and Uganda', IDS Discussion Paper 353, Brighton: Institute of Development Studies, Nov.

Healey, J., and Robinson, M. (eds.) (1992), *Governance, Democracy and Economic Policy: Sub-Saharan Africa in Comparative Perspective*, London: Overseas Development Institute.

Held, D. (1987), *Models of Democracy*, Cambridge: Polity Press.

Holm, J. D. (1988), 'Botswana: A Paternalistic Democracy', in L. Diamond, J. J. Linz, and S. M. Lipset (eds.), *Democracy in Developing Countries*, ii: *Africa*. Boulder, Colo.: Lynne Rienner.

—— (1996). 'Development, Democracy and Civil Society in Botswana', in A. Leftwich (ed.), *Democracy and Development: Theory and Practice*, Cambridge: Polity Press.

Huntington, S. (1965), 'Political Development and Political Decay', *World Politics*, 18/7: 286–330.

—— and Nelson, J. M. (1976), *No Easy Choice: Political Participation in Developing Countries*, Cambridge, Mass.: Harvard University Press.

Keemar, G., and Ghosh, B. (1996), *West Bengal Panchayat Elections 1993: A Study in Participation*, New Delhi: Institute of Social Sciences and Concept.

Kohli, A. (1989), *State and Poverty in India*, Cambridge: Cambridge University Press.

Landell-Mills, P. (1992), 'Governance, Cultural Change and Empowerment', *Journal of Modern African Studies*, 30/4: 543–67.

Lehmbruch, G., and Schmitter, P. (eds.) (1982), *Patterns of Corporatist Policy-Making*, Beverly Hills, Calif.: Sage.

Lipset, S. M. (1959), 'Some Social Requisites of Democracy: Economic Development and Political Legitimacy', *American Political Science Review*, 53: 69–105.

Luckham, L., and White, G. (eds.) (1996), *Democratization in the South: The Jagged Wave*, Manchester: Manchester University Press.

Ministerio de Desarrollo Humano (1996), *Bolivia: La participación popular en cifras*, La Paz: Secretaria Nacional de Participación Popular.

Molutsi, P. P., and Holm, J. D. (1990), 'Developing Democracy when Civil Society is Weak: The Case of Botswana', *African Affairs*, 89/356: 323–40.

Moore, M., and Hamalai, L. (1993), 'Economic Liberalization, Political Pluralism and Business Associations in Developing Countries', *World Development*, 21/12: 1895–912.

Nelson, N., and Wright, S. (eds.) (1995), *Power and Participatory Development: Theory and Practice*, London: Intermediate Technology.

Nie, N. H., and Verba, S. (1975), 'Political Participation', in F. I. Greenstein and N. W. Polsby (eds.), *Handbook of Political Science*, iv: *Nongovernmental Politics*, Reading, Mass.: Addison-Wesley.

Nordlinger, E. (1981), *On the Autonomy of the Democratic State*, Cambridge, Mass.: Harvard University Press.

Nyang'oro, J. E., and Shaw, T. M. (eds.) (1989), *Corporatism in Africa: Comparative Analysis and Practice*, Boulder, Colo.: Westview.

Oakley, P., et al. (1991), *Projects with People: The Practice of Participation in Rural Development*, Geneva: International Labour Office.

Orsini, D. M., Courcelle, M., and Brinkerhoff, D. W. (1996), 'Increasing Private Sector Capacity for Policy Dialogue: The West African Enterprise Network', *World Development*, 24/9: 1453–66.

Parry, G., and Moyser, G. (1994), 'More Participation, More Democracy?', in D. Beetham (ed.), *Defining and Measuring Democracy*, London: Sage.

Pateman, C. (1970), *Participation and Democratic Theory*, Cambridge: Cambridge University Press.

Phillips, A. (1991), *Engendering Democracy*, Cambridge: Polity Press.

Pretorius, L. (1996), 'Relations between State, Capital and Labour in South Africa: Towards Corporatism?', in M. Faure and J.-E. Lane (eds.), *South Africa: Designing New Political Institutions*, London: Sage.

PRIA (Society for Participatory Research in Asia) (1997), 'Local Self Governance: Myth or Reality of Gram Panchayat and Gram Sabha', paper prepared for the Seminar on 'Strengthening Panchayati Raj Institutions in India', New Delhi, Aug.

Rahman, M. A. (1995), 'Participatory Development: Toward Liberation or Co-optation?', in Craig and Mayo (1995*b*).

Riddell, R. C., and Robinson, M. (1995), *Non-governmental Organizations and Rural Poverty Alienation*, Oxford: Clarendon Press.

Robinson, M. (1996), 'Economic Reform and the Transition to Democracy', in R. Luckham and G. White (eds.), *Democratization in the South: The Jagged Wave*, Manchester: Manchester University Press.

Schönwalder, G. (1997), 'New Democratic Spaces at the Grassroots? Popular Participation in Latin American Local Governments', *Development and Change*, 28/4: 753–70.

Shastri, V. (1997), 'The Politics of Economic Liberalization in India', *Contemporary South Asia*, 6/1: 27–56.

Singh, H. (1994), 'Constitutional Base for *Panchayati Raj* in India', *Asian Survey*, 34/9: 818–27.

Skalnes, T. (1995), *The Politics of Economic Reform in Zimbabwe: Continuity and Change in Development*, Basingstoke: Macmillan.

Slater, D. (1995), 'Democracy, Decentralization and State Power: On the Politics of the Regional in Chile and Bolivia', in D. J. Robinson (ed.), *Yearbook, Conference of Latin Americanist Geographers*, 21: 49–65.

Smith, B. C. (1996), 'Sustainable Local Democracy', *Public Administration and Development*, 16/2: 163–78.

Stone, C. (1980), *Democracy and Clientelism in Jamaica*, New Brunswick, NJ: Transaction Books.

Toye, J. (1992), 'Interest Group Politics and the Implementation of Adjustment Policies in Sub-Saharan Africa', *Journal of International Development*, 4/2: 183–97.

van de Walle, N. (1994), 'Political Liberation and Economic Policy Reform in Africa', *World Development*, 22/4: 483–500.

Wade, R. (1990), *Governing the Market: Economic Theory and the Role of Government in East Asian Industrialization*, Princeton: Princeton University Press.

Webster, N. (1990), *Panchayati Raj and the Decentralisation of Development Planning in West Bengal: A Case Study*, CDR Project Paper 90.7, Copenhagen: Centre for Development Research.

—— (1992), 'Panchayati Raj in West Bengal: Popular Participation for the People or for the Party?', *Development and Change*, 23/2: 129–63.

—— (1995), 'Democracy, Decentralized Government, and NGOs in Indian Rural Development', *Journal für Entwicklungspolitik*, 11/2: 187–212.

Williams, P. J. (1989), *Corporatism in Perspective*, Beverly Hills, Calif.: Sage.

Wiseman, J. A. (1986), 'Urban Riots in West Africa, 1977–1985', *Journal of Modern African Studies*, 24/3: 509–18.

World Bank (1997), *World Development Report 1997: The State in a Changing World*, Washington: World Bank.

Zakaria, F. (1997), 'The Rise of Illiberal Democracy', *Foreign Affairs*, 76/6: 22–43.

....

6

....

The Developmental Implications of Federal Political Institutions in India

ROB JENKINS

It is widely accepted that a democratic state's developmental performance can be influenced profoundly by the specific configuration of its political institutions. This chapter argues that a particularly important axis of institutional variation is whether state power is constituted as a unitary government or a federal system comprising multiple levels of political contestation and authority. Any attempt to assess the developmental implications of federalism as an independent institutional variable is complicated by the variety of federal systems in existence and the broad range of social and political contexts within which they operate. While we cannot isolate federalism as a distinct and uniform variable for comparative analysis, it *is* possible to examine the ways in which political dynamics created by multi-level systems facilitate or inhibit the achievement of developmental aims within particular countries.

In order to provide further analytical focus, this chapter explores not development generally, but rather the prospects for attaining both efficiency- and equity-related developmental objectives within the specific context of market-oriented economic reform, using India as a case study.

This chapter's argument can be summarized as follows:

1. Several de jure and de facto features of India's federal system do not conform to the institutional arrangements which the theoretical literature considers most likely to increase developmental performance.
2. Nevertheless, other features of India's federal system which are not explicitly addressed in the theoretical literature—particularly

the way in which it shapes party competition—help to offset these shortcomings. In particular, the organization of state power on multiple levels provides opportunities for political elites to overcome the opposition of powerful groups to market-oriented economic reform.

3. Thus, the structure of its federal institutions has helped India to escape from the change-resistant tendencies to which democratic states are prone. In this sense, federalism can be said to have had a beneficial impact on efficiency.

4. However, some of the very same political dynamics which enabled India's federal system to increase efficiency by making reform politically sustainable have simultaneously reduced certain dimensions of equity. (This is not, it must be stressed, the same as arguing that economic reforms themselves—unmediated by political-management tactics—have had negative distributional consequences, or that there has been a *net* decline in equity, measured along all of its dimensions.)

1. Theoretical Grounding

By analysing the role of federal institutions in helping to make economic reform in India politically sustainable, this chapter contributes insights to two sets of theoretical literature. The first concerns the developmental implications of various federal arrangements, while the second focuses on the interaction between democracy and policy implementation. The analysis of the Indian case material suggests that theories of federalism and economic performance suffer from an excessive orientation towards explaining static environments. They need to incorporate an understanding of the relationship between federal systems and the political processes underlying policy change. If they did, then their assessments of the developmental impacts of various federal systems might be altered dramatically, given that an ability to adapt to new circumstances may be one of the most important developmental attributes of any institutional environment. On the other hand, the second body of literature on the interaction between democracy and policy implementation is already fundamentally concerned with change. It has, however, been much less sensitive to federalism as an institutional variable that can influence a democratic state's capacity for policy implementation—in some cases, for the better. Before turning to the case-study evidence, it may be useful to consider some of the major propositions in each of these bodies of literature.

(a) Federalism and economic performance

Academic debate and political discourse in India are filled with heart-felt pleas for a realignment of relations between the centre and the states, usually in the direction of greater 'autonomy' for the latter. These are usually made on grounds of both equity and efficiency. Two strands of the theoretical literature on the economic impacts of federal institutions also lead to a fairly harsh indictment of the inefficiency and (to a lesser extent) inequity of Indian federalism—one relating to 'fiscal federalism', the other, an offshoot of more recent origin, concerned with what has been termed 'market-preserving federalism'.

(i) Fiscal federalism

The first subset of the literature relates to 'fiscal federalism'. This body of theorizing is concerned with 'the optimal degree of decentralization of public sector decisions of different sorts', particularly regarding taxation, expenditure, and regulation (Boadway et al. 1994: 3). The aim is to create institutions which provide disincentives for citizens to free-ride or for decision-makers at various levels of government to either overgraze the fiscal commons or evade responsibility for citizens whose needs place disproportionate burdens on public expenditure.

The way in which functions are 'assigned' in India's federal system is generally considered sub-optimal, in terms of both equity and efficiency. The central problem is one of practical operation: while its mixture of 'subnational provision and central oversight is consistent with [desirable] theoretical principles . . . the role of the central government is larger than these assignments suggest' (Boadway et al. 1994: 47). Through the extra-constitutional Planning Commission, and the discretionary transfers made by central ministries to state governments, the central government's influence over taxation, spending priorities, and regulatory decisions has become greatly expanded. More-over, '[m]ost specific purpose transfers are allocated without a formula, allowing the central government considerable discretion' (Boadway et al. 1994: 59).

Other peculiarities of the system of fiscal relations between governing units in India tend to create unhealthy side-effects. For instance, one comparative analysis noted that 'India [perhaps] is the only federation where an inter-state sale is subject to tax by the exporting state in addition to the tax levied by the importing state' (Rao 1995: 290). Not only does this benefit some states more than others, particularly those with large manufacturing capacities; 'the inter-state sales tax has also led to distortions in tax structures, as the states tend to levy higher tax rates on commodities predominantly exported out of the states' (Rao 1995: 291).

According to the principles set forth in the literature on fiscal federalism, India's particular form of federalism does not possess the features most likely to assist in the attainment of efficiency objectives. It is also found wanting in terms of promoting equity—either between regions, or between groups of people classified according to non-geographic characteristics. In some areas, such as intergovernmental transfers, the negative implications for equity and efficiency are closely intertwined:

the design of general purpose transfer schemes from both the Finance and Planning Commissions do not adequately offset the fiscal disadvantages to enable 'competitive equality'. The designs for transfer schemes also have dis-incentive effects and tend to promote laxity in fiscal management. In the event, the system of federal transfers evolved in India has not helped to reduce inter-state disparities in the levels of services or incomes. (Rao 1995: 304–5)

(ii) Market-preserving federalism

A second strand of the literature which attempts to theorize the links between multi-level systems and economic outcomes is centred around the notion of 'market-preserving federalism' (Weingast 1995). Its central premiss is that federal institutions can, under certain conditions, provide credibility to government commitments to honour the legal rights and rules which are required to 'maintain the economy' by 'protecting markets'. The purpose of this 'special form of federalism' is largely to constrain the capacity of political actors to encroach upon markets (McKinnon 1994).

Market-preserving federalism can only be said to exist if the system displays five characteristics that govern the allocation of re-sponsibilities among levels of government: (1) a delineated scope of authority; (2) subnational government control over the economy in their jurisdictions; (3) common-market policing functions assigned to the national government; (4) an effective hard budget constraint through strict controls on revenue-sharing and borrowing; and (5) institutional features which make the assignment of responsibilities and powers impervious to political interference (Montinola et al. 1995: 55). According to these criteria, India does not qualify. The authors of a study on China specifically point out that '[m]any de jure federalisms are nothing like market-preserving federalisms, for example, in Argentina, Brazil, and India. In these cases, conditions 2 and 5, and often condition 4, fail' (Montinola et al. 1995: 57).

These two strands of the theoretical literature—on fiscal and market-preserving federalism—are premissed on sound analytical principles. But they do not necessarily tell the whole story. Even granting all of the flaws that are said to mar the economic efficiency of India's federal system—whether stemming from design or practical operation—there remain hidden aspects of its role in shaping political behaviour that must be taken into account when assessing its *net* impact on developmental performance. To apprehend these we must, in some respects, move beyond the fairly narrow concerns which have informed the modelling of fiscal and market-preserving federalism. This does not mean abandoning all of the rational-choice preoccupations of these writers: still very much at the forefront are issues of how the incentives facing various actors are shaped by both uncertainty and behaviour-constraining institutions. But if we shift the emphasis a bit to include the types of political conflict, and techniques for waging it, that are found in the real world of democratic politics, some functional aspects of Indian federalism can be appreciated. These provide a more balanced picture of federalism's developmental impact. The most significant of these is the contribution of the federal structure to the Indian state's capacity to carry out a programme of market-oriented reform which has, on balance, increased economic performance by reducing systemic inefficiencies (World Bank 1996).

(b) Democratic governance and policy implementation

Making the case for federalism's role in the political sustainability of India's economic reform programme brings us into contact with another body of literature, on the politics of economic reform. While this contains a large and varied set of theoretical propositions, for the purposes of this chapter only one relatively small subset need be addressed—that portion which asks why democratic regimes have over the last several years proven less constrained by political factors in implementing far-reaching policy reform than earlier theories had predicted.

Three lines of thinking can be discerned. The first has tended to focus on the nature of political transitions, largely because the main developing-world democracies involved in implementing economic reform have been those which recently emerged from authoritarian rule (Haggard and Kaufman 1995). Issues of political sequencing have been at the forefront of this school of thought. The second set of studies has been concerned with the ways in which political leaders in democratic settings use the tools that a relatively transparent, liberal political system puts at their disposal. These involve 'selling' reform to the electorate (Husain 1994), promoting an inclusive form of policy-making that involves extensive consultation with key interest groups (Harvey and Robinson 1995), and building new coalitions for reform that can give a greater voice to the poor (Graham 1994: 252). The third analytical stream consists of studies which seek to evaluate the impact of various institutional variables on the capacity of democratic states to achieve their reform objectives (Haggard and Webb 1994). The institutions most often studied are electoral systems, party systems, and the structure of relations between politicians and civil servants.

This chapter's analysis of the Indian case material will reveal the extent to which each of these approaches could be strengthened were they to consider how relations between a political system's various levels influence the shape of political conflict and the prospects for political compromise. First, while India is a long-established rather than a fledgeling democracy, the political dynamics produced by its federal setting clearly have some relevance for post-authoritarian federations such as Russia, Brazil, and Argentina. Second, the Indian experience suggests that the operation of a federal system provides avenues for political tactics that rely less on salesmanship and transparency than on blame-shifting between competing parties and collusive arrangements between the state and privileged economic interests. Third, while electoral systems, party systems, and the structure of relations between politicians and civil servants can each have a substantial impact on the prospects for successful policy implementation, the nature of these impacts is likely to vary significantly, depending on whether they occur in a federal or unitary polity.

While this chapter does not argue that federalism is a 'meta'-variable, it does seek to highlight the importance of federalism as a potentially important cross-cutting variable. The central point is that a failure to assess the impact that the existence or absence of a multi-level polity might have on efforts to implement policy reform renders conclusions based on other (admittedly important) institutional variables far less robust. Although it is impossible conceptually to separate the federal system from the many other formal institutions which make up the structure of Indian government, this chapter highlights the mechanisms through which the federal ordering of state power helps to reduce the political pressures facing reformers at the apex of the political system, allowing the reforms to take root, create new economic incentives, and generate efficiency gains.[1]

---

[1] An analysis which highlights the role played by informal institutions, as well as the formal institution of a federal system, can be found in Jenkins (1999, forthcoming).

2. About Indian Economic Reform and Federalism

Before turning to the ways in which India's federal institutional form has provided the flexibility required to bring about changes that many other countries (including several authoritarian regimes) have found difficult to sustain, it is important to make the case that the policy reforms in question are far-reaching.

Clearly the most substantial reforms have taken place in the area of trade and industrial policy. While it is true that India still has some of the highest tariff levels in the world, when compared to the pre-reform system (which had *the* highest) the current policy environment represents an enormous transformation of the trade regime. Much of the progress in trade reform consisted of doing away with the system of bureaucratic controls which governed various aspects of international commerce. Examples include the drastic scaling back of the import licensing system and the withdrawal of the Cash Compensatory Scheme for exports, which had been a major subsidy item on the federal budget.

On the industrial side, progress has also been gradual, but it began with a big bang. The centrepiece of reform was the drastic scaling back of the industrial licensing system for all but eighteen 'core' sectors, announced at the beginning of the reform process in 1991. By 1992 the system had been effectively dismantled. The government of India also opened up to the private sector industries that had previously been the sole preserve of state-owned enterprises. Combined with substantial relaxation of the Monopolies and Restrictive Trade Practices (MRTP) Act, which had severely restricted the activities of large business houses, industrial delicensing and dereservation resulted in a spurt of private sector investment and corporate restructuring. This increased business activity, in turn, led to further regulatory anomalies that (over time) necessitated additional reforms in policies relating to taxation, share markets, foreign joint ventures, and infrastructure.

The considerable liberalization of foreign direct investment and foreign portfolio investment began in the form of modification to the Foreign Exchange Regulation Act (FERA), 1974. It was subsequently revised on many occasions before a replacement was proposed, in the form of the far more liberal Foreign Exchange Management Act (FEMA). Like most other areas of reform, financial-sector liberalization has also occurred in a phased manner. Very early reforms included substantial lowering of the statutory liquidity ratio and the incremental cash reserve, instruments through which the government has access to the resources of commercial banks. Interest rates have, with important exceptions, been given relative freedom to seek their natural market levels. The government has also taken numerous steps to create the conditions under which deregulated financial markets could operate. For instance, after the post of Controller of Capital Issues was abolished in 1992–3, many reforms were introduced which strengthened the regulatory capacity of its successor, the Securities and Exchange Board of India (SEBI).

To many economists, a government's capacity to meet targets for reducing the fiscal deficit (measured as a percentage of GDP) is the *sine qua non* of true structural adjustment. The rise in India's fiscal deficit to 7.3 per cent of GDP in 1993–4 was often cited as a watershed, the Narasimha Rao government's first step on the slippery slope back to populism. Nevertheless, when measured over the longer term, the fiscal deficit as a percentage of GDP has come down significantly, and has certainly broken free from the escalating trend that was evident in the pre-reform period. When considered alongside the 1990–1 figure of 8.3 per cent (and growing), it is clear that India has made significant progress in the area of fiscal reform. While the government has consistently failed to meet IMF and World Bank targets for fiscal discipline, a fixation upon the fiscal deficit : GDP ratio is misleading, for it obscures many others of importance, such as substantial reductions in net bank credit to the government, the ratio of indirect to direct taxes, and the proportion of the budget devoted to non-interest expenditure.

One of the main scourges of the Indian economy, according to neo-liberal economists, is the prevalence of subsidies. And, indeed, subsidies are still ubiquitous. But while the two largest subsidy items —for food and fertilizer—have continued to rise, the growth in the overall subsidy burden of the central government has been arrested. Moreover, as a percentage of total central government expenditure, subsidies accounted for just 7.5 per cent in 1995–6, as opposed to 11 per cent in 1990–1. The share of subsidies in GDP was reduced from 3.5 per cent in 1990–1 to 2.8 per cent in 1995–6.[2]

Clearly, this type of summary of reforms is vulnerable to a critique of the 'glass-half-empty' variety (Datta-Chaudhuri 1996). This inexhaustive list is provided in the hope that the depth and diversity of reform measures, as well as an appreciation of their considerable secondary effects, will indicate the scope of what has taken place. This is important, because the main reason why such reforms were once considered unthinkable—why development was seen to be arrested, sacrificed at the altar of democracy—was that the Indian state was

---

[2] The data in this paragraph are drawn from an analysis of government budget documents performed by the Business Standard Research Bureau, with commentary from the EPW Foundation (Bombay). It was reported in the *Business Standard*, 12 Aug. 1996.

systemically averse to growth-enhancing change. It was viewed as a hostage to a coterie of powerful interests capable of preying on the short-termism of elected politicians, who were themselves among the main beneficiaries of the status quo (Bardhan 1984). Indeed, this stranglehold over the state was the predominant explanation given for why earlier attempts at reform in India (particularly in the early and mid-1980s) had come unhinged, before being abandoned by their initiators (Harriss 1987, Kohli 1989). To the extent that a substantial reorientation of economic policy has been achieved in the 1990s— one which has speeded development in terms of many important indicators—the 'enemy of change' vision of India's democratic state has been dispelled. The federal system played a large role in under-mining the strength of those groups who had once been considered the system's main hostage-takers.

The federal political structure, which encompasses a range of in-stitutions such as state and national legislatures, national finance and planning commissions, and inter-state co-ordinating bodies, is a defining feature of Indian democracy—one which is a clear response to the regional diversity of Indian civilization. The frequency with which identity-based politics asserts itself at the regional (or 'state') level invests Indian federalism with a substance not found in many putatively federal political systems, and provides an important de-centralizing tendency that runs like a thread through politics since independence (Brass 1982).

And yet, the division of political labour between the centre and the states in independent India has been the subject of much political debate and almost as much academic theorizing. As the Congress Party has slowly lost its dominant position in Indian politics, a pro-cess which has been underway at least since the 1967 general election, tensions between national and provincial political forces have taken on an increasingly partisan character. Efforts to reverse this trend, such as the increasing abuse of the constitutional provision known as President's Rule to supersede state governments, have not been successful, and have arguably accelerated the deterioration in federal relations. It is also generally accepted that attempts by Congress prime ministers over the past twenty-five years to undercut up-and-coming Congress state chief ministers have, paradoxically, dimin-ished the national party's ability to influence events in the states where Congress held power (Manor 1978, 1983). In recent years, the Congress has been reduced to a marginal force in electoral politics in important states like Uttar Pradesh, Bihar, and Tamil Nadu. Over the past decade it has usually governed fewer than half of India's twenty-five states, though under Prime Minister Narasimha Rao it presided over the national government during the crucial first five years of economic liberalization, from July 1991 until May 1996, after which the electorate replaced it with a coalition of left and regional parties which relied on Congress support to maintain its parliamentary majority. As this volume was going to press, the Hindu nationalist Bharatiya Janata Party (BJP), in alliance with several regional parties, had been in power for three months, following its victory in the general election of February 1998.

Often, state governments are viewed, by both Indians and foreign observers, as obstacles to coherent and effective implementation of policy reforms. The constitution's unclear division of powers in several areas where responsibility is meant to be exercised jointly by state and central governments (the 'concurrent list') leads to ceaseless attempts from both sides to grab power and abdicate responsibility. This is particularly rife when a state is controlled by a party different from the national governing party. It is also clear that the existence of multiple levels within the political system introduces the potential for administrative linkage problems to emerge. Policy directives formulated in New Delhi can become hopelessly distorted by the time they reach a state capital, let alone a district or subdistrict headquarters. Public resources—whether for productive activity or poverty alleviation—are vulnerable to illegal appropriation at the many decision points along the chain of political and bureaucratic command. The inefficiency inherent in this system was one of the stated reasons for reforming the economy by divesting the public sector of some of its responsibilities.

3. How Federalism Contributes to the Political Sustainability of Economic Reform

Despite the complications and uncertainties it introduces, India's federal political structure has been an extremely important ingredient in helping to make its economic reform programme politically sustainable—that is, in reducing the pressure on political decision-makers in the central government to abandon reform. This process operates through four stages of causally related action, each of which stems from the altered incentives facing important economic and political actors.

(a) Inter-state disparities, inter-state rivalries

The first, and most basic, advantage of a federal system to political managers in New Delhi is that the impact of liberal economic reform varies from state to state. Some states' economies benefit—from, for instance, employment growth, foreign investment, and more buoyant tax bases—while others do not. Politicians from states that benefit have fewer reasons to oppose the centre's reform programme. Those from states that suffer relative declines in economic performance (or autonomy in determining economic policy) have both less clout and fewer allies (among their counterparts in states that perceive themselves as beneficiaries) with which to mount a serious challenge to liberalization. Even among states that can be considered *net* losers—that is, when the balance of gains and losses from various policy changes are assessed—there is often little commonality in the *nature* of their grievances: almost all states have gained in at least some areas, and these small compensations tend to be jealously guarded. As a result, efforts to mount a campaign of resistance to reform from this crucial tier of the Indian political elite—a group that has long been considered hostile to market-oriented reform because of the threat liberalization represents to its powers of patronage (Kohli 1990)—have suffered from collective-action difficulties.

A good illustration of this problem was the reaction of state governments to the central government's approach to the 'freight equalization' scheme, a classic piece of statist industrial regulation which attempted to negate disparities in transport costs between India's regions. The scheme had long worked to the disadvantage of states in the eastern part of India. Successive chief ministers in the three main states in the eastern region—Bihar, West Bengal, and Orissa—had been decrying the unfairness of freight equalization for years. When, as part of its efforts to marketize the economy, the Narasimha Rao government announced the abolition of the scheme, all three states were governed by non-Congress parties who were officially critical of efforts to dismantle the regulatory state.[3] And yet, because of the popularity of the abandonment of the freight equalization scheme among interests within their states, three usually liberalization-bashing chief ministers found themselves politically constrained from opposing it.[4] Their self-interested acceptance of this policy shift not only dulled the edge of their public fulminations against other aspects of the central government's reform programme; it sent a signal to chief ministers in other regions that the prospects for a united front against liberalization would

[3] Orissa's Janata Dal government lost power to the Congress as a result of assembly elections held in late 1994.

[4] Buddhadeb Bhattacharjee, West Bengal's minister for information and cultural affairs, captured the dilemma facing state leaders when he stated: 'While we are opposed to the philosophy and approach of the Centre's New Economic Policy, we must take advantage of the withdrawal of the freight equalisation scheme and delicensing in regard to some major industries.' *Sunday*, 3–9 Apr. 1994: 68.

be fruitless in the face of chief ministers willing to cave in on particular reforms that suited their particular circumstances.

In time, the every-state-for-itself logic became an entrenched feature of political life. For instance, states which were in a position to
take control over their natural resources as a result of new central
policies had less reason to oppose liberalization in the mining sector,
regardless of objections from their colleagues in non-mining states
who claimed that such tacit approval lent further political credibility
to the reform process as a whole.[5] With each state holding a soft spot
for liberalization measures that worked to its advantage, co-ordinated
resistance to the overall redirection of economic policy became extremely difficult.

Even in the one area in which virtually all states have fared poorly,
the devolution of resources from the central government, the specific
sources of forgone income varied from state to state. Moreover, some
states were much better equipped than others to regain a part of the
lost revenue by adapting to other aspects of the central government's
liberalization policies. These sorts of adaptations further delink
states' economic fates from one another—contributing to the pattern
of provincial Darwinism alluded to above. In short, while discontent
could be found among political elites in every state in India, there
was no common *basis* for welding that discontent into a unified programme of opposition to reform. This worked (and continues to work)
to the advantage of reformers in New Delhi, who would have found it
far more difficult to implement efficiency-enhancing economic reforms
in the face of co-ordinated resistance from state chief ministers and
other subnational political elites.

The most overtly divisive area of reform has been liberalization
of industrial policy. Under the 'licence-permit raj', business-location
decisions were effectively taken by central planners in New Delhi. With
the abolition of this system, both Indian and foreign capital have been
freed to seek locations offering the best returns. Given the centre's
reduced regulatory role, state governments have become a crucial point
of contact for entrepreneurs keen to take advantage of many of the
new reforms. State government agencies are where industrialists
must go if they want environmental and labour clearances, water
and electricity connections, land and zoning permits, and so on. This
has set off an intense competition among state governments to attract
investment, resulting in a proliferation of tax-incentive schemes and

---

[5] Among these states was Rajasthan. At a press conference announcing the state's
'New Mineral Policy 1994', Chief Minister Shekhawat openly thanked the Prime
Minister for going out of his way to remove bottlenecks relating to environmental
regulation so that Rajasthan could make the most of its natural resources. *Hindu*, 17
Aug. 1994.

promises of speedy administrative procedures, the expedition of land acquisition for industrial uses, and efforts to maintain a 'conducive' industrial-relations climate.

This sort of competition exacerbates the collective-action dilemmas facing state-level political elites (particularly non-Congress chief ministers) who would otherwise be inclined to band together in opposition to what, in more militant moments, they unsubtly refer to as the 'anti-people/pro-rich' policies of the central government.[6] The air of resignation surrounding the prospects for reversing the liberalizing tide reinforces the perceived need to get whatever share of the investment pie might be available. Since not every state will be materially better off (nor will every chief minister be politically better off), there is a strong element of confidence-trick politics at work in the political-management strategies of reformers in the central government. Creating a perception of reform's permanence is as important with respect to political actors, who will only take the go-along-to-get-along bait when convinced that resistance is futile, as it is with respect to economic agents, whose investment and consumption decisions are well known to be conditioned upon expectations of future policy scenarios (Rodrik 1990).

(b) Novel opportunities for corruption among state-level political elites

The new salience given to state governments in the industrial-development process contributed to reducing resistance to reform among state-level political elites (and thus to sustainable reform and, in turn, efficiency-related developmental performance enhancements in the economy as a whole) in a second way as well: through the allure of illicit income. If competition among states in a climate of fiscal retrenchment represented the stick imposed by the new policy dispensation, then the prospect of enhanced opportunities for corruption was the carrot. Given the investment boom, and the newfound demand for their 'investment-facilitation services', leaders of state governments had suddenly increased their earnings potential enormously.

This has taken many forms. One of the most important has been 'dereservation' of core infrastructure sectors. This is distinct from privatization and disinvestment in that it denotes not the selling of Public Sector Enterprises (PSEs), but the opening up to private sector investors of economic activities previously reserved for government

---

[6] During the early Narasimha Rao years, the discontent among state leaders was reportedly vented regularly at meetings between state-level party presidents and the Prime Minister—for instance on 23 Oct. 1992. This was considered a major threat to the political sustainability of the reform process. *Sunday*, 8–14 Nov. 1992: 14–15.

departments or PSEs. The keen interest expressed in infrastructure industries by well-funded multinational corporations, and the possibility of diverting illicit income to difficult-to-trace foreign currency bank accounts, has made dereservation one of the most important new sources of political funding. As one commentator has argued, 'rent-seeking—relentlessly objected to in the past in respect of the political-bureaucratic nexus of decision-makers by renowned expatriate Indian economists—is now practised more vigorously, more openly, with greater assurance (verging on arrogance) by private foreign capital in India' (Ghosh 1994: 13).

But the most noteworthy example of liberalization enhancing the prospects for deriving illegal funding is the case of land transactions. Over the years, politicians in various states have developed a variety of illegal means for profiting from land speculation. The registering of co-operative housing societies in the names of friends and relatives, for example, has provided privileged access to an extremely rare resource. Politicians have also employed criminal gangs to intimidate residents into abandoning their rights under heavily pro-tenant legislation, allowing them to obtain possession of and sell prime land in city centres. Special exemptions from local land-ceiling acts are another means by which real-estate developers with political connections can derive lucrative economic rents from projects such as suburban shopping centres.[7] These practices continue today,[8] as do others with an even longer tradition, such as tampering with village land records.[9] But they are considered relatively small time by those who have witnessed the scramble to manipulate the process of acquiring land for private sector industrial and infrastructure projects. Indeed, this area has emerged as one of the primary avenues through which state-level politicians have been able to benefit financially from the process of liberalization.[10]

---

[7] The 'Baldev Plaza affair' in Rajasthan, dating from the early 1980s but still the source of much controversy, involved such a mechanism, allegedly benefiting the son of prominent Congress MP Ram Niwas Mirdha. *Frontline*, 9 Oct. 1992: 133.

[8] An investigatory committee in Madhya Pradesh, for instance, identified several anomalies in land deals in Mandsaur district which allegedly benefited the brother of former BJP chief minister Sunderlal Patwa. *Asian Age*, 27 Feb. 1995.

[9] For instance, several cases involving the nephew of the Rajasthan chief minister have been documented by opposition politicians and have figured prominently in assembly debates. These cases are cited in page 3 of a letter from Surendra Vyas, MLA, to Home Minister S. B. Chavan, dated Oct. 1992, requesting the government of India to withhold its assent to the Rajasthan Tenancy (2nd Amendment) Bill 1992, passed by the Rajasthan Legislature on 26 Sept. 1992. See also *Observer of Business and Politics*, 18 Mar. 1994.

[10] Interviews with a senior IAS officer in the West Bengal government, 27 Apr. 1995, Calcutta; a member of the Rajasthan BJP, 9 Dec. 1993, Jaipur; an opposition MLA from Karnataka, 23 Mar. 1994, Bangalore; and a dissident member of the Maharashtra cabinet, 5 Apr. 1994, Bombay.

The standard practice by which politicians benefit from land transactions for infrastructure projects is to use the state government's official land-acquisition procedures, which commonly involve a tribunal consisting of MLAs elected from the region, local politicians, and district bureaucrats.[11] The tribunal offers landowners either nominal compensation, or if politicians are worried about electoral implications in that constituency, prices above the market rate, with a 'commission' then going to one or more local politicians and bureaucrats. Often, the senior politicians involved arrange for friends or relatives to buy back the land from the state at a later stage when the project finds that it has 'surplus' land. Bought for the same price at which it was sold, this land is then more valuable because of the commercial potential stemming from its proximity to the venture in question.

Delicensing and dereservation has led to a large increase in the number of project proposals, and it is the power that the legal system gives elected officials to deliver land to promoters of private industrial projects that they regard as the biggest benefit of liberalization. One particularly egregious example is Reliance Petroleum's use of 'dubious means and underhanded tactics', with the alleged help of political patrons, to acquire 4,000 acres of land in Gujarat needed for a refinery project (*Indian Express*, 8 Oct. 1993). But virtually any firm contemplating a new facility requires the assistance of the relevant state government. Subsequent to the announcement of the state's industrial policy in 1993, for instance, the Maharashtra Industrial Development Corporation (MIDC) acquired more than 30,000 hectares of land, with plans to acquire an additional 28,000 hectares over the next three years (*Observer of Business and Politics*, 25 Mar. 1994). This was in anticipation of investment flows, and in response to more liberal guidelines. In the name of promoting market-led industrialization, MIDC has been allowed to acquire land for purposes other than setting up its own government-operated industrial estates.[12] As a 'facilitator' in the process of providing the necessary inputs for investors, it has been permitted to acquire land for private entrepreneurs. In at least four cases, the entrepreneurs involved had ties to the ruling Congress Party, which left power when it was defeated at the polls in 1995. Their intention, not to mention capacity, to establish functioning

[11] This process was described to the author in interviews with a middle-ranking bureaucrat in the Rajasthan land-revenue bureaucracy, 19 Nov. 1993, Jaipur; the president of an agro-processing firm in Rajasthan, 12 Nov. 1993, Jaipur; an expert on agro-processing business practices for a major Indian consulting firm, 4 Feb. 1994, Bombay; and by a Congress MLA from Rajasthan, 22 Apr. 1994, Jaipur.

[12] The land acquisition process, especially the issue of compensation to farmers, has been the subject of much discussion in the state legislature. See, for instance, *Observer of Business and Politics*, 31 Mar. 1994.

business ventures was open to serious question.[13] The lucrative possibilities continued to increase as various arms of the Maharashtra government became more active in land-related activities[14]—a process which has continued under the coalition of Hindu nationalist parties which succeeded Congress.

Two additional points need to be made about the new opportunities created by the liberalizing environment. First, the very same interstate competition which undermined the structural cohesiveness of the anti-reform lobby among state-level political elites should also, in theory, provide a systemic check on the ability of ministers in state governments to derive illegal income from their suddenly pivotal positions. The competition to create an investor-friendly climate should penalize states that impose heavy 'corruption taxes' on businesses. In fact, this has not been the case. Some states, such as the industrial powerhouses of Maharashtra and Gujarat, began the race for investment pre-eminence with such an advantage in terms of human and physical infrastructure that any implicit threats by entrepreneurs to take their projects elsewhere were relatively empty. This may be changing,* but in the early phases of reform, when the perceptions of state-level elites are crucial to political sustainability, this was not the case. Just as a World Bank research report found that competition for investment among Indian states did not lead to a race to lower environmental standards—that is, lowering them did not attract investment, controlling for other factors affecting business decisions (Mani et al. 1997)—levels of corruption among state-level politicians have been similarly unaffected by competitive pressures.

The second point concerns changes in the way in which the corruption pie is shared between the central and state levels of India's political system. One prominent feature of the transition towards a greater reliance on markets has been, paradoxically, the emergence of new means of profiteering and patronage for *national* politicians. In particular, the new sources of corrupt income provided by foreign capital have, as Pranab Bardhan had predicted in the mid-1980s, reduced the reliance of national elites on domestic business interests for funding political activities (1988: 224). This helps to explain why national politicians were willing to relax investment policies in ways which gave *state*

---

[13] Interviews with two local journalists with intimate knowledge of Congress politics, 31 Mar. 1994 and 11 Apr. 1995, Bombay.

[14] For instance, the development commissioner (industries) announced in early April 1994 the acquisition of 250 hectares for each of three export processing zones in Pune, Aurangabad, and Nagpur; 500 hectares for a software technology park in Pune; and 350 hectares for a hotel-convention centre in Bombay. *Observer of Business and Politics*, 6 Apr. 1994.

* During 1996 until early 1998, Tamil Nadu managed to steal away a number of high-profile proposed investment projects from Maharashtra, including a Ford motor factory.

governments new responsibilities, in the process providing the politicians that run them with access to new resources.

(c) *States as the central government's accomplices in the political management of interest-group resistance to economic reform*

This brings us to the third aspect of federalism which assists the sustainability of economic reform: its tendency to disperse the political energies of economic interests, as opposed to political elites, by forcing them to battle in twenty-six states rather than in just one unitary political authority at the national level. The result is a significant fragmentation among certain interests along regional lines. This often reduces their political potency. Quarantined within individual states, where they are often less effective to begin with (Weiner 1989: 36), many socio-economic interests find it difficult effectively to influence policy. The issues that concern them have tended to get bound up with the day-to-day political mudslinging of state politics, further reducing their potency, and making the maintenance of a co-ordinated national lobbying effort even more difficult.

What needs to be emphasized is that the tendency for central government policy reforms to have different impacts in different states has affected not only the incentives and collective-action prospects facing state-level politicians, but also the way in which socio-economic interests respond to economic reform.

Moreover, liberalization is increasingly implemented in the form of successive micro-reforms in different states, at different times, and under different political circumstances. This combination means that the political impact of economic reform is refracted through the prism of federal India. This results in a slower pace than many proponents of reform would prefer. But it also helps to blunt the edge of opposition. Efforts to mount co-ordinated political resistance to one or another reform tend to become severely dissipated in such a fragmented environment.

One of the main assets of the Indian political system on which reformers in the central government rely is the political-management capacity of state-level governments. The existence of functional competitive arenas at various levels of the political system helps to spread the burden of conflict resolution over a broader institutional base. The political pressure facing reformers at the apex of the political system is reduced in proportion to the capacity of state governments, acting as the first line of political defence, to outmanœuvre and/or reach agreements with interests which might be aggrieved by either central- or state-level policy reforms.

The example of the trade union response to economic reform provides a useful illustration of the way in which the actions of state governments help to sap the political potency of interest groups. With state
governments, in the words of one labour activist, 'doing the centre's
dirty work', the resources of trade unions have been spread thin.[15] They
have been unable to respond to the many trespasses upon labour's
collective interests that have occurred in isolated incidents in different states.

These have taken various forms. For instance, invoking the Industrial Disputes Act of 1947, the Maharashtra government declared
the products of four companies 'essential' public-utility items, thus
making them immune to strike action (*India Today*, 15 Apr. 1994: 97).
Chief Minister Sharad Pawar also worked assiduously to effect splits
in various powerful unions.[16] And despite laws forbidding firms from
dismissing workers, many chronically loss-making companies have
simply locked their factory gates as elected state governments looked
the other way, preferring to let this practice proceed quietly. Representatives of a workers' rights organization which held a rally in Bombay
in January 1994 stated that more than 20,000 workers had lost jobs
in the Bombay area alone due to the failure of the Maharashtra government to prevent the closing of factories.[17] Labour disputes were often
used as a pretext for effecting an 'indefinite lockout'. By failing to pay
water and electricity bills, employers who find their enterprises no longer
profitable—or who would like to start up business with a docile workforce made up of contract labourers—thus invite a 'de facto closure,
obviating the necessary legal permission from the government under
section 25 of the Industrial Disputes Act' (Bidwai 1994).

Union leaders argue that while they have shown flexibility by ton-
ing down labour stridency, 'management militancy' has been on the
rise, abetted by state governments. This is borne out by the statistics:
while the number of person-days lost because of strikes decreased almost by half, from 12.43 million in 1991 to 6.6 million in 1994, the

---

[15] Interview with a trade union activist and writer, 11 Sept. 1996, Bombay. The involvement of state governments in this process, rather than the central government acting
alone, was considered politically effective because it was 'like the police interrogating
suspects individually, and working them over one at a time'.

[16] He played a role in the exit of former MLA Sharad Khatu, along with four other
central committee members of the Maharashtra General Kamgar Union, controlled
by independent trade unionist Datta Samant, in late 1993, as well as the earlier departure of T. S. Bhokade, once a trusted lieutenant. Interview with Datta Samant, 26
Mar. 1994, Bombay, and with an independent labour activist, 29 Jan. 1994. See also
Business India, 27 Sept.–10 Oct. 1993: 23.

[17] Interview with two organizers of the Bandh Karkhana Samgharsha Samiti, 24 Jan.
1994, Bombay.

number lost due to management lockouts actually increased over the same period (*Business World*, 7–20 Feb. 1996: 114).

Because such tactics have been used only sporadically—under diverse circumstances in different states—and because of the pre-occupation of national trade union federations with national labour reform (the much-talked-about 'exit policy'), local unions have had fewer financial and organizational resources with which to oppose state government actions and inactions.[18] The result is that the trade union movement—already fragmented on the basis of party affiliation and the public–private sector divide—is becoming more regionally frag-mented as well.[19] The ability of federalism to weaken interest groups by quarantining them within state-level political systems is of immense value to reformers in New Delhi, who would like to see the strength of the trade union movement reduced before embarking on major national legislative reform.[20] Governments in many, though not all, states possess the capacities needed to accomplish this task without fomenting levels of dissent that can threaten their own survival.

(d) Undercutting anti-reform dissidence among national opposition parties

Many non-Congress state governments, in response to both the pres-sures of competition and the new sources of rent-seeking thrown up by liberalization, eventually 'fell into line with liberalization'.[21] This complicity not only helps to provide greater depth to the technical aspects of the reform agenda, it also makes the process more politic-ally sustainable.

The reform measures enacted by non-Congress state governments undermine the heated anti-reform rhetoric emanating from their

---

[18] For instance, the Orissa government's crushing of a strike among workers at the state electricity board, which was backed by the All-India Trade Union Congress (*Frontline*, 14 Jan. 1994: 23). The Maharashtra state police were alleged to have tortured striking workers at automotive manufacturer Mahindra and Mahindra (*Independent* (Bombay), 8 Sept. 1994).

[19] The involvement of state governments as brokers often results in workers in one state reaching agreement with employers, thus undercutting the union's representat-ives at a location of the same company in a different state. This happened in the case of Philips India. See *Observer of Business and Politics*, 3 Sept. 1996.

[20] Interview with an ILO official who has held extensive consultations with members of government, industry, and labour, 6 Sept. 1996, New Delhi.

[21] This expression is often used in India—for instance, with reference to the actions of the Janata Dal chief minister of Bihar (Laloo Prasad Yadav) and the Shiv Sena chief minister of Maharashtra (Manohar Joshi), *Financial Express*, 27 Apr. 1995.

parties' MPs in the national Parliament.[22] Finance Minister Manmohan Singh was able to deflect opposition parties' criticism of the government's accession to the 1994 GATT agreement, including the creation of the World Trade Organization, by claiming that it was a decision around which consensus had formed in India:

Economic reforms are no more an object of contention among political parties. This is evident from their manifestos and speeches of various leaders, and more so from the recent industrial policy statement of the left-ruled West Bengal which is virtually an endorsement of the Centre's policy. (*Economic Times*, 22 Nov. 1994)

A year later, in West Bengal, the Communist Party of India (Marxist)-ruled government's embrace of market-oriented reform was even more highly visible. The CPI (M)'s parliamentary leader, Somnath Chatterjee, was greeted with derisive laughter from all sides when he launched a broadside on the floor of Parliament against 'the [central] government's total surrender to the IMF and World Bank' (*Hindustan Times*, 27 Apr. 1995). Parliamentary debates generally have little influence over policy, but when well orchestrated they can help to frame public debates in advantageous ways for groups that are out of power. To the extent that discrepancies between national rhetoric and state-level reality undermine this, they are a blow to opposition efforts on economic policy.

Federalism provides political shelter for politicians operating at all levels of the political system. Reluctant reformers at the state level are able to claim that actions taken by the central government leave them no option but to liberalize. And when state governments liberalize under duress, reformers in the central government (or their party colleagues in state capitals) are then able to declare that consensus has been reached. The chief minister of Rajasthan stated in 1994 that the state's new mining policy, which was significantly more liberal towards the private sector, was a matter of necessity: 'the new economic policies being pursued by the centre had left the states to fend for themselves' (*Hindu*, 17 Aug. 1994). These and other liberalizing moves were rejected as 'sheer hypocrisy' by the Rajasthan Congress president, Paras Ram Maderna: 'It is shocking that while the state BJP leadership charges the Centre with taking loans from world bodies, burdening the nation with debts, it is itself securing huge loans running into thousands of crores [tens of billions] from international

---

[22] A leaked memo from BJP national executive committee member and economic adviser Jay Dubashi to party president L. K. Advani admitted as much. The damage-control efforts of the party's spokeswoman only revealed further divisions within the party. *Economic Times*, 18 Jan. 1994.

agencies.' Maderna's words were picked up by Congress MPs from the state and used to blunt the edge of anti-reform criticism pouring forth on the floor of Parliament from BJP MPs (*Rashtriya Sahara*, Apr. 1994: 47).

4. *Federalism, Political-Management Tactics, and Developmental Equity*

Many of the same dynamics which made federalism a useful institutional form for breaking down resistance to reform—by 'parochializing' the concerns and actions of both political elites and economic agents—possess negative implications for the equity side of the developmental equation. Again, this does not demonstrate, in general, a positive correlation between the extent of federalism and the extent of inequality. The concern here is with a particular, though important, moment within the development process: the effort to sustain market-oriented economic reform in the face of political obstacles. In attempting to achieve this, reformers in India's central government passed much of the burden onto state governments, deriving significant political benefits for themselves in the process. Unloading thankless responsibilities onto others is part of the time-honoured tactic of shifting blame, one not confined to developing countries: it was a successful tactic for both Reagan and Thatcher in the pursuit of their policy objectives (Pierson 1995). An idealized notion of democracy should not blind us to its pervasiveness in the process of promoting policy change in democratic India. The *conflictual* nature of federalism, as we have seen, provided some of the tools with which accomplished buck-passers in the central government were able to generate competition as a way of furthering their preferred agenda.

While the central government's tactics concealed the extent to which, for instance, the costs of fiscal adjustment were passed on to state governments, they also conceal the great variance in the inclination or ability of states to pass these costs on to the poor. In other words, while it is not clear that the poor are worse off nationally as a result of economic reform—i.e. that national income-group inequality has increased—it is nevertheless true that poorer groups have been less cushioned from adjustment's shocks in some states than they have been elsewhere. The existence of federal institutions, therefore, influences the *pattern* of inequality from region to region in so far as state-level political elites pursue customized strategies to cope with the opportunities and constraints furnished by the new policy environment. This is quite distinct from the extent to which states are unequally affected by liberalization in its politically unmediated form, and will form the basis of what follows.

The response of state governments to the centre's approach to containing the food-subsidy bill reveals the extent to which federalism helps to mask expedient but inequitable means for passing the cost of adjustment on to the most vulnerable sections of society. The government has loudly trumpeted its steadfast refusal to comply with World Bank recommendations that it drastically curtail the public distribution system (PDS), through which rice, wheat, sugar, kerosene, and other essential commodities are sold at subsidized prices to 'ration card' holders. National leaders are able to portray this as a determined stand against attempts to undermine its sovereignty.[23] It is held up as proof of their continued commitment to India's poor and downtrodden. Government officials make frequent mention of the fact that the budgetary allocation for the food subsidy has risen steadily in the years since liberalization began.

What this conceals, however, is that even this increased budgetary allocation for the food subsidy has not been sufficient to offset the steep rise in government support prices offered to cultivators of wheat and rice. As a result, poor consumers have been forced to pay far higher prices. The fact is that it would have required *even higher* increases in the level of budgetary support in order to stabilize the price at which grains are sold in the PDS's 'fair-price shops'. While 'increasing the level of budgetary support' for the PDS, the government has nevertheless made essential commodities more expensive for the poorest of the poor. Through a deft display of political legerdemain, it has transferred a substantial portion of the subsidy from consumers to farmers. This was deemed necessary to compensate for the government's failure to take other measures demanded by farmers. It therefore offered massive 'price incentives' to farmers, while recouping as much of this outlay as possible from those who rely on subsidized foodgrains, the poor. While maintaining the appearance of continuity (continued, though slower, growth in food-subsidy outlays), the government effected a dramatic change (massive increases in the prices at which consumers bought them through the PDS). The rise in the prices at which foodgrains are sold through the PDS tended to lessen the distance between the 'subsidized' and market prices, leading to a very large

---

[23] In order to quell speculation that India was considering the abolition of food subsidies in response to international pressure, Civil Supplies and Public Distribution Minister A. K. Anthony told a press conference: 'Whatever may be the constraints, there is no question of reducing or abandoning the food subsidy because food security is as important as national security, if not more.' *Asian Age*, 9 July 1994.

decline in consumption through the PDS, from 20.8 million tonnes in 1990 to 14 million tonnes in 1994.

But how has the cost of this political sleight-of-hand been apportioned? Would not the large numbers of poor people reliant on the PDS for cheap foodgrains and other essential commodities revolt? The answer is that it depends on how assertive these groups are, which is in turn closely related to the region in which they live. One reason the central government was able to get away with such sins of omission stems from the federal structuring of political authority: it is, after all, state governments, acting as the first line of political defence, that must face the irate public. S. Guhan has argued that, compared to the central government,

States are much closer to the electorate and also much more vulnerable to instability. . . . The States are responsible for much that affects the daily lives of people. . . . [T]hese several activities that lie at the cutting edge of administration expose State governments more intimately and continually to popular demands, conflicting pressures, and diverse local grievances. (1995: 101)

Electorates vent their frustrations at the most accessible level of government, not necessarily the one most responsible for their problems. The laying of blame is a political process, one that by no means follows strict rationality. Tactics matter, as the Republican-controlled US Congress learned when it lost the battle of public opinion against President Clinton over which arm of government was responsible for shutting down essential services during a prolonged deficit-reduction standoff in 1995. Faced with protests, and the futility of blaming New Delhi, many state governments in India felt compelled to substitute their own food subsidies to compensate for some of what the central government had withdrawn. The most notable example was the highly expensive Rs. 2 per kilogram rice scheme in Andhra Pradesh, which emerged as a result of a campaign promise during the 1994 assembly elections. In that case, not only was the newly installed non-Congress state government forced to clean up the mess created by the central government's PDS price increases, it was also blamed by the Congress for its lack of fiscal prudence when it had done so.

Andhra Pradesh had the most expensive subsidy scheme, but others took similar actions, and for similar reasons. In Karnataka the Congress government of Veerappa Moily in 1994 reduced the prices at which PDS outlets in the state sold rice and wheat. This cost the state's exchequer Rs. 420 million. As a newspaper editorial noted:

The decision to reduce the end prices of grains also represents the additional financial burden that the States are forced to carry on account of the Centre's fiscal stabilisation programme. While the Centre raised issue prices to contain food subsidies, Mr. Moily reduced it to ensure demand among the weaker sections. (*Deccan Herald*, 24 Mar. 1994)

As the central government continued its withdrawal from the PDS, Moily's non-Congress successor as chief minister felt compelled to extend the state-level subsidized rice scheme, at a cost of Rs. 2.2 billion per year, more than five times the amount Moily was willing to commit. In 1995, he announced that the scheme would be extended to urban consumers (*Pioneer*, 18 Oct. 1995).

If we recognize that only *some* states found it necessary to cushion the blow of the central government's PDS price rises, it is possible to gain an even greater perspective on the extent to which federalism not only allows state governments to tackle resistance to reform among powerful interests, but also assists in isolating geographically defined sections of the poor in arenas in which they are less capable of defending their interests. The politically unpalatable consequences of the central government's reform-management legerdemain are masked by federal institutions.

In practice, the distribution of public resources thus takes a *politically* more efficient form: it apportions the price rises in accordance with regional, rather than national, thresholds at which such hardships translate into widespread political discontent. After all, poorer groups are not as politically assertive in Rajasthan and Orissa as they are in Karnataka and Andhra Pradesh. In this sense, it is valid to ask, as Mick Moore's study of the politics of adjustment in Sri Lanka did, whether one unintended consequence of how liberalization has been implemented in India has been to 'remedy an historic "weakness" of the . . . political system: the relatively indiscriminate and inefficient distribution of relatively large volumes of material patronage such that they purchase little lasting support for the party in power' (1990: 352).

Inequalities, in so far as they are exacerbated or simply reconstituted, are not the consequence of federalism *per se*, but of the incentives it creates in the context of economic adjustment—that is, for governing elites at the national level to pass to their state-level counterparts a package of carrots (opportunities for corruption) and sticks (responsibility for filling gaps in social spending and tackling interest-group responses to reform); and for state-level governing elites to respond to their newfound dilemmas by, in many instances, passing whatever costs they can to the poorest groups. This is often the result of several interlocking trade-offs.

Some states, for instance, have been able to compensate for losses to centrally devolved revenue by taxing economic activities within their jurisdictions that have been rejuvenated as a result of other aspects of the central government's reform programme. One example is the government of India's gradual reform of the coffee-marketing system. In 1992, coffee growers were for the first time permitted to sell 30 per cent of their crop in the open market, having previously been required to sell to the government-controlled Coffee Board at what were usually below-market rates. In 1993 the Free Sale Quota was increased to 50 per cent. In April 1995, in a long-anticipated move, all obligations to the Coffee Board were removed for 'small growers' (those with landholdings of less than 10 hectares). In need of new sources of revenue, states with substantial coffee-growing operations began to cast an avaricious eye towards coffee growers who had received 'windfall' profits. The Karnataka government, for instance, was able to raise resources in this way, justifying the new tax by saying that the coffee growers who had benefited should be prepared to contribute resources for the welfare of the poor (*Hindu*, 18 Apr. 1995).

In fact, the true victims of this policy were not the members of the well-organized 'coffee lobby'. The tax increase was just one part of a complex political understanding, arranged through informal networks connecting leaders from three different parties, which resulted in unofficial permission for large-scale coffee growers to encroach on lands nominally designated for extremely poor and vulnerable 'scheduled-caste' (or ex-untouchable) groups.[24] The log-rolling of favours-for-concessions transactions ended with the poor, and at the kind of localized level that only a state government could manage with any degree of effectiveness. When considered alongside the type of unsavoury tactics used by state governments to undercut the resistance of labour unions to economic reform, it becomes apparent that the intervention of state governments in the politics of reform—a form of involvement on which reformers in the central government rely—serves to shift burdens to poorer groups, but (crucially) in ways that vary from region to region.

5. Conclusion

The reliance of national political elites on the ability of federalism to create intra-state rivalries capable of dampening resistance to their policy agenda, and on state-level political systems to reduce interest-group potency, has generated a new set of political forces. The regionalization of Indian politics that the outcome of the 1998 general

---

[24] Interview with one of the party leaders involved in this process, 19 Apr. 1995, Bangalore.

elections seems to have confirmed cannot be ascribed solely, or even primarily, to political trends associated with liberalization. But it has certainly been reinforced by them (Jenkins 1996: 511–15, Jenkins 1998). This is perhaps the most lasting contribution of federalism to the sustainability of efficiency-enhancing economic reform. It bears a striking resemblance to the dynamic described by the authors of the study on market-preserving federalism in China: 'These changes [in the relations between central and provincial political authority] endow the economic reforms with a degree of political durability. Each serves to raise the costs of a recentralization of political authority and an economic retrenchment' (Montinola et al. 1995: 72–3). Indian federalism, in other words, may have more market-preserving features than theorists, operating within the confines of their self-devised modelling parameters, are capable of recognizing.

This chapter has not claimed that federal politics is the missing institutional link between democracy and positive developmental performance. However, its analysis of the ways in which this particular institutional variant of democracy can affect the evolution of economic policy—and thus development performance in terms of both efficiency and equity—highlights the desperate need for detailed studies of how individual democracies function in practice. These are required in order to aid our understanding of the extent to which institutional differences among democracies can explain variations in the success of achieving what are widely considered desirable policy shifts. There are many additional features of India's social, political, and economic life that influenced the direction of policy change, and indeed shaped the nature and functionality of the federal system itself. This is surely true of other countries as well. But in seeking to understand the factors which inhibit or promote policy change, and those which influence the developmental impact of such changes, analysts must pay careful attention to the way in which the distribution of authority among levels of a political system can alter the terrain upon which political battles are waged.

REFERENCES

Bardhan, Pranab (1984), *The Political Economy of Development in India*, Oxford: Basil Blackwell.

—— (1988), 'Dominant Proprietary Classes and India's Democracy', in Atul Kohli (ed.), *India's Democracy: An Analysis of Changing State–Society Relations*, Princeton: Princeton University Press.

Bidwai, Praful (1994), 'May Day! May Day!', *Times of India*, 1 May.

Boadway, Robin, Roberts, Sandra, and Shah, Anwar (1994), 'The Reform of Fiscal Systems in Developing and Emerging Market Economies: A Federalism Perspective', Policy Research Working Paper 1259, (Washington: World Bank.

Brass, Paul (1982), 'Pluralism, Regionalism and Decentralising Tendencies in Contemporary Indian Politics', in A. Jeyaratnam Wilson and Denis Dalton (eds.), *The States of South Asia: Problems of National Integration*, London: Hurst.

Datta-Chaudhuri, Mrinal (1996), 'Liberalisation without Reform', *Seminar*, 437 (Jan.): 32–5.

Ghosh, Arun (1994), ' "Rent-Seeking" and Economic Reform', *Economic and Political Weekly*, 1–8 Jan.: 13.

Graham, Carol (1994), *Safety Nets, Politics, and the Poor: Transitions to Market Economies*, Washington: Brookings Institution.

Guhan, S. (1995), 'Centre and States in the Reform Process', in Robert Cassen and Vijay Joshi (eds.), *India: The Future of Economic Reform*, Delhi: Oxford University Press.

Haggard, Stephan, and Kaufman, Robert R. (eds.) (1995), *The Political Economy of Democratic Transitions*, Princeton: Princeton University Press.

—— and Webb, Steven B. (eds.) (1994), *Voting for Reform: Democracy, Political Liberalization, and Economic Adjustment*, New York: Oxford University Press/World Bank.

Harriss, John (1987), 'The State in Retreat: Why has India Experienced Such Half-Hearted Liberalisation in the 1980s?', *IDS Bulletin*, 18/4: 31–8.

Harvey, Charles, and Robinson, Mark (1995), 'The Design of Economic Reforms in the Context of Political Liberalization: The Experience of Mozambique, Senegal and Uganda', IDS Discussion Paper 353, Brighton: Institute of Development Studies, Nov.

Husain, Ishrat (1994), 'Why Do Some Economies Adjust More Successfully than Others? Lessons from Seven African Countries', Policy Research Working Paper, no. 1364, Washington: World Bank, Africa Regional Office, Oct.

Jenkins, Rob (1996), 'The Continued Democratization of Indian Democracy: Regionalization, Social Change and the 1996 Elections', *Democratization*, 3/4 (Winter): 501–16.

—— (1998), 'India's Electoral Result: An Unholy Alliance between Nationalism and Regionalism', *Briefing Paper No. 42*, London: Royal Institute of International Affairs, March.

—— (1999, forthcoming) *Democracy & the Politics of Economic Reform in India* (Cambridge: Cambridge University Press).

Kohli, Atul (1989), 'The Politics of Liberalisation in India', *World Development*, 17/3: 305–28.

—— (1990), *Democracy and Discontent: India's Growing Crisis of Governability*, Cambridge: Cambridge University Press.

McKinnon, Ronald I. (1994), 'Market-Preserving Fiscal Federalism', Working Paper, Department of Economics, Stanford University, Stanford, Calif.

Mani, Muthukumara, Pargal, Sheoli, and Huq, Mainal (1997), 'Does Environmental Regulation Matter? Determinants of the Location of New Manufacturing Plants in India', Policy Research Working Paper no. 1718, Washington: World Bank, Feb.

Manor, James (1978), 'Indira and After: The Decay of Party Organisation in India', *Round Table*, Oct.: 315–24.

—— (1983), 'The Electoral Process amid Awakening and Decay', in Peter Lyon and James Manor (eds.), *Transfer and Transformation: Political Institutions in the New Commonwealth*, Leicester: Leicester University Press.

Montinola, Gabriella, Yingyi Qian, and Weingast, Barry R. (1995), 'Federalism, Chinese Style: The Political Basis for Economic Success in China', *World Politics*, 48/1 (Oct.): 55.

Moore, Mick (1990), 'Economic Liberalisation versus Political Pluralism in Sri Lanka', *Modern Asian Studies*, 24/2: 341–83.

Pierson, Paul (1995), *Dismantling the Welfare State*, Cambridge: Cambridge University Press.

Rao, M. Govinda (1995), 'Indian Fiscal Federalism from a Comparative Perspective', in Balveer Arora and Douglas V. Verney (eds.), *Multiple Identities in a Single State: Indian Federalism in Comparative Perspective*, Delhi: Konark Publishers/Centre for Policy Research.

Rodrik, Dani (1990), 'How Should Structural Adjustment Programs be Designed?', *World Development*, 18/7: 933–47.

Weiner, Myron (ed.) (1989), *The Indian Paradox: Essays in Indian Politics*, New Delhi: Sage Publications.

Weingast, Barry R. (1995), 'The Economic Role of Political Institutions: Market-Preserving Federalism and Economic Growth', *Journal of Law, Economics, and Organization*, 11 (Spring).

World Bank (1996), *India: Country Economic Memorandum. Five Years of Stabilization and Reform: The Challenges Ahead* (Washington: Country Operations, Industry and Finance Division, Country Department II, South Asia Region, 8 Aug.).

Democratic Institutions and Development in Post-apartheid South Africa

NICOLI NATTRASS and JEREMY SEEKINGS

In the last years of apartheid South Africa was distinguished not only by a political system based on racial discrimination against the majority of the population, but also by a very high level of economic inequality. Extensive poverty existed amidst considerable wealth. The open, democratic general election of April 1994 marked the achievement of representative democracy—and transferred responsibility for development to the new, democratically elected government. The developmental challenge facing the new democracy is twofold: to bring about sustainable growth and to facilitate redistribution—in part through job creation, and in part through the redirection of state expenditure. Both goals require an efficient and appropriate institutional framework to succeed.

In the 1990s, as White points out, the orthodox view of development is that 'development can best be promoted through a market-friendly state presiding over a predominantly capitalist economy operating within the political "shell" of a liberal democratic polity' (1995: 27). In the 'new' South Africa a commitment to this orthodoxy is widespread among political and economic elites. In practice, however, the political 'shell' of a liberal democratic polity can be filled with a wide range of different institutions, and the precise character of each set of institutions has very important consequences for both growth and redistribution.

A key feature of liberal democratic polities is the dispersion of authority between different state institutions. In South Africa, historical and political considerations have accentuated this dispersion. In this chapter we examine the implications for development of the relationships between key institutions: between different government departments, between parliamentary and corporatist modes of representation, and between central and provincial government (paying special attention to 'fiscal federalism'). The dispersion of authority between institutions also affects delivery. Given that there may be a relationship between delivery and the legitimacy (and hence sustainability) of democracy, we also examine this aspect of South Africa's political institutions.

Overall, the South African experience points to the severe difficulties facing democratic institutions in addressing poverty and inequality in a labour-surplus, middle-income economy. Redistribution in a democracy requires the co-ordination of public policy and the political empowerment of the poor. In order to enhance co-ordination, and sometimes to override sectional interests, governments are encouraged to centralize, curtailing the dispersion of authority. But the poor, rarely well organized and lacking resources, have weak voices at the national level. An egalitarian, democratic state must thus find a way of combining strong central direction with forms of institutional decentralization that strengthen the voices of the poor.

1. Visions of Development in the 'New' South Africa

In the 1994 elections, almost two-thirds of the electorate voted for a party—the African National Congress (ANC)—which was committed to a 'people-centred' vision of development, in which democracy and development dovetailed seamlessly at national and local levels. The ANC's vision of democracy and development was set out in its 1994 election manifesto, the Reconstruction and Development Programme (RDP). The RDP, which described itself as 'an integrated, coherent socio-economic policy-making policy framework' (ANC 1994: 1), identified an attack on poverty and deprivation as the first priority of a post-election, democratic government. The government's efforts would focus on infrastructural development—i.e. providing access to 'modern and effective services like electricity, water, telecommunications, transport, health, education and training' (ibid.: 6)—but extending to include also land reform, social security (and public works programmes), and labour policy reform. The Programme set some concrete goals, including the construction of at least one million houses and the redistribution of 30 per cent of the country's agricultural land within five years (ibid.: 22). But the RDP was not a plan with detailed targets, let alone mechanisms or costings. It was a statement of a vision, in which development meant, first and foremost, the satisfaction of basic needs.

Such a vision of development was unsurprising for a party with the overwhelming support of the poor in a country characterized by an extreme level of inequality. Life expectancy and adult literacy are lower, and infant mortality is higher, than in other middle-income economies. About 40 per cent of the population live in households with a per capita caloric intake below 2000 Kcal per day. About the same proportion have incomes below locally calculated poverty lines (World Bank 1995: 6–8). The incidence of poverty might be lower than in many other African countries (see World Bank 1997: 6–9), but its existence is especially glaring given that it coexists with considerable affluence. South Africa has as unequal a distribution of income as any other country for which there are reliable data. Data for 1993 indicate that the top income decile earns approximately half of the total income, or 100 times the share of the bottom income decile. The poorest five deciles earn just 11 per cent of the total (Seekings 1997: 6). South Africa's Gini coefficient is variously estimated at between 0.58 and 0.68 (World Bank 1997, Whiteford et al. 1995, McGrath and Whiteford 1994).

South Africa's very high level of inequality is the result of one and a half centuries of capitalist development—first in farming, then mining, and later manufacturing—unmatched in sub-Saharan Africa, and compounded by racial discrimination. By the 1970s South Africa's smallholder (or peasant) agricultural sector had been destroyed, through land dispossession in 'white'-owned areas and massive overcrowding in the 'reserves' (or 'homelands' and 'bantustans' as they were variously termed) (Simkins 1981, 1984). For well over thirty years, South Africans' incomes have depended on what is earned through the sale of labour power, mitigated somewhat through public welfare transfers. But large numbers of South Africans have been unable to find employment. Estimates of the unemployment rate in the 1990s range from 14 per cent to 43 per cent (Nattrass and Seekings 1996). A majority of households in each of the poorest four deciles has no members in employment—confining them to poverty and accentuating inequality (Seekings 1997: 11–14, 21–2).

Given the extent of inequality, it might have been expected that the RDP would have a more explicit focus on redistribution. In its first policy documents after its unbanning in 1990 the ANC had indeed called for 'growth through redistribution'. The ANC supported the call of its ally, the Congress of South African Trade Unions (COSATU), for a 'high-wage, low-cost' economy, with massive increases in social spending, land reform, and nationalization (ANC 1990; see Nattrass 1994: 346–50). The ANC retreated from this position in the face of warnings (from business, political opponents, and economists within as well as outside the ANC) of the dangers of macro-economic populism and increased unemployment. More conventional, market-friendly policies were proposed (ANC 1991, 1992), and endorsed at the ANC's Policy

Conference in 1992 (Nattrass 1994: 350–5). Unhappy with this strategic shift—and accompanying statements by ANC leaders that the trade unions' influence on the future government's macro-economic policies would be 'limited'—COSATU sought to bind the ANC to a 'reconstruction pact' in return for its electoral support. Unwilling to enter into any such pact, the ANC did agree to the trade unions making a substantial contribution to the drafting of the RDP (ibid.: 355–9). The result was a manifesto that combined an uneasy mix of radical and moderate themes and discourses.

One of the more radical aspects of the RDP vision was its emphasis on democratization. 'Thoroughgoing' democratization was represented as being central to the RDP vision of development. The RDP described development as a 'people-driven process'; it 'is not about the delivery of goods to a passive citizenry', but is rather 'about active involvement and growing empowerment' (ANC 1994: 5). The RDP laid stress on its 'commitment to grassroots, bottom-up development which is owned and driven by communities and their representative organizations' (ibid.: 15). The RDP also referred to 'deepening' democracy: 'Democracy is not confined to periodic elections. It is, rather, an active process enabling everyone to contribute to reconstruction and development' (ibid.: 7). Government institutions were called on to involve organizations in civil society in decision-making, and to 'facilitate direct democracy' through popular forums and referenda (ibid.: 120–1).

The RDP was undoubtedly a radical document in terms of its vision of egalitarian development and deepened democracy, but it was silent on many of the key issues. As Wolpe argued, it portrayed the challenges of reconstruction and development as free from contradiction and conflict.

What is absent . . . is any discussion of the politics of implementation. Indeed the very terms in which the RDP and the [subsequent] White Paper are cast submerges the central political issues. By this I mean the following: (a) firstly, while the RDP operates on a deeply contested terrain, in crucial respects it eradicates sources of contradiction and probable contestation and conflict by asserting harmony, (b) secondly, on this basis it constructs a consensual model of society which is the premise for the accomplishment of the goals of the RDP; and (c) thirdly, on the basis of this premise it also conceptualises the state as the unproblematic instrument of the RDP. (Wolpe 1995: 91)

This was manifested, on one level, in the absence of references to 'redistribution' in the RDP (with the 'R' in RDP standing resolutely for 'reconstruction' instead). In so far as resources were needed to fund the envisaged expenses, they would be released through 'restructuring' the budget and 'redirecting' existing revenues, and (quite explicitly) not through raising taxation as a share of GDP. At a deeper level, the RDP avoided any discussion of trade-offs between objectives. This enabled a wide range of parties to declare their support for it—and, indeed, following the election President Mandela insisted that the National Party (NP) and Inkatha Freedom Party (IFP) accept the RDP as a requirement for participation in the Government of National Unity. The RDP could—and did—become something that politicians could sprinkle over their speeches like holy water, an 'icon of the new South Africa' (Munslow and Fitzgerald 1995: 53).

2. *Central Government Co-ordination of Development*

The RDP said little about implementation in practice, but in a some-what airy final section did refer to the need for the 'thoroughgoing reform' of state institutions. This was deemed to be necessary to over-come 'structural weaknesses', including 'excessive departmentalism' and poor co-ordination, over-centralization at the national level, inadequate consultation, and a lack of transparency and accountability. Moreover, it continued, the RDP vision represented such a 'fundamental break' with the past that 'specific'—i.e. new—institutions would be required for its implementation at every level of government (ANC 1994: 136–9). The government's attempt to build new state institutions proved a failure. Notwithstanding the denunciation of 'over-centralization', the incoming government sought to centralize economic co-ordination through the establishment of a new institution—an RDP Office, run by a cabinet minister (the former trade unionist Jay Naidoo). The RDP Office had power over some of the funds formally allocated to the government departments, and so soon became embroiled in tense relationships with them. In a polity and society where government departments are responsive to different interests and pursue differ-ent agendas, such attempts to impose central direction are unlikely to be viable politically unless they are backed by powerful actors. The poor and unemployed are unlikely to be sufficiently powerful.

It is unclear why the ANC was so insistent on forming a new, co-ordinating institution. It may have been a legacy of a commandist approach to economics (the other rhetoric of the RDP notwithstand-ing). Alternatively, it might have been a concession to the ANC's allies and partners in drafting the RDP—i.e. COSATU, the South African Communist Party (SACP), and the South African National Civic Organization (SANCO)—who wanted institutions that would allow much greater participation by 'civil society' than was normal among government departments. It is also possible, of course, that the ANC

genuinely believed that it needed a co-ordinating structure to counter
'departmentalism' and so on. Two specific factors in the transition surely
reinforced such factors. First, the ANC itself did not control the Ministry of Finance. The interim constitution provided for a Government of
National Unity, although the ANC assumed a predominant role by
virtue of its massive electoral victory. An NP-nominated business-
man was appointed as Minister of Finance, in an apparent effort to
reassure local and international investors that there would be sound
macro-economic management. Secondly, many senior bureaucrats
appointed by the NP were guaranteed continued employment, and the
ANC may have felt that they would exert negative influence even in
departments with ANC ministers.

Whatever the initial motivation, the role of the RDP Office was soon
transformed. In June, an RDP Fund was established as part of the
first, post-election budget. The Fund received its income through
'top-slicing' departmental budgets. In line with the government's commitment to redirecting rather than simply increasing revenues (see
ANC 1994: 142–3), a share of the departmental budgets was transferred to the RDP Fund, and the departments then had to apply to
the Fund for disbursements. If the RDP Office decided that the projects were in line with the objectives of the RDP, then funding was
allocated. Departments who failed to come up with acceptable projects
would experience a real decline in their resources. R2.5 billion was
allocated to the RDP Fund in the 1994/5 budget, and it was proposed
that the allocation would rise by the same amount annually until it
reached R12.5 billion in 1998/9. The RDP Office was also responsible
for managing a set of high-profile 'Presidential Lead Projects', including sanitation projects, targeted free health services, and school feeding schemes.

The RDP Office and Fund were designed to have a catalytic influence on the process of budget reprioritization. In practice, financing
the Fund through top-slicing departmental budgets generated inevitable tensions between the line departments and the RDP Office.
Ministers resented having their budgets sliced and then having to apply
to the RDP Office for funding. Furthermore, departments were subject to delays in getting access to the money which (in many cases)
would have been allocated directly to them if the RDP Office did not
exist. Departmental hostility was further compounded when the RDP
Office proved to be dogged by inefficiency. In its first year of operation
the RDP Office only managed to allocate 55 per cent of the initial
RDP Fund. The image of the RDP Office was further dented by its
attempts to extend its control over the developmental activities of the

NGO sector. It instructed donors to channel their finance through the RDP Office, supposedly to ensure a co-ordinated process of integrated development. Although the policy was abandoned after donors withdrew their funding and many NGOs were forced to close down, the debacle reinforced a perception that the RDP Office was more concerned with control than delivery.

The publication of an RDP White Paper in late 1994 did little to clarify underlying uncertainty, or to propose ways round the growing institutional problems. By mid-1995 'the programme was clearly in difficulties, both practically and politically' (Blumenfeld 1997: 67). The RDP Fund was unable to allocate its budget in 1995–6 for the second year running. Eventually, in March 1996 the government shut down the RDP Office (ibid.: 69). The government has continued to claim that it is committed to the RDP in some general sense of commitment to basic needs provision and poverty alleviation, with control over the RDP passed to the vice-president's office, but in practice the experiment in institutional redesign was ended. Henceforth, the executive branch of central government was organized along orthodox departmental lines, with a heavy hand being wielded by the Department of Finance. There is thus some irony in the government's claim that the lack of delivery in the first half of its term of office was because 'the main emphasis . . . has been on planning and setting up the machinery for delivery' (RSA 1997: 2).

The RDP failed largely because it was unable to bridge the different interpretations of its role. As Blumenfeld writes, 'the RDP simply could not sustain its duality of purpose as both a general vision for transformation and a strategic mechanism for change' (1997: 87–8). Its attempts to gather control over development prompted, quite predictably, a series of institutional disputes with other government departments. Its inefficiency undermined further its arguments for central control. Finally, it seems to have made little headway in promoting a 'people-driven' and 'people-centred' process of development. Indeed, such a process might be at odds with the notion of an integrated and sustainable programme of development, since the latter requires a certain amount of control and direction. Certainly, the NGO sector might be more appropriate than a government department as a vehicle for people-centred development.

Soon after closing down the RDP Office, the government announced its new 'Growth, Employment and Redistribution Programme' or 'GEAR' (RSA 1996). GEAR presented a new vision in which growth generated new jobs and hence 'redistribution' (the term, so conspicuously absent from the RDP, now elevated into the very title of GEAR)

(Nattrass 1996). GEAR was produced by the Department of Finance, now under the control of an ANC minister, and at one level clearly reflected the triumph of that department within an orthodox pattern of institutional politics. GEAR provided the fullest expression yet of the ANC's commitment to fiscal conservatism. Whilst that commitment can be traced back at least as far as 1992 (as we saw above), the primacy of GEAR indicated a new sensitivity to financial markets and willingness to defy critics in COSATU, the SACP, and elsewhere.

At a deeper level, the adoption of GEAR reflected the weaknesses of the impulse towards centralized, commandist developmental institutions in the mid-1990s, especially in South Africa. Without strong support from the very top, and without a supportive consensus within the cabinet, an institution like the RDP Office was too vulnerable to orthodox patterns of institutional politics—patterns that seem to be entrenched in liberal democratic polities. Neither Nelson Mandela (the President) nor Thabo Mbeki (Vice-President) showed much concern with poverty and inequality (with Mandela, especially, focusing on reconciliation), and Jay Naidoo lacked seniority. Given the tight fiscal constraints, greater co-ordination might have been provided on a sustainable basis through a process of monitoring the line departments (and other levels of government) rather than by administering a budget directly.

The Department of Finance might have envisaged that it would co-ordinate the government's economic policies in the GEAR era, but it has not proved able to do this. There are important inconsistencies between the policies developed by different government departments. Whilst GEAR refers to the need for flexible labour markets, for example, the Department of Labour has been promoting inflexibility through aspects of the 1996 Labour Relations Act and the 1997 Basic Conditions of Employment Bill. The division of responsibility between numerous line departments (Labour, Public Works, Housing, Education, Welfare, Finance, Trade and Industry, and so on) has meant that no single institution has responsibility for addressing the big issues, most notably the need for policies to reduce unemployment and thereby poverty and inequality. The Department of Labour, for example, seems concerned with industrial relations to the exclusion of job creation. A system of central government comprising relatively autonomous departments might be appropriate in a society in which the challenges facing government are amenable to piecemeal reform. But in a society with such major developmental challenges as South Africa, a much higher degree of institutional co-ordination is surely necessary.

3. Corporatist Institutions

The closure of the RDP Office and the inability of the Department of Finance to secure a co-ordinating role in the GEAR era has left a major gap in the institutional architecture of the 'new' South Africa. One institution which has been touted as able to fill this gap is the corporatist National Economic, Development, and Labour Council (NEDLAC). The idea was to build a form of societal corporatism which would operate at the macro level (see Schmitter 1979, Cawson 1986). This ambitious role for NEDLAC was proposed by the ANC's more radical allies in the trade union movement (and elsewhere), whose influence seems to have waned with the closure of the RDP Office and the elevation of fiscal conservatism in GEAR.

Corporatism has been advocated widely as 'a way of organising the links between state, political society and civil society so as to create the political consensus, stability and capacity needed for longer-term developmental decision-making' (White 1995: 34). The South African experience affirms the warning made by White, that corporatism 'may have problematic distributive and redistributive consequences if the dominant coalition . . . only includes a relatively narrow, and relatively influential, section of society, the remainder being weakly represented or unrepresented in the political process' (ibid.). The poor and unemployed are largely excluded from South Africa's corporatist institutions at the national level, although those institutions play a major role in determining policies that have drastic implications for them.

NEDLAC's origins lie in part in the pre-1994 government's concerns to maintain stability in the face of the fast-growing independent trade unions, led by COSATU. COSATU-led protests and strikes against proposed reforms of labour relations legislation forced the NP government in 1990 to revamp the existing National Manpower Commission (NMC) into a tripartite body. After negotiations with labour and business, the NP Minister of Manpower conceded that 'no future legislation on labour relations shall be put before parliament unless considered by a (restructured) National Manpower Commission broadly representative of all the major actors in the labour relations area' (quoted in Baskin 1993: 1). In 1991 COSATU led a wide-reaching campaign against the introduction of value added tax (VAT), culminating in a threatened income tax boycott. Although the campaign did not prevent the introduction of VAT, COSATU was successful in its broader demand for the creation of a tripartite 'National Economic Forum' (NEF)—through which the unions envisaged having a greater voice in the design and implementation of economic policy.

The new NEF and restructured NMC gave COSATU a powerful base from which to negotiate with government and business about proposed economic and labour market policies. Agreements over South Africa's position on GATT, public works programmes, and drought relief were hammered out in the NEF during 1993 and 1994. But apart from the agreement on tariff reduction (which in any event was ignored by the Minister of Trade and Industry), these agreements tended to be over marginal aspects of state spending.

By the time the first democratic elections were held in April 1994, 'the corporatist current' was flowing strongly in South Africa (Maree 1993). In addition to the NEF, a range of more narrowly focused tripartite bodies had sprung up at the national level—including a National Housing Forum and a National Electricity Forum—as well as development forums at regional and local levels. At each level, the NP government had been forced to accommodate mass-based organizations —including, besides trade unions, SANCO and other 'civic' organizations in the townships—in order to avoid continuing protest. This move towards corporatist intermediation reflected the weakness of the old apartheid state which had neither the institutions nor the legitimacy to deal with the demands of previously excluded communities.

But the flowering of such corporatist institutions was not simply a 'managerial' form of concertation, as the close political relationship between COSATU (and the civic organizations) and the ANC also constituted a 'foundational pact' (to use the distinction made by Karl (1990), cited in Haggard and Kaufman (1995: 340)). In South Africa, as in Spain in the 1970s, a pact between organized labour and other political groupings was central to the success of democratization. This was in large part a consequence of the strength of the independent labour movement and the role it played in resisting apartheid, which in turn reflected social and economic conditions in South Africa. By the 1970s industrialization had produced a large urban, industrial working class, with a large semi-skilled workforce providing fertile soil for unionization. Industrialization had also produced capitalist elites who relied on the market rather than on state repression to secure labour power, and were willing to concede trade union rights (and accept democratization) in return for a degree of industrial (and political) stability. The labour movement was thus able to play major roles in the struggle for political change, leading to their inclusion in a foundational pact with the ANC.

South African corporatism thus involved the institutions of managerial concertation alongside the politics of a foundational pact. Haggard and

Kaufman note that such foundational pacts generally do not lead to the resolution of key economic questions (1995: 340–1). The South African experience conforms to this general pattern.

NEDLAC was established in 1995, under parliamentary legislation enacted the previous year. The Nedlac Act set the following objects and functions for the Council:

(a) to strive to promote the goals of economic growth, participation in decision-making, and social equity;
(b) to seek to reach consensus and conclude agreements on matters pertaining to social and economic policy;
(c) to consider all proposed labour legislation relating to labour market policy before it is introduced in Parliament;
(d) to consider all significant changes to social and economic policy before it is implemented or introduced in Parliament;
(e) to encourage and promote the formulation of co-ordinated policy on social and economic matters.

'Social and economic policy' is defined in the Act as including 'financial, fiscal and monetary policy, socio-economic programmes, trade and industrial policy, reconstruction and development programmes and all aspects of labour market policy, including training and human resource development'. The NMC and NEF were disbanded and their functions were taken over by NEDLAC.

NEDLAC is a statutory body with four chambers, focused on the labour market, trade and industry, public finance and monetary policy, and 'development' respectively. NEDLAC is for the most part tripartite in nature, with representatives from government, organized labour, and business. The development chamber also provides for representation of the 'community', through four nationwide so-called 'community' organizations—SANCO, the National Women's Coalition, the National Youth Development Forum, and the Federal Council for the Disabled.

In practice, NEDLAC's role has been restricted to a relatively limited range of 'social and economic policy'. Only with respect to labour policy has NEDLAC played a major role. The Council's major success has been the negotiation of a new Labour Relations Act, with other agreements concerning small business policy and training. NEDLAC has not contributed significantly to policy-making in other areas of 'social and economic policy', including the whole GEAR programme.

Moreover, NEDLAC has not functioned smoothly even with respect to labour policy. Having agreed to the inclusion of employers' right to lock out workers alongside labour's right to strike in the Labour Relations Act, COSATU took to the streets in April 1996 to pressurize

Parliament not to accord lockouts and strikes equal status in the constitution. This caused anger and resentment within business ranks (Lundahl and Petersson 1996: 21), and cast doubt on labour's commitment to negotiated agreements in NEDLAC. More importantly, business and labour were unable to reach consensus in NEDLAC over a Basic Conditions of Employment Bill in 1997. When negotiations stalled, COSATU threatened widespread strike action in support of its demands for a forty-hour week and various forms of protection. The Minister of Labour negotiated with labour and business, but eventually lost patience and submitted a bill to Parliament. Amidst howls of protest from labour, the director-general of the Department of Labour stated that NEDLAC needed a 'shake-up' and that NEDLAC's powers should be curtailed because 'government could not be conducted by collective bargaining' (*Business Day*, 2 Sept. 1997). Moreover, as NEDLAC's executive director admits, business and labour are still very far from consensus on the 'bigger issues' of labour market flexibility, employment creation, and fiscal and monetary policy (*Business Day*, 4 Sept. 1997).

The dispute over the Basic Conditions of Employment Bill raises fundamental institutional and distributional questions. What is the appropriate mix between corporatist and parliamentary modes of democratic representation? How should resources be distributed between business and labour (i.e. between profits and wages) and between employed workers and the unemployed (i.e. wages, and total labour costs, and jobs)? Each of these issues has profound implications for the others. Do—or how can—corporatist institutions in a labour-surplus economy play roles that are conducive to 'development', if by development we mean rising living standards for the poor?

In South Africa, both inequality and poverty are rooted in the labour market. Data for 1993 indicate that over half of the households in each of the bottom four income deciles had no members in employment. There are low-paid workers—mostly farmworkers and domestic workers—in the poorest half of the population. But the bases of the trade union movement, i.e. the industrial working class and public sector workers—are concentrated in the top five deciles (Seekings 1997: 21–3). Bhorat et al. (1995), using the same data, found that the income gap between the unemployed and the employed is a major determinant of inequality. They estimated that wage income inequality contributed 73.5 per cent of total inequality, and that the gap between the unemployed (with no wage income) and average wage earners contributed a staggering 45 per cent to the wage income Gini coefficient. There is currently no public welfare provision for most unemployed people. Remittances sent by workers to other, poorer households serve as one mechanism for redistribution, but the total value of inter-household remittances is just one-twentieth of the total value of wage income in society (Seekings 1997: 9).

In a labour-surplus economy where poverty is so closely linked to unemployment, job creation has a significant impact on poverty (and inequality) even if wages are low in the new jobs. An egalitarian development strategy must involve, above all, labour-intensive growth. There are doubts, however, over whether corporatist institutions such as NEDLAC will support the kinds of policies required for labour-intensive growth. Whatever disagreements there may be between organized labour and business, neither articulates the concerns of the unemployed except in so far as these happen to overlap with their own interests. The representation of the 'community' is tokenistic, and in any case is confined to the development chamber. None of the 'community' organizations represents the unemployed. There are some sections of the Labour Relations Act which illustrate the prospective pitfalls of excluding the unemployed. These provide for the extension of centrally bargained agreements to firms—and workers—that were not party to the negotiations, thereby allowing high wages to be protected at the cost of low-wage jobs (Nattrass and Seekings 1997a). Similarly, the 1997 Basic Conditions of Employment Bill contains a number of provisions likely to inhibit job creation.

Not only might NEDLAC be of mixed value in developmental terms, but it might also be of questionable democratic value. Should labour get 'two bites at the cherry', the first through elected representatives in Parliament and the second through representatives on NEDLAC? In practice, organized labour would continue to have two bites at the democratic cherry even if NEDLAC was abolished, through lobbying their allies in the ANC. Indeed, organized labour might have an even greater impact on economic policy if it devoted its activities entirely towards lobbying the ANC.

One answer to these questions is social democratic in origin. If NEDLAC can facilitate an agreement which dampens the inflationary consequences of distributional conflict, then this will be a win–win situation for everybody. In such a situation, there is no necessary conflict of interest between employed labour, the unemployed, and consumers. By solving a collective-action problem, each party stands to secure benefits on a sustainable basis. The ideal type was the experience of the 'Scandanavian model' which operated by keeping wage growth in line with productivity—to the advantage of both workers and employers (Henley and Tsakalotos 1993: 156). NEDLAC's strategic documents support this social democratic slant (NEDLAC 1995). There have also been calls in various government documents for

NEDLAC to forge national-level agreements between labour and capital which would promote favourable macro-economic outcomes. The report of the Presidential Commission of Inquiry into Labour Market Policy (LMC 1996), for example, goes as far as suggesting that a national social accord should be struck in NEDLAC over wages, prices, and investment, i.e. a type of incomes policy. Similarly, a gesture in the direction of a national agreement to ensure that wages rise in line with productivity can be found in the government's macro-economic strategy document, GEAR (RSA 1996), although how this could be forged is left unclear.

It is questionable, however, whether organized labour and business are really in a position to start negotiating ambitious accords at the national level. First, there is little indication that organized labour is interested in social accords which entail wage restraint (see NEDLAC Labour Caucus 1996). Trade unions are under pressure to deliver benefits to their members now, whilst the government has a longer time horizon. The ANC's time-horizon is probably 2004, i.e. the country's third general election (the second being scheduled for 1999), when its majority may no longer be assured. Secondly, it is a moot point whether the 'social partners' are sufficiently strongly and comprehensively organized that they could articulate a coherent position and deliver their membership in support of such accords even if they wanted to (Sellars 1997). Organized labour experiences capacity problems when negotiating in NEDLAC—in part because many of the most able union organizers left to take up state employment and those that remained had hectic work schedules (Naledi 1994, Sellars 1997: 16–17, Lundahl and Petersson 1996: 25–7). Furthermore, COSATU is a federation of unions which bargain over wages at the industry level, limiting the scope for COSATU itself to enter into agreements about wages at national level. Likewise, business representation in NEDLAC comprises a loose coalition with no capacity to ensure that members comply with agreements (Nattrass 1997a). These organizational limitations, coupled with the existence of industrial-level wage-bargaining institutions, constrain the range of feasible bargains which could be negotiated in NEDLAC.

If NEDLAC is unlikely to deliver the social accord desired by government, and if it continues to block or delay legislation, then government criticisms of NEDLAC are likely to intensify. The fall-back justification of NEDLAC, i.e. that it is better to have organized interest groups negotiating in a transparent manner in NEDLAC than engaged in private lobbying of government, will be less and less compelling as organized labour and business continue to engage in both. The Labour Minister has warned the social partners on several occasions that unless they show increased commitment to NEDLAC and to reaching compromises within its structures, the government will take over decision-making entirely (Lundahl and Petersson 1996: 35).

The existence of corporatist institutions, especially NEDLAC, gave rise to an expectation that there would be a high degree of concertation around social and economic policy-making, but in practice there has been very little. Having disbanded the RDP Office, the government was certainly not going to cede control of the overall direction of public policy to either labour or business, especially when the dominant government department—Finance—was particularly suspicious of labour. It would be reassuring if the government was motivated by a concern with inequality and job creation, and therefore sought to curtail an institution that empowered business (concerned with profits and accumulation) and organized labour (concerned with wages and the protection of existing privileges). But the low priority attached to job creation by the government suggests that the real reason for the hostility to NEDLAC might be institutional jealousy and a concern for control *per se*.

The exclusionary character of corporatist institutions has led some scholars to advocate a complementary 'micro-strategy . . . based on a commitment to associational mobilisation of politically marginalised groups which function both as an alternative development agency to the state and as a source of political pressure on the state' (White 1995: 34). Certainly, such mobilization would help to deepen democracy (and, in South Africa, would be consistent with the RDP). But such a strategy does not exclude other institutional reforms which enhance the voices of the poor in public policy-making and implementation. A degree of decentralization is important here, as local political institutions are likely to be more responsive to the needs of the poor locally.

This is true of corporatism as much as of electoral forms of representation. Furthermore, the optimal mix of corporatist and other democratic forms of representation may be obtained more easily at local levels where development needs can be clearly identified, collective-action problems are more easily overcome, and where transparent and accountable forms of governance can be forged (see Nattrass 1997b). Corporatist negotiations at community level are more likely to be sensitive to the unemployment problem and the need to redistribute resources to the needy. In the Eastern Cape, for example, COSATU initiated an accord in the city of Port Elizabeth, whereby workers would allow the compulsory deduction of mortgage and municipal service charges from their wages as part of their contribution to improving local government finances and resolving the housing crisis. In that the unemployed and poor benefit from municipal services, this results in redistribution. This is the first example of COSATU agreeing to a deal where the benefits extend beyond union members (although

COSATU rejected the extension of this scheme on a provincial basis) (ibid.). In the South African case (as, no doubt, in many others), over-decentralization can constrain redistribution, if powers are decentralized to pockets of affluence which use those powers to maintain their privileges. But there remains considerable scope for decentralization to provincial and local levels.

4. Problems of Developmental Delivery

It is widely held that, in new democracies characterized by poverty and inequality, the legitimacy and sustainability of democracy as a political system depend on the performance of governments in delivering developmental benefits to the citizenry. The capacity of institutions to deliver supposedly thus assumes an importance beyond improving living conditions to sustaining democracy itself. In South Africa, contrary to conventional wisdom, the evidence suggests that most citizens do not expect their living standards to rise quickly as a result of the transition to democracy; a lack of delivery is unlikely to lead to disillusionment with democracy itself in the short or medium terms (Nattrass and Seekings 1997*b*). None the less, it remains important to examine the delivery capacity of institutions in democratic polities. Institutional capacity has distributional implications regardless of its effects on the legitimacy of the political system. Redistributive policies are worthless if they cannot be implemented.

In South Africa, in 1994, the ANC promised the voters 'A Better Life For All' (Lodge 1994, Eldridge and Seekings 1996). Two and a half years later, the ANC-led government claimed it had 'laid the foundation for a better life'—but acknowledges that such a foundation is not the same thing as a better life already. The ANC claimed that its major successes had been in the political field, with lower levels of political violence and no civil war. In terms of 'reconstruction and development', the ANC claimed significant progress in areas such as school feeding schemes, primary health care, access to clean water, and electrification (see RSA 1997, Mandela in *Hansard*, 15 Apr. 1997). But in the key areas of employment and housing, progress had been limited. Of course, the government's finances have been constrained, but poor institutional co-ordination and efficiency were important factors in the lack of delivery.

All the provinces are struggling to get housing projects going (Cattell 1997). As can be seen in Table 7.1, all except two provinces have failed to spend even half of the total funding available for housing subsidies.

TABLE 7.1. *Indicators of provincial capacity problems*

	Community-Based Public Works Programme (% of funds)		Provincial housing subsidy[a] allocation
	Allocated	Disbursed	% spent
Eastern Cape	82	70	16
Mpumalanga	100	69	53
Free State	58	n/a	63
KwaZulu/Natal	79	8	28
Northern Cape	97	70	42
Northern Province	73	66	18
North-west Province	92	73	30
Western Cape	84	80	47
Gauteng	100	69	55

[a] Includes housing commitments from the previous dispensation.
Sources: Abedian (1997), Cattell (1997).

One of the biggest problems facing the new government has been the lack of capacity to deliver at all levels of government. This is partly to do with the chaos which surrounded the reintegration of the old homeland bureaucracies into provincial governments, and partly to do with the lack of skilled manpower, particularly at local and regional levels. An example of how delivery problems have affected government's attempts at development is the saga of the Community-Based Public Works Programme (CBPWP). When the RDP Fund was created, R250 million was put into a dedicated fund to facilitate the rapid delivery of much needed community facilities through labour-intensive methods. The short-term component of the fund was officially implemented as the CBPWP. Government bodies and NGOs would be given access to these funds for acceptable projects. This institutional arrangement for development delivery ran into a set of practical and political problems. Conflict immediately ensued between the Department of Labour, the Department of Public Works, and the RDP Office. Control of the public works programme was won by the Department of Public Works. R150 million of the CBPWP funds was allocated to the provinces (with more going to the poorer provinces than the richer ones), with most of the remaining R100 million allocated to NGOs (including R70 million to the Independent Development Trust (IDT), R12 million to the 'Sikhaya' project of the South African Sugar Association, and R4 million to the Transkei Community School Building Trust).

The provinces and NGOs had very mixed success in allocating and disbursing the funds. Bureaucratic delays resulted in the NGOs only receiving their allocations in late 1995. Nevertheless, by the final quarter of 1996, the IDT and Sikhaya project had spent their allocations on about 500 employment projects in poor areas (Abedian 1997). Delivery was poor, by contrast, on the part of the provinces (and the Transkei Community School Building Trust). As can be seen in Table 7.1, the worst performer was KwaZulu/Natal Province which succeeded only in dispersing a mere 8 per cent of its allocation in 1996/7. Only Gauteng and Mpumalanga had earmarked all of their funds for specific projects and they were only able to disburse 69 per cent of the money. The poor delivery seems to have been due to poor management, uncertainty about financial flows, and unclear lines of accountability (ibid.), i.e. a generally 'weak institutional base from which to assess, plan and manage public works applications and programmes' (Breslin et al. 1997: 34). Only R140 million of the original R250 million was spent by 1997 (most of this by the IDT and Sikhaya project). Available data indicate that 3.8 million labour days of employment were created. Taking dependency ratios into account, about 2 million poor people were direct beneficiaries of the programme (Abedian 1997).

The Department of Public Works has not had much success in promoting the use of labour-intensive construction methods. The public works programme in the Northern Province—South Africa's poorest province with the highest unemployment rate—is in fact capital intensive, with only 9 per cent of the total budget allocated to labour costs (Breslin et al. 1997: 35). As Breslin et al. (ibid.) comment:

It is alarming that project proposals with such low proportions of their budget allocated to labour are accepted by the tender boards as 'labour-intensive'. This suggests that a great deal of capacity building remains to be done. The end result is that fewer jobs are being created than is feasible, even with the currently low levels of disbursement, and the potential direct and indirect impact that increased levels of income could have had locally have not been realised.

Other problems include inadequate training at community level to service and maintain new infrastructure (such as local water supply) provided through public works programmes, and the failure to co-ordinate with other departments over the design and implementation of projects. Thus, for example, thirty clinics, built as part of a public works programme, lie abandoned in the Northern Province because the Department of Health lacks the resources to staff them (ibid.).

The poorer provinces, like the Eastern Cape and the Northern Province, experienced the most difficulties with budgeting, planning, and delivering—largely due to the chaotic state of administration in the former homelands or bantustans (Khumalo 1997, Mamabolo 1997). Across the whole country, however, administrative problems have been compounded by the effects of 'fiscal federalism'.

5. Fiscal Federalism

The relationships between different levels of government are of great importance in a country, such as South Africa, where inequality has a geographical dimension. Decentralization can strengthen the political voice of poorer sections of the population—but it can also enable relatively privileged groups to maintain their privileges beneath the rhetoric of democratic self-determination. In South Africa, historical and political circumstances produced a quasi-federal constitution, but the national government has sought to restrict the provinces' room for manœuvre. The result is an untidy system in which neither developmental nor democratic goals are fully realized.

In South Africa, poverty is concentrated in the predominantly rural provinces (most markedly, in the Northern Province and Eastern Cape). These provinces have the highest dependency ratios, the lowest monthly household incomes, poor access to running water, and relatively low per capita health spending (see Table 7.2). As the majority of the population live in these provinces, any development strategy clearly requires a redistributive allocation of funding to these provinces.

Inter-provincial redistribution by fiscal means is complicated, however, by the quasi-federal character of South Africa's political arrangements. Whilst falling short of federalism, the interim and final constitutions grant the provinces a range of powers and functions. These include heavy responsibilities in the delivery of social services, health, education, and welfare (comprising primarily non-contributory old-age pensions). Together, these three functions absorb about 80 per cent of provincial budgets (Simkins 1997: 8). The framework created by the national legislation supposedly gives the provinces considerable discretion in resource allocation. In practice, much provincial spending, including public sector salaries, is set nationally. Provinces are obliged to comply with the wages and conditions bargained at national level. As Ajam (1997: 10) puts it, 'There seems to be a tension emerging between fiscal decentralisation and centralised wage bargaining, provincial autonomy versus national standards and

TABLE 7.2. *Provincial indicators*

	Poverty rate %	Dependency ratio	% distribution of pop.	% urban	% with water supply[a]	Monthly household income	Govt spending per capita[b] Health	Welfare
Western Cape	23	1.2	9.2	94.9	93.3	R3,234	R532	R537
Northern Cape	57	1.8	1.4	90.0	88.5	R1,225	R345	R532
Eastern Cape	78	2.0	16.0	28.1	31.0	R1,098	R328	R370
KwaZulu/Natal	53	2.3	20.6	34.6	45.7	R1,705	R337	R341
Free State	66	1.4	6.9	61.6	49.9	R2,161	R388	R301
Mpumalanga	52	1.7	8.7	25.7	50.4	R2,057	R225	R244
Northern Prov.	77	2.6	12.3	7.8	21.4	R971	R256	R273
North West	57	1.4	8.2	12.2	52.9	R1,301	R260	R276
Gauteng	19	1.1	16.9	98.9	94.5	R3,442	R470	R223
Total	53	1.7	100.0	46.7	59.1	R2,089	R364	R321

Note: The poverty rate is defined as the poorest 40 per cent of households.

[a] Internal water supply or yard tap.
[b] Health (1997/8), welfare (1996/7).

Sources: SALDRU (1994), Strachan (1997), World Bank (1995: 10), De Bruyn (1997: 6).

redistributory objectives.' The level of welfare benefits is also set nationally. Given their limited capacity to raise additional revenue (own revenue is generally less than 5 per cent of total provincial expenditure), the provinces have little room for manœuvre.

Nevertheless, this emerging (albeit limited) form of fiscal federalism is a distinct improvement over the way that the old apartheid government dealt with government expenditure at second-tier level. According to Simkins (1997: 1):

That system was ramshackle and particularist, in that it had different arrangements for provinces, self-governing territories and TBVC [i.e. the four supposedly independent states of Transkei, Bophuthatswana, Venda, and Ciskei]. All these arrangements were subject to arbitrary political intervention. Although there were moves towards equality of entitlement in some aspects of expenditure, equality was not the main concern of the system as a whole.

Two new institutions have been created to help with the allocation of funding to the provinces, and to co-ordinate national and provincial budgeting: a Financial and Fiscal Commission (FFC) and a Budget Council. The FFC is a constitutional body which was created to help depoliticize the allocation of funding to the provinces. The FFC is empowered to make recommendations regarding the financial and fiscal requirements of all three tiers of government. This includes matters relating to taxation, borrowing, and the division of resources between the provinces. For the 1997/8 budget, the FFC suggested that resources be divided between the provinces according to a formula which essentially allocates funding in accordance with population distribution, with an added weighting of 1.25 for rural people as a proxy for deprivation. As can be seen in Table 7.2, the poorest provinces are indeed those with the lowest level of urbanization. These recommendations were broadly followed by the Budget Council.

The Budget Council is an executive institution consisting of the national minister and deputy-minister of Finance, the provincial ministers for finance, and officials from the Departments of Finance and State Expenditure and the provincial treasuries. For the 1997/8 budget, the Budget Council first subtracted from total revenue the interest due on government debt and amounts set aside for improvements in the conditions of service. After these 'top-slice' amounts were set aside, the Budget Council recommended that the remainder be divided between national and provincial tiers in the same ratio as had applied previously. The allocation between the provinces was then determined according to the FFC's formula. Revenues are allocated to the provinces as 'block grants'. Provinces are then free to allocate the money as they please—subject of course to meeting existing obligations and complying with nationally determined minima and salaries. This means that the national government cannot know for sure exactly how much money is going to be spent in the country on health, education, and welfare, as the allocation decisions will be made in nine separate budgets. This situation is a far cry from the centralizing and co-ordinating notion behind the original RDP.

Decentralizing spending decisions in this way has potential benefits for development. It could facilitate greater public participation in debates about resource allocation, spending decisions may be more sensitive to local needs and lines of accountability and responsibility may be clearer. But the national government's provision of 95 per cent of provincial revenues means that lines of fiscal accountability run more from provincial to national government rather than from provincial government to the provincial electorate. It is also easy for provincial governments to shift the blame for any of their own inefficiencies and poor decisions to the national government, attributing them to supposedly inadequate funding. The NP-controlled Western Cape government has developed this strategy into a fine art, accusing the ANC-led national government of discriminating against the province.

There is also considerable doubt about the capacity of the provinces to deliver, as we have already seen. Barnes and Morris (1997) provide a case study of the institutional problems in KwaZulu/Natal—which (like the Western Cape) is not controlled by the ANC (but by the Inkatha Freedom Party). They start off by pointing to problems with the relationship between national and provincial development activities. Poor co-ordination between national departments (such as Water Affairs and Forestry, Land Affairs, and Mineral and Energy Affairs) and the provincial government results in poor strategic planning. Furthermore, national departments have often undermined local government structures by setting up specific 'community' structures to deal with water and electricity provision.

Most importantly, in this province, institutional responsibilities reflect past and present political concerns. The institutional system was not designed in an ahistorical and apolitical vacuum, but was instead the outcome of political bargaining and calculations at different levels, with powerful political groupings often aligned with pre-existing institutions. The KwaZulu/Natal administration comprises the amalgamated administrations of the former white province of Natal and the KwaZulu bantustan. The result was an unwieldy and incompetent bureaucracy, structured more to alleviate political discord than to establish competent provincial governance. For example, the provincial Department of Conservation and Traditional Affairs operates independently of the other nine departments and has complete jurisdiction over all those areas previously classified as 'tribal' under apartheid. Barnes and Morris argue that the primary aim of this department is to establish political hegemony over the tribal areas, and that this goal militates against co-operation with other departments and NGOs in the development field. In their view, there is an urgent need to reorient that department from being a jurisdictional department encompassing specific geographical areas, to a line function department focusing specifically on traditional cultural issues. They make a similar argument with respect to the Department of Agriculture and Rural Development, which also operates with a geographical jurisdiction. The Inkatha Freedom Party draws most of its support from rural areas, and is keen to maintain its hegemony there through supportive chiefs and specialist provincial government departments. The result is, however, an inefficient mix of departments with geographical jurisdiction (controlled by Inkatha) and ones with line functions (some of which are headed by ANC ministers in the 'government of provincial unity').

The other rural provinces do not share the politically driven problems of KwaZulu/Natal, but most seem to suffer severe administrative problems. In the Eastern Cape, for example, where the part of the old (white) Cape provincial administration was amalgamated with the homeland administrations of Transkei and Ciskei, government is not organized solely along line functions. The difficulties experienced in this province concern mismanagement (Khumalo 1997) and the complete collapse of service provision at local level within the former homeland areas.

If there is a bright side to the Eastern Cape story, it is perhaps the fact that the manifest capacity problems facing the Eastern Cape government led to the creation in 1995 of an Eastern Cape Socio-Economic Consultative Council (ECSECC), a forum bringing together the provincial government, labour, business, and the NGO sector, and modelled loosely on NEDLAC. ECSECC's principal objective is:

to advise and assist the provincial government to achieve an integrated development strategy for the province and its constituent regions, in order to address the economic development of the province in terms of the RDP, and in particular the needs of the deprived communities and underdeveloped areas. (quoted in Nattrass 1997*b*: 108)

Although ECSECC has experienced problems as a result of internecine conflict within the business caucus as well as conflict between organized labour and business (Nattrass 1997*b*), ECSECC's 'Operational Team' introduced a set of projects which have proved helpful to the regional government. These include a pilot project to provide performance evaluations within government structures; mobilizing local expertise to prevent government from wasting money on expensive outside consultants; helping government to co-ordinate its various strategic planning initiatives; and helping the government to transform the old planning infrastructure.

6. Conclusion

Development in a highly inegalitarian, labour-surplus economy such as South Africa requires institutions that are both responsive to the poor and capable of co-ordinating potentially disparate public policies. Building such institutions requires overcoming different kinds of obstacles. Some of the obstacles are institutional, in that line departments will oppose the transfer of resources and powers to other institutions (such as the RDP Office). In a conventional demarcation of departmental responsibilities, it can be the most serious problems (such as unemployment) which fall through the cracks. Other obstacles are political, in that the poor are generally weakly organized and do not have loud voices in the political arena. Still others are entrenched in the constitution, such as the division of responsibilities without corresponding powers of taxation to the provinces.

The precise form of these obstacles might be specific to South Africa, but these kinds of obstacles are endemic in liberal democratic polities in the inegalitarian societies where many 'new' democracies have been established. Liberal democratic polities are generally characterized by the dispersion of power between government departments and often between different levels of government. How the tensions between different parts of the state are managed is of great importance to the quality of both democracy and development. Liberal democratic polities are also generally characterized by marked political inequalities, despite the formal equality of the vote (the importance of which can be reduced through electoral arrangements such as, in South Africa's case, proportional representation with centralized party lists). The voices of the poor can seldom compete with those of privileged groups (capital, the professional middle class, the organized working class, and—in South Africa—the aspirant black bourgeoisie). Finally, many of the 'new' liberal democracies have been established in pacted transitions, with the constitutions reflecting political bargaining between old and new elites. In many cases the former elites seek to retain some power through constitutional provisions for coalition governments as well as restrain the incoming elites through constitutionally entrenched divisions of powers. This can have the effect of emaciating democracy, through removing political opposition after the transition (Jung and Shapiro 1995), and producing chronically poor co-ordination with respect to development.

In the South African case, the failure and closure of the RDP Office, the narrow scope of the Department of Finance, and the reluctance of the president and deputy president have left central government without an institution capable of providing co-ordination and direction to social and economic policy. The government has been unwilling to allow NEDLAC to play this role (and the other participants in NEDLAC might stymie any attempt to play this role even if the government allowed it). The result is that policy-making and implementation have been subject to inconsistency and a lack of direction, notwithstanding the visions provided in the original RDP and, later, GEAR.

The major problem with allowing NEDLAC to play a more important role is its exclusive composition. NEDLAC excludes, in practice, the voice of the very poor, providing instead for the expression of the interests of the urban working class and middle class, as well as business. The electoral system (based on proportional representation) may insulate political parties from local electoral pressure, but the ANC will have to be more responsive in the long term to the concerns of the rural poor than the unions have ever been. In South Africa, therefore, there is a strong argument that parliamentary forms of representation and voice should take clear precedence over corporatist forms of representation at the national level. At the provincial and local levels, there is a stronger case for corporatist institutions, such as the Eastern Cape and Port Elizabeth initiatives discussed above, as well as initiatives at the local level elsewhere—for examples, see Ndlovu and Fairhurst (1996) and Nel and Hill (1996).

If the mix of corporatist and political institutions is more likely to be conducive to development at local level, then Barnes and Morris are correct to emphasize the need to build democratic and effective democratic institutions at the local level. By creating the institutional environment for meaningful popular participation in development, the developmental vision behind the RDP may well eventually take shape. But it would be wrong to think that local, democratic institutions can be effective without effective co-ordination at the top. A democratic, developmental state must combine decentralization with strong central direction. This combination is politically unlikely in that any government which achieves its desired centralized co-ordination is unlikely to decentralize authority. But South Africa, unfortunately, seems to be some way away from either goal.

REFERENCES

Abedian, I. (1997), 'Provincial Delivery Hamstrings Successful Programme', *Budget Watch*, 3/2, June: 7.

Ajam, T. (1997), 'The Evolution of Devolution: Fiscal Decentralisation in South Africa', paper presented at the Development Policy Research Unit, University of Cape Town, 16 Sept.

ANC (1990), *Discussion Document on Economic Policy*, Johannesburg: ANC, Department of Economic Policy.

—— (1991), *Draft Resolution on ANC Economic Policy for National Conference*, Johannesburg: African National Congress, May.

—— (1992), *ANC Policy Guidelines for a Democratic South Africa: Document for Discussion*, Johannesburg: ANC, Department of Economic Policy.

—— (1994), *The Reconstruction and Development Programme: A Policy Framework*, Johannesburg: ANC.

Barnes, J., and Morris, M. (1997), 'KwaZulu-Natal's Rural Institutional Environment: Its Impact on Local Service Delivery', *Development Southern Africa*, 14/2: 185–210.

Baskin, J. (1993), 'Corporatism: Some Obstacles Facing the South African Labour Movement', Centre for Policy Studies, Social Contract Series, Research Report no. 3, Johannesburg, Apr.

Bhorat, H., Leibbrandt, M., and Woolard, I. (1995), 'Towards an Understanding of South Africa's Inequality', paper delivered at the African Economic Research Consortium Conference, Johannesburg, Dec.

Blumenfeld, J. (1997), 'From Icon to Scapegoat? The Experience of South Africa's Reconstruction and Development Programme'. *Development Policy Review*, 15: 65–91.

Breslin, E., Delius, P., and Madrid, C. (1997), 'Strengthening Institutional Safety Nets in South Africa: Sharing Operation Hunger's Insights and Experiences', *Development Southern Africa*, 14/1: 21–41.

Cattell, K. (1997), 'Housing Vote Allocations under Spotlight', *Budget Watch*, 3/2, June: 5.

Cawson, A. (1986), *Corporatism and Political Theory*, Oxford: Basil Blackwell.

De Bruyn, J. (1997), 'FFC: No Bite, but a Lot of Bark', *Budget Watch*, 3/2, June: 6.

Eldridge, M., and Seekings, J. (1996), 'Mandela's Lost Province: The African National Congress and the Western Cape Electorate in the 1994 South African Elections', *Journal of Southern African Studies*, 22/4, Dec.: 517–40.

Haggard, S., and Kaufman, R. (1995), *The Political Economy of Democratic Transitions*, Princeton: Princeton University Press.

Henley, A., and Tsakalotos, E. (1993), *Corporatism and Economic Performance: A Comparative Analysis of Market Economies*, Cheltenham: Edward Elgar.

Jung, C., and Shapiro, I. (1995), 'South Africa's Negotiated Transition: Democracy, Opposition and the New Constitutional Order', *Politics and Society*, 23/3, Sept.: 269–308.

Karl, T. (1990), 'Dilemmas of Democratisation in Latin America', *Comparative Politics*, 23: 1–21.

Khumalo, B. (1997), 'Eastern Cape: Legacy of Homeland Civil Service Poses Challenge', *Budget Watch*, 3/1, Mar.: 7.

LMC (Labour Market Commission) (1996), *Restructuring the South African Labour Market*, Report of the Presidential Commission of Inquiry into Labour Market Policy, Cape Town.

Lodge, T. (1994), 'The African National Congress and its Allies', in A. Reynolds (ed.), *Election'94 South Africa: The Campaigns, Results and Future Prospects*, Cape Town: David Philip.

Lundahl, H., and Petersson, C. (1996), 'NEDLAC: A Boxing Ring or a Negotiating Forum?', Lund: Lund University, Department of Political Science, Autumn.

McGrath, M., and Whiteford, A. (1994), 'Inequality in the Size Distribution of Income in South Africa', Occasional Paper no. 10, Stellenbosch Economic Project.

Mamabolo, S. (1997), 'Northern Province: System Marked by Competition for Resources', *Budget Watch*, 3/1, Mar.: 8.

Maree, J. (1993), 'Trade Unions and Corporatism in South Africa', *Transformation*, 21: 24–54.

Munslow, B., and Fitzgerald, P. (1995), 'The Reconstruction and Development Programme', in P. Fitzgerald, A. Mclennan, and B. Munslow (eds.), *Managing Sustainable Development in Southern Africa*, Cape Town: Oxford University Press.

Naledi (1994), *Unions in Transition: COSATU at the Dawn of Democracy*, Johannesburg: Naledi.

Nattrass, N. (1994), 'Politics and Economics in ANC Economic Policy', *African Affairs*, 93/372, July: 343–59.

—— (1996), 'Gambling on Investment: Competing Economic Strategies in South Africa', *Transformation*, 31: 25–42.

—— (1997*a*), *Business and Employer Organisations in South Africa*, Occasional Report no. 5, Geneva: Employment and Training Department, International Labour Office.

—— (1997*b*), 'Collective Action Problems and the Role of South African Business in National and Regional Accords', *South African Journal of Business Management*, 28/3: 105–12.

—— and Seekings, J. (1996), 'Changing Patterns of Inequality in the South African Labour Market', paper delivered to the 16th Arne Ryde Symposium at the University of Lund, Aug.

—— —— (1997*a*), 'Constitutional and Legislative Provisions Governing Citizenship, Class and the Labour Relations Act', in N. Steytler (ed.), *Human Rights, Democracy and Economic Development in Southern Africa*, Johannesburg: Lex Patria.

—— —— (1997*b*), 'Growth, Democracy and Expectations in South Africa', unpublished paper.

Ndlovu, F., and Fairhurst, J. (1996), 'The Ogies-Phola Development Forum as an Example for South African Communities?', *Development Southern Africa*, 13/2: 265–75.

NEDLAC (1995), *Discussion Document on a Framework for Social Partnership and Agreement-Making in NEDLAC*, Johannesburg: NEDLAC, 16 Oct.

NEDLAC Labour Caucus (1996), *Social Equity and Job Creation*, Johannesburg: COSATU.

Nel, E., and Hill, T. (1996), 'Rural Development in Hertzog, Eastern Cape: Successful Local Economic Development?' *Development Southern Africa*, 13/6: 861–70.

RSA (Republic of South Africa) (1996), *Growth, Employment and Redistribution: A Macro-economic Strategy*, Johannesburg: Ministry of Finance, unpublished.

—— (1997), 'The Foundation for a Better Life Has Been Laid: The Government's Mid-term Report to the Nation', Johannesburg: South African Communication Services.

SALDRU (South African Labour and Development Research Unit) (1994), *South Africans Rich and Poor: Baseline Household Statistics*, Cape Town: SALDRU, University of Cape Town.

Schmitter, P. (1979), 'Still the Century of Corporatism?', in P. Schmitter and G. Lehmbruch (eds.), *Trends toward Corporatist Intermediation*, London: Sage.

Seekings, J. (1997), 'Inequality and Social Stratification in Post-apartheid South Africa, Part I: A Profile of Inequality', mimeo.

Sellars, C. (1997), 'The Organisation and Behaviour of Interest Groups: A Theoretical Review and Application to South Africa', SANER Working Paper no. 1, Cape Town.

Simkins, C. (1981), 'Agricultural Production in the African Reserves of South Africa, 1918–1969', *Journal of Southern African Studies*, 7/2: 256–83.

—— (1984), 'African Population, Employment and Incomes on Farms outside the Reserves, 1923–1969', conference paper no. 25, Carnegie Conference, Cape Town.

—— (1997), 'Reconciling Equity and Diversity: Provincial Budgets in Perspective', *Budget Watch*, 3/2, June: 1–8.

Strachan, B. (1997), 'Need for New Budget Framework', *Budget Watch*, 3/2, June: 3.

White, G. (1995), 'Towards a Democratic Developmental State', *IDS Bulletin*, 26/2: 27–36.

Whiteford, A., Posel D., and Kelatwang, T. (1995), 'A Profile of Poverty, Inequality and Human Development', Pretoria: Human Sciences Research Council.

Wolpe, H. (1995), 'The Uneven Transition from Apartheid in South Africa', *Transformation*, 27: 88–101.

World Bank (1995), 'Key Indicators of Poverty in South Africa', Report for the Office of the RDP, Pretoria.

—— (1997), *World Development Indicators 1997*, Washington: World Bank.

PART III

Deepening Democracy

'Fiddling with Democracy'

Translating Women's Participation in Politics in Uganda and South Africa into Gender Equity in Development Practice

ANNE MARIE GOETZ

Has political liberalization in developing countries enhanced women's participation in politics, and the representation of their interests in development policy-making? In some currently democratizing countries, the answer to the first part of this question is increasingly positive. There is nothing in democratic institutions or processes *per se* which favours gender equity, indeed, democratically constituted governments have long been able to deny women equitable participation (let alone the vote). But gender-sensitive cultural and structural changes in the institutions of rule can bring more women into politics, as is being demonstrated today in both Uganda and South Africa, which now rank above many developed countries in terms of women's numerical representation in national legislatures. Whether greater numbers of women in politics translates into the effective representation of their interests in development policy-making is, however, another matter. It cannot be assumed that women politicians are necessarily committed to representing women's interests; indeed, few of them will have succeeded in politics by promoting a feminist platform. Much more critical to the promotion of gender equity in economic development policy than the number of women in power is the character and capacity of the state; whether it promotes class and gender equity in social and

For comments and advice on this chapter I am grateful to Gordon White, Mark Robinson, Julie Oyegun, Debbie Budlender, and Robert Jenkins. A first draft of this chapter was presented on 10 Apr. 1997 to the joint Gender Colloquium of the University of the Western Cape's Gender Equality Unit, and the University of Cape Town's Africa Gender Institute, where I received useful comments which I acknowledge with thanks.

economic policy, and has the capacity to implement such policies even against the resistance of dominant patriarchal interests both in society and in the institutions of the state itself. In the current environment of intolerance of any restraint on the free functioning of markets, to which liberal democracy is the handmaiden, the room for promoting women's interests in economic policy-making can be limited.

Gender equity is still considered by many people—and certainly by many political scientists and economists—as a human rights matter which will be a by-product of economic growth and greater democracy. In contrast, this chapter is premissed on the assumption that gender equity is critical to the achievement of economic growth and to genuine democracy. It is a matter of concern for economic development policy because unequal gender relations create market distortions by raising transaction and information costs. Gender equity is also a welfare issue; it is about enhancing the quality of human and social reproduction through women's improved education or health. But more than that, it is a matter of social justice and social transformation aimed at redistributing resources and social value more equally between women and men, a process which includes undermining the gendered public/private segregations which marginalize women in the worlds of politics and economic production. These kinds of changes can be profoundly threatening to men's privileges, individually and collectively, and unsurprisingly arouse considerable resistance. At stake in considerations of developmental democracy from a gender perspective, then, is whether democratic institutions can achieve enough autonomy from dominant gender interests to challenge male privileges and promote the policies necessary for this kind of social change. Whether democracy can bring gender-equitable development depends on whether its institutions admit not just of women's participation, but of the representation of women's interests as a gender.

It is important to specify at this stage what is meant by 'women's interests as a gender'. The notion that women share certain interests by virtue of their gender is central to feminist politics, but is deeply contested, because women's interests, like men's, vary according to their circumstances and identities by class, race, ethnicity, occupation, life-cycle stage, and so on. However, the fact that most women, whatever their other circumstances, tend to be constrained in their life choices to a range of reproductive functions in the private sphere, and marginal positions in public arenas of the economy and politics, suggests that gender affects the way other social cleavages (class etc.) are experienced, and hence generates specific interests. Since a basic way in which gender inequality is organized is through gendered segregation between public and private worlds, it is in women's interests to seek presence and power in public arenas of politics and the market (Jonasdottir 1988). Beyond this, feminists argue that women have 'strategic' gender interests in changing aspects of the gender division of labour and power which disadvantage them.[1] This could mean a strategic gender interest in undermining gendered segmentation in the labour market, or abolishing men's greater rights to land ownership or property inheritance in certain cultures, or defending women's personal autonomy in decisions over reproduction or sexuality—but the exact nature of these strategic interests cannot be specified in advance in some kind of feminist prescription; they must be determined through women's political struggles in particular contexts. These 'strategic gender interests' thus are a political advance on women's more 'practical' interests in gaining access to development resources to enhance their livelihood securities. Achieving these practical interests may contribute to women's well-being but not necessarily challenge the structure of gender relations which has put them in a disadvantaged position in the first place.

This chapter discusses institutional changes which can enhance women's participation in politics and development decision-making, drawing on contemporary processes in Uganda and South Africa, and it considers whether these changes have contributed to an improved representation of women's interests in policy-making. Three key processes of institutional change are investigated: new developments amongst women's associations in civil society to improve interest articulation and aggregation amongst women; changes to electoral systems to admit of greater participation by women; and changes in state bureaucracies to facilitate the representation of women's interests. First, I will situate this discussion in debates on women and democracy.

1. The Relationship between Democracy and Development for Women

A debate animating the 'good government' agenda regards the relationship between economic development and political democracy: which comes first? which institutional arrangements in politics favour positive developmental performance? Since the democratic transitions in Eastern Europe in 1989 this debate has seen a growing presumption in favour of democratic representation and more accountable

---

[1] The clearest and certainly best-known theorization of women's 'strategic' and 'practical' gender interests is found in Molyneux (1985).

government, which have been seen as key to the efficient operation of the market and to healthy growth. When we approach these debates from a gender perspective we must include considerations of participation in governance, and distributional equity in the economy; considerations of deepening democracy and sharing the benefits of growth. Does democracy enhance women's participation in politics? Is it associated with welfare gains for women?

From the point of view of women's participation in formal politics, political freedom does not seem to have a significantly positive effect. Globally, there has been a remarkable consistency in the figures for female representation in national and local polities. Regardless of the political system, with the notable exception of Scandinavian countries, women represent between 0 and 12 per cent of national assemblies, and rarely exceed 15 per cent of local governments (Inter-Parliamentary Union, 1994). Indeed, numbers of women in legislatures tend to plummet during democratic transitions, especially where these are accompanied by economic liberalization, which puts great strain on women's market position and adds to their reproductive responsibilities, cutting into their time for politics. In Eastern European countries, women have been wiped out as political contenders in multi-party competition since 1989, declining to less than 10 per cent of members of national assemblies compared to an average of 33 per cent before democratic transitions. Transitions to democracy out of either right-wing or neo-patrimonial authoritarian regimes similarly often fail to bring a broadening of women's participation; in Latin American, as in African countries, women's participation has either dropped somewhat or remained at its previous average of less than 7 per cent of national assemblies. As pointed out by Molyneux, in narrow institutional terms the restoration of political rights in the global wave of democratization since 1989 has led to a 'masculinization' of the public sphere as the numerical representation of women in institutional politics has declined (1994, also Waylen 1994). It must be noted that this does not necessarily indicate electoral failure on the part of women in ex-socialist or right-wing authoritarian regimes, as in large part it is due to the elimination of seats reserved for women. Nevertheless, there does not appear to be a positive correlation between increases in political freedom and women's participation in legislatures.

Nor does there appear to be a strong relationship between levels of women's participation in democratic political institutions and levels of development and women's welfare. Historical and contemporary evidence from developed countries suggests that a country's level of development is not a reliable indicator of women's numerical representation in politics. In 1975, women were fewer than 10 per cent of legislators in 30 out of the 32 most developed countries reporting electoral data, with women accounting for 2 per cent or less of their legislatures in France, Greece, and Japan (Jaquette 1997). In the United States, where women's socio-economic status is very high, democratic institutions remain resistant to their participation, admitting women to just 5 per cent of Congress seats in 1987, and 11.2 per cent today.

It is difficult to generalize from any of this evidence because none of it differentiates sufficiently between the many regime forms which democracies take. The most positive examples of connections between women's political participation, national wealth, and women's status come from the Nordic countries, with distinctively social democratic regimes embedded in egalitarian societies and welfare states, and in economies kept relatively stable (until recently) by corporatist decision-making structures. In Nordic countries, women have been a substantial presence not just in parliaments but in top political positions. As Anne Phillips notes, Norway took the record for this in 1985, with women representing 34.4 per cent of the national assembly, holding eight out of eighteen cabinet posts, making up 40.5 per cent of county councils, and 31 per cent of municipal councils (1991: 83).

The story of women's achievement of political prominence in Scandinavia offers lessons for other contexts. It began with the adoption of voluntary 40 per cent quotas for female representation at all levels of elected delegation within a range of Scandinavian parties. These were mostly social democratic and communist parties, adopting these principles in response to pressure which the women's sections of these parties had been exerting since the 1950s, pressures which were not out of place in a culture known for its 'passion for equality' (Phillips 1991: 86). This was eventually extended to a voluntary quota of 40 per cent women candidates on electoral lists in the 1980s, which, in combination with a proportional representation system, brought substantial numbers of women into power. However, the real power of Parliament was being eroded during this same period through the growth of corporate structures in Nordic countries. Ironically, this had the effect of creating new political space for gender sensitivity in social democratic compacts. As key economic decisions were debated and taken increasingly outside of Parliament, party politicians turned to 'women's concerns', or social welfare issues, as new terrain for politicization and party competition. One result of this was equal opportunities legislation and Equal Status Councils at national and local government levels, set up in the 1970s. These stressed sexual equality in labour and business arenas, and as a result women have been able to permeate corporate structures and exert influence over employment and industrial policy. Anne Phillips attributes women's political and policy successes[2] to three factors. The first is systems of proportional representation; the second is the strength of women's structures within the traditional social democratic parties. The third is the way social democracies can legitimize efforts to change relationships between the public and private spheres by interfering in the market to create a more level playing field for those whose capacities are constrained by social relations in the private sphere.

2. A Feminist Perspective on Democracy, Development, and the State

However inconclusive, the above discussion suggests at the least that women are in a rather different relationship to the polity and the economy from men. Gender relations affect women's political effectiveness. Women's disproportionate responsibilities in the domestic sphere impose enormous constraints on the time they can devote to politics. Their lack of access to material and social resources undercuts their capacity to generate political power. These constraints inhibit the political performance of individual women and the political capacity and clout of women's associations. Gender relations will also affect the impact of economic policies on women, which calls for development policy to provide public responses to challenge private sphere patriarchy. This could include state support for women's public and private autonomy, such as guarantees of property rights, equal access to paid employment, welfare measures which compensate women for time devoted to reproductive work (such as pensions, maternity leave, etc.), measures to defend their physical security and to combat sexual violence, and so on.

Beyond these practical constraints, there is a more fundamental obstacle: the gendered construction of political authority and subjectivity which makes the realm of political competition profoundly hostile both to women's participation and to the representation of women's interests as a gendered group. So hostile is this arena to the association of women with public power that women are simply not electable, particularly if they promote feminist concerns with social and gender equity.

---

[2] Scandinavian women themselves do not always consider that they have been successful in politics and public policy. Some remain critical of their governments' commitment to gender equity and suggest that women in politics, although they have demonstrated a greater concern with women's issues than do men (Dahlerup 1988), have not yet ushered in a social revolution in relations between women and men, let alone fundamental changes to labour markets or the domestic division of labour (Hernes 1987). See Phillips (1991: ch. 3) for a full discussion.

Electability is contingent upon identifying with the masculine political culture, as Germaine Greer suggests:

We have had female rulers but they presided over the masculine hierarchies and they did so in the approved masculine fashion. They have never stacked their governmental bodies with women or enacted policies that were in women's interest. They have never been pacifist, egalitarian, non-authoritarian, sororal, or even faintly green. If they had been any of these things they would never have come to power in the first place. (Greer 1996)

Thus women representatives, even if their numbers expand significantly, cannot be expected automatically to be representatives of women. A feminine presence in politics is not the same as a feminist one. Getting more women into politics is a worthy project from the point of view of democratic justice, but the real challenge is in institutionalizing gender equity goals in government policy, and developing autonomous power bases in civil society to promote these concerns. Unfortunately, the first and easier project—increasing the numbers of women in politics—is often mistaken for the second. This is a confusion between the numerical and strategic representation of women. Improving the representation of women's interests calls for a transformation of politics to legitimize the political status of gender conflict, and a transformation of state institutions to eliminate institutionalized male preference (Connell 1990).

Any efforts to enhance women's participation in politics have to respond to both types of constraint—women's lack of political leverage as individuals and as a broad social group defined by their gender, and the lack of legitimacy of gender issues in politics. As Anne Phillips points out, this is a familiar catch-22; a democracy requires gender equality policies before women and feminists are able to participate equally in politics, but without the second, how can the first be achieved (Phillips 1991: 79)? Efforts to respond to this dilemma have involved relatively undemocratic forms of political engineering to get women into office, such as quota systems to include women on party lists (as in Scandinavian countries), or reserved seats for women (as in South Asian countries). In tandem with what has come to be known as 'state feminism', or state support for women-friendly welfare and employment policies, this has resulted in significant improvements in women's social and economic welfare in some countries.

Whereas efforts to gender-sensitize political processes are about increasing the numbers of women representatives in politics, the concern to transform administrative institutions is about improving state accountability to women's needs. The persistent frustration of gender equity policy initiatives at the level of implementation has led to a growing awareness of the gendered nature of the state itself, and of the need for a politics of gender sensitivity at all levels of state bureaucracies. A considerable number of studies have shown that male-dominated state institutions tend to promote men's interests (Connell 1990, Charlton et al. 1989, Agarwal 1988, Staudt 1990). So pervasive is this bias that even social policies intended to promote gender equity have been shown to transfer the condition of female dependency from private patriarchy to a public form of patriarchy (Fraser 1989: ch. 7). Many developing states have adopted principles of gender equity in order to appear progressive in the international arena, but the lack of commitment in the administration scuppers gender equity initiatives or else reduces them to welfare measures which reinforce women's secondary position in the labour market.

This problem casts a new light on conceptualizations of state capacity and autonomy. State capacity to implement policies to tackle the poverty and disprivilege of women and girls requires not just autonomy from dominant class interests, but relative autonomy from dominant gender interests. It is not customary in political science to discuss state autonomy in this manner; autonomy from social relations is never understood to include autonomy from gender relations. In discussions of governance and economic reform, the concern is to expand the state's room for manœuvre amongst, and relative independence from, competing class interests. Leftwich, for example, suggests that such autonomy is the bedrock of sound public administration, and, from a developmental point of view, is more important than democracy to state capacities to deliver development efficiently (1996: 18). He argues that successful development outcomes depend on:

such factors as internal stability . . . on the relative autonomy of the state in both democratic and non-democratic polities; on sound infrastructure and competent administration; on low levels of corruption; on a critical minimum degree of consensus between groups and regions about the objectives of growth and the rules of the game for achieving it . . . and on an increasing degree of both regional and social equality in the distribution of the costs and benefits of that growth. (1996: 20)

Feminists would not disagree about the importance of good governance to strong development performance, but would add that gender equity must be included explicitly as one of the objectives of growth and as part of the rules of the game for achieving it. And given social resistance to gender equity, democracy is critical to women's chances of building and sustaining a political imperative behind their demands. Democratic principles such as political equality and popular sovereignty create expectations and opportunities for the inclusion and promotion of women's interests—opportunities that simply are not available to women under authoritarian regimes, even if they are good developers.

Strategies to deal with administrative indifference or hostility to gender equity concerns in development have included the establishment of a range of state 'machineries' to represent women's interests, such as national offices on the status of women, a process which has been under way since the first of the UN Conferences on Women in 1975. However, these kinds of units have tended to be under-funded and side-lined in the administration and in political decision-making (Goetz 1995). A new, but still rather incipient, strategy involves promoting institutional change to establish gender equity in the structure and culture of a range of state institutions, particularly the police, agricultural extension services, social services, and local administrations. This includes augmenting the presence of women in these services, and encouraging gender-sensitive practices ranging from more sensitive approaches to policing violence against women, to training agricultural extension officers to respond to the needs of women farmers.

The second half of this chapter turns to Uganda and South Africa, two countries which have emerged from turbulent and protracted transitions, and which stand out as trail-blazers in efforts to achieve gender equity in formal politics. They now rank alongside Scandinavian countries in terms of women's numerical representation in legislatures: women are 18 per cent of the National Assembly (previously the National Resistance Council) in Uganda, and 27 per cent of the National Assembly in South Africa (ranking South Africa seventh in the world for women's representation in national-level politics). Women are building on this democratic presence to establish a strategic impact on public policy. The following sections investigate three aspects of efforts to institutionalize women's interests in development through democratic processes: first, efforts to improve interest articulation and aggregation amongst women in civil and political society—to amplify their political 'voice'; second, changes to electoral systems to augment women's presence in formal politics; and third, bureaucratic measures creating dedicated space for gender equity issues in the public administration.

3. Women's Mobilization in Civil and Political Society: Enhancing their Impact on Politics

In both Uganda and South Africa there is a phenomenal number and diversity of women's associations, reflecting a rich African tradition of women's organizing which makes it the world region with the most extensive female solidarity networks (Staudt 1987: 199), with most structured around the self-help survival 'politics of everyday life' (Nelson and Chowdhury 1994: 18). But like women's associations elsewhere, they generally fail to constitute an effective political base for women's interests in politics because of a range of constraints on their capacities for interest articulation and aggregation beyond the local level. These constraints include:

- women's limited time for political activism because of their double duty of work in productive and reproductive arenas;
- women's lack of financial and social resources and political experience, which, coupled with the relatively fluid organizational forms their associations tend to adopt, undermines their capacity to generate effective leadership and make an impact on public decision-making;
- male domination of the main democratic institutions of civic voluntarism—political parties—which fail to promote women either individually or collectively (while exploiting women as party workers and as potential vote banks);
- a tendency amongst women's associations to seek distance from, rather than engagement with, the state, because of histories of the abuse of women's rights by public authorities, or because of fears of co-optation by the state;[3]
- difficulties in establishing a coherent set of women's interests in politics because of differences between women by class, ethnicity, race, region, and so on.

The first constraint—the impact of the gender division of labour on women's time for political activism—is the most intractable, and, as noted earlier, cannot be resolved without a revolution in social relations. But as the recent history of women's involvement in democratic transitions in Uganda and South Africa demonstrates, the other constraints have been challenged through a combination of deliberate strategies to make a political resource out of women's strength of numbers in the electorate, and through the political opportunities created by temporary suspensions of conventional party politics.

---

[3] This constraint and the previous one can be taken by some observers as positive advantages in that women's alternative organizational forms and their marginalization from formal politics enhance their autonomy from the politics of patronage and corruption in Africa, creating all-women spaces where women's resources can be defended from predatory interests. Some students of women's forms of political engagement in Africa suggest that their low-visibility, autonomous self-help groups represent a distinctive form of politics in civil society, modelling alternative social values (Tripp 1996, Hirschmann 1991, MacGaffey 1986).

(a) Uganda

The main institutional factors which have strengthened women's civil society presence and their engagement with politics have been the suspension of multi-party politics and the personal support of President Yoweri Museveni for women's rights. This has helped the women's movement grow from a negligible and politically co-opted social presence under the Obote regime, to 'one of the strongest mobilized societal forces in Uganda' (Tripp 1997: ch. 1). Museveni's personal support for women's equality and for their participation in politics reflects his appreciation of women's role in the civil war as supporters of his National Resistance Army (Tripp 1994: 115), his awareness of their key role in agricultural development and family welfare, and also his recognition of the potential contribution of women's organizations to consolidating the NRM's political dominance in Uganda (Mugyenyi 1994: 1). Museveni's support has been a tremendous piece of political luck for the women's movement. This contingent variable—support for gender equity issues from a top national leader—is a critical yet unpredictable ingredient for success in feminist politics.

The suspension of multi-party politics in Museveni's 'no-party' system reflects a desire to build a national government of democratic reconciliation without returning to the sectarian multi-party system which proved so destructive in the past. Uganda's Constituent Assembly agreed in 1995 to suspend multi-party politics until 2001. Parties in Uganda, which still operate openly, if unofficially, are constituted primarily along religious and ethnic lines, which is why multi-partyism has come to be associated with sectarianism. Obote's Uganda People's Congress, for instance, draws its support primarily from non-Baganda Protestants, while the Democratic Party is made up mainly of Catholics. Even Museveni's inclusive NRM is dominated by people from the Ankole region in the south-west of the country. In the traditional parties, the importance of ethnic identity, combined with religion, has left little space to pursue gender equity politics. In the 'no-party' system people stand for free and open elections as individuals independent of party affiliation, and join the government as part of a broad-based National Resistance 'Movement' without having to join the NRM itself. Because party loyalties interfere less to inhibit co-operation between women politicians, this extended transition period has made it easier for women activists and legislators to build coalitions to promote an agenda for gender equity in public policies. It has also created space in civil society for women to form new associations and promote their interests independently of sectarian party interests.

However, the bulk of these women's organizations remain fairly isolated from national and even local politics. This reflects a dual process: women continue to be marginalized from male-dominated local councils and other key community bodies, and also deliberately seek to distance themselves from public authorities because of experiences of corruption and fear of co-optation (Tripp 1997: ch. 4). In other words, effective forms of coalition politics and interest aggregation aimed at influencing national decision-making still elude women's associations. There is a persistent divide between rural women's organizations which avoid registering themselves out of a concern to preserve autonomy from local and national authorities, and urban feminist groups which engage with the state to promote women's professional prospects, secure legal reform in family and customary law, combat violence against women, and promote women's participation in politics.

New democratic structures established to broaden popular participation in national decision-making have not always been more inclusive of women and more receptive to their concerns. An example of this was the process of soliciting people's views in early debates on the new constitution. The 1988 Constitutional Commission, which consisted of two women and nineteen men, was intended to identify issues for debate by the Constituent Assembly through an open and consultative process. However, the majority of women were left out of this because of the inappropriateness of consultative mechanisms used: mixed-sex public discussion groups all over the country, and written memoranda. Neither of these mechanisms for participation recognized constraints on women's voices imposed by the presence of men in public fora or by the illiteracy of the majority of poor rural women. Thus, for example, few of the reputed 15,000 memos to the Constitutional Commission were from women.

The resolution of this problem was, in the end, a good example of state–society co-operation to amplify women's voice in politics. Urban women's organizations recognized the need for gender-sensitive facilitation and, together with the Department of Women in Development, researched women's understanding of constitutional issues, designed a simple illustrated manual explaining constitutional matters, and facilitated focus group discussions with rural women all over the country to elicit their views on the constitution. These were submitted to the Constitutional Commission in 1991–2. Later, women delegates to the Constituent Assembly were able to argue that this process gave them a mandate for their efforts to promote the progressive gender equity provisions in the 1995 constitution, acknowledged at the time as one of the most 'woman-friendly' constitutions in the world (Tamale 1997: 146).

While women acknowledge the key role which NRM support has played in strengthening their political prospects, they have recently become increasingly wary of being too closely associated with Museveni or the NRM, partly out of concerns that the NRM is trying to capture and control the female constituency (Tamale 1997: 134), and partly out of a worry that exclusive association with Museveni will undermine the prospects of the women's movement under future leaders.

(b) South Africa

In contrast to Uganda, women's organizations were central to the struggle for democracy, which gave them a mandate and leverage to impress their needs on the politicians negotiating the transition. In consequence they have had more direct ownership over the new democratic institutions and are in a stronger position in political society.

Women in South Africa have made a substantial contribution as an organized group to popular struggle against apartheid since at least the turn of the century (Walker 1991). As in Uganda, a period of suppression of party activity has opened some space for women to assert themselves as political actors. This was in the long suspension of the opposition mass-based parties such as the African National Congress (ANC) and the Pan-Africa Congress (PAC) from the mid-1960s to 1990. Some of this struggle has occurred in the framework of multi-party competition—even when anti-apartheid parties were banned from the mid-1960s to 1990, a great deal of women's activism took place through party-linked associations. This has made it particularly important for women to raise the political status and legitimacy of gender equity issues *within* parties. This has been an uphill struggle. As pointed out by analysts of gender politics in South Africa:

There is no history or tradition within South Africa which recognizes gender conflict as political conflict. South Africans unquestioningly accept the idea of racial conflict, ethnic conflict and religious conflict as being political. . . . The construction of racism and class exploitation by the national liberation movement precludes a gendered analysis of both class and race in South Africa. (Charman et al. 1991: 55–6)[4]

Tremendous struggle by women within the ANC has made it the standard-bearer of gender equity concerns in politics today. The South

[4] Two efforts to overcome the resistance and determined myopia of mainstream parties involved creating women's parties: the South Africa Women's Party, and the Women's Rights Peace Party. Unsurprisingly, both performed poorly in the 1994 elections, where the priority for most voters was to endorse strongly the leading organizations of the anti-apartheid struggle.

Africa Communist Party has tended to see gender conflict as secondary to other forms of social conflict as does the Pan-African Congress (PAC).[5] The Democratic Party is committed to a classically liberal approach to gender equality. The Inkatha Freedom Party, in step with its emphasis on tribal identity, follows the route more conventional to African politics of sporting a massive Women's Brigade (reputed to have 400,000 members) which is described as promoting a secondary role for women in politics and the economy (Hassim 1991*b*).[6] The National Party, the party of apartheid, has taken a more traditional perspective on women in politics, opposing affirmative action and abortion.

There is a strong tradition in South Africa of women seeking an autonomous organizational expression for interests which transcend party lines—such as the Federation of South African Women formed in 1953 by women from trade unions and political organizations, which drafted a Women's Charter in 1954 and participated in drawing up the Freedom Charter in 1955. The most dramatic example of cross-party collaboration was the Women's National Coalition (WNC) formed in 1992 to promote women's demands for inclusion and equity in the negotiations for a new South Africa. The WNC represented over 90 national organizations and 13 regional coalitions by the time it had researched and presented the 'Women's Charter for Effective Equality' in February 1994. It brought women from the ANC together with their counterparts in the NP; the Congress of South African Trade Unions (COSATU) and the Business and Professional Women's Club, the Vroue Landbou-Unie (the white Afrikaner Women's Agricultural Union) and the Rural Women's Movement from the Transvaal. The political, racial, linguistic, and class differences between these groups were tremendous. The diversity this represents made for an unsustainable coalition, and since the 1994 elections the WNC has been unable to retain its membership or sustain its impact. Nevertheless, the urgency of ensuring women's participation in the rapidly unfolding democratization process was enough to weld the widely different and often opposed groups of women in the WNC into a distinct constituency.

---

[5] This is suggested by a statement from Patricia de Lille, the PAC's representative at the transitional negotiations in 1993: 'I am an African before I am a woman . . . This is the way that all African women should see themselves. Liberal feminists say women face a triple oppression, on the basis of race, gender and class. This is a move away from the main problem' (cited in Kemp et al. 1995: 149).

[6] On the other hand, as testimony to the relative autonomy of the political realm, IFP women representatives and MPs (particularly Suzanne Vos) have certainly not held back from taking a feminist stance on politics since the 1994 elections (Gowans 1997).

The impetus for the WNC's creation was the imperative of participating in the transitional negotiations. There were only 23 women amongst over 400 delegates to the formal negotiations in the Convention for a Democratic South Africa (CODESA). The 'mechanics' of participation—essentially a series of highly technical and legalistic negotiations, and conversations between men in closed bilaterals between the two main parties, the ANC and the NP—excluded the majority of women in the country. The WNC lobbied to make this process more accessible to women. Its most publicized success was in pressing for the inclusion of a woman on every delegation to the Multi-Party Negotiating Process (MPNP) which replaced CODESA in March 1993.[7]

Some observers of the women's movement in South Africa consider this a phenomenal achievement: 'No other constituency had achieved such recognition during the negotiation process, and no single women's organization had been able to achieve this kind of legitimacy for women's issues on its own' (Kemp et al. 1995: 151). Others are less sanguine, pointing out that women were still excluded from the heart of decision-making, which was the closed bilaterals between the main contenders (Albertyn 1994: 56). Women's lack of technical legal expertise[8] detracted from their capacity to act in women's interests.

The strategy of seeking a numerical expansion of women at the talks was an example of confusing numerical representation with strategic representation. The liberal democratic framework of the MPNP did not admit of the representation of social movements, as opposed to political parties and legal experts. There were no mechanisms for the formal representation of group interests. Women did not act as a caucus within the MPNP, neither did they wield political or economic influence in the way that organized labour did.[9] The WNC set out to enhance communications between women negotiators and women's organizations, but it was extremely difficult to establish a sense of political clout behind the individual women negotiators compelled to operate in roles dictated by their membership in disciplined political parties.

Nevertheless, there is no doubt that the interventions of the WNC made the parties involved in the transition aware of an organized

[7] For a detailed account of this particular negotiation and of women's participation in the transitional negotiations generally, see Albertyn 1994.

[8] Whereas the majority of male delegates were politicians or lawyers, most of the women were from caring professions such as nursing, education, or social work (Finnemore 1994: 16).

[9] The Congress of South African Trade Unions, COSATU, organized a march of 100,000 workers on the MPNP to demand reconsideration of the constitutional entrenchment of the right to lockout.

women's constituency. Women's interests in gender equity were written into the draft constitution, and women and their concerns became important targets in the election campaign in 1994. Research by the ANC's Elections Commission identified women's issues as one of the four major areas, along with education, housing, and jobs, upon which its campaign should concentrate. This made women aware of their potential leverage on the electoral process, enabling some women politicians to campaign on feminist issues.

Since the 1994 elections the WNC has retreated in importance, and women's associations, like other key anti-apartheid groups, have been literally decapitated, as their leaders have moved from civil society into politics. This has somewhat weakened women's civil society presence, although new leadership capacities are developing. In spite of the loss of a unifying apex organization, there is still structured engagement by women's associations in policy-making, as will be shown in the next section.

To summarize, temporary suspensions of party politics-as-usual in both countries have given women opportunities to organize and express an autonomous position in politics—a position promoting gender equity as a political project. They have also prepared women for democratic competition by providing some space for women's organizations to institutionalize themselves more firmly. However, starting from a weaker position in Uganda, women's associations have been more dependent on state patronage than in South Africa.

Women activists and politicians in Uganda and South Africa have targeted constitution-writing processes as a first step in deepening democracy from a gender perspective. The impressive results are state-of-the-art constitutions which have guaranteed women's equal rights with men. Many of the mechanics of governance and norm-creation in these new democracies have been designed with a view to respecting minorities in these highly diverse and divided societies—a form of 'democratic counter majoritarianism' (Devenish 1993)—although in the case of South Africa, of course, the objective was to liberate oppressed majorities. Women, though in fact a numerical majority of the population, experience the stigma and marginalization associated with politically powerless sociological minorities. This is particularly so for poor, rural, and, in South Africa, black and coloured women. Consequently, they benefit from constitutional minority rights protections such as a Bill of Rights, a public ombudsman or public protector, commissions on human rights and equal opportunities, and proportional representation which facilitates minority representation in a multi-party system (ibid.). Women in civil society in both countries have made a point of trying to ensure that guarantees of gender equity overrule protections to cultural rights and the juris-diction of customary law. In this they have not been unambiguously successful, reflecting the extent to which traditional patriarchs remain critical power brokers even under the new democratic dis-pensations. The challenge to customary law by women is a critical first step, however, in translating public democracy into democracy in the home, and into economic democracy, as customary law stands in the way of some women's equal rights to property ownership and legal adulthood.

4. 'Fiddling with Democracy': Political Measures to Bring Women into Electoral Politics

The second aspect of efforts to consolidate women's 'democratic pres-ence' has been institutional reform in the electoral process. In both Uganda and South Africa, women have been able to impress upon the leading political movements—the ANC and the NRM—the need to take measures to guarantee space for women in legislatures to bypass the entrenched male preference of voters and of male-dominated party selectorates.

(a) Uganda

In Uganda, affirmative action has been the basic political mechanism used by Museveni to encourage women's political participation in the Local Council (until 1996 this was known as the Resistance Council) governance system. This five-tier system starts from the village, in which Local Councils are directly elected. Village LCs send representatives to the next tier of government, and so on up to the National Assembly in Kampala.[10] A special seat for women—the secretary for women's affairs—is mandatory amongst the nine seats at each of the five LC levels. The objective is to institutionalize representation of women as a special group. Each district elects a woman representative to sit in the National Assembly. Although initially the existence of this special seat associated women's participation in local politics solely with women's issues, women have been competing in ever greater numbers in local elections over the last decade for other seats on these councils, with a few winning the chairperson's seat in the 1992 local elections.[11]

---

[10] Each of the country's thirty-two districts is divided into five administrative zones, with Local Councils at each level.

[11] Interview with Gertrude Njuba, Director of Women's Affairs, NRM Secretariat, Apr. 1995.

The system has resulted in an increasingly substantial presence of women in government: since 1989 women have occupied 18 per cent of National Assembly seats—the majority of these seats being those reserved through affirmative action. In addition, although there is no explicit affirmative action provision in the civil service, by 1995 women were reasonably well represented by virtue of both direct appointments and regular promotional processes: 21 per cent of permanent secretaries, 26 per cent of under-secretaries, and 16 per cent of district administrators. Museveni has made a point of putting women in politically sensitive, extremely high-profile positions, such as the 1988 appointment of Betty Bigombe as Minister for the Pacification of the North, where she was the most prominent negotiator in Uganda's persistent civil war. In a country whose agriculture is dominated by women, the President has insisted on appointing women as ministers of agriculture. In 1994 he appointed a woman, Specioza Wandira Kazibwe, as Vice-President, a first for Africa. He has appointed very few women to cabinet posts, however.

There is considerable debate amongst feminists in Uganda on the merits of the affirmative action system (see especially Tamale 1997, Ahikire 1994). While its success in bringing more women into politics has been applauded, it is clear that it has not been an effective tool for ensuring the representation of women's interests. Right from the village level, the women elected as secretary of women's affairs tend not to be the more radical women involved in women's associations. This is because male voters tend to reject those candidates in favour of more malleable women who are linked to the local male power structure; women who are related to dominant village men, who will participate in sustaining the hold of a traditional group over a local community (Tripp 1994: 116). In some areas where women local councillors are not in a painful minority of one, there is some evidence that women have made an impact on decision-making at local levels over women's practical needs for water, sanitation, and schools (Elson and Evers 1997: 21). However, they face pressures from husbands and local communities not to stand for election at the county and district levels (LC 4 and 5) where strategic policy and budgetary decisions are made (ibid.).

The presence of a greater number of women at the national level does seem to offer more opportunities for building support for gender equity concerns, as evidenced by the effectiveness of caucusing amongst women Constituent Assembly delegates (where they were 18 per cent of delegates) over women's issues in the constitution. A Women's Caucus has also been formed in the National Assembly. It also includes representatives of workers, the disabled, and a category of men labelled 'Gender Sensitive Males' by Women's Caucus members. As a result it constitutes the largest organized caucus in the National Assembly. In spite of this, its impact has been limited. Only a minority of women representatives project themselves as feminists in political debates. The women who are in affirmative action district seats are selected through an all-male electoral college,[12] which can favour the selection of fairly conservative women (Tamale 1997: 124). Women representatives who are interested in gender equity have faced considerable opposition to efforts to promote women's interests, particularly in relation to development planning decisions. The Women's Caucus has, however, been able to bring women together across the Assembly on the issue of domestic violence, resulting in substantial support for legislation to enforce better policing and sentencing of perpetrators of domestic violence.

One problem with the affirmative action system is that it risks creating a gendered enclave for women's political participation, with electorates assuming that the reserved seats are the only legitimate spaces for women candidates. This became apparent in the 1994 Constituent Assembly elections, in which 39 women ran against male candidates for county seats (9 won). Some of these were told by voters not to fight in the election for county representatives, but to wait for the separate election a few weeks later for the seats representing special groups, including the seat of the women's LC delegate for each district (Kasente 1994).

Precisely these kinds of problems with the affirmative action system have spurred greater numbers of women to contest open seats. They seek to base their political legitimacy on constituency support, and sometimes also campaign on women's rights issues. Some women have treated the affirmative action seats as the first step into competitive politics, with ten of the women who were in affirmative action seats in the 1989 parliament competing against men for county seats in the 1996 elections (six won) (Tamale 1997: 119).

The affirmative action system has had the great value of providing space for increasing the numerical representation of women in politics, pending the development of a women's movement better able to mobilize electoral support for them. The absence of party divisions has created opportunities for feminist activists amongst women politicians

---

[12] The electoral college for women National Assembly representatives in affirmative action seats is composed of people elected from the first three levels of the Local Council system; since the majority of LC officials are men, the electoral college for women national representatives is overwhelmingly male. This system is now under review, with many women affirmative action representatives interested in opening up their electorate to all district residents.

to galvanize others into acting as genuine representatives of women. For instance, some women MPs are promoting a new Domestic Relations Bill to ensure that women's rights are respected within marriage. Others are raising public awareness of problems of domestic violence and child abuse. Effective collaboration was also demonstrated in the Constituent Assembly by the Women's Caucus, a non-partisan organization animated largely by feminist politicians such as the county seat holder Winnie Byanyima. This Caucus was responsible for the progressive provisions on gender written into the 1995 constitution, ensuring that the final Ugandan constitution recognizes gender equality under the law, prohibits laws, customs, and traditions that undermine the position of women, provides for the establishment of an Equal Opportunities Commission to see that constitutional principles are enforced, and provides for an expansion of the numbers of women representatives to a minimum of one-third of local government bodies. This last provision suggests that in spite of ambivalence regarding the perceived legitimacy of access to politics through affirmative action, it is still seen as necessary in overcoming gender biases in the electoral system.

(b) South Africa

In South Africa the party list version of the proportional representation system has been a key electoral tool for bringing large numbers of women into office, confirming research which shows the greater amenability of this system to the inclusion of women (Norris 1985). The 1994 elections returned 109 women to the National Assembly—27 per cent of the seats. Political scientists such as Hyden have celebrated PR as a means of 'de-localizing' the vote to promote the representation of marginalized social groups in ethnically fractured societies (Hyden 1995). This can work to women's advantage too; the party list version of PR helps to undermine voter reluctance to select women candidates because the focus of the vote is on the party, not the individual candidates. Another advantage of the 'de-localizing' effect of the PR system is that it allows candidates to campaign on issues which are sometimes controversial, such as women's gender interests, which would otherwise be downplayed when candidates are responding to the conservative common denominator of voters in a constituency.

Dramatic evidence of the power of PR in overcoming local prejudices against women is to be seen in the results of the local government elections in South Africa, which were a combination of PR and ward-based voting. For every party except the right-wing Freedom Front and the left-wing PAC (from which, respectively, just nine and two women were elected), the PR system returned far more women to local government office than did the ward system. In the ANC, of the 911 women elected (24.6 per cent of the total ANC winners), 717 won through the PR system and only 194 through the ward system (election results fact sheet, IDASA, 1997). The impact of ward-based conservatism in selecting women candidates resulted in the poorer showing women made at the local level compared to the national level; in total women won just 19 per cent of local councillor positions across the country.

The PR system cannot promote women candidates in male-dominated parties without an explicit commitment, usually underlined by clear quotas, to fronting women candidates.[13] After considerable internal struggle, in October 1993 women in the ANC succeeded in winning agreement to a self-administered quota of 30 per cent women on the ANC party list, and most other parties joined in this voluntary quota for the 1994 elections. The ANC's list of 200 candidates, which included 66 women, clustered most of them on the bottom 15 per cent of the list. There were only two women, Winnie Mandela and Albertina Sisulu, in the top 30 positions, and 19 women in the bottom 30. Commenting on this with some resignation, Nomatyala Hangana, the Western Cape ANC Women's League chairperson, remarked that while there was 'disappointment' that more women candidates were not placed higher, 'if that happened . . . the leadership would stand accused of fiddling with democracy. Delegates at the conference made their choice and this has to be respected. That, I suppose, is one of the drawbacks of democracy' (*South*, 28 Jan.–1 Feb. 1994).

Quotas on party lists for women, however much resented by the male rank and file, are more effective than reserved seats. Women who win are seen as having a legitimate presence as political participants, and if they have campaigned partly on gender issues, they can claim a legitimate mandate to represent these issues in government. However, a serious problem with this system—the reverse side of the detachment or 'de-localization' of candidates from particular constituencies—is that it places great power in the hands of the central or provincial party which compiles these lists, making women candidates beholden primarily to the party hierarchy, not to a particular constituency.[14]

---

[13] In Namibia, for example, a PR system has not automatically ensured women's numerical representation. There were no official quotas for women on party lists, and only SWAPO placed women on lists to ensure that at least one woman would be elected out of every ten candidates. Each party submitted a list of seventy-two candidates for the National Assembly, seven parties participated in the elections, and among these, only six women were elected. In contrast, for the local authority elections in 1992 an affirmative action provision stipulating a minimum of 25% of women on party lists resulted in women being elected to approximately 30% of local authority councils.

[14] This problem affects men too, as attested by the fate of Patrick Lekota, who was withdrawn from his premiership of the Free State in 1996, in spite of his enormous local support.

Women face a difficult trade-off: the price of access to power is subordination to the party hierarchy, unless they can establish themselves as national electoral assets to their party—in the way Winnie Mandela has done.[15] And as the case of Winnie Mandela suggests, it is not through taking explicitly feminist positions that women cultivate electoral loyalty, but rather, as in her case, by pursuing a very populist political agenda and developing a personality cult.

On the one hand, the PR system makes women's position in politics more tenable and legitimate because they have achieved it through popular election (with just a little 'fiddling with democracy' to get onto the party list). On the other hand, their freedom to raise feminist concerns, particularly if these are seen as oppositional and divisive, is more tenuous. Without a constituency they cannot threaten to deliver their local popularity—their seat—to another party in the next election, since no one voted for them specifically. They have no leverage to exert if their party neglects issues of importance to them. Ideally, the women's movement could serve as a constituency for women in government, and to some extent it does. The break-up of the Women's National Coalition after the 1994 elections has weakened the capacity of women's organizations to support cross-party action in women's interests, or to make demands on politicians with a single voice. Women's associations now coalesce across social and ethnic divisions on specific issues, such as violence against women, rather than seeking expression as a coherent and singular women's movement.

These kinds of constraints have undermined women's capacities to act across party lines in the National Assembly. A parliamentary women's caucus does exist but has not risen above party competition between ANC and NP parliamentarians. In two major gender-specific debates held in Parliament in 1996, women divided along party lines: the debates over pornography, and abortion. The women's caucus within the ANC, on the other hand, is very strong, and the ANC's majority in government means that this group has been able to press Parliament into acting on some of the constitutional protections of women's rights.

Notable successes so far have included passage of an abortion rights bill, and challenging the government to appoint powerful feminists on its Commission on Gender Equality. ANC women MPs are behind the creation of the '*Ad Hoc* Parliamentary Committee on Improvement of the Quality of Life and Status of Women in South Africa'

---

[15] The allegations of extensive criminal activity made against Winnie Madikizela Mandela at the Truth and Reconciliation Commission hearings in November and December 1997 have deeply undermined her value to the ANC as an electoral asset.

to review government legislation for its gender implications, and to monitor the situation of women in the country. In late 1996 the ANC Women's Caucus initiated a Parliament/NGO task force on Violence against Women, and in early 1997, in response to the rape of a prominent feminist activist on Robben Island, women across most parties joined in supporting the task force's campaign against violence against women, which included lobbying for the reform of magistrates' courts and the police system to sentence offenders more systematically, and to police more sensitively. Women's strength in civil and political society is evident from the fact that the campaign generated a rapid response: by mid-1997 the Departments of Justice, and Safety and Security, had declared violence against women a priority crime.

Through each of these legislative battles, the women's movement has been strengthening its capacity to recover from its post-transition exhaustion and to engage in politics in a structured way. Democratization has multiplied fora and opportunities for consultation, and women's associations have been particularly involved in policy debates over the reform of the country's social welfare system, particularly debates in early 1997 over the reorientation of the child benefit system to respond to the needs of poor coloured and black women. As will be shown in the next section, however, women in both civil and political society have found it harder to break into debates on economic policy.

In sum, political measures which involve 'fiddling with democracy' have been necessary in both Uganda and South Africa to increase the numbers of women in legislatures. But whether these women are able to bring the developmental concerns of all women into the political process depends purely on their individual proclivities; on a contingent and not structural variable. This issue is blurred by the language used to justify special measures to bring women into legislatures; in Uganda, affirmative action is justified as a means to represent women as a group, without measures to enhance connections between women representatives and the women's movement. In South Africa, the strength of women's associations and their support for women politicians gives the latter a stronger and more direct mandate to represent women's interests.

A problem for women both in Uganda and South Africa is that they have no realistic political options outside of the NRM or the ANC. There are no other social democratic alternatives with any prospects for electoral success. The lack of political alternatives rather restricts the political leverage of women within their parties, both of which are likely to continue to dominate politics in their respective countries for some time to come.

5. From Politics to Policies

In both countries democratization processes have been relatively sensitive to the need to enhance women's political participation, but has this resulted in a feminist impact on development policy-making? In both countries there are growing numbers of women in power who profess a commitment to gender equity, and they are backed up by a substantial civil society presence of organized women—this is particularly so in South Africa. This ought in principle to lead to an impact on economic decision-making, but it has not been this simple. For a start, it is too early to make a fair assessment of the impact of women politicians on policy, as it takes a long time for a group which is so new to politics to learn the rules and to use them effectively. Secondly, it is difficult to trace direct connections between women politicians and policy outcomes because of the many different factors which affect the making, adopting, and implementing of policy. Thirdly, as the women politicians interviewed for this chapter suggested, to look for a direct policy impact is to overestimate the power of parliamentarians. Many of them had been surprised by their relative lack of power when they entered office, particularly in the arena of economic reform policy, which is shaped by international economic forces and fashions which seemed to these politicians to be relatively impervious to domestic political manipulation. And finally, to expect an immediate feminist impact on policy even if there is a feminist presence in political and civil society is greatly to underestimate the obstructive effect of the very masculine culture and environment of politics on women's political effectiveness. Although this chapter cannot investigate this problem, it is discussed in a study by Sylvia Tamale for the Ugandan National Assembly, and by Hannah Britton for the South African Parliament, who describe problems faced by women representatives ranging from ridicule, through exclusion from key informal discussions, to sexual harassment.[16] So intense is the sense of alienation this produces that, in the South African Parliament, half of a sample of women representatives interviewed by Britton claimed they would not seek office again (Britton 1997: 1).[17]

[16] See Tamale (1997) and Britton (1997) These problems are also discussed in a report on the achievements of women in the first two years of the multi-racial Parliament South Africa: Serote et al. (1996). In both countries efforts are being made to challenge the masculine culture of politics and to build the political skills of women new to politics. In Uganda, the Forum for Women in Democracy, an NGO, supports women in the National Assembly. In South Africa, the multi-party caucus, the Parliamentary Women's Group, tries to give practical support to women politicians, while the Speaker's Office will house a Women's Empowerment Unit to build women's political skills and to make efforts to transform the culture of Parliament.

[17] Britton interviewed 30% of women parliamentarians (Britton 1997).

This section examines primarily the impact of formal measures to institutionalize a concern with gender equity at the heart of economic policy-making. The difficulty of both legitimizing feminist politics and gender-sensitizing state institutions has promoted the pursuit of bureaucratic strategies to institutionalize a space for women in the state—strategies such as creating special bureaucratic 'machinery' for the representation of women's interests.

(a) Uganda

In an analysis of gender issues in Uganda's economic reform programme, Diane Elson and Barbara Evers conclude that women have not shared equally in Uganda's impressive growth—averaging 6 per cent a year since 1987. Its structural adjustment programme has taken a particular toll on women, whose labour obligations have increased on new export crops, without a commensurate growth in their control of the proceeds (Elson and Evers 1997: 24). This is suggested by persistently poor welfare indicators for women and children, who would have benefited had there been increases in women's income. Furthermore, there is some evidence of a drop in the access of women and girls to health care and education, because user fees for health care are too high for women, and because girls are withdrawn from school to assist in export crop production or housework (ibid: 25).

Elson and Evers note that the increased numbers of women in national political decision-making have had little impact on public expenditure decisions, which do not reduce gender-based price distortions or lift institutional barriers to women's capacities to profit from their labour. They posit that: '[t]his may be because, in absolute terms, there are not yet enough women in positions of power; or it may be that women have insufficient voice in public expenditure decisions; or that the few women in positions of power do not share the priorities of poorer women' (ibid: 25).

All three points may be right, but certainly it is true that there have been barriers to women's participation in public expenditure decisions. In Uganda the gender issue has been institutionalized through the establishment of a separate women's ministry: the Ministry of Gender and Community Development. Although responsible for initiating and co-ordinating 'gender-responsive development' across economic development sectors, it has a limited capacity to do this because it is small and under-funded.

The gender interest in policy remains a step behind major economic planning initiatives; neither the Gender Ministry nor powerful feminist politicians are included in national economic planning processes. This seems obvious from the exclusion of gender equity concerns from

Uganda's national planning document, the 1993–6 *Rehabilitation and Development Plan*, which is the 'single most comprehensive statement of Government's principal social and economic policies' (GoU 1993: 1). This plan is primarily concerned with co-ordinating macro-economic stabilization measures and structural adjustment in agriculture, industry, and the social sectors. There is an emphasis on encouraging private initiative and a stronger export orientation in productive sectors through privatization and market liberalization. Three paragraphs under a small subheading on 'Women in Development' reiterate the government's commitment to integrating gender in development, and acknowledge that women 'are the overwhelming majority of the producers in agriculture which is the mainstay of the economy' (ibid.: 58). But in the rest of the document, gender is not integrated into planning assumptions regarding the impact of liberalization on patterns of labour and asset deployment in productive sectors such as agriculture, nor the impact of higher prices for basic commodities on domestic consumption budgets.

The Ministry of Gender and Community Development has been excluded from key economic policy discussions in other areas where gender issues are recognized as critical, such as poverty reduction. For example, the Ministry has not been invited to join a Poverty Assessment Consultative Group which was formed in 1995 for line ministries and donors to develop a National Action Plan for Poverty Reduction in Uganda (Elson and Evers 1997: 20). An important constraint has been the difficulty of building skills in gender-sensitive economic analysis in the Ministry itself or amongst sympathetic bureaucrats. Linked to this is the lack of economic analysis capability in women's civil society organizations. This emerged in 1996–7, when the normally secretive World Bank and Uganda's Ministry of Finance and Economic Planning threw open their joint economic planning process in highly publicized consultations with 'civil society' over the Country Assistance Strategy (a World Bank/government policy paper). Women's groups were invited to participate, but as Hellen Wangusa of the African Women's Policy Network, suggested in feedback to the World Bank, women were unable to make much of an impact, having no idea what a CAS is. She argued that many of the conditions of 'participation' were insensitive to women. The technical language was an enormous obstacle, with economic planners making few allowances for women's lack of economic literacy (or even basic literacy). And the time frame for involving them in 'participation' or 'consultation' was too short; the nine months provided by the Bank and the government's tight economic planning and project preparation framework were insufficient for women's groups to develop sufficient policy knowledge and bargaining skills (World Bank 1997: 18).

According to Tamale, the Ministry maintains formal and informal links with women legislators through conferences at district and national levels (1997: 112). The Ministry's political role of representing women was implicit in the symbolically powerful fact that its Minister was created the Vice-President in 1995. But clearly neither the Ministry nor women politicians have been able to make a significant impact on economic planning. Their impact has been greater in other areas, particularly: raising the political legitimacy of combating violence against women; protecting war and AIDS orphans; working to end female genital mutilation in the east of the country; improving legislation on domestic violence; and building the awareness of women all over the country about their rights through civics education. These are not insignificant achievements and are also, strikingly, issues which male legislators and bureaucrats have tended to ignore in the past. Since these kinds of issues deal with very fundamental forms of gender oppression, they tackle a first-order constraint on women, a set of obstacles to their capacities to benefit from economic policy opportunities. They tackle a set of problems around women's physical security and knowledge about their own human rights which are in their strategic gender interests to resolve.

(b) South Africa

In South Africa, likewise, the representation of gender equity concerns at economic planning levels has remained a step behind policy developments. To begin with, much of the bureaucratic machinery for the representation of gender issues in the public sphere has yet to be fully installed. In response to widespread debate amongst women in civil society, the option of a Women's Department was rejected out of a concern to avoid ghettoizing the gender equity interest (Mabandla 1994). Instead, a package of mechanisms to allow for the cross-institutional promotion of gender equity—measures such as departmental gender equity focal points, an Office on the Status of Women to develop a national women's emancipation policy, and a Commission on Gender Equality to keep an independent eye on the promotion of gender equity and the status of women (section 119 (3) of the constitution), and the building of similar structures at the provincial level.

There has been some delay in enacting these measures. Not until two years into the new administration was legislation enacted detailing the remit of the Commission on Gender Equality, and indicating that the Office on the Status of Women would be established in the Office of the Deputy President. The composition of the Commission was not finalized until early 1997, when it became clear that its budget was to be just one-third of budgets for other commissions, such as those on human rights or youth. More generally, women parliamentarians have complained that gender equity concerns have been forced into second place as other issues, such as the crime situation, are declared greater priorities, without, however, attention being given to the gendered dimensions of these issues.[18] Although there is considerable political will for action on gender equity, a central obstruction has been the limited capacity of the relevant departments to make new resource commitments and create new institutional structures in the environment of strict fiscal discipline which has been imposed by the economic reform programme adopted by the government. The 1996 neo-liberal Growth, Employment, and Redistribution (GEAR) programme is framed in the language of current economic orthodoxy of tightly controlled government deficits and in a political context which obliges compromises with business interests. Under these economic and political conditions, and in the absence of either an independent watchdog mechanism in the state, or a vigilant civil society presence, women's interests as a gender in redistribution and in participating in economic restructuring are easily overruled. Another problem is the difficulty of pursuing new agendas in bureaucracies which are little changed from apartheid days—this is a problem which afflicts many other government programmes addressing the vast socio-economic disparities between the races in South Africa.

As a result of the tremendous amount of caucusing amongst women which occurred during the transition to democracy, and included consultations with women across the country, and the elaboration of visionary plans for women's participation in political and economic democracy, women politicians in South Africa and women in civil society have developed significant skills in strategic planning. A draft Women's Empowerment Programme which is the result of consultations by the Gender Unit of the Reconstruction and Development Programme (the ANC's national development plan prior to 1996) will be finalized as the national gender equity policy by the Office of the Status of Women. As in other national contexts, however, there is still a lack of means and skills to 'mainstream' gender equity concerns across all government departments. An important and highly innovative response to this problem and to bureaucratic resistance to internalizing gender analysis is the Women's Budget initiative.

The Women's Budget initiative calculates the impact of government expenditure and revenue-raising policies on women, providing

[18] Interviews with four women parliamentarians in Cape Town: Brigitte Mbandla, Deputy Minister of Arts and Culture (22 Apr. 1997), Pregs Govender (23 Apr. 1997), Melanie Vorwoerd (24 Apr 1997), Nozizwe Madlala-Routledge (24 Apr. 1997).

a mechanism to audit the impact of public spending on women, and to sensitize economic planning departments to women's different experience of policy measures.[19] It also serves the critically important function of translating highly technical and political discourses surrounding public expenditure into accessible language for women's organizations. The capacity for financial analysis developed through this initiative, coupled with the relationships developed between women politicians, academics, and activists, enhances the prospects that this will prove an effective tool for working 'in and against' the state. Prospects that it will feed into policy-making processes may be enhanced by the appointment in 1996/7, for the first time, of two women to high positions in the Department of Finance: Gill Marcus as the deputy minister, and Maria Ramos as the director-general; both are considered potential allies for the women's movement.

Another arena in which efforts have been made to institutionalize women's interests is in the national corporatist body: the National Economic Development Labour Council (NEDLAC). NEDLAC has four chambers: the first three follow corporatist convention in housing representatives of labour, business, and the state. These chambers negotiate economic and trade policies. The fourth chamber houses representatives from civic organizations—and this has provided an arena for women's organizations which have national coverage to articulate women's interests in economic policy. To date, civic organizations have not had an appreciable impact on NEDLAC negotiations—they are constrained by the fact that they have no powers to formulate economic policy, and any proposals they make must be approved by an executive committee on which all four chambers are represented. There is no formal mechanism for the representation of women's interests in the other chambers, although the trade unions have well-established mechanisms for representing women; they were the first institutions in South Africa to have women's caucuses and gender equity units. Although women are still badly under-represented in the leadership of COSATU, the Congress of South African Trade Unions (Nyman 1996: 31), this has not prevented COSATU from defending gender equity concerns, lately in its campaign to include extended paid maternity and parental leave rights in the government's 1997 Basic

[19] This initiative is a joint project of the Working Group on Gender and Economic Policy of the Joint Standing Committee on Finance, the Institute of Democracy in South Africa (IDASA), the Law, Race, and Gender Research Unit (University of Cape Town), and the Community Agency for Social Inquiry. In its first year the emphasis was on employment, welfare, housing, education, public service, and taxation (Budlender 1996). In its second year it focused on the budgets for health; police, corrections and justice; transport; energy; land and agriculture; home and foreign affairs. It also looked at budget reform (Budlender 1997).

Conditions of Employment Bill. The toe-hold for women within South
Africa's corporatist institutions holds out promise that women may
develop influence in the arena of employment and industrial policy via
the same routes used in Scandinavia: enhanced influence on social equity
policy in Parliament feeding into greater representation of women on
corporate bodies.

In sum, the relative lack of political leverage of women and feminists both in and outside of the state in Uganda and South Africa has
obliged women to seek a bureaucratic form of representation for the
gender equity interest in policy-making. This strategy has had mixed
results: while it has raised the general level of awareness of gender
issues and heightened rhetorical commitments to women's rights, it
has not yet resulted in a substantive change to the concepts and priorities guiding economic planning, nor has it yet led to a transformation in the structure of bureaucracies and the character of the state.
These kinds of changes take time, and it is unrealistic to expect profound change yet. Given the difficulty of making a direct impact on
economic policy, women in both countries have chosen to pursue
policy change in other arenas, most notably in policies affecting
women's physical security in contexts where violence against women
is insufficiently proscribed socially, let alone prosecuted legally.
These efforts are highly significant: they promote policies which male
politicians and bureaucrats are less interested in pursuing, and they
are a critical step towards enabling women to participate equitably in
the economy and society. They aim to reduce one of the most fundamental transaction costs on women's access to social, economic, and
political opportunities, which is the fear, and experience, of gender-
based violence.

6. Conclusion: Interrupting Conversations between Men

More women in politics and a mobilized feminist presence in civil
society is probably a good indicator of the extent to which democratic
freedoms are shared in a society, but it does not translate automatically into higher well-being for women and more gender-sensitive
development policies. Political liberty and liberal constitutionalism
in Uganda and South Africa have been important, but not sufficient,
conditions for seeking changes to the institutions of democratic competition and public administration which would improve the representation of women's strategic interests. Political liberty has provided
women with the space in civil society to organize autonomously and
gain respect for feminist politics, while women's participation in

writing new constitutions has provided the opportunity to challenge customary law and the social power of private sphere patriarchy. Different measures to ease, however slightly, elite male control of party hierarchies—from the extreme of banning party politics in Uganda to the efforts to share space on party lists with women in South Africa— have enabled women to engage in political competition. The creation of new institutions in the state bureaucracy to perform a watchdog function over the impact of government policy on women—such as the Commission on Gender Equality in South Africa—demonstrate political will to improve women's status.

These processes have, however, been slowed by the masculinity of party politics, elite bargaining, and the functioning of state bureaucracies. The latter, particularly, are extremely slow to react to new gender equity legislation, as witnessed, for example, by the resistance of magistrates and the police system in South Africa to enact gender-sensitive measures to combat violence against women in ways which would challenge male sexual prerogatives. However, the very fact that women in both countries have been able to come together, both within political and civil society, to address issues of violence against women does indicate that important changes have been initiated. By demonstrating that violence in gender relations is a development and justice issue, not a private matter, women have politicized an issue which their male counterparts have, historically, failed to take as seriously as women do. This shows that women politicians and activists have been able to make some difference to the conduct and concerns of politics, and are beginning to enhance the accountability of government to women.

States do not achieve autonomy from socially entrenched gender relations merely by including more women in government, although greater numbers of women in policy-making fora is definitely a critical step to changing the culture, concerns, and capacities of government. Thus it is not whether government is liberal democratic or not which affects women's capacity to participate in politics and influence decision-making, but the degree to which it promotes and implements policies on social equality, and the degree of legitimacy enjoyed by feminist social movements and politicians. This does imply a significant degree of political liberty for women to politicize their needs, special measures to get women into politics, and economic policies compensating for their reproductive burden. The latter implies some version of a welfare state, and serious limits are put on gender-sensitive economic policies by the prevailing environment of economic austerity. Like liberal democratic politics, neo-liberal economic planning can admit of measures to enhance women's *access* to economic opportunities, but denies the legitimacy of efforts to level the playing field (and tamper with the market) in order for women to have substantive *control* over these opportunities.

REFERENCES

Agarwal, Bina (ed.) (1988), *Structures of Patriarchy: State, Community and Household, in Modernising Patriarchy*, Delhi: Kali for Women.

Ahikire, Josephine (1994), 'Women, Public Politics and Organization: Potentialities of Affirmative Action in Uganda', *Economic and Political Weekly*, Bombay, 29 Oct.

Albertyn, Catherine (1994), 'Women and the Transition to Democracy in South Africa', in Christina Murray (ed.), *Gender and the New South African Legal Order*, Cape Town: Juta Press.

—— (1996), 'Gender Equality in the Provinces: The Question of Structures', *Agenda*, 30: 6–17.

ANC Women's League (1994), *Reader: Women and Reconstruction*, Johannesburg: ANCWL Policy Division, Jan.

Annecke, Wendy (1990), 'The Launch of the Women's League', *Agenda*, 8: 1–3.

Boyd, Rosalind (1989), 'Empowerment of Women in Uganda: Real or Symbolic', *Review of African Political Economy*, 45–6.

Britton, Hannah (1997), 'Women have the Numbers, but not the Power', *Parliamentary Whip*, Cape Town: IDASA, Parliamentary Information and Monitoring Service, 18 Apr.

Budlender, Debbie (ed.) (1996), *The Women's Budget*, Cape Town: IDASA.

—— (ed.) (1997), *The Second Women's Budget*, Cape Town: IDASA.

Charlton, Sue Ellen, Everett, Jana, and Staudt, Kathleen (eds.), (1989), *Women, the State, and Development*, New York: State University of New York Press.

Charman, Andrew, de Swardt, Cobus, and Simons, Mary (1991) 'The Politics of Gender: Negotiating Liberation', *Transformation*, 15: 40–64.

Connell, R. W. (1990), 'The State, Gender and Sexual Politics', *Theory and Society*, 19: 507–44.

Dahlerup, Drude (1988), 'From a Small to a Large Minority: Women in Scandinavian Politics', *Scandinavian Political Studies*, 11/4: 275–98.

Devenish, George (1993), 'Democratic Counter-majoritarianism: Protecting Ethnic Minorities in a Liberal Democracy with Special Reference to South Africa', in Pearson Nherere and Marina d'Engelbronner-Kolff (eds.), *The Institutionalisation of Human Rights in South Africa*, Copenhagen: Nordic Human Rights Publications.

Elson, Diane, and Evers, Barbara (1997), 'Gender Aware Country Economic Reports: Working Paper Number 2: Uganda', produced to support the DAC/WID Task Force on Gender Guidelines for Programme Aid and Other Forms of Economic Policy Related Assistance, University of Manchester, July.

Finnemore, Martheanne (1994), 'Negotiating Power', *Agenda*, 20: 16–21.

Fraser, Nancy (1989), *Unruly Practices: Power, Discourse, and Gender in Contemporary Social Theory*, Cambridge: Polity Press.

Friedman, Elisabeth (1998), 'Why "Machismo was Stronger than a Military Dictatorship": The Paradoxes of Gendered Political Opportunities and Women's Organizing in the Venezuelan Transition to Democracy', *Latin American Research Review*.

Geisler, Gisela (1994), 'Troubled Sisterhood: Women and Politics in Southern Africa: Case Studies from Zambia, Zimbabwe and Botswana', paper presented at the 37th Annual African Studies Association Meeting in Toronto, Canada, 3–6 Nov.

Goetz, A. M. (1995), 'The Politics of Integrating Gender to State Development Processes', UNRISD Occasional Paper no. 2, Geneva.

GoU (Government of Uganda) (1993) *Rehabilitation and Development Plan, 1993/4–1995/6*, vol. i, Kampala: Ministry of Finance and Economic Planning.

Gouws, Amanda (1996), 'The Rise of the Femocrat?', *Agenda*, 30: 31–43.

Gowans, Jill (1997), 'Under-representation Linked to Abuse of Women', *Sunday Tribune*, 9 Mar.

Greer, Germaine (1996), 'Come the Revolution', *Sunday Times*, 3 Mar.

Hassim, Shireen (1991a), 'Where have All the Women Gone? Gender Politics in South African Debates', unpublished conference paper, 'Conference on Women and Gender in Southern Africa', Natal University.

—— (1991b), 'Gender, Social Location and Feminist Politics in South Africa', *Transformation*, 15: 65–82.

Hernes, Helga Maria (1987), *Welfare State and Woman Power: Essays in State Feminism*, Oslo: Norwegian University Press.

Hirschmann, David (1991), 'Women and Political Participation in Africa: Broadening the Scope of Research', *World Development*, 19/12: 1679–94.

Hyden, Goran (1995), 'Political Representation and the Future of Uganda', in Holger Hansen and Michael Twaddle (eds.), *From Chaos to Order: The Politics of Constitution-Making in Uganda*, Kampala: Fountain Publishers.

Inter-Parliamentary Union (1994), *Plan of Action to Correct Present Imbalances in the Participation of Men and Women in Political Life*, Geneva: Inter-Parliamentary Union.

Jaquette, Jane (1997), 'Women in Power: From Tokenism to Critical Mass', *Foreign Policy*, Autumn: 23–37.

Jonasdottir, Anna (1988), 'On the Concept of Interest, Women's Interests, and the Limitations of Interest Theory', in Kathleen Jones and Anna Jonasdottir, *The Political Interests of Gender: Developing Theory and Research with a Feminist Face*, London: Sage.

Kasente, Deborah (1994), 'Women in the Constituent Assembly in Uganda', discussion paper, presented to the Public Forum of the African Women and Governance Seminar and Training Workshop, Entebbe, 24–30 July.

Kemp, Amanda, Madlala, Nozizwe, Moodley, Asha, and Salo, Elaine (1995), 'The Dawn of a New Day: Redefining South African Feminism', in Amrita Basu (ed.), *The Challenge of Local Feminisms*, Boulder, Colo.: Westview Press.

Leftwich, Adrian (1996), 'On the Primacy of Politics in Development', in Adrian Leftwich (ed.), *Democracy and Development: Theory and Practice*, Cambridge: Polity Press.

Lewis, Desiree (1994), 'Women and Gender in South Africa', in Vincent Maphai (ed.), *South Africa: The Challenge of Change*, Harare: SAPES Books.

Liatto-Katundu, Beatrice (1993), 'The Women's Lobby and Gender Relations in Zambia', *Review of African Political Economy*, 56: 79–125.

London–Edinburgh Weekend-Return Group (1979), *In and Against the State*, London: Pluto Press.

Mabandla, Brigitte (1994), 'Choices for South African Women', *Agenda*, 20: 22–9.

MacGaffey, Janet (1986), 'Women and Class Formation in a Dependent Economy: Kisangani Entrepreneurs', in Claire Robertson and Iris Berger (eds.), *Women and Class in Africa*, New York: Africa Publishing Company.

Molyneux, Maxine (1985), 'Mobilization without Emancipation? Women's Interests, the State, and Revolution in Nicaragua', *Feminist Studies*, 11/2: 227–54.

—— (1994), 'Women's Rights and the International Context: Some Reflections on the Post-communist States', *Millennium*, (London: LSE), 23/2: 287–313.

Mugyenyi, Mary (1994), 'Gender, Empowerment, and Development in Uganda', Kampala: Department of Women's Studies, Makerere University, mimeo.

Nelson, Barbara J., and Chowdhury, Najma (eds.) (1994), *Women and Politics Worldwide*, London: Yale University Press.

Norris, P. (1985), 'Women's Legislative Participation in Western Europe', *West European Politics*, 8.

Nyman, R. (1996), 'The Glass Ceiling: The Representation of Women in COSATU', *South African Labour Bulletin*, 20/5.

Parpart, Jane (1988), 'Women and the State in Africa', in Donald Rothschild and Naomi Chazan (eds.), *The Precarious Balance: State and Society in Africa*, Boulder, Colo.:, Westview Press.

—— and Staudt, Kathleen (1989), *Women and the State in Africa*, Boulder, Colo.: Lynne Rienner.

Phillips, Anne (1991), *Engendering Democracy*, Philadelphia: Pennsylvania University Press.

Robinson, Jennifer (1995), 'Act of Omission: Gender and Local Government in the Transition', *Agenda*, 26: 7–18.

Serote, Pethu, January-Bardill, Nozipho, Liebenberg, Sandra, and Nolte, Jacqui (1996), 'A Report on what the S. A. Parliament has Done to Improve the Quality of Life and Status of Women in S. A.', Cape Town: Office of the Speaker of the National Assembly of South Africa, mimeo.

Staudt, Kathleen (1987), 'Women, Politics, the State, and Capitalist Transformation in Africa', in I. L. Markovitz (ed.), *Studies in Power and Class in Africa*, New York: Oxford University Press.

—— (ed.) (1990), *Women, International Development, and Politics: The Bureaucratic Mire*, Philadelphia: Temple University Press.

Tamale, Sylvia (1997), 'When Hens Begin to Crow: Gender and Parliamentary Politics in Contemporary Uganda', unpublished Ph.D. thesis, University of Minnesota.

Tripp, Aili Mari (1994), 'Gender, Political Participation and the Transformation of Associational Life in Uganda and Tanzania', *African Studies Review*, 37/1: 107–31.

—— (1996), 'Women's Associations and Challenges to Neopatrimonial Rule in Africa', MSU Working Paper no. 15, East Lansing: Michigan State University.

—— (1997), 'Women and Politics in Uganda: The Challenge of Associational Autonomy' (provisional title), draft unpublished manuscript, University of Wisconsin-Madison.

Walker, Cheryl (1991), *Women and Resistance in South Africa*, Cape Town: David Philip.

Watson, S. (ed.) (1990), *Playing the State*, Sydney: Allen & Unwin.

Waylen, S. (1994), 'Women and Democratization: Conceptualizing Gender Relations in Transition Politics', *World Politics*, 46/3: 327–54.

World Bank (1997), 'A Report on the Second Annual Meeting', External Gender Consultative Group, Gender Analysis and Policy Unit, Washington: World Bank.

Yeatman, Anna (1994), *Postmodern Revisionings of the Political*, London: Routledge.

Young, Iris Marion (1990), *Justice and the Politics of Difference*, Princeton: Princeton University Press.

Democratization and Sustainable Rural Livelihoods

SUSANNA DAVIES

1. Introduction

Elites and analysts of the so-called third wave of democratization have very different agendas from those of the rural poor.[1] This majority are largely invisible both in the theory and practice of democratization in sub-Saharan Africa (SSA) in the 1990s, despite the simultaneous pre-occupation with promoting sustainable development and livelihoods on their behalf.[2] Democratization in SSA has been conceived of and is being implemented by a narrow urban and largely middle-class elite (with some urban working-class support for its initial establishment), often in alliance with northern donors. This bias is reflected in recent polit-ical analyses and exacerbated by their emphasis on formal political systems and formal civil society. It echoes the enduring liberal and Marxist belief that the rural 'peasantry' are essentially conservative and reactionary and need to be shown the route to political enlightenment by their urban neighbours.

One of the questions explored in this book is how democratic regimes can tackle developmental problems effectively, a crucial dimension of which is what democratization means for the rural poor and their developmental objectives. It is now widely accepted that

---

[1] The term 'rural poor' refers to the majority of subsistence or near-subsistence agri-cultural and pastoral producers in SSA and is not restricted to the rural poorest. The interests of rural elites, while still less visible than those of their urban counterparts, have always been better represented via formal political channels.

[2] Sub-Saharan Africa conventionally refers to all of continental Africa, excluding the North African states of Morocco, Algeria, Tunisia, Libya, and Egypt. In this chapter, South Africa is excluded from the analysis on the grounds of the specific nature of the democratic transition from apartheid.

development is not simply a matter of economic growth, but also is centrally concerned with reducing vulnerability and poverty in sustainable ways. In addition to growth and distributional issues, this entails improving risk management and protecting future capacity to survive, as well as increasing security to meet current needs. Donors have become vociferous advocates and paymasters of both democratization and sustainable development, without adequately addressing the relationship between the two. The World Bank (1989: 60, cited in Rasheed 1995) has argued that 'history suggests that political legitimacy and consensus are a precondition for sustainable development', although most historians would argue that the opposite is true. Developmental breakthroughs which have generated economic benefits for the majority tend to precede reforms to extend political participation. In Britain, for example, men were only gradually enfranchised once economic growth was well established; and women did not get the vote until nearly a century after the industrial revolution. Historically, the rural poor have been excluded both from the benefits of economic growth and from formal politics and policy-making, irrespective of regime type (see Gore 1994).

Failing to tackle the link between democratization and sustainable development matters because democratization is being experimented with in some of the poorest and 'least developed' countries in the world. Of the forty-eight countries classified as having low human development by the Human Development Index in 1996, thirty-seven were in SSA (UNDP 1996). Taking the bottom ten countries in the world, nine of which are in SSA: three have undergone democratic reforms in the 1990s after relatively short periods of political unrest (Burkina Faso, Mali, Niger); two have done so after prolonged civil wars (Ethiopia and Mozambique); two have only just signed peace agreements after protracted wars (Angola and Sierra Leone); and one continues to be in the grip of political uncertainty (Burundi).[3] It is in such poorest, least developed countries that sustainable development is strongly advocated as the only alternative to worsening impoverishment and marginalization. Yet these very conditions mean that democratic breakthroughs are chronically weak. This fragility is due to the dearth of economic and institutional resources available to democratically elected governments to meet the expectations of the newly enfranchised electorate, expectations which are raised in the fever of electoral campaigns. A vicious circle between faltering and unsustainable growth and development on the one hand, and political instability on the other, is created; generating the conditions for a return to authoritarian forms

---

[3] The tenth country is Afghanistan.

of rule, in the name of restoring order and stability. This spectre hovers over many of the new democracies of SSA today.

No one claims that the process of democratization in SSA is going to be easy or that it can overturn entrenched political and social norms overnight. The concern here is not with teething problems alone, but with a more fundamental characteristic of democratization in SSA: its inappropriateness to the livelihoods of the rural poor, which is reinforced by formal civil society–state relations. The term 'inappropriate' describes our concerns better than 'irrelevant' because it cannot be assumed that democratization is inconsequential for, or has a purely benign effect on, the rural poor. Democratization may damage their interests, not simply fail to address them, by undermining or bypassing local political institutions and so reduce their options to pursue sustainable livelihoods. If so, the rural poor can only appropriate democratization by a more inclusive approach to state–society relations, in which informal civil society is part of the process. The exclusion of the rural poor is not simply a transitional problem, for as Fox (1995: 13) correctly argues, 'the "deals" (rules) that are worked out during the transition phase not only affect who will participate in the immediate shaping of the new regime, but will ultimately determine "winners and losers" under the new regime'.

Just because informal social and political institutions exist and work to some degree in rural communities, this does not make them virtuous, efficient, or intrinsically better than democratic alternatives, however new and imperfect. As Manor (in this volume) argues, there is little practical sense in having unrealistic expectations of local-level contexts. Conversely, it is vital not to *under*estimate the capabilities of local groups and institutions to support livelihoods (in however an archaic and imperfect way), especially in relation to the very limited capacity of the centre in much of SSA to reach the rural poor. The aim here is to redress the imbalance of much debate about democratization which concentrates on the nation-state, in alliance with formal civil society; *not* to construct and defend an idealized notion of customary political and social organization. This debate needs, first, to include questions about how and whether informal rural political systems can be incorporated into the process and rendered more democratic. This might include, for example: the election of village chiefs and councils, in place of existing hereditary or appointed systems; or the explicit and conscious reinforcement of intersections and channels of communication between local polities which do represent the poor to some extent and democratically elected representatives at higher levels of government. Secondly, the question needs to be tackled of how those elements of livelihoods which are *already* decided in inclusive and participatory ways can be reinforced. Examples include: decisions about how to manage drought and other shocks to livelihoods; when to switch between the exploitation of different key resources; or how to resolve conflicts over such resources. Although it tends to be assumed by outsiders that such livelihood decisions are either random or based on individual choice, in fact there are often well-established (though legally unrecognized) institutional rules for arriving at consensus.

2. Politicizing Sustainable Development

Initially, sustainable development focused on environmental sustainability, but it is now recognized that—much like economic growth —there is little to be gained from singling out environmental sustainability from the web of conflicting and overlapping development challenges.[4] Increasingly, sustainable development is concerned with how trade-offs are made optimally between environmental, economic, and social sustainability. As such, the idea encapsulates reduction of vulnerability, poverty and welfare issues, social justice, environmental protection, as well as economic growth and equitable distribution of its gains. Focusing on the more specific subset of issues about how the livelihoods of the rural poor can be more sustainable, as a minimum people must have the capacity not only to subsist today, but to do so in such a way as not to compromise both their own and subsequent generations' capacity to survive in the future. To do this, people seek to minimize fluctuations in well-being, consumption, and incomes; to adapt to anticipated risks and sudden shocks in smooth and positive ways; to be economically viable in the medium to long term; to manage exploitation of natural resources in ways that will secure their future availability; and to cement and reproduce reciprocal social ties which insure against failures in production, exchange, and employment. Inevitably, the poor are forced to make trade-offs between these often competing objectives.

A predominant feature of colonial and post-colonial governments in SSA has been their failure to assist the poor in optimizing these trade-offs. All too often, governments (sometimes with the collusion and financial support of donors) have *reduced* the capacity of the rural poor to manage risk, based on misapprehensions of how the rural poor try to make their livelihoods more secure and sustainable (e.g. by

---

[4] See WCED (1987) for one of the earliest expositions of sustainable development and, for a more recent view, see Lele (1991).

privatizing common property resources or forcing sedentarization), coupled with policies designed to enrich elites and urban populations at the rural poor's expense (e.g. usurious and untimely taxation which is not reinvested in rural areas or maintaining artificially low producer prices). The security of rural livelihoods can be increased on many fronts, the achievement of which is contingent upon state and societal support, not just for rural elites, but for the poor as well. It is most simply encapsulated by the idea of increased entitlements: to land and other natural resources; to affordable, needed inputs, including flexible credit; to appropriate technology to raise output and productivity; to food when production fails; to functioning labour markets; to social services; to extended kinship networks to insure against illness or desertion and so on. But these material and social provisions tell only part of the story. The rural poor also need the more intangible benefits ascribed to democracy if their livelihoods are to be more sustainable: accountability from those who exercise power in their name; representation in a range of fora; and greater rights to a share of the national cake than they conventionally receive.

The success or failure of people's attempts to pursue more sustainable livelihoods is contingent on the interaction of state–society relations to a significant extent. Yet little mention is made of the political dimension of sustainable livelihoods, although implicit in the idea are political stability and managed institutional change. In so far as it is addressed, it is in the context of the need for peace and security in the sense of absence of armed conflict. While important, this recent emphasis on the acute, destabilizing impact of war in SSA on rural livelihoods (see Duffield 1990, de Waal 1996a) has tended to divert attention away from the political dimension of livelihoods under more peaceful—but nevertheless stressful, changing, and uncertain —political conditions. Chronic instability affects both the formal dimension of state–society relations, in which the rural poor interact with the state and formal civil society organizations (notably non-governmental organizations (NGOs), but also well-resourced and established community organizations); and the informal one, in which they interact with local indigenous political and social institutions and organizations.[5]

The significance of this second dimension has been underestimated in the current process of democratization, not least because debates about democratization and sustainable development are to a great degree hermetically sealed from each other. To the extent that the

---

[5] 'Institutions' is used in the sense of regularized patterns of behaviour or the rules of the game and 'organizations' as the players in the game (see North 1990).

sustainable development literature does address democratization, it has an essentially optimistic view of political liberalization. Those concerned with democratization have more nuanced views of this relationship, but rarely explore it specifically in terms of the rural poor. Recent attention has focused at a more macro level, on the links between economic reform via structural adjustment and political liberalization (see Robinson 1996). The implicit assumption on both sides of the debate is that successful democratic transitions and better governance go hand in hand with the promotion of more sustainable livelihoods. Yet there is little evidence, let alone systematic research, to support the belief that they are mutually reinforcing at this juncture in Africa's political economy.

One apparent area of overlap concerns participation, but just how do the rural poor participate in democratization other than as vote fodder? Conventionally, rural development has not been democratic, with respect either to the political system controlling it, or to the manner in which it has been implemented. These two trends have been mutually reinforcing: the rural poor made no input into rural development policy and it followed that, in the implementation of development initiatives, there was little genuine participation. Top-down approaches to rural development were underpinned by dirigiste and clientelist political systems, with donors content to fund such initiatives without, until recently, insisting on greater democratization as a precondition for their assistance. Pressure for democratization has come both from within certain strata of African societies, most of which are urban and professional (e.g. students, teachers, lawyers, and civil servants), with some popular, urban backing; and from without in the form of donor political conditionality. But it is by no means automatically true that greater democratization leads to greater participation of the rural poor in policy decisions and implementation which affect their lives.

Both 'democrats' and 'sustainable developers' are strong advocates of the developmental benefits to be gained from increased participation, yet the two sides mean significantly different things by current usage of the term. For democrats, it is participation in formal political processes, and in some cases in formal civil society organizations, which counts.[6] Democratization has, of course, facilitated the possibility for such participation, not least by holding elections, but self-exclusion remains high. Failure to vote has resulted in only 20 to 50 per cent of the registered electorate voting in the recent wave of multiparty elections in SSA (Rasheed 1995). In the presidential elections

[6] See Robinson in this volume for a discussion of political participation.

in Mali in 1992, for example, the rural turnout was only 21.3 per cent (compared to a still low, but significantly higher, 28.5 per cent in urban constituencies). Despite this low figure, the success of the winner, Alpha Konaré, has been attributed to his personal visits to many rural areas during the campaign (Vengroff 1993). Low turnouts are explained by a range of factors, which tend to start from the premiss that people would vote if only they were more aware of or better equipped to embrace the intrinsic value of democratic participation. Much less often are they explained in terms of *conscious* and *critical* self-exclusion, on the basis of failing to perceive any self-interest in or developmental gains from participation. Fowler (1996: 24) argues that, 'at its simplest, democracy is a condition where people effectively control those who exercise authority in their name. In other words, those in power have gained a mandate and hence have earned legitimacy with the polity.' But this mandate does not come from rural areas, and especially not from poor people within them.

In contrast to democrats, sustainable developers see participation as a more practical, continuous input into local decision-making which affects immediate, tangible development outcomes (e.g. which intervention donors will fund, how a given government or NGO policy will be implemented in a particular locality). At best, such an approach empowers marginal local groups via the acquisition of resources, skills, and strengthened associational activity. At worst, the fervour for more participatory approaches to rural development is politically simplistic, implying that greater participation of the poor and marginalized in such decisions will, as if by magic, do away with entrenched political, class, and gender interests both within rural communities and between them and the wider political economy.

The two sides come together in asserting that participation in local civil society organizations engenders a gradual process of greater empowerment, leading to a greater desire or capacity to participate in other spheres. Participation in local rural development decisions thus makes them more democratically active in formal political arenas. It is in this vein that Ndegwa (1996: 2) claims that 'a clear effect of NGO grassroots development work is to enable local communities to independently engage in political actions, with important implications for democratisation'. But such reasoning is often normative or based on anecdotal evidence, and fails to account adequately for the fact that formal participation in Africa has long been restricted to a small minority. There is little history of broad-based Western-style social coalitions in SSA; rather, 'power is based on loose alliances of elite factions with followings grounded in clientelism' (Bratton and van de Walle 1992: 436). However, as Gore (1994) notes, clientelism is paradoxical with regard to its inclusionary/exclusionary nature and is by no means uniformly exclusive of the poor. Although highly undemocratic, participation in patron–client relations is rational in certain conditions even for those who are excluded from some choices by virtue of their inclusion in the clientelist network. These same conditions relate directly to the ability to sustain livelihoods: control of key resources such as land and employment by one particular group in society; the inhibition of organization and co-operative mobilization by the client group to gain access to the resources controlled by the patron group; and the absence of universalist criteria for allocating and exchanging resources and, in their place, private and personalistic criteria (Gore 1994: 66, citing Clapham 1982). Current debates about participation thus provide only limited insights into the ways in which democratization affects the livelihoods of the rural poor. The implication that participation in local decisions automatically leads to participation in formal political processes at higher levels, for which there is little or no historical or cultural precedent, belies how power is distributed and decisions are made both by and for the rural poor in SSA.

3. *The Inappropriateness of Democratization*

The idea of democracy being inappropriate is not new, but conventional reasoning is based on democracy's incompatibility with existing forms of government, especially clientelism. The concern here is a different one: how democratization is inappropriate to the ways in which the rural poor pursue their livelihoods. The tendency of authoritarian regimes to perpetuate or increase rural poverty is much better documented, and attributed to limited pluralism and political competition, hierarchical and one-way communication, and dependence on the distribution of resources between elites to maintain power, making them unavailable for reallocation to rural areas and marginalized groups within them. In a study of six Asian countries, it was found that resources were more likely to be distributed in favour of the rural poor when regimes were democratic and political elites were dependent on their electoral support, than when regimes were authoritarian (King 1981). But this implied causality between democratization and poverty-reducing agendas presupposes rural participation in elections and availability of resources to distribute which can make a significant difference to the material position of the poor, neither of which is currently the case in SSA.

White (1995) has identified four variant views of the links between democratization and development, none of which quite captures the essence of inappropriateness. The most dismissive of these is the school which argues that the political regime is not the central issue. Instead, building up the capacity of the developmental state will deliver developmental objectives to the greatest number, whether authoritarian or democratic in type. In some ways this echoes the charge of inappropriateness due to existing forms of government, focusing instead on government capacity. At the opposite end of the debate is the optimistic school mentioned above, which downplays or rejects incompatibility between democratization and sustainable development for the rural poor. The two remaining schools hint at inappropriateness, but for different reasons. Pessimists hold that it is hard to combine democratic politics with sustained economic growth, however laudable an objective democracy may be in its own right. One variation on this theme is that Africa is not 'ready' for multi-party democracy, a claim made by colonial rulers and fading one-party states alike (Bratton and van der Walle 1992). Another is the critique that democracy in Africa is a façade and has been imported, not by popular demand and organic momentum, but by the influence and insistence of foreign donors (Rasheed 1995). None of these views adequately describes the dissonance between democratization and the livelihoods of the rural poor, they only infer that their needs are unlikely to be met without economic growth and that democratization may not be the surest route to achieve this, especially if it is imposed from outside. The don't-expect-anything school comes closest to inappropriateness, correctly rejecting the optimists' claim that political freedom and economic growth go hand in hand. As White (1995) argues, this linkage is especially problematic in countries which are characterized by extreme poverty, massive inequality, and rising mass expectations as a result of democratic openings, an accurate description of many of the new democracies in SSA.

4. Rights, Resources, and the Rural Poor

Interpretations of what democratization means range from narrow one person one vote definitions, implicit in which are rights of citizenship and collective rights to organize, to broad ones of increased plurality and participation in a variety of political fora and processes. In the following discussion, the concern is with democratization as it is currently being played out in SSA, and not with an idealized notion of a theoretical democratic polity.

Rights-based views of democracy are especially problematic for the rural poor for two reasons. First, such a view (whether narrowly defined in terms of individual rights of political representation, or more broadly as rights of citizenship) implies no urban or class bias in democratic objectives. In a study of democratic change since 1989 in thirty African states, Bratton and van der Walle (1992: 436) found that the social composition of protesters was almost exclusively urban, with no evidence of rural unrest in any of the countries in their sample. They purposively excluded countries undergoing civil wars where, as they correctly point out, organized political opposition clearly originates from rural areas (e.g. in Angola, Ethiopia, Mozambique, Somalia, and Sudan). The urban bias in the transition to democracy is explained in terms of the relative benefits which have accrued to rural surplus producers as a result of structural adjustment. This, however, belies the fact that the rural poor are not simply (or not even) producers of agricultural surplus, but food purchasers and they too have had to contend with price rises. They may, however, have lost less than their urban counterparts given how little they benefited from state employment and service provision *before* structural adjustment. Class is given as the second explanatory variable for the lack of involvement of rural people: the democratic wave has been the concern of the middle class, itself predominantly urban (students, teachers, and, in West Africa, civil servants). Other reasons for the failure of the rural poor to participate are indicative of their wider social exclusion: low literacy rates and educational enrolment levels; limited access to formal sources of information; physical distance from decision-makers and political parties; and lack of time due to the exigencies of their livelihoods. The apparent universality of democratization masks the fact that democrats continue to express their own urban elitist perceptions of rural people's needs and interests, rather than giving a voice to the rural poor's own understanding of what rights they require in order to pursue sustainable livelihoods.

This leads to the second problem: democratization defined in terms of rights (especially individual ones) and values directly contradicts most existing customary mechanisms and institutions for distributing power in rural SSA. As Bangura (1994) has argued in the context of the ineffectiveness of institutions in SSA to respond to economic crisis— a point equally relevant to democratization—there is a fundamental contradiction between the formal institutional set-up itself and what goes on in wider society. Power is distributed, managed, and bargained over on the basis of gender, age, kinship, lineage, and customary rights and other sources of hierarchy, which are not necessarily—or indeed usually—compatible with those rights associated with democracy (see Berry 1989). It is on the basis of these criteria that social and political interaction in Africa is determined; and not on the basis of individual or collective rights shared by equals as commonly understood in Western liberal democracies. Such interactions are not equal in a democratic sense, but can be equitable in so far as they operate according to a set of rules, based on a set of values, which participating members agree to. More important is that they are often perceived to *work* in that they allow people to manage the resources on which they depend for their livelihoods in a relatively stable and predictable way. Certainly, they are regarded as working better than the alternative provided by the state, often viewed as a major source of instability and unpredictability, no matter what its political hue.

An obvious example is the nationalization of natural resources, access to which is subsequently granted on the basis of state-issued licences. Such equality of access flies in the face of customary natural resource management regimes. These have evolved to take account of the variability in resource availability between seasons and years and the need to manage fragile ecosystems in ways which reflect the nature of the resources concerned and the multiple demands of conflicting interest groups (e.g. of strangers and founding lineages, of herders and farmers) which depend on them. Critically, *customary regimes manage people in relation to the resources on which their livelihoods depend*. As Metcalfe (1996: 97) argues in the context of natural resource management in Zimbabwe, 'democracy looks good in theory but when the leadership positions are all dominated by a centralised party hierarchy sometimes customary leadership seems more representative and accountable . . . what needs governing is not so much the people in isolation but the people in relation to the communal area resource base.'

Defining democratization as a deliberate process of institutional construction and accumulation[7] is more compatible with a sustainable development approach than either a rights-based view or a narrow definition based on participation in formal political processes. Democratization in the sense of 'the deliberate construction of new political institutions and the development of a pluralistic political culture actively favouring participation and contestation' (Robinson 1996: 70) appears to be flexible enough to incorporate existing informal institutions. But this institutional view *only* helps if local indigenous institutions are regarded as being legitimate by the democratic system (part of the plurality), despite the fact that they are rarely based on Western liberal democratic values, and hence easy to dismiss as being anti-democratic. Thus when democratization is interpreted as a

---

[7] See O'Donnell and Schmitter (1986), cited in Bratton and van der Walle (1992); White (1995).

technique of government based on a set of values which determines how power should be distributed within society, the critical issue for the rural poor is whether these values are consistent with the ways in which *they* manage the resources on which they depend to make their livelihoods. Invariably this is not the case. A great deal hinges on whether the values of ruling elite include pro-poor or anti-poor attitudes. If pro-poor, there is scope for democratization developing a more enabling climate. But even if elites at a central level are advocates of greater inclusion and distribution in favour of the poor, this can be thwarted by prevailing anti-poor attitudes at lower levels of government, where the distinction between poor and not quite poor (including low-level civil servants) is not all that great. Popular democracy is much harder to promote in resource-scarce economies, where the not-poor hover just above the poverty line.

The case for the inappropriateness of democratization starts from the premiss that political rights are not the driving force behind the rural poor trying to make their livelihoods more sustainable. Other rights are more likely to be compatible with this objective: the right to secure tenure to land and access to other resources; the right to food and other economic securities; the right to credit on terms that are not usurious; the right to pay taxes at moments which take account of seasonal income and expenditure flows; or the right to protection from preventable illnesses. This is not to argue that issues about the distribution of power and civil and political rights have no bearing on the interests of the rural poor, but rather that there is a need to focus on *rights to resources as well as to political power*. The Indian famine relief system provides an illustration of this key connection. It not only provides resources in times of famine, but also—critically—state provision of these resources is underwritten by a legal right to famine relief and an effective judicial system through which these rights can be claimed (de Waal 1996*b*). In India, freedom from famine is part of a social contract, developed through political struggle. In stark contrast, there has been little or no opportunity for famine prevention to emerge as a right in Africa because 'famine never became the politicised issue in the same way that it was in India' (ibid.: 199). Consequently, there is no social contract between those in power and famine-prone people, nor any means of holding the powerful to account if they fail to respond. This belies the optimists' view that 'secondary' economic and social rights will only be achieved once fundamental political rights have been established.

The inappropriateness of democratization is further justified by Bayart's (1993) argument that marginal groups, including the rural poor, are unwilling to participate in government-driven change, as long as the regime in power lacks legitimacy and appears only to be interested in self-enrichment via bureaucratic and all other means available. Although developed in the context of authoritarian regimes, this argument is equally pertinent to democratizing ones, if the rural poor are excluded from the agenda and benefits of democratization in ways that are understood by them positively to affect their livelihoods. The distinction made by Luckham (in this volume) between popular democracy and liberal democracy is important in this respect. Only popular democracy emphasizes social and economic rights as well as political ones, and the eradication of social as well as political inequalities. Few of the new democracies in SSA today fit Luckham's category of popular democracies, especially in the context of popularity among the rural poor.

Emphasizing alienation from government, irrespective of its political hue, echoes the don't-expect-anything school, as does the implication that legitimacy is not conferred on government simply because elections have been held. But inappropriateness goes one step further and suggests that democratization may actually harm the interests of the rural poor, by actively undermining the ways in which power and resources are distributed within rural livelihood systems, given democracy's emphasis on equality and tendency to render invisible informal and undemocratic customary institutions. Further, although the objective of democratization may be institutional accumulation, this takes time and many new democracies are quicker to destroy existing institutions perceived to be undemocratic than they are to embark on the long process of establishing new ones and, crucially, legitimizing them in the eyes of the poor. This is inevitable in democratization that is conceived of and imposed by agents from outside (urban) and above (middle class). Marginalizing the rural poor from processes of democratization means that their interests are either only indirectly addressed, or are treated as a by-product of other groups' democratic gains. For those who are not mainstreamed in the process of democratization, there is a need to be much more precise about its costs and benefits—what it replaces and destroys, as well as what it adds— before its developmental effects on particular groups can be assessed.

5. Formal and Informal Civil Society–State Relations

The charge of inappropriateness does not mean that maintaining authoritarian regimes is preferable to experimenting with democratization, but it does force the question of how democratization affects the livelihoods of the rural poor, and how it might contribute to their improved sustainability. Civil society appears to be the most obvious route via which democratization can be appropriated by the rural poor, not least because it is in part comprised of organizations and associations formed by people disenfranchised or disempowered by the state (Bayart 1986). Further, the nature of associational life in civil society is one of the key areas of difference between developmentally effective and ineffective democratic regimes (White 1995). A vibrant civil society grounded in rural areas will be better able to promote the rural poor's interests, than either a low level of associational life or one which is predominantly urban.

Relations between civil society and the state have been vigorously debated in the context of democratization in SSA. In rural contexts, much of this debate revolves around NGOs (or the associations which they spawn and promote), as the most visible and often vociferous actors within rural civil society. In contrast to democratic movements, NGOs are regarded as significant agents to provide the link to sustainable livelihoods because they tend to focus on poor rural people (Thérien 1991). The role of civil society *vis-à-vis* the state has undergone a number of fashions since independence in SSA. Under authoritarian regimes, local civil society was severely constrained by extractive state policies and purposive attempts to undermine both non-governmental and 'traditional' institutions. It is important to note, however, that within many authoritarian states, customary rules and political systems continued to operate even though hidden or not formally acknowledged. In contrast, foreign civil society, as manifested in international NGOs, thrived in rural SSA, especially in the aftermath of the drought in the early 1980s in much of East and West Africa. Since the late 1980s, democratic change has gone hand in hand with a more active interest in local formal civil society as an agent of political change (Fowler 1993), although its contribution is greatly contested.

Those in favour of formal civil society's transformatory powers begin from the premiss that it has gradually replaced the failing state, initially in delivering social services (MWENGO 1993, Ng'ethe and Kanyinga 1992, Mwansa 1995). As it gains momentum, some even go so far as to argue that civil society organizations can be the 'official opposition' in absence of a functioning party system (Ndegwa 1996), or at least can act as a conduit for people to reach the state and so promote regime change. Conversely, when civil society is weakly and informally organized, it is much easier for incumbent governments to ride out pro-democracy protests (Bratton and van der Walle 1994). Once the transition to democratization is under way, there is an iterative relationship between it and civil society. Supporters argue that democratization will create the conditions under which civil society can flourish, as part of the development of institutional plurality. But such arguments have yet to be tested in the context of SSA, not least because the democratic transition is still so recent.

Sceptics of the contribution civil society can make identify a number of reasons for its limited potential both to bring about and benefit from democratization. These relate to the relationship between civil society, the state, and wider society (or community) and to the internal culture of civil society organizations (especially NGOs). Of particular importance is that civil society does not exist in splendid isolation from the state: associational life is a function of the predatory state, social incoherence, and economic decline. As Fatton (1995: 72) correctly argues, many civil society organizations are the mirror image of the predatory state: 'by generally reflecting the lopsided balance of class, ethnic and sexual power, the organisations of civil society tend inevitably to privilege the privileged and marginalize the marginalized.' Marginalized people adapt to this, not by embracing formal civil society, but by developing strategies which generate alternative economic opportunities and an alternative society, with parallel social and religious institutions alongside official ones: the constantly evolving informal civil society. Their scepticism of civil society is easily transferred to a more general scepticism about the democratic project advocated by the same people and interests. Further, the organizations which make up civil society are themselves problematic champions of democratization: they are frequently undemocratic in their internal structure and workings (Edwards and Hulme 1996); often dominated—much like one-party states—by an individual or oligarchy, and hence in a poor position to advocate more representative and accountable political processes (Monga 1995).

Greater political pluralism has tended to shift emphasis away from the extremes of both arguments: either that civil society can replace the state, or that it is irrelevant to wider political processes. Few analyses exist of what happens to civil society once democratization is under way. An exception is a recent study in Niger, which argues that 'without question, institutions of civil society have flourished—they have become much more numerous and diverse as new formal rules of political liberalisation and democratisation have been put into place, and as a combination of external pressure and internal changes have made the operation of these institutions a practical working reality' (Charlick et al. 1994: 9). They also note, however, that despite constitutional changes to guarantee political liberty to civil society organizations, the state still exercises considerable power and a system of political patronage still prevails. In other words, the informal rules of the preceding regime have been maintained, extend down to local level, and conflict with more recent democratic reforms. It is thus by no means clear that changes to formal rules or other improvements in the working conditions of civil society organizations necessarily mean improvements in functional capacity or in outcomes. Civil society is not a magic wand that can create or reinforce democratic institutions overnight.

The recent burst of interest in formal civil society tends towards the impression that associational life in Africa is new or, if it did exist, was impotent. In fact, there are webs of social and political networks which run from top to bottom, from the centre to rural areas, in both public and private spheres (Agbaje 1990). As Fowler (1996: 14) notes, 'externally imposed forms of "civicness"—in the form of legally incorporated or formally registered associations and organisations, Western norms of behaviour, written Constitutions and rigidly divided institutional relations—overlay pre-existing indigenous ways of associating and relating which are often familial in the broad sense of the term, non-formal in the legal sense and highly resilient'.

Civil society is multifaceted and needs to be analysed in the plural (Fatton 1995), to include this informal dimension. This provides a crucial link between rural livelihoods and democratization, because it defines in important ways how people pursue their livelihoods. People 'wire' themselves into numerous networks, based on family, alliance, and friendship, in order to sustain their livelihoods (Bayart 1993).[8] These networks are not static, because as livelihoods become more vulnerable, thresholds are reached beyond which reciprocal and other ties can be severed because neither patrons nor clients are able to deliver what is expected (Roniger 1994). Even within more horizontal reciprocal arrangements, the insurance premium of reciprocity becomes too costly. Others must then be negotiated, invested in, and relied on. The significance of such informal elements of civil society is that they come closer to the principle of governing people in relation to resources. As such, they have the potential to be building blocks for linkages between existing rights to resources and potential rights to political power based on democratic principles, as well as more democratically decided rights to resources. Simply because they have not yet been included in the democratization project does not mean that they lack local legitimacy: the same cannot be assumed for newly democratic governments in rural areas.

[8] This informal dimension of civil society is part of the 'moral economy', or the range of redistributive processes which occur within larger and smaller communities, from households to extended families, through kinship networks, and upwards to political structures (Scott 1976, Swift 1989).

Such institutions and organizations have proved remarkably adept at adapting to changing political circumstances. In the post-independence era

groups which saw themselves as the custodians of the traditions of society, such as chiefs, networks of elders, religious leaders, Koranic and traditional teachers, herbalists, hunters, secret society organizers etc., were downgraded to the informal, 'unseen', traditional arena, *even though their influence on the wider society and on many of those in the modern sector remained enormous* . . . [such] traditional actors have entered the social stage not so much by taking over modern institutions, but by articulating a new power of relevance at local levels where states are no longer effective in mobilizing their populace for national projects. (Bangura 1994: 810–11, emphasis added)

Informal civil society was more or less ignored by international actors under authoritarian regimes and in the run up to democratization, but its capacity to adapt has persisted, especially with post-adjustment states becoming ever more ineffectual in providing even basic levels of material welfare. The rural poor have responded by investing their political energies into informal organizations, as African states repressed formal participatory structures (Chazan 1982, 1994). Democratic regimes have ceased some of the more excessive forms of destruction of informal customary institutions and organizations, but they continue to be excluded from many discussions of the contribution of civil society to democratization. This is on the grounds 'that they either do not exist, or are up to no good' (Fowler 1996: 15), being seen as irrelevant, backward, and hence intrinsically undemocratic (Gyimah-Boadi 1996). This perception is coloured by the persistence of institutions which have ceased to be influential in Western liberal democracies, in particular, the extended family and complex webs of patron–client relationships; and to the preoccupation with (international) NGOs' catalysing role.

6. The Twilight Zone [9]

These networks and informal arrangements are not easily categorized. Several attempts have been made to do so, in order to redress the tendency to ignore or undervalue them. The first option is to incorporate them as part of civil society, but to subdivide civil society to take account of variations within it. Fox (1995) uses organizational type as the basis for subdivision into three groups: specialized civic organizations; multi-purpose civic organizations; and primary-level associations.

---

[9] This term is taken from Lund (1996).

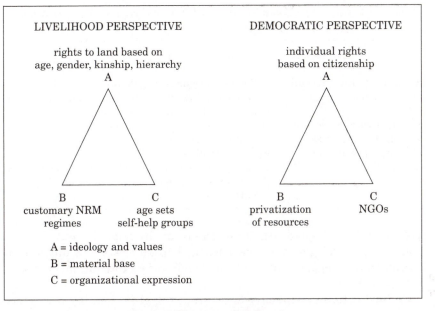

FIG 9.1: *Elements of civil society*

Note: NRM = natural resource management. *Source*: Adapted from Fowler (1996).

It is into this last category that primary-level self-governing associations (users of natural resources, service providers, and economic interest groups) and primordial ascriptive-based associations (kinship, lineage, age-grade, and gender groups) are put. These, he argues, are the building blocks of development and democracy but 'are unlikely to engage the state directly, although their function as self-governing associations is an important civic function and should be encouraged, however indirectly' (ibid.: 12). The trouble is that this encouragement rarely takes place. An alternative is to use level of operation as the basis for subdivision. Thus Jorgensen (1996) differentiates between national, middle-range, and grass-roots civil society. It is in this last category that informal forms of association are located, but again this implicitly keeps such forms of association well down in the hierarchy of democratic institutional accumulation and fails to account for their key characteristic of vertical as well as horizontal linkages within society.

A second option is to define civil society in terms of its basic dimensions, around which variation occurs according to the society in question. Fowler (1996: 15) identifies three such elements of civil society: ideology and values (A); material base (B); and organizational expression (C). Fig. 9.1 illustrates how such variation can occur *within* the same society, depending on whether a democratic or a livelihood

TABLE 9.1. *Categorization of formal and informal civil society institutions and organizations*

	Informal/civil society	Twilight zone	Formal/civil society	
S	Local natural resource	Religious associations;	Professional and	S
O	management regimes;	traditional political	business associations;	T
C	informal credit	alliances; federations	trade unions;	A
I	networks; gender- and	of lower-level self-	pro-democracy	T
E	age-based groups;	governing associations	organizations; policy	E
T	kinship networks	e.g.: co-operatives,	institutes and think-	
Y		credit unions, pastoral	tanks; independent	
		associations, women's	media; developmental	
		groups	NGOs	

perspective is adopted. All three points in the triangle may directly conflict, depending on the view chosen. This suggests how difficult an incremental incorporation of informal civil society into formal civil society is likely to be.

A third option is explicitly to embrace the grey area between more formal manifestations of informal civil society (e.g. village-level credit associations) and more informal ones of formal civil society (e.g. genuinely participatory, indigenous NGOs). Lund (1996: 1) has identified a 'twilight zone' between state and society, which he describes thus: 'some state institutions like the government or the army are "state" and not civil society while some social institutions like e.g. the family can hardly be considered "state". However, a number of *institutions are less clearly ordered*. In the African context, the traditional village political hierarchies are probably the most conspicuous examples . . . [operating] . . . in the *twilight zone between state and society*.' The significance of recognizing a twilight zone is that it draws attention to institutions that are otherwise ignored or categorized as being less important than more visible, vociferous, and obvious contributors to institutional plurality and democratization. The *twilight zone* is, however, more accurately described as *the space between formal and informal civil society*. This categorization allows for fluidity between informal and formal sectors of associational life. It opens the door to the possibility of currently informal forms of associational activity becoming incorporated into the formal, legally recognized plurality of organizations and institutions under a democratic regime. Examples of how formal and informal civil society institutions and organizations, and the twilight zone between them, can be categorized are shown in Table 9.1.[10]

---

[10] The organizations listed in Table 9.1 are based on Fox's (1995) civic organizations.

Those institutions and organizations which most directly affect the rural poor are found in the 'informal' column. As they enter the twilight zone (e.g. when local credit groups join forces to form a credit union or when people sharing customary rules of access to pastures form a pastoral association) they move closer towards formal civil society, but remain some way from it. The point is not to advocate that all informal civil society should seek to move into this category; but rather to emphasize the *continuum between formal and informal civil society*, and to situate the claims to recognition and support for informal institutions and organizations during democratization in the context of civil society as a whole. It is in the twilight zone that energies to build institutional capacity and to initiate institutional change need to be directed if democratization is to be appropriated by the rural poor.

In this process, it is important to note that democratic openings do not remove entrenched inequalities or undemocratic forms of association overnight. The very opening up of channels between different parts of civil society is likely to engender new sources of conflict, or to unearth existing ones. In an analysis of the difficulties encountered when trying to introduce a rights-based family code in recently democratized Niger, Villalón (1996) clearly shows the problems when individual democratic values and rights clash with customary institutions affecting such vital interests as inheritance, marriage, divorce, and adoption. Different civil society organizations (Islamic associations, women's groups, human rights associations, and international actors) all now have the freedom to express their views and to lobby for support, but 'at root the debate is one between competing, and ultimately irreconcilable, value systems' (ibid.: 55–6). He concludes that probably the only way to achieve constitutional individual rights would be via undemocratic means, exhibiting the fundamental dilemma at the heart of democratization in SSA: 'as long as the democratic debate is about which value system should prevail, rather than about *finding a means for the two to coexist*, no resolution is possible' (ibid.: 65, emphasis added). Conversely, when he examines the case of Senegal, he finds scope for customary institutions (Islamic brotherhoods) forming a link between state and society in the twilight zone. Sufi orders are 'undoubtedly the single most important feature of the contours of Senegalese society which the state confronts in its efforts to elaborate a basis for the exercise of power. This pre-eminence is due to the fact that the orders have facilitated and provided the incentives for the vast majority of the population to participate in mass social organisations which exist outside of—and largely autonomous from—the state, but which interact both with each other and with the state' (Villalón 1994: 434). In contrast, whereas Villalón sees the power of Islamic brotherhoods as contributing to a balance between state and society in Senegal, Coulon and Cruise O'Brien (1989) are more sceptical and argue that it can be at the expense of a more fundamental democratization and politicization of civil society.

The message from these cases is clear: there is no simple transition from customary to democratic values, nor always scope for a fusing of the two. But the significance of customary values, and the institutions which underpin them, cannot be swept away by the tide of democratization. They need to be provided with political space, bargained over, and assimilated, however unpalatable they may be to democrats, especially those who view customary institutions as the cause of rural poverty and social exclusion. There are historical precedents for this approach. As Rasheed (1995: 352) notes, 'if the colonial powers were shrewd enough to use [traditional leaders and systems] as instruments of control and repression, the new democrats should be able to co-opt the traditional leaders and adapt the traditional systems to reach out to the small communities and build national consensus and cohesion'.

In some instances, democratic governments have helped to promote their rehabilitation, on the grounds that they represent one of the few forms of organization remaining at local level. In Mali, for example, local public hearings were held to solicit the views of rural people about changes to codes regarding control of bush fires (Brinkerhoff 1995) and in the relatively prosperous cotton-producing zone, farmers have begun to form their own associations and are making a range of demands on state organizations (Degnbol 1996). But all such attempts to include informal civil society in processes of democratization show that co-option is not problem free. Attempts to reform the anachronistic and much-detested forestry service in Mali as part of the process of democratization, by incorporating traditional natural resource management mechanisms into policy reform, are constrained by: the history of conflict between rural people and the policing, quasimilitary forestry service and its continuing inaccessibility; the invisibility of customary institutions in Malian law; and the persistence of extractive and top-down attitudes amongst much of the service's staff (Brinkerhoff 1995). Writing in the context of land tenure reform in Niger, Lund (1996) describes how the very opening up of opportunities for multiple civil society organizations provided by democratization leads not only to the challenging of the authority of traditional institutions, but also to increased politicization of and competition between formal and informal civil society. This, in turn, can result in greater livelihood insecurity for those dependent on functioning and predictable institutions to set the rules for how access to key resources is managed, however undemocratic those rules may have been in the past. In other words, change can increase livelihood insecurity, especially if the conflict between competing institutions persists.

7. Conclusions

Incorporating informal civil society into processes of democratization is not to advocate a return to 'merrie Africa'. There are strong critics of the role that it can play, especially from those who regard customary political systems as feudal, anti-democratic, and conservative. They often are, but this does not mean that they fail to provide people with some of what they need. Customary political systems are especially unpopular amongst democrats because they are seen to mirror the neo-patrimonialism of African authoritarian regimes, being based on relationships of loyalty and dependence, the award by public officials of personal favours in exchange for clients mobilizing political support and referring all decisions upward in deference to patrons. Thus Bratton and van der Walle (1992: 489) argue that although such organizations (market women's associations, ethnic associations, credit clubs) may improve welfare (and indeed the sustainability of livelihoods) and by sapping the government's legitimacy may have helped paved the way for democratization, only formal institutions (human rights organizations, political parties) can force governments to change because they appear as plausible alternatives to governments in power. Thus, although such critics recognize the importance of such organizations, they do not believe they are up to the task of promoting democratization.

In contrast, it has been argued here that the key connection between rural people and the resources on which they depend necessitates a reformulation of prevailing conventional wisdom, which holds that Africa is in need of Western-style democracy (implicitly in order to create the conditions under which market capitalism can flourish), leading to economic growth and in turn sustainable development (Fowler 1993). A more plural definition of state–society interaction is needed if local political processes and structures are to be incorporated into the layering of institutions that appropriate democratization implies. There is a need to understand what customary versus democratic systems offer to people trying to achieve sustainable livelihoods. A process of rapprochement between the two is more likely to succeed than the imposition of one on the other. In other words, a synergistic approach to state and society relations to redress the balance between either state-centric approaches or society-centric ones is needed.

Degnbol (1996: 4) refers to this as the interactive approach which 'sees the state as only one form of organisation among many which implies that state elites do not automatically enjoy a monopoly of political power'.

If increased security now and in the future is the driving force behind the rural poor's pursuit of sustainable livelihoods, what are their requirements of an appropriate form of democratization? First, it must formally recognize institutions which already represent the interests of the rural poor and address their livelihood needs. Second, it must provide mechanisms for negotiation and conflict resolution within them or reinforce such mechanisms where they already exist. Third, it must underwrite the stability and predictability of these institutions. Fourth, it needs to build on, adapt, and reform these institutions to confront changing economic and political conditions, including more democratic forms of distributing power and resources. Finally, in so doing, it must link informal civil society to other domains of institutional control, especially in formal civil society and in the state; and provide effective channels of communication between them, including accountability to the rural poor of those institutions which fail to meet these criteria.

The idea of 'livelihood democracy' would better encapsulate these democratic requirements of the rural poor than current manifestations of political democracy in SSA. Livelihood democracy is defined as a system of *governing people in relation to the resources on which their livelihoods depend, and hence providing rights to resources as well as to political power*. This would entail a process of institutional accumulation which merges existing customary institutions and nascent democratic ones. Plurality in such systems would be defined in terms of the multiple institutions and organizations which make up formal and informal civil society, and the interaction of both with the state. Maps of political and livelihood democracy would look completely different: whereas geographical boundaries and constituencies predominate in conceptions of political democracy; the boundaries of livelihood democracies would be based on resource availability and use, kinship, patron–client relations, and social fences. Power within livelihood democracies would be distributed not on the basis of equality of individual participation, but in terms of a range of social institutions, including kinship, wealth, age, and gender. Many of these are hierarchical and exclude categories of people (e.g. women, the rural poorest) and would require reform to merit a democratic label. Even so, many of the decisions taken about livelihoods are *already* democratic within a bounded group.

Unless democrats in SSA and their external allies recognize the need to manage people in relation to the resources on which their livelihoods depend, and to build on and reform what already exists, the democratic experiment in Africa is likely to continue to be inappropriate to the rural poor and to be short-lived.

REFERENCES

Agbaje, A. (1990), 'In Search of Building Blocks: The State, Civil Society, Voluntary Action and Grassroot Development in Africa', *Africa Quarterly*, 30/3–4: 24–40.

Bangura, Y. (1994), 'Economic Restructuring, Coping Strategies and Social Change: Implications for Institutional Development in Africa', *Development and Change*, 25/4: 785–827.

Bayart, J. F. (1986), 'Civil Society in Africa', in P. Chabal (ed.), *Political Domination in Africa: Reflections on the Limits of Power*, Cambridge: Cambridge University Press.

—— (1993), *The State in Africa: The Politics of the Belly*, London: Longman.

Berry, S. (1989), 'Social Institutions and Access to Resources', *Africa*, 59/1: 41–55.

Bratton, M., and van de Walle, N. (1992), 'Popular Protest and Political Reform in Africa', *Comparative Politics*, 24/4: 419–42.

—— (1994), 'Neopatrimonial Regimes and Political Transitions in Africa', *World Politics*, 46/4: 453–89.

Brinkerhoff, D. W. (1995), 'African State–Society Linkages in Transition: The Case of Forestry Policy in Mali', *Canadian Journal of Development Studies*, 16/2: 201–28.

Charlick, R., Fox, L., Gellar, S., Robinson, P., and West, T. (1994), 'Improving Democratic Governance for Sustainable Development: A Study of Continuity and Change in Niger', summary version of draft report, Washington: Associates in Rural Development Inc. in association with Management Systems International, mimeo.

Chazan, N. (1982), 'The New Politics of Participation in Tropical Africa', *Comparative Politics*, 14/2: 169–89.

—— (1994), 'Engaging the State: Associational Life in Sub-Saharan Africa', in J. S. Migdal, A. Kohli, and V. Shue (eds.), *State Power and Social Forces: Domination and Transformation in the Third World*, Cambridge: Cambridge University Press.

Clapham, C. (1982), 'Clientalism and the State', in C. Clapham (ed.), *Private Patronage and Public Power: Political Clientelism in the Modern State*, London: Frances Pinter.

Clayton, A. (ed.) (1996), *NGOs, Civil Society and the State: Building Democracy in Transitional Societies*, Oxford: INTRAC.

Coulon, C., and Cruise O'Brien, D. (1989), 'Senegal', in D. Cruise O'Brien, J. Dunn, and R. Rathbone (eds.), *Contemporary West African States*, Cambridge: Cambridge University Press.

de Waal, A. (1996a), 'Contemporary Warfare in Africa: Changing Context, Changing Strategies', *IDS Bulletin*, 27/3: 6–16.

de Waal, A. (1996*b*), 'Social Contract and Deterring Famine: First Thoughts', *Disasters*, 20/3: 194–205.

Degnbol, T. (1996), 'Changing Patterns of State–Society Inter-action in Mali', paper presented to the seminar on 'Civil Society, Public Sphere and Organizational Behavior—Approaches to the Study of State–Society Relations in the Non-western World', Oslo, 22–3 Apr. 1996, International Development Studies, Roskilde University, mimeo.

Duffield, M. (1990), 'War and Famine in Africa', Oxfam Research Paper no. 5, Oxford: Oxfam.

Edwards, M., and Hulme, D. (1996), 'Too Close for Comfort? The Impact of Official Aid on Non-governmental Organizations', *World Development*, 24/6: 961–73.

Fatton, R. (1995), 'Africa in the Age of Democratization: The Civic Limitations of Civil Society', *African Studies Review*, 38/2: 67–99.

Fowler, A. (1993), 'Non-governmental Organizations as Agents of Democratization: An African Perspective', *Journal of International Development*, 5/3: 325–39.

—— (1996), 'Strengthening Civil Society in Transition Economies—from Concept to Strategy: Mapping an Exit in a Maze of Mirrors', in Clayton (1996).

Fox, L. (1995), 'Civil Society: A Conceptual Framework', Washington: USAID Global Center for Democracy, prepared by Thunder and Associates Inc.

Gore, C. (1994), 'Social Exclusion and Africa South of the Sahara: A Review of the Literature', Discussion Paper no. 62, Geneva: International Institute for Labour Studies.

Gyimah-Boadi, E. (1996), 'Civil Society in Africa', *Journal of Democracy*, 7/2: 118–32.

Jorgensen, L. (1996), 'What are NGOs Doing in Civil Society?', in Clayton (1996).

King, D. Y. (1981), 'Regime Type and Performance: Authoritarian Rule, Semi-capitalist Development and Rural Inequality in Asia', *Comparative Political Studies*, 13/4: 477–504.

Lele, S. (1991), 'Sustainable Development: A Critical Review', *World Development*, 19/6: 607–21.

Lund, C. (1996), 'Approaching Twilight Institutions: Some Preliminary Reflections on Politico-legal Institutions', paper prepared for 'Civil Society, Public Sphere and Organizational Behavior—Approaches to the Study of State–Society Relations in the Non-western World', Centre for Development and the Environment, University of Oslo, 22–3 Apr. 1996, International Development Studies, Sahel-Sudan Environmental Research Initiative, Roskilde University, mimeo.

Metcalfe, S. (1996), 'Local Governance and Natural Resource Management in Zimbabwe', in Clayton (1996).

Monga, C. (1995), 'Civil Society and Democratisation in Francophone Africa', *Journal of Modern African Studies*, 33/3: 359–79.

Mwansa, Lengwe-Katembula (1995), 'Participation of Non-governmental Organisations in Social Development Process in Africa: Implications', *Journal of Social Development in Africa*, 10/1: 65–75.

MWENGO (1993), *Civil Society, the State and African Development in the 1990s*, Nairobi: All Africa Conference of Churches and Reflection and Development Centre for NGOs in Eastern and Southern Africa (MWENGO).

Ndegwa, S. (1996), *The Two Faces of Civil Society: NGOs and Politics in Africa*, West Hartford, Conn.: Kumarian Press.

Ng'ethe, N., and Kanyinga, K. (1992), 'The Politics of Development Space: The State and NGOs in the Delivery of Basic Services in Kenya', Working Paper no. 486, Nairobi: University of Nairobi, Institute of Development Studies.

North, D. C. (1990), *Institutions, Institutional Change and Economic Performance*, Cambridge: Cambridge University Press.

O'Donnell, G. and Schmitter, P. (1986), 'Transitions from Authoritarian Rule: Tentative Conclusions about Uncertain Democracies', in G. O'Donnell, P. C. Schmitter, and L. Whitehead (eds.), *Transitions from Authoritarian Rule: Prospects for Democracy*, Baltimore: Johns Hopkins University Press.

Rasheed, S. (1995), 'The Democratization Process and Popular Participation in Africa: Emerging Realities and the Challenges Ahead', *Development and Change*, 26/2: 333–54.

Robinson, M. (1996), 'Economic Reform and the Transition to Democracy', in R. Luckham, and G. White (eds.), *Democratization in the South: The Jagged Wave*, Manchester: Manchester University Press.

Roniger, L. (1994), 'Civil Society, Patronage and Democracy', *International Journal of Comparative Sociology*, 35/3–4: 207–20.

Scott, J. C. (1976), *The Moral Economy of the Peasant: Rebellion and Subsistence in Southeast Asia*, New Haven: Yale University Press.

Swift, J. (1989), 'Why are Rural People Vulnerable to Famine?', *IDS Bulletin*, 20/2: 8–15.

Thérien, J.-P. (1991), 'Non-governmental Organizations and International Development Assistance', *Canadian Journal of Development Studies*, 12/2: 263–80.

UNDP (1996), *Human Development Report 1996*, United Nations Development Program, New York: Oxford University Press.

Vengroff, R. (1993), 'Governance and the Transition to Democracy: Political Parties and the Party System in Mali', *Journal of Modern African Studies*, 31/4: 541–62.

Villalón, L. (1994), 'Sufi Rituals as Rallies: Religious Ceremonies in the Politics of Senegalese State–Society Relations', *Comparative Politics*, 26/4: 415–37.

—— (1996), 'The Moral and the Political in African Democratization: The *Code de la Famille* in Niger's Troubled Transition', *Democratization*, 3/2: 41–68.

WCED (1987), *Our Common Future: Report of the World Commission on Environment and Development*, Oxford: Oxford University Press.

White, G. (1995), 'Towards a Democratic Developmental State', *IDS Bulletin*, 26/2: 27–36.

World Bank (1989), *Sub-Saharan Africa: From Crisis to Sustainable Growth*, Washington: World Bank.

······················

10

······················

Are There Alternatives to Liberal Democracy?

ROBIN LUCKHAM

> Would it not be easier
> In that case for the government
> To dissolve the people
> And elect another.
> > (Bertolt Brecht, 1953)

1. Introduction

This chapter differs from analyses of 'developmental democracy' which treat popular participation as a clamorous inconvenience to be managed in the interests of economic efficiency.[1] Instead it asks what follows from prioritizing participation both as a defining feature of democracy, and as an integral part of what is meant by development.

The analysis will be developed in two parts. First I will contrast the narratives of popular and of liberal democracy, showing they come to different conclusions about participation and its role in development. But I will also argue that there are potential complementarities. These were obscured when socialist 'people's democracies' were (misleadingly) seen as popular alternatives to liberal democracy. But since the end of the Cold War there is much less interest in whole-system alternatives to liberal democracy. Instead the debates focus on democratizing the latter, to ensure it is responsive to the needs of

[1] Though as White's contribution to this volume makes clear, not all analyses of developmental democracy follow such an approach. Indeed Sklar (1987) originally introduced the term to argue against the previously fashionable view that developmental dictatorship was more conducive to economic progress than democracy.

citizens, as active participants in development and not just targets of state policy.

Second I shall review the experience of two popular democratic experiments, in Tanzania and Nicaragua, which sought to extend participation beyond the confines of representative democracy, and to link it to participatory development. My analysis might be read as a requiem for their apparent failure. But I shall also hope to show that their vicissitudes raise broader questions: about the contradictions between popular participation and 'people's democracy' as a system of rule; about the structures and procedures (elections, political parties, civil society bodies, mass organizations, etc.) through which participation is organized; and about the problems of harmonizing participatory development with the management of complex national economies.

2. Popular versus Liberal Democracy?

In *The Real World of Democracy*, C. B. Macpherson (1966: 3) asserted that democracy is not to be equated with Western liberal democracy, as 'the clearly non-liberal systems which prevail in the Soviet countries, and the somewhat different non-liberal systems of most of the underdeveloped countries of Asia and Africa, have a genuine historical claim to the title democracy'. Seen from the 1990s, this assertion seems anachronistic. The liberal version of democracy is everywhere celebrated, whilst socialist and non-Western democracies have been banished to the footnotes of history. Yet the paradox is that Western liberal democracies are falling into disrepair at their moment of triumph. A democracy deficit has opened, manifest in public apathy about politics, an erosion of standards in public life, and widening socio-economic inequality. Globalization has eroded the capacity of elected governments to take decisions affecting their own citizens, even in advanced industrial countries (Held 1993: 23–8). A double disempowerment has apparently occurred, both of democratic institutions and of the citizens they serve.

Contrasts between the triumphal image and the disempowering reality of democracy are even more striking in the developing world (Ake 1994). Not only has the jagged wave of democratization started to recede, pulling unstable new democracies into whirlpools of authoritarian rule or state collapse. Major doubts surround the nature and extent of democracy in those countries alleged to be making the transition, such as Ghana, Argentina, or the Philippines; which are reflected in a proliferation of terms like 'limited', 'low-intensity', 'exclusionary', or 'delegative' democracy.

These contrasts are no historical accident: they are tangled in the discourses of democracy itself. Democracy is simultaneously a (contested) set of values; an (inherently contradictory) system of rule; and a (necessarily unfinished) emancipatory process. Its moral force derives from the original Greek term 'rule by the people', though the latter is sprung with conceptual traps for the unwary and explicitly repudiated by some democratic theorists. Rule by the people implies in turn the twin principles of popular control and political equality (Beetham 1994*a*); which are valued not only as means to ends such as good government, political stability, or development, but as goals worth pursuing in their own right.

But how the democratic principle of rule by the people is realized in the real world of politics is much disputed. One may distinguish two competing narratives: that of political realists who regard democracy primarily as a system of rule or set of institutions; and that of those who ask that it should live up to its emancipatory or popular promise. Broadly speaking, the former has tended to be the discourse of politicians and mainstream academics; the latter of activists and the critical left.

On the whole liberal democratic theory has been determinedly realist, tending to detach democracy from its ethical moorings. According to Schumpeter (1965: 284, 269), its most influential modern exponent, democracy is not 'an end in itself, [but] a mere method that could be discussed rationally like a steam engine or a disinfectant', being 'that institutional arrangement for arriving at political decisions in which individuals acquire the power to decide by means of a competitive struggle for the people's vote'.

Not all liberal theorists go as far. Most hold that democracy requires moral as well as practical justification. Nevertheless to the extent that they base democracy on party competition this emphasizes 'institutions rather than direct popular participation, and leaders rather than citizens' (Kasfir 1992: 59). Representative institutions and procedures embody a 'sovereign' view of power (Foucault 1980), since the leaders of parties winning electoral contests are authorized to take charge of the commanding heights of the state and make decisions on behalf of their fellow citizens. To be sure, they are restrained by constitutional and legal arrangements, and by the existence of plural sources of power, especially in Madisonian versions of liberal democracy. Yet the main object is to circulate elites and ensure accountable and effective government, rather than to assure popular participation as such. Indeed, too much participation may endanger the social arrangements that underpin party competition, including a capitalist economy, class inequality, and an autonomous state (as elegantly argued by Przeworksi 1991).

The ultimate test of the superiority of liberal or representative democracy, as Schumpeter suggests, is its capacity to deliver the collective goods its citizens desire: be they political stability, national security, lower taxes, social welfare, or development. To the extent that it is 'developmental' it would seem to be its liberal rather than its democratic aspects that are most decisive: notably the alleged synergy between political and economic freedoms; and the role of constitutional government in assuring stable property relations and predictable, transparent decision-making. That is, it is *liberal* democracy and *capitalist* development which are held to be mutually reinforcing. To be sure, popular participation is needed to assure the legitimacy of institutions, and to help spread the benefits of development to the poor and excluded. Yet it is also regarded as a potential threat, for instance by liberal economists who warn new democracies of the dangers of 'macro-economic populism' deviating from the 'Washington consensus' on market-oriented economic reform (Dornbusch and Edwards 1990, Williamson 1993). Whilst the masses are invited to the liberal democratic feast, and are the assumed beneficiaries of development, they must not spit, swear, or speak too loudly, or they will spoil the meal.

But there exists another, more subversive, narrative or set of narratives, according to which democracy has come into being precisely because the masses have dared speak out and even rebel. Democracy in this view is less a set of institutions than an unfinished emancipatory process, kept in motion by the failure of existing political arrangements (including liberal democracy) to assure social justice, protect marginalized groups, and overcome public apathy. Hence it tells a shifting tale of ideals proclaimed and betrayed, struggles won and lost, tyranny and freedom. Its intellectual origins can be traced to a variety of different sources, depending on who is telling the tale: for instance the direct democracy of ancient Athens; Rousseau's conceptions of citizen self-government; Marx's account of the Paris commune; Gramsci's analysis of counter-hegemony; or the communal democracy of traditional society idealized by certain Third World leaders.

Yet these popular narratives cannot be reduced neatly to any single theory or model of democracy. Nor can one easily identify them (like liberal democracy) with particular institutions and procedures. Rather, they are constructed around the aspirations and historical experience of those who have experienced subjugation in complex modern states and class-divided societies. They tend to function both as utopias or visions of the good society, and as ways of confronting power, extending choice, and creating spaces for participation in the framework of modern states . They do not reside in sovereign authorities or institutions; rather they are to be asserted against power at every level of state and society.[2] They are inherently suspicious of the hegemonic, patriarchal states that lurk behind liberal democratic façades; and challenge hierarchy and inequality wherever they occur. They are highly contingent, speak many voices, are easily subverted, and therefore must be continually defended, even against those who speak in their name.

Popular versions of democracy are as fraught with contradictions as liberal democracy. Most political thinkers before the nineteenth century indeed mistrusted *all* forms of democracy, fearing they would generate anarchy and unrest. In the West, such fears were eventually put to rest by the emergence (*before* the franchise was extended, as Parekh (1993) emphasizes) of liberal doctrines of a constitutional state that placed firm limits on popular sovereignty, and prepared the way for representative democracy. Yet the contemporary world still yields many examples of previously subjugated groups voicing popular aspirations only to trample on those of others: as in Algeria, where popular Islam has collided with an equally popular tradition of secular nationalism, to the detriment of both. Civil society has often become warlike and uncivil, as in Somalia or Bosnia. Charismatic moments, like the 'people's power' revolution in the Philippines, have ushered in formal democracy, without guaranteeing it will remain democratic. 'The people' have frequently been mobilized to support, not democrats, but authoritarian populists like Perón, Nasser, or Rawlings, or religious ideologues like Khomeini.

Moreover, popular democracy has been associated with varying approaches to development. Before the 1980s Marxist and neo-Marxist political economists were the sharpest critics of development orthodoxy. According to them (to simplify brutally) capitalist development was responsible for mal-development; and only socialism would both sustain accumulation and assure a more equitable distribution of resources. To achieve socialism, subaltern social classes (workers and peasants) had to be empowered as the agents of revolutionary transformation. Only socialist revolutions could liberate the masses from exploitation and poverty and bring true or people's democracy into being.[3]

But the empowerment of the masses seldom continued once the charismatic moment of revolution had passed. The people's democracies that

---

[2] Hence they are the mirror image of Foucault's (1980) conception of power as 'capillary', or rooted in social practices at every level of society, rather than being 'sovereign' or exerted from the top.

[3] Though of course there were differences between official Marxists, neo-Marxists, dependency theorists, and a significant minority of Marxist theorists who held (with Warren 1980) that only sustained capitalist economic progress could lay the foundations for transition to socialism.

emerged in the communist states of the East were founded upon the heroic assumption that popular participation would be energized in the course of transforming the material conditions of life of the masses. Yet, 'democratic centralism' effectively subordinated popular participation to the party, the state, and the plan; implying an even more 'sovereign' and centralized practice of power in people's than in liberal democracies. The goals of socialist development—defined largely in terms of capital accumulation and rapid industrialization —were as confining as those of capitalist development orthodoxy. Indeed it was the failure of socialist states to keep pace with the material progress of the capitalist West that ultimately sealed their fate (Przeworksi 1991).

Nor did the people's democracies that emerged from anti-colonial struggles in the south fare better. Most were preoccupied with national self-determination and capturing the state (epitomized in President Kwame Nkrumah of Ghana's maxim 'seek ye first the political king-dom') rather than empowering the people, despite noble statements of intent about socialist development and grass-roots participation. Even committed leaders like President Nyerere in Tanzania and the Sandinistas in Nicaragua found themselves presiding over sclerotic state and party apparatuses, failed socialist development models, and hungry and disillusioned citizens. In sum, though popular struggles against colonialism and dictatorship spawned an immense variety of democratic movements and grass-roots organizations, whether they brought people's *democracies* into being is far more doubtful.

Hence one needs to distinguish 'people's democracy' as an (outmoded) type of polity from popular democracy as a goal and process. The latter is not confined to socialist states or left-wing parties; but calls on a much wider range of groups and social actors in civil and polit-ical society. Moreover, though the narratives of popular and liberal democracy remain distinct, they are not mutually exclusive, even in the liberal democracies of the West. Indeed the latter only became democratic, as Rueschemeyer et al. (1992) remind us, because of the empowerment during the nineteenth and early twentieth centuries of previously subaltern groups, including the urban working class and women. Conversely growing social exclusion in present-day Western democracies diminishes the vitality of democratic institutions and calls liberal democracy itself into question.

The changing goals of popular struggles have renewed criticism of the nature and purposes not only of democracy, but also of develop-ment. The latter faces the familiar criticisms of market-oriented growth: that it ignores poverty and exploitation, gives short shrift to culture and values, downplays the destructive impact of adjustment and globalization, etc. However, the critique has been extended to state-managed accumulation, and indeed to the entire enterprise of development as such: as ideologically based and disempowering (Escobar 1995), an 'anti-politics machine' (Ferguson 1990), and 'against democracy' (Loomis 1991), by denying agency to the groups and individuals who are 'developed' by states and development institutions.

Seen in this perspective, whole-system people's democracies were little or no better at assuring equitable development and popular control than liberal democracies; whilst their record on liberal rights and freedoms was typically worse. At the same time liberal democracies too have been flawed by socio-economic inequality and 'democracy deficits' (Beetham 1994*b*), reinforced by trends in the global economy disempowering both national governments and local communities. In sum, each of the previously opposed grand narratives, of people's democracy and socialist development on the one hand, and of liberal democracy and capitalist development on the other, have come into question.

It might seem to follow that democracy and likewise development are best advanced 'in parts' (Sklar 1987): that is, through incremental changes which start from the empowerment of individuals and groups in civil society, before extending into the upper reaches of the state and corporate decision-making. Such an emphasis on the sources of democratization in civil society would seem to be compatible with classic pluralist or Madisonian versions of democratic theory, as well with recent thinking about the role of 'social capital' in sustaining local-level democracy and development (Putnam 1993).

But any seriously emancipatory strategy of democratization and likewise development would need to empower subaltern or marginalized classes and groups, and not simply the 'bourgeois' groups in civil society (organized business, the professions, community influentials, etc.), which are the mainstay of pluralist democratic theory. For capitalism and the liberal democratic state have dug formidable trench-systems (Gramsci 1971: 235) against the empowerment of the poor, oppressed minorities, and women, inside the major institutions of civil society as well as within the state.

Indeed it is precisely for this reason that the revolutionary left used to hold that democracy could only be built on the ruins of capitalist society. But revolutionary transformation failed to deliver a viable popular alternative to the latter. Morover, it was the empowerment of groups in civil society that brought down the edifice of people's democracy at the end of the Cold War. Yet it has proved enormously difficult to construct stable and legitimate democratic institutions in post-communist societies riven by unfettered capitalism and deepening socio-economic inequality.

Hence, even though popular struggles no longer propose whole-system alternatives to liberal democracy and capitalism, and focus instead on the opening of democratic spaces from below, the precise strategies vary. In established liberal democracies the issue has remained how to make democracy more democratic; or more negatively (in the 1990s) how to prevent the increasing power and global reach of capital from demobilizing subaltern classes and eroding the remnants of social democracy. In the few popular democracies which have not collapsed before the advance of liberal capitalism, it is how to liberalize their economies and introduce the mediating institutions of the liberal state (constitutionalism, the rule of law, freely contested elections, etc.) without the two conflicting, or entirely demolishing existing social programmes and popular organizations.

But if democracy is to be rebuilt from below, and linked to broadly based development, there is still little agreement how to turn this into practical politics. One may distinguish four relevant traditions of analysis. First, there is an extensive literature on alternative, participatory, deliberative, discursive, or radical democracy (Gould 1988, Pateman 1970, Benhabib 1996, Mouffe 1992). The terms used vary, and there are differences in emphasis. However, most thinkers in this tradition advocate a more active conception of citizenship, the reinvigoration of civil society, especially through new social movements, the recognition of difference, and the extension of democracy beyond the public sphere into the workplace and the household; in the belief that democratic empowerment in civil society can begin to transform power relations within the state too.

However, there are a number of difficulties inherent in such an approach. Not least of these is the paradox of participation, namely that those who participate and accumulate social capital tend not to be the poor and socially excluded. Thus more focused strategies of empowerment are needed to ensure participation does not merely perpetuate existing class, gender, and other inequalities. Nor, with the decline of class-based politics and partial erosion of the nation-state, is it clear what groups and social forces might be mobilized in support of democratic transformation from below, or in which institutional arenas they can be effective. Radical democrats, especially in Latin America (Escobar and Alvarez 1992), emphasize the capacity of new social movements to form local and global political alliances to bypass the limitations of national-level politics and institutions. Yet their enthusiasm about the transformative capacity of such movements is often tempered by a salutary realism about their enormous diversity; about the need to engage with rather than attempt to replace existing organizations such as political parties and trade unions; and about the difficulties of scaling up political action on behalf of the disenfranchised and oppressed to the national and international levels, in an increasingly complex global environment (ibid.: 1–5, 325–9).

A second school of thought starts from reform of liberal democratic institutions themselves, and of the mediating institutions which link them to political and civil society. It may be subdivided into two groups. First, those (like the Democratic Audit in Britain: Beetham 1994b) who have concentrated on holding liberal democratic institutions to their own promise of providing popularly sanctioned and accountable government. And second, the advocates of more far-reaching changes in the philosophy and practice of democratic governance: for example the introduction of more deliberative or consensual modes of decision-making (Miller 1993); direct democracy (e.g. through plebiscitary voting, making use of new communications technologies); 'consociational' power-sharing (Lijphart 1977 and 1996);[4] or decentralizing powers and functions to local communities under different versions of 'municipal democracy' (Castañeda 1993).

Such proposals face the limitations inherent in engineering democratic change from above. However, they may be of some interest to developing countries, where there has been much criticism of the adversarial and individualistic bias of Western liberal democratic institutions (Parekh 1993). To be sure, such criticism has often been deployed to restrict democratic participation (as in current debates about 'Asian values') rather than to extend it. Yet it is a useful antidote to much existing literature on democratization which tends to ignore institutional innovation and concentrate on the consolidation of Western liberal models and on the 'good government' or 'governance' agendas of the donors (IDS Bulletin 1995).

In contrast, a third perspective arises from the recent explosion of interest in participatory development across a wide spectrum, from grass-roots activists to the World Bank. Exponents of participatory development have not only concentrated on the empowerment of the rural and urban poor; they have developed practical methodologies to bring it about (Chambers, 1997; Fals-Borda and Rahman 1991). In spite of the potential links with participatory democracy (Stiefel and Wolfe 1994), the focus has often been on productive participation, i.e. mobilizing popular energies for shared developmental tasks, rather than democratic participation as such. Hence, participatory development risks 'capture' by donors, state elites, and development NGOs hoping to extend and legitimize their own policies and programmes. Such a risk is clearly greater where participatory techniques are regarded primarily as a

---

[4] Despite the conservative bias of much of the literature in consociationalism, and its preoccupation with political stability, it does at least address the problem of protecting rights and extending the political participation of minorities.

developmental tool, than where they are used to mobilize the poor and oppressed through social movements pressing the state to respond to popular demands (Fals-Borda 1992).

For participation can mean many things, from mere consultation, to active involvement in externally decided programmes, to self-mobilization by people and groups who take the initiative themselves (Pretty 1995: 1251–3). In so far as it is genuine and not simply managed it is bound to challenge established interests and generate political conflict. Indeed the 'dilemma for many authorities is that they both need and fear peoples' participation' (ibid.: 1252), and this tends to be one of the more fundamental constraints upon participatory development. Moreover, the latter has complex and sometimes contradictory relationships to what Davies (in this volume) calls 'livelihood democracy', founded upon the real conditions of life of the poor and excluded; who may sometimes be embedded in local-level clientelistic relationships that cater to their perceived needs better than even genuinely participatory democratic institutions. Grass-roots movements also tend to be constrained by wider structural limitations on political action, including those imposed through donor conditionality or economic globalization. Gains made at a local level may be put at risk by decisions taken in remote bureaucracies, corporate boardrooms, or international agencies, which they have little capacity to influence, except by forging broader political alliances.

Hence a fourth approach has focused upon piecing together fresh counter-hegemonic strategies aimed at 'democratising democracy' (Castañeda 1993: ch. 12), to ensure that democratic structures at all levels address the concerns of the great mass of citizens and not merely those of political elites. The elements of such an approach can be found in the work of a number of critical intellectuals in the south who have struggled to disentangle themselves from the ideological baggage of the Cold War, such as Ake (1994) and Mamdani (1990, 1996) in Africa, Castañeda (1993) and Vilas (1996) in Latin America, and Kothari (1988) in South Asia.

Despite being a highly diverse group, most of them have emerged from Marxist and neo-Marxist theoretical traditions, with which they keep cautious critical engagement. Historical experience may have alerted them to the traps liberal democracy and market capitalism can set for projects of social transformation, as in Allende's Chile, Sandinista Nicaragua, or present-day South Africa. Yet none still believe (if they ever did) that outright rejection of capitalism and revolutionary capture of state power are the way forward. They have gained a new appreciation of liberal rights and freedoms; and tend to be critical of the commandist proclivities of revolutionary movements and democratic centralism in socialist states. Like proponents of participatory democracy and grass-roots development, they tend to argue that democracy and socialism have to be reconstructed from the bottom up, and should also affirm gender and minority rights.

They tend to support the restoration of one form or another of social democracy (widely canvassed in Latin America: Vellinga 1993). And though the latter is not a distinct form of democratic rule like liberal or representative democracy (with which it can coexist) it nevertheless has distinctive implications for democratic governance. These include a commitment to broader conceptions of citizenship than assured by liberal democracy on its own; insistence on social and economic as well as political rights; and greater emphasis upon political participation, including 'double democratisation' of both state and civil society (Held 1989).

At the same time they are under some pressure to show that popularly based projects for change are also politically feasible. This requires some basic understanding of present-day realities, such as the declining capacity of governments to manage national economies, or the political and economic forces ranged behind the Washington consensus on liberal economic and political reform. Yet rather than regarding the latter as *faits accomplis*, they tend to treat them as the starting point for reasoned analysis of how they can be challenged, to ensure broader-based development and a democracy that does not merely protect the rights of the few.

Despite important differences in emphasis, none of the approaches summarized above is mutually exclusive. All may be regarded as utopias, or desirable projects for change. But it is much harder to say whether they pass muster as *feasible* utopias, that will not be wrecked upon the shores of history, as with the experiments in popular democracy in Tanzania and Nicaragua, to which I turn next.

3. Popular Democracy in Tanzania and Nicaragua: *A Reassessment*

Tanzania following the 1967 Arusha Declaration and Nicaragua after the 1979 revolution pursued transformative development policies, with the state playing a leading role in mobilizing resources for development. In this sense they held themselves out as people's democracies founded upon heroic assumptions regarding their capacity to mobilize popular participation around socialist projects. Yet they also claimed to offer alternatives to the Cold War polarity of capitalism and communism, liberal and non-liberal democracy, they maintained mixed economies, and they sought both capitalist and socialist assistance. And the leaders of both countries made apparently genuine efforts to mobilize popular support at the grass roots, rather than merely orchestrating it from the top.

Tanzania rejected multi-party (though not electoral) democracy, though preserving other features of a liberal state, and trying to deepen popular participation. Nicaragua's 'dual transition' (Williams 1994) sought to combine multi-party democracy with the instruments of popular power created during the Sandinista revolution, including grass-roots organizations and a revolutionary party and army. In both countries people's democracy faced adverse international pressure, in Nicaragua from American-orchestrated destabilization, in Tanzania from donors pressing for economic and political liberalization.

Both countries changed political course in the early 1990s. In Nicaragua, the Sandinista Liberation Front (the FSLN) was defeated in the 1990 elections, and lost again in 1996, this time to opponents committed to rolling back the remaining gains of the revolution. In Tanzania former President Nyerere himself opened the debate on the introduction of a multi-party system in 1990; though in contrast to Nicaragua, the ruling Chama Cha Mapinduzi (CCM) won the first contested elections in 1995.

The democratic and socialist credentials of the regimes in each country have been disputed. In Tanzania the left's criticism was even more severe than the right's, although its principal target was the shortcomings of utopian socialism, rather than the lack of democracy as such (there are summaries in Barker 1979, Pratt 1979, and McHenry 1994; among the more influential critiques are Shivji 1976 and Coulson 1982). In Nicaragua, the left was initially more supportive, partly in reaction to the Cold War orthodoxy emanating from Washington. However, since 1990 the critiques of the revolution's failures and contradictions have become sharper (Vilas 1991, Serra 1993, Dore and Weeks 1992, Castañeda 1993). For with the benefit of hindsight it is easy to criticize Tanzania's and Nicaragua's experiments. This does not necessarily mean they should be written off as 'failures', nor that they were misconceived in the first place. But it does oblige one to look behind the stereotypes propagated by both supporters and opponents, before drawing conclusions about how far they were really popular, socialist, or democratic.

What were the historical origins and goals of the two countries' popular democratic projects? In what ways, if any, did they offer alternatives to liberal democracy and capitalist development?

In Tanzania popular democracy formed part of a broader commitment to socialist development made by President Nyerere and the party leadership, formalized in the 1967 Arusha Declaration prioritizing 'socialism and self-reliance' based on rural development. Democracy and socialism were inseparable in Nyerere's view, for 'a political democracy which exists in a society of gross economic inequalities, or of social inequality, is at best imperfect, and at worst a hollow sham' (Nyerere 1968: 5).

By the time of the Declaration, Tanzania had already established a presidential executive and a one-party system, justified by Nyerere (1965, 1968: introduction) on the grounds that Western multi-party democracy tended to subordinate public to private interests, politicize ethnic differences, and threaten national development. Single-party rule did not, he contended, preclude voting or public debate of government policy, which might indeed be more robust than in multi-party systems. Moreover, it was more compatible with the consensual decision-making methods of indigenous governance. Nyerere translated 'socialism' as 'ujamaa', literally 'family-hood' in Swahili, to emphasize 'the African-ness of the policies we intend to follow' (Nyerere 1968: 2). It implied 'government by discussion' (Nyerere 1965: 106), designed to elicit the active participation of the mass of the people in development. And it did not preclude the protection of basic rights and freedoms under the rule of law (Nyerere 1968: 5–8).

Nyerere's central role as progenitor of the Tanzanian socialism raises serious questions about the sustainability of a system so dependent on his own leadership. Critics hold that the Arusha Declaration was decisive, not for the socialist principles it enunciated, but because of other agendas behind them: such as Nyerere's preoccupation with political stability after a series of post-independence crises, including the 1964 army mutiny and the Zanzibar revolution (Hartmann 1985); the consolidation of the country's bureaucratic *vis-à-vis* its commercial bourgeoisie (Shivji 1976: ch. 8); and the centralizing tendencies of the ruling party and state apparatuses.

But even if Nyerere's principles must be evaluated in the light of the real politics behind them, they cannot be reduced to the latter. To do so is to obscure key features of post-independence Tanzanian history. These include real popular support for the Arusha Declaration; the sense of public purpose that pervaded development policies (however defective they might be in practice); surprisingly frank intra-party debates about the widening gap between theory and practice; Nyerere's efforts to revitalize atrophying state and party machines; his reopening of the debate on multi-party democracy in 1990–1; and the CCM's ability to keep control over the political agenda and win the 1995 elections.

The Sandinistas in Nicaragua had to overcome a legacy of brutal author-itarian rule and rebuild an economy devastated by war and capital flight, in circumstances seemingly even less propitious for democracy than in Tanzania. Democracy in both popular and liberal forms emerged from prolonged armed struggle against dictatorship, which (from early 1978) broadened into popular insurrection across the country, sometimes with little or no direction from the FSLN (Vanden and Prevost 1993: 54). This had contradictory implications for the construction of popular democracy. The FSLN's military vanguardism sometimes made it unresponsive to the popular sectors. Yet it also enjoyed real legitimacy and mass support. Moreover it was obliged to accommodate a variety of potentially conflicting social interests which had helped bring it to power.

The FSLN's commitment to socialist development was likewise ambiguous. Despite the tendency of both supporters and opponents 'to accept the Sandinista movement's definition of itself as Marxist, or some form of revolutionary socialist, and then construct history back-wards' (Dore and Weeks 1992: 2), its programme was at least as much nationalist and populist as Marxist-Leninist. Indeed, the incoming Government of National Reconstruction adopted political pluralism, non-alignment, and a mixed economy with a socialist orientation as its three guiding principles (Vanden and Prevost 1993: 90).

Political pluralism was implicit in the counter-hegemonic strategy of the revolution itself. The Sandinista leadership was collective and presided over a coalition of ideologically differing groups formed to over-throw the Somoza dictatorship. Whilst the coalition's more conservat-ive members resigned from the government, those not joining the rebel Contra movement remained able to organize, and to press the gov-ernment to operate within liberal democratic parameters.

Yet, the Sandinistas did not believe pluralism by itself assured 'ef-fective democracy', which, according to Vice-President Sergio Ramirez, depended on

the people who suggest, construct and direct, organise themselves; [it is] a daily democracy and not one that takes place every four years. [At elections] the people don't go as a minority but in totality, and they consciously elect the best candidate and not one chosen like a soap or a detergent . . . For us democracy is not merely a formal model, but a continual process capable of giving the people . . . the real possibility of transforming their living conditions (cited in Dunkerley 1988: 280–1)

—though the practice was to fall short of this ideal.

In contrast to the CCM in Tanzania, the FSLN never made itself the sole institutional expression of popular democracy. It remained a vanguard, rather than a mass party, with strong organizational ties to the Ejército Popular Sandinista (popular armed forces) whose officers were party members. Instead it was the mass organizations that were the most vibrant practitioners of democracy: including the neighbourhood Sandinista Defence Committees (CDSs), the national women's organization (AMNLAE), the Sandinista Youth (JS), the Sandinistas Workers' Central (CST), the Rural Workers' Association (ATC), and the National Union of Farmers and Ranchers (UNAG). Though allied to the FSLN, these bodies were separately organized, had substantial mass memberships of their own, and made major contributions to development, notably through the mass literacy and agrarian reform programmes.

Did popular democracy complement or compete with liberal democracy? How far was democracy in both these forms subordinated to the ruling party and the state?

The veracity of the official claim that Tanzania remained a democracy under single-party governance hangs upon two assertions: first, that the party practised internal democracy; second, that the government acted in accordance with the wishes of the party (McHenry 1994: 49). Pratt (1979) argues with some cogency that these two requirements were satisfied. Members of Parliament and even ministers lost their seats at elections. Intra-party democracy was manifest in ongoing debates between 'pragmatic' and 'ideological' socialists (McHenry 1994: 16–18), with a tangible impact on policy, for instance the abolition and subsequent reinstatement of co-operatives. The party claimed to be rooted in the 'ten-cell' system at grass roots, rather than being a state-dominated shell, as in many other one-party states. It assumed political control over major state institutions, notably (via a network of political commissars) the armed forces, which never developed the praetorian, anti-democratic tendencies found elsewhere in Africa (Tungaraza 1998).

Yet despite Nyerere's claim that nonconformists were valued for 'the irritation' they caused, preventing 'society from ceasing to think' (quoted in Nursey-Bray 1983), the limits within which dissent was tolerated were narrow. Development policy was enunciated in a somewhat militaristic discourse according to which the President 'commanded' the population to move into *ujamaa* villages, and the party carried out 'operations' in the countryside to put this into effect, giving rise to a 'political culture of intolerance' in which critics were co-opted or watched by the state security agencies (Shivji 1991: 86). Despite Nyerere's proclaimed support for the rule of law, constitutional protections for human rights were not enacted until 1984, not put into effect until 1988, and were held to have inferior status to Acts of Parliament (McHenry 1994: 60–1).

In practice power circulated between President, party, and government. Though this ensured broad-based discussion of government policy, it also contributed to policy instability, notably during the prolonged hiatus with donors and the IMF over structural adjustment between 1979 and 1986. It depended heavily on Nyerere's capacity to interpellate the party and the public in the classic style of a populist leader, so that he 'failed to build and consolidate a system' (Hartmann 1988: 170–1). At the same time the practice of *kofia mbili* (two hats, i.e. leaders holding joint party and government responsibilities) enmeshed public servants in patronage networks, subverted the leadership code established under the Arusha Declaration, and prevented effective development administration (McHenry 1994: ch. 3).

Intra-party debate tended to be concentrated within the closed circles of the National Executive Committee, with little accountability toward ordinary members (Shivji 1991: 84–6, von Cranenburgh 1990: ch. 4). According to the Presidential Commission (1992: 112) which ultimately recommended the dismantling of the single-party system, the party 'which had historically acquired legitimacy from the people, began to usurp that legitimacy' by transforming itself from a mass to a state party (an indictment which carries all the more weight because the Commission's members were party insiders).

The National Assembly increasingly became a 'residual', legislature, with not much capacity to act as a watchdog of the administration (McHenry 1994: 7–8). Proposals for legislation were usually initiated by the government and discussed in specialized committees of CCM's National Executive Committee, before ratification by Parliament. Although MPs were competitively elected, candidates were selected and could be deselected by the party. The legislature's authority was eroded because party guidelines were frequently treated as if they supplemented or even overrode legislation (notable examples were the party guidelines on villagization, and on co-operatives).

The CCM's monopoly of power and espousal of directed development brought the media and educational institutions under the hegemony of the state, demobilized civil society, and curtailed the autonomous expression of differences within it (Shivji 1991: 85). Mass organizations, including the Union of Tanzanian Workers (JUWATA), the Co-operative Union of Tanzania (CUT), the Tanzanian Youth Organization (VIJANA), and the Union of Tanzanian Women (UWT), were subordinate to the party, and undermined by frequent changes in development policy. The trade unions were used to suppress labour militancy, notably during the labour unrest of the early 1970s. Under the UWT the 'women's movement in Tanzania' was more 'fragile and fragmented . . . than in Kenya, reflecting its longer history of complete demobilisation' (Nzomo 1995–6: 94), and did not do enough to promote grass-roots initiatives.

In Nicaragua the coexistence of people's with liberal democracy opened a wider potential space for autonomous organization by mass bodies. Yet one finds wildly varying assessments of the extent of popular participation, ranging from Ramirez's claim (ibid.) that the Sandinistas established a genuinely participatory democracy, to the contrary assertion that the FSLN remained 'a hierarchical military movement, preoccupied in institutionalising its rule in a country with no tradition of democracy', with leaders who were 'masters of the form of mass participation, while facilitating little in practice' (Dore and Weeks 1992: 32).

During the initial post-revolutionary phase (1979 to 1984) there did seem to be substance in the claim that new democratic forms were replacing rather than merely reconstituting the traditional organs of state power. Mass organizations flowered at grass roots; and popular corporatism prevailed at the centre, with the mass organizations represented in the Council of State (the legislature) alongside the FSLN, other political parties, and private sector bodies. Even so, the nine-man Sandinista National Directorate of revolutionary _comandantes_ firmly controlled policy at the centre. It acted as a government within the Governing Junta of National Reconstruction (JGRN). And its supporters, together with the representatives of the mass organizations, commanded a large majority in the legislature.

Yet the Sandinistas faced considerable domestic as well as international pressure to move toward orthodox multi-party democracy. Opposition members of the Council of State shaped the legislation setting out the ground rules for the 1984 elections. Under these, mass organizations ceased to be represented in the legislature; free competition between political parties was guaranteed; and parties rather than mass organizations were recognized as the building blocks of political society. The 1984 elections were free and fair, despite US and opposition attempts to discredit them, and the FSLN was returned with a two-thirds majority. Drafts of a new constitution were presented in television debates and open fora across the country (boycotted, however, by much of the opposition). The result was a standard-issue liberal democratic constitution, whose only novel features were gender equality provisions, protections for women's rights, and emphasis on economic and social as well as civil and political rights.

This shift toward democratic orthodoxy had contradictory implications for the Sandinistas' popular democratic project. Whilst it gave the opposition political space within which to confront the FSLN, it also strengthened the latter *vis-à-vis* its own grass-roots supporters. The FSLN's relationships to popular democracy were already ambiguous. Though claiming to be a national movement following the 'logic of the majority' (Dore and Weeks 1992: 22–3), its members comprised virtually all those holding sensitive positions in government, local government, the armed forces and police, and the senior management of the state sector of the economy. It remained a vanguard party with a small membership (about 12,000 in the mid-1980s), accountable only to the Sandinista Assembly, composed mainly of former guerrillas selected by the national directorate. It did not hold a Party Congress until 1991 after its defeat at the polls (Wright 1990, Vanden and Prevost 1993: ch. 6).

The new constitution added to these centralizing tendencies by redefining political participation in terms of inter-party electoral competition, with the government controlled by the electorally dominant party (i.e. the FSLN up to 1990). The Contra war led to states of emergency, which partially suspended constitutional protections during most of 1985–9. Even so, the legal opposition remained free to organize, was active in the legislature, had its views taken into account during the constitution-making exercise, and regrouped (with US assistance) to fight and win the 1990 elections. American and opposition accusations that the Sandinista regime was authoritarian were disingenuous, not least because they themselves subverted democratic processes in supporting the Contras.

Instead, the two groups with most reason to complain about exclusion were the ethnic minorities of the Atlantic coast, and the Sandinistas' own mass organizations. The FSLN's militant *mestizo* nationalism made it insensitive to the political and developmental needs of oppressed non-Hispanic minorities (Dunkerley 1988: 312). The Atlantic region was overrun by the Contra insurgency and alienated by government counter-insurgency tactics. Subsequent efforts to address minority concerns, including the Autonomy Law of 1987, came too late to effect a reconciliation.

As for the mass organizations, they were disempowered from two directions. On the one hand formal democratization displaced them from the legislature and marginalized them from national politics. On the other hand the FSLN treated them as adjuncts of administration, charged with assisting land reform, adult literacy programmes, distributing rationed goods, and organizing municipal services. Although they initially appeared to constitute a form of municipal or local power, popular organizations failed to develop into distinct arenas for political debate, remaining 'firmly within the orbit of Sandinismo' (Dunkerley 1988: 281–3). The top-down relationship between state, party, and mass organizations proved to be a central flaw in Sandinista governance, especially when sacrifices were imposed on the masses under the 'survival economy' of the mid- and late 1980s (Stahler-Sholk 1995: 240).

Some mass organizations were more affected than others. The supposed linchpins of local democratization, the CDSs, had become defunct in many areas of the country by the mid-1980s (Jonas and Stein 1990: 28–9). The industrial and agricultural workers' unions, CST and ATC, followed state and party 'directives for voluntary labour, more participation in defence, and austerity in wage demands . . . This, combined with a verticalist decision-making style . . . caused many workers to see [unions] as representing the interests of the state and the party rather than their own' (Vanden and Prevost 1993: 65). A rival industrial labour federation emerged, and wildcat strikes spread during the late 1980s. But in contrast UNAG, whose base was among farmers in the co-operative and independent sectors, agitated successfully for agrarian reform including redistribution of land to individual peasants; and continued to mount challenges against the revolutionary authorities.

The Sandinistas failed to build on an initially positive record of promoting the empowerment and interests of women. Though the women's AMNLAE lacked internal democracy (it did not hold proper leadership elections until 1991), it intervened in the policy-making process, and could even challenge the government and the FSLN (Vanden and Prevost 1993: 59). It engaged in debates over women's participation in the military, helped secure divorce and family law reform, and insisted on recognition of women's rights in the constitution, besides achieving tangible gains in education, health, and child care. In the mid-1980s it was claimed women constituted 50 per cent of the militia, 22 per cent of FSLN members (down from 33 per cent in 1979), and 37 per cent of the party leadership cadre (Molyneux 1985: 150–2); though they remained under-represented in the FSLN national directorate, ministerial positions, and Parliament. Yet 'from 1987 the FSLN leadership promoted the slogan "women are not a sector," dodged the issue of equal pay, and became increasingly mealy-mouthed about abortion' (Dunkerley 1993: 17). Women bore the brunt of the economic dislocations of the late 1980s, a high proportion of women's employment being concentrated in the informal sector. Their disaffection was reflected in the higher proportion of women than of men voting against the Sandinistas in 1990.

By the late 1980s the mass organizations had started retreating from the spaces opened up in civil and political society. And into these spaces began moving the bourgeois elements they had displaced: the churches, employers' federations, professional associations, the independent press (headed by the opposition *La Prensa*), and opposition parties. During the period of revolutionary government the Catholic Church hierarchy became the Sandinistas' single most dangerous adversary, its antagonism directed at least as much against radical Christians in Ecclesiastical Base Communities and Catholic worker, student, and youth movements as against the Sandinistas themselves (Dunkerley 1988: 287–90). Civil society was by no means coextensive with the popular sectors, nor self-evidently supportive of the Sardinistas' project of economic and social transformation.

Why was it difficult to build popular participation into the political design of development policy? How far did this explain the failure to generate development from below?

Tanzanian socialism was constructed around two potentially conflicting principles: first, state control, including nationalism of key sectors of the economy (though not the entire private sector); second, commitment in principle to participatory methods of development. The latter was above all embodied in the theory and practice of *ujamaa* villages. These passed through two main phases. In the first, initiated by the Arusha Declaration in 1967, emphasis was on communal production and transformation of village society through grass-roots initiatives supported by economic incentives. In the second, after 1973, priority was given to compulsory villagization to facilitate delivery of administrative and social services, a policy which proved inconsistent with the goal of creating self-reliant village communities.

There is a substantial literature on why *ujamaa* villages failed to expand agricultural production, or transform the living conditions of the rural masses. Explanations fall into four categories.[5] An influential stream of Marxist analysis (Shivji 1976, Coulson 1982) contended that the policy never confronted capitalist relations in the rural areas; rural socialism being frustrated by an alliance between wealthy peasants and the bureaucratic bourgeoisie. Party militants incorporated this critique into the CCM's own 1981 Guidelines, attributing the country's economic problems to the 'glaring weaknesses of the party' and 'lack of implementation of socialist policies' (summarized in van Cranenburgh 1990: 117–20).

Market liberals in contrast have argued that expansion of peasant output required more capitalism and rural inequality, not less

---

[5] See Barker (1979), who makes a related distinction between the critiques of 'production socialists' and of 'production liberals', though placing those emphasizing institutional and political factors in the latter category, along with true market liberals.

(Lofchie 1989), requiring (in line with the policy reforms advocated by international donors) liberalization of agricultural marketing, less party interference in rural development, and an end to villagization.

Others, thirdly, have argued against reducing Tanzania's 'development equation . . . to a choice between capitalism or socialism without realising her predicament of not being easily accessible to both' (Hyden 1980: 176), due to institutional barriers deriving from the rural 'economy of affection' which make peasants resist 'capture' by either the state or the market.

A final, and in my view more convincing approach, focuses on contradictions in the political design of development policy (Sundet 1994, van Cranenburgh 1990). It argues that these explain the inability of the Tanzanian government to implement its own commitment to self-reliant and participatory development, or even to allocate resources in accord with its own declared priorities, agriculture receiving a lower share of the state budget than industry during the entire period up to 1986 (Costello 1996: 31).

A pertinent example of these contradictions is the government's treatment of co-operatives, as described by van Cranenburgh (1990). These began as mainly societal organizations responding to peasant needs, but from the 1960s were 'officialized', becoming the lowest level of an increasingly corrupt and inefficient state-controlled marketing system. Then following the introduction of *ujamaa* villages, 'friction developed between the conception of co-operatives as voluntary organisations serving member needs and the rival claims of the party to represent the people' (ibid.: 141, 147). The co-operatives were forcibly dissolved and replaced 'by villages, in which the party occupied leadership posts, and by the parastatal crop authorities which were controlled by the state' (ibid.: 191). Having been reinstated in 1980 because of failures in state marketing, co-operatives again became hostage to bureaucratic struggles, between those maintaining they should return to their previous semi-autonomous form, and those proposing they be reorganized as multi-purpose village co-operatives implementing 'the party policy of *ujamaa* and self-reliance' (1985 party guideline, cited ibid.: 170).

Similar problems of reconciling party control and grass-roots initiatives plagued industrial sector reforms. The 1970 Presidential Directive on workers' participation, along with the 1971 Mwongozo (Party Guidelines) were designed in theory to break the grip of capitalist management practices in parastatals. In practice they tamed the workers politically by introducing party and party militia structures into the workplace, undermined management, and disastrously reduced public sector efficiency (Hyden 1980: ch. 6).

Likewise with local government reform. According to Nyerere, the 1972 Decentralization Act was not supposed to mean 'transfer of a rigid and bureaucratic system from Dar Es Salaam to lower levels. . . . We are trying to eradicate the thicket of red tape and the tyranny of "the proper channels," not to plant them out all over the country' (cited in Hill 1979–80: 189). Yet it had the precisely contrary effect, by simultaneously eliminating citizen participation through elected village, district, and regional councils. Far from empowering village authorities, villagization 'replicated the bureaucratisation process which had grown roots in districts and regions . . . Local government authorities do not really represent the people. This is more evident at village level, [where] the party leadership is really supreme [and] the majority of the people who are not members of the CCM hardly have any say' (Presidential Commission 1992: 56, 117).

In sum, the Arusha Declaration's policies of self-reliant development failed not because there was too much grass-roots participation, but because there was too little. Some see this as a triumph of administration over politics (Costello 1996, Boesen 1979), arguing that the bureaucracy frustrated the party's proposals for socialist transformation; being able to do so because the CCM lacked a coherent strategy to link its ideology to practical implementation of rural development. For others, however, the party itself was just as much part of the problem, being dominated by its own bureaucrats, who ultimately stifled the intra-party debates which the Arusha Declaration had fostered (Hill 1979–80). Nyerere's efforts to build intra-party democracy were frustrated, because the one-party state provided too narrow a space for political participation (Mmuya and Chaligha 1992: 14). Indeed, as van Cranenburgh (1990) argues, it was *because* CCM remained a single-party structure of the conventional socialist type that it failed to catalyse the self-reliant development promised by the Arusha Declaration.

The Sandinistas were no less committed to socialist development; but from the start emphasized they would work within the framework of 'a mixed planned economy', transformed to meet the needs of the 'poor majority' (MIPLAN, the planning bureau, cited in Dijkstra 1992: 2). This transformation was to be achieved through four principal methods. First, there was to be central planning, based on exchange relations (control of foreign exchange, prices and credit, including de facto nationalization of the banking system), rather than full-scale state ownership of the means of production. Second, redistributive policies would assure food security and an adequate social wage for all. Third, land reform would transform relations of production in the country-side. And fourth, the mass organizations would actively participate in these transformations: i.e. development was to be led from below.

The commitment to participatory development was by no means a formality. The popular literacy and public health programmes owed much of their success to the neighbourhood CDSs (for an urban case study see Higgins and Coen 1992). The ATC and UNAG, represent-ing rural wage workers and the co-operative and independent farm sectors, were consulted and brought into agricultural management struc-tures, from enterprise up to ministry levels. Their top cadres (and those of other mass organizations) enjoyed direct access to the Sandinista leadership, being represented in the Sandinista Assembly and (until 1984) the Council of State. Yet whether this gave popular sectors significant influence over the formulation of government development policies and programmes remains doubtful.

It was in the agrarian sector where one could make the strongest case that development was partly democratized. Yet, far from re-inforcing the Sandinistas' socialist project, this induced a peasant revolution within the revolution that ultimately contributed to their downfall. Peasant land occupations, initially led by the ATC, started soon after the revolution, but were halted when the government introduced its own land reform programme. The latter produced a more comprehensive redistribution of rural resources than anywhere else in Latin America, first targeting the estates of the Somoza family and supporters, then being extended to abandoned or unutilized land. Though initially the emphasis was on agroindustrial development in state enterprises and state control of marketing, the peasant move-ment eventually succeeded in diverting the course of agrarian reform toward a labour-intensive strategy, based on the co-operative and inde-pendent peasant sectors (Serra 1993: 34).

This pro-peasant strategy was driven to a considerable extent by political imperatives, especially the realization that peasant political support was essential to military victory over the Contras. A leading role was played by UNAG, which seceded from the ATC in 1981 to become a militant mass organization representing the heterogeneous interests of the peasantry, and demanding the redistribution of land to individual peasant households (Dore 1990: 112–13). By 1988, only 12 per cent of agricultural land was in the state sector (down from 21 per cent in 1983), 23 per cent was in the co-operative sector, and no less than 39 per cent was in the hands of small and medium peas-ant producers. At the same time large individual estates had declined from 52 per cent in 1978 to only 21 per cent a decade later (Dijkstra 1992: 80).

Even so, development from below failed to produce tangible material benefits for small farmers and other members of the 'poor majority' the Sandinistas claimed to represent. Partly it was thwarted by the war-induced crisis which ravaged the economy. But government policies, together with poor economic management, also aggravated the impact on the popular sectors, who bore the brunt of the consequent imbalances, including hyper-inflation and declining real incomes. Rural food producers were squeezed at one end by price controls on their produce and at the other end by the scarcity of productive inputs and credit. Whilst partial liberalization of the rural sector began to ease their situation, resulting in modest food production rises, they remained vulnerable to economic dislocations; and they suffered a sharp drop in real incomes during the economic adjustments of the late 1980s (Utting 1991: 4, 27). The disillusion of the popular sectors was all the sharper because 'economic policies were often out of co-ordination with Sandinista structures for political mobilisation. Workers and peasants were mobilised to seize factories and lands, but then the state took control of most confiscated properties. [The CDSs] were called on to distribute rationed goods, but then inflationary policies fed a flourishing inflation that made "speculators" out of the most loyal revolutionaries' (Stahler-Sholk 1995: 240).

Did liberal displace popular democracy because of external destabilization, donor conditionality, economic failure, or the contradictions of popular democracy itself?

Although Western powers criticized Tanzania for turning to socialism, the latter never faced a concerted campaign of destabilization, such as that waged against the Sandinistas in Nicaragua. To the contrary, its development model initially attracted some admiration, and for many years it attracted more external assistance relative to GNP than any other sub-Saharan African country; though this funded state expansion and thereby reinforced imbalances in the economy (Crouch 1987).

The combination of foreign dependence and economic stagnation made Tanzania vulnerable to external pressure; all the more in the difficult international economic conditions of the 1980s, when per capita GNP declined after slow increases up to the late 1970s. Nyerere opposed the stabilization and adjustment measures proposed by international financial institutions, contending that they imposed an inappropriate market-oriented model of development. But in 1986, the year after he stepped down from the presidency, an IMF-approved Economic Recovery Programme (ERP) was introduced to restore internal and external balance in the economy, cut back the role of the state, and rebuild the private sector. Tanzania became a policy-taker and not a policy initiator, with policies and programmes, including proposals for political reform, coming in packages to be implemented with little change in content or timetable (Mmuya and Chaligha 1992: 20). Moreover, the donors' democracy promotion efforts became all the more insistent following the transitions in Eastern Europe. As Nyerere reminded the CCM leadership in 1990 when opening the debate on a multi-party system, 'when a colleague gets shaven, better wet your hair lest you get a dry shave' (quoted ibid.: 23).

These external forces impinged on a crisis in the Tanzanian state and development model. Efforts to transform rural society had already run out of steam by the end of the 1970s, and state revenue and expenditure went into decline. Cuts in education, health, and welfare budgets represented not only a retreat from socialism, but also a loss in state legitimacy. The decline was marked by an exponential growth of corruption and of the informal economy (from 10 per cent of GDP in 1978 to 31 per cent in 1986 according to Maliyamkono and Bagachwa 1990: 144). Indeed a recent effort to counter stereotypes, by asking 'what went right in Tanzania?' (Swantz and Tripp 1996), concentrates on the retreat from 'directed development' and the emergence of new coping strategies in the informal sector. If official people's democracy was in tatters, this was because the people found their own ways of surviving, starting to 'ridicule and cajole . . . the institutions they most revered: CCM was no longer *Chama cha Mapinduzi* (Party for Revolution) but *"Chukua Chako Mapema"* (pocket what is at your disposal quickly)' (Mmuya and Chaligha 1992: 16).

Nyerere initiated the debate on multi-party democracy in 1990, following the frustration of his efforts (as party chairman) to revitalize an atrophying CCM. His intervention propelled a hesitant government and party into appointing a commission chaired by the Chief Justice to enquire into the merits of multi-party democracy (Presidential Commission 1992). Existing mass organizations began to loosen bonds with the CCM, and a number of new pro-democracy groupings, women's groups, professional associations, and trade unions emerged. Although 77 per cent of those consulted by the Commission in public meetings across the country endorsed continuation of a single-party system,[6] most supported reforms (separation between party and government structures; greater accountability to Parliament and the public; better protection for rights and freedoms) which added up to

---

[6] However, those consulted were not a random sample, being more representative of political society than of the general population. The party influenced the process of consultation, and not everybody felt able openly to criticize the existing system (interviews with members of the Commission, 1996).

a change of system. The party and the government were finally persuaded to introduce multi-party democracy; doing so by changing existing legislation, rather than by convening a constituent assembly, as recommended by the Commission. Their change of strategy paid off, since a reinvigorated CCM won the first multi-party elections in 1995.

In Nicaragua in contrast, the FSLN sponsored political reform only to suffer unexpected electoral defeat in 1990. This defeat, however, was the culmination of political and economic shifts commencing well before the elections. US hostility was the single most crucial factor (Helwege 1989); in particular the CIA's prolonged campaign of attrition, forcing the Sandinistas into concessions despite the failure of the Contra rebels on the battlefield. According to ECLAC figures the war inflicted property damage and production losses totalling $1.42 billion during 1980–8; Contra targeting of export crops squeezed foreign earnings; and defence spending rose from 7 per cent of the national budget in 1980 to more than 50 per cent during 1985–8 (Dijkstra 1992: 114–15, 124). Multilateral assistance, loans, and foreign investment virtually ceased, leaving Nicaragua to repay debts incurred by the Somoza regime until its meagre foreign earnings were exhausted in 1985, reinforcing the breach with the private sector. After positive rates of growth up to 1983, GDP went into sharp decline, and by 1989 per capita GDP was 33 per cent less than in 1981.

At the same time the United States redefined the conflict in terms of the neo-liberal agenda of international financial institutions. As a confidential World Bank report put it, 'the ideological struggle between economic models is, in the final analysis, a power struggle'. Lending to Nicaragua should cease until the Sandinistas accepted the Bank's proposals for revitalizing the private sector (IBRD Country Program Paper: Nicaragua, 1982, cited by Leogrande 1996: 336); but this was impossible so long as the USA was funding the Contras and discouraging private investment.

Nevertheless, the revolutionary government's response to these economic pressures defies ideological stereotyping. In the rural sector, as we have already seen, it changed tack to emphasize market incentives, land redistribution, and small-scale production; and by 1988 the markets for grain and other basic foodstuffs were decontrolled. Stabilization and adjustment measures introduced during 1988–90 (including massive devaluation) were as draconian as those that might have been imposed by international financial institutions, though their impact was more adverse because they were poorly designed and not cushioned by IMF balance of payments support. They neither restored macro-economic equilibrium, nor stimulated the output of peasant farmers, who responded to uncertainty by withdrawing into non-monetary relationships (Dore 1990: 116–17).

Economic reverses translated into defeats in class and power relations. The government's loss of control over the economy forced abandonment of its redistributive programmes, and hence sacrifice of grass-roots support. Trends in consumption are a useful indicator. To start with, basic wage goods remained available at low prices, offsetting the impact on the poor of the decline in GDP and total private consumption. But after 1986 consumption of these basic wage goods began to decline even faster than non-basic consumption (Dijkstra 1992: 128). The immiseration of the masses was aggravated by swingeing cuts in government services, subsidies, and employment, with especially regressive impacts on wage earners and the urban poor.

The Sandinistas found it all the harder to prevent erosion of their popular support, because they had not converted the latter into durable party-political relationships. The FSLN had remained a vanguard party rather than a broadly based structure like CCM in Tanzania. Neither the party nor the mass organizations were consulted about the 1988 economic stabilization package, introduced in a technocratic manner, consistent with the Sandinistas' 'military approach to economic decision-making' (Serra 1993: 27–8). The latter insulated economic decision-makers from populist pressures to continue unsustainable redistributive policies. But it also made the government dangerously complacent about its grass-roots support.

The pressure was increased by the Esquipelas accords ending the Central American conflicts, which tied cessation of external military intervention to internal political reform (Dunkerley 1993: 38–9). The 1990 elections were brought forward and the fourteen parties composing the UNO opposition coalition secured strategic concessions, including international observers and access to foreign (i.e. US) funding (Robinson 1992). The electorate confounded the pollsters, who had predicted a FSLN victory, by decisively rejecting the latter and returning UNO with a margin of 55 to the FSLN's 41 per cent.

There is little doubt that the crisis of the economy and the government's stabilization measures were factors in this defeat, along with the perception that confrontation with the USA, war, and compulsory military service would drag on under the Sandinistas. But the election also reflected important structural changes, notably the transformation of the bulk of the peasantry into small independent farmers. Only 36 per cent of all rural voters and just 29 per cent of independent small and middle farmers voted for the FSLN, which gained a majority only among agricultural co-operative members and state farm workers (Utting 1991: 102). Likewise in urban areas (where the FSLN vote was 44 per cent), UNO won majorities among owners and employees of private businesses, in the informal sector, among the un-employed, and among women. In contrast the FSLN vote was strongly correlated with education, and with state and formal sector employ-ment (Anderson 1992). That is to say, the Sandinistas' support held up within the revolution's bureaucratic and technocratic core, but not in the popular sectors beyond the formal economy.

What have been the legacies of popular democracy and socialist development? Have they made it more difficult to consolidate liberal democracy and market-oriented development or easier?

In neither country was the apparent defeat of people's democracy the end of the story. In Tanzania the fact that the CCM won the 1995 elec-tions against an opposition led by former CCM notables was evidence of the depth of its political roots, and the popularity of ex-president Nyerere, who campaigned for the party. It was also testimony to CCM's capacity to reinvent itself as a party of liberal modernizers, pro-moting state technocrats (like President Mkapa himself) over the old ideological barons, reflecting shifts in the political balance initiated during the 1980s debates over the IMF and structural adjustment.

However, in reinventing itself as a party of government in a multi-party framework, the CCM has withdrawn from a number of institu-tional arenas in civil society it previously dominated, including trade unions, the co-operative movement, and the women's and youth organizations (Luanda 1994). Likewise it has severed links with the Tanzanian People's Defence Force (TPDF), which kept the latter loyal to party and government. Under multi-party governance the country will be protected from coups on the possibly less secure foundations of military professionalism and adherence to a democratic constitution.

Another issue is the potential erosion of some positive achievements of the Arusha Declaration era: including preservation of national unity (albeit by restricting public debate about ethnic, religious, and regional divisions: Kaiser 1996); reduction of social and economic in-equality; and expansion (up to the early 1980s) of basic social services like health and education. There is some evidence that the burden of economic adjustment has been shouldered by the poor and that social inequality has increased (useful summaries of the data are Ferreira 1996 and Wangwe 1996[7]). If the lesson of the 1970s is that an economic

[7] However, some of the studies summarized by Wangwe (1996) suggest a rather more complex picture: because of real growth in incomes and consumption, the proportion of the population who are poor have declined, at the same time that the *gap* between the better off and the poor has widened.

strategy based on the fulfilment of basic needs became unsustainable due to the neglect of macro structural adjustment considerations, the lesson of the 1980s and 1990s is that sole focus on the latter is equally perilous (Wangwe 1996: 29). The potential sharpening of class antagonisms heads a lengthening list of issues that could threaten political stability and national unity, including the politicization of previously suppressed ethnic, national, and religious identities and the political status of Zanzibar (a contentious issue during and after the 1995 elections). The issue is whether Tanzania can find democratic solutions to such problems, now that Nyerere's original conception of the state as a moral community in which ordinary citizens have a stake has been eroded.

In contrast to the CCM in Tanzania, the FSLN not only presided over transition to multi-party democracy, but also lost the 1990 election. Its autocritique blamed defeat on 'Authoritarianism. Lack of sensitivity to the problems put forward at grass roots. The stifling of criticism. Bureaucratic forms of leadership and the imposition of leaders and organisational structures' (cited in Serra 1993: 26). That the Sandinistas could be so candid is arguably evidence of an underlying commitment to popular democracy and participatory development. Whilst this commitment has complicated economic adjustment under post-1990 governments, it may also have preserved Nicaragua from ending up with a largely formal 'democracy by default' (Whitehead 1993).

After their 1990 electoral defeat the Sandinistas made use of the fact that they still controlled the army, the police, and the mass organizations to hammer out a *concertación* or cohabitation pact with the incoming Chamorro government. Under this the government held back from the counter-revolutionary agenda of its more right-wing supporters, modified its privatization programme to permit worker ownership of some properties, and refrained from tampering with the armed forces. For their part the Sandinistas co-operated in controlling the armed forces, reining in the unions, balancing the economy, demobilizing former combatants, and restoring political order.

The economy stabilized, more through massive external assistance than because of recovery in the real economy. During the early 1990s Nicaragua received more foreign aid per capita than any other developing country, this being in effect political rent paid for ejecting the Sandinistas. From 1991 the principal threats to economic recovery came not from popular militancy, but from elsewhere: including disturbances arising from failure to resettle ex-government and ex-Contra combatants; lack of credit and other inputs needed to revive peasant production and halt parcellization of land; the right's ideologically driven efforts to secure return of redistributed properties; and over-enthusiastic economic liberalization which, rather than contributing to the recovery of agricultural production, stimulated a 'jungle capitalism . . . in which short-term profit motives are dominant' (Spoor 1994: 200; Dijkstra 1996 makes a similar assessment of the industrial sector).

The relative health of democracy may be partly attributable to the democratic norms instilled through the Sandinistas' popular education and mass participation programmes. A comparative public opinion survey in the late 1980s (Seligson and Booth 1993) found support for popular participation was almost as high in Nicaragua as in Costa Rica, and support for the right to dissent was even higher; despite the latter's longer established democratic culture.[8] The mass organizations did not disappear (except the CDSs, partly absorbed by the Community Movement). Some indeed received a new lease of life after their ties with government and the FSLN were loosened (Prevost 1996: 320), especially those already enjoying autonomy under the Sandinistas, notably the farmers' UNAG and the women's AMNLAE. The trade unions lost ground after their initial resistance to economic restructuring, partly because they co-operated with redundancies and privatization, and partly due to government strike-breaking and anti-union policies.

As for the FSLN, it embarked on a partial democratization of party structures following its 1991 National Congress, but found itself caught in a contradiction, since greater responsiveness to its grassroots activists would risk 'wrecking a capitalist truce' (Dunkerley 1993: 55). The de facto coalition with the Chamorro administration not only resulted in a major schism at the 1994 FSLN National Congress, it also triggered the defection from the government of most UNO National Assembly members, producing a protracted crisis in relations with the legislature, and a near breakdown in constitutional governance. The consequent realignment of political forces opened the way for the election of a hardline conservative administration in 1996, headed by the former Somocista President Aleman, who promised wholesale reversal of the gains of the revolution, including the land reforms.

In sum, the FSLN's silent pact with the Chamorro administration marked an apparent return to the established Latin American

---

[8] Seligson and Booth (1993) argue that political attitudes were strongly influenced by the 1990 election campaign, which was then commencing. They point out that support for the right to dissent was stronger among opposition than FSLN supporters, which is what one might expect in the light of government restrictions on rights during the Contra emergency. However, overall support for democratic norms was strong among *both* groups, suggesting it was not just contingent, but also based on a broad popular consensus.

pattern of elite negotiation of democracy, in contrast to the popularly based democratization of the Sandinista period. Yet at least three important legacies from the latter remained in place. First, the transformations in the agrarian sector which freed the peasantry from patrimonial relationships (though these are now threatened by the right's efforts to reverse land reform). Second, a pattern of grass-roots militancy which partially offset the worst excesses of economic liberalization. And third, a disputatious political culture which enlivens formal liberal democratic institutions.

4. Conclusion

Why did Tanzania and Nicaragua have such difficulty establishing a form of popular rule that was sustainable and capable of delivering socialist development? One obvious answer is the hegemonic pressures exerted by the capitalist West. Another is their own governments' failures of economic and political management. But despite impressive empirical evidence for both explanations, neither is enough.

Both countries' experiments were beset by problems inherent in the contradictions between popular democracy and state-induced socio-economic change. Some of these were specific to the socialist models of state-managed, autocentric development followed in Tanzania and Nicaragua, together with the modes of political organization historically associated with them, including the dominance of centralized party apparatuses. Yet, as shown above, in neither country can one say with much confidence that the extent and quality of participation and governmental accountability were increased as a result of the adoption of more liberal political and economic models; in many respects indeed they may be less.

Hence part of the difficulty may be at an even deeper level, namely the problems of harmonizing high levels of popular participation with the requirements of the modern developmental state as such. The liberal democratic form of the latter, as Schumpeter (1965) argued, may not be any more consistent with 'rule by the people' than the people's democracies it has replaced. In Nicaragua indeed it was the competitive multi-party system introduced by the Sardinistas during their 'dual transition' that shut mass organizations out of national-level politics. Moreover, the opening of the two countries to global markets imposed *different* constraints upon the ability of citizens to shape the economic decisions affecting their daily lives, rather than fewer constraints; and it came with new forms of state intervention in support of markets, rather than greatly reduced intervention as such.

What lessons, if any, can be extracted by other new democracies, especially those like South Africa, Uganda, Eritrea, or Ethiopia, which have recently emerged from popular struggles against dictatorial regimes? The first is a lesson their leaders seem to have absorbed already, that there is little to be gained and much to be lost from recreating the party-states and closed economies of yesterday's people's democracies. Some of these leaders have indeed taken developmental realism even further by demobilizing the popular organizations which helped bring them to power in order to safeguard liberal democracy and market-oriented development from mass discontent.[9]

Nevertheless I do not believe the evidence presented above would justify the view that the requirements of development and those of popular participation are necessarily incompatible. Despite real contradictions, the balance between them is open to negotiation; and there may also be synergies. In Tanzania, *ujamaa* would have enjoyed better success had the CCM been more responsive to its own grass-roots constituencies. In Nicaragua, peasant mass organizations changed the course of rural development in ways that departed significantly from the Sandinistas' own blueprint for rural transformation. Even in post-Sandinista Nicaragua, technocratic blueprints for economic restructuring could not be imposed 'by riding roughshod over groups which, through a decade of revolutionary transformation, had come to expect and demand both social justice and a degree of participation in the policy process' (Utting 1991: 103).

But what happens when popular participation is no longer part of the official design of the developmental state? In some respects this may be a blessing, as party and state bureaucrats can no longer hide behind populist rhetoric to impose development from above. The burden of holding governments and development administrators accountable thus shifts to the grass-roots organizations most capable of mobilizing subaltern classes and groups, through and outside the regular channels of the liberal democratic state. Popular participation of this kind is bound to be messy, decentralized, and divisive; and to challenge development orthodoxy. It may also become rudderless if not guided by well-formulated counter-hegemonic strategies (of the type discussed on pp. 315–16 above). Furthermore, isolated local initiatives are easily swamped without national (and international) infrastructures to support them. Whatever their faults, the Arusha Declaration in Tanzania and Sandinisino ideology in Nicaragua contained strategic visions of how development could empower their citizens, even if

---

[9] See the heated debate on the South African left over the ANC government's efforts to rein in the grass-roots organizations which were active in the struggle against apartheid: Bond and Mayekiso (1996) and Cherry (1994).

they were flawed by being imposed upon the latter, not evolved in partnership with them.

REFERENCES

Ake, Claude (1994), *Democratization of Disempowerment in Africa*, CASS
   Occasional Monograph no. 1, Lagos: Malthouse Press.
Anderson, Leslie (1992), 'Surprises and Secrets: Lessons from the 1990
   Nicaraguan Election', *Studies in Comparative International Development*,
   27/3: 93–119.
Barker, Jonathan (1979), 'The Debate on Rural Socialism in Tanzania', in
   Mwansasu and Pratt (1979).
Beetham, David (1994*a*), 'Conditions for Democratic Consolidation', *Review of
   African Political Economy*, 60: 157–72.
—— (ed.) (1994*b*), *Defining and Measuring Democracy*, London: Sage.
Benhabib, Seyla (1996), *Democracy and Difference: Contesting the Boundaries
   of the Political*, Princeton: Princeton University Press.
Boesen, Jannik (1979), 'Tanzania: From Ujamaa to Villagisation', in Mwansasu
   and Pratt (1979).
—— Storgoard Madsen, Birgit, and Moody, Tony (1977), *Ujamaa: Socialism
   from Above*, Uppsala: Scandinavian Institute of African Studies.
Bond, Patrick, and Mayekiso, Mzwande (1996), 'Developing Resistance,
   Resisting "Development": Reflections from the South African Struggle',
   Socialist Register 1996, London: Merlin Press: 33–61.
Castañeda, Jorge G. (1993), *Utopia Unarmed: The Latin American Left after
   the Cold War*, New York: Knopf.
Chambers, Robert (1997), *Whose Reality Counts? Putting the First Last*,
   London: Intermediate Technology Publications.
Cherry, Janet (1994), 'The Politics of Hegemony and the Politics of Develop-
   ment: The 1994 Elections in South Africa's Eastern Cape', *Democratization*,
   1/3: 406–22.
Costello, Matthew J. (1996), 'Administration Triumphs over Politics: The
   Transformation of the Tanzanian State', *African Studies Review*, 39/1:
   123–48.
Coulson, Andrew (1982), *Tanzania: a Political Economy*, Oxford: Clarendon
   Press.
Crouch, Susan (1987), *Western Responses to Tanzanian Socialism, 1967–1983*,
   Aldershot: Avebury.
Dijkstra, Geske (1992), *Industrialisation in Sandinista Nicaragua: Policy
   and Practice in a Mixed Economy*, Boulder, Colo.: Westview.
—— (1996), 'The Impact of Structural Adjustment Programs on Manufactur-
   ing: Lessons from Nicaragua', *World Development*, 24/3: 535–47.
Dore, Elizabeth (1990), 'The Great Grain Dilemma, Peasants and State Policy
   in Revolutionary Nicaragua', *Peasant Studies*, 17/2: 96–120.

—— and Weeks, John (1992), *The Red and the Black: The Sandinistas and the Nicaraguan Revolution*, London: Institute of Latin American Studies, University of London.

Dornbusch, Rudiger, and Edwards, Sebastian (1990), 'Macroeconomic Populism', *Journal of Development Economics*, 32: 247–77.

Dunkerley, James (1988), *Power in the Ithsmus: A Political History of Modern Central America*, London: Verso.

—— (1993), *The Pacification of Central America*, London: Institute of Latin American Studies, University of London.

Escobar, Arturo (1995), *Encountering Development: The Making and Unmaking of the Third World*, Princeton: Princeton University Press.

—— and Alvarez, Sonia (eds.) (1992), *The Making of Social Movements in Latin America: Identity, Strategy and Democracy*, Boulder, Colo.: Westview.

Fals-Borda, Orlando (1992), 'Social Movements and Political Power in Latin America', in Escobar and Alvarez (1992).

—— and Rahman, Mohammad Anisur (eds.) (1991), *Action and Knowledge: Breaking the Monopoly with Participatory-Action Research*, London: Intermediate Technology Publications.

Ferguson, James (1990), *The Anti-politics Machine: 'Development', Depoliticisation and Bureaucratic Power in Lesotho*, Cambridge: Cambridge University Press.

Ferreira, M. Luisa (1996), *Poverty and Inequality during Structural Adjustment in Rural Tanzania*, World Bank Policy Research Paper 1641, Washington: World Bank.

Foucault, Michel (1980), *Power/Knowledge: Selected Interviews and Other Writings*, Hemel Hempstead: Harvester-Wheatsheaf.

Gould, Carol (1988), *Rethinking Democracy*, Cambridge: Cambridge University Press.

Gramsci, Antonio (1971), *Selections from the Prison Notebooks*, trans. and ed. Q. Hoare and G. Nowell-Smith, London: Lawrence & Wishart.

Hartmann, Jeanette (1985), 'The Arusha Declaration Revisited', *African Review*, 12/1: 1–11.

—— (1988), 'President Nyerere and the State', in Michael Hodd (ed.), *Tanzania after Nyerere*, London: Pinter.

Held, David (1989), 'The Contemporary Polarisation of Democratic Theory: The Case for a Third Way', in D. Held, *Political Theory and the Modern State*, Cambridge: Polity Press.

—— (1993), 'Democracy: From City-States to a Cosmopolitan Order', in D. Held (ed.), *Prospects for Democracy: North South East West*, Cambridge: Polity Press.

Helwege, Ann (1989), 'Three Socialist Experiences in Latin America: Surviving US Economic Pressure', *Bulletin of Latin American Research*, 8/2: 211–34.

Higgins, M. J., and Coen, T. L. (1992), *Oigame! Oigame! Struggle and Social Change in a Nicaraguan Urban Community*, Boulder, Colo.: Westview Press.

Hill, Frances (1979–80), 'Administrative Decentralisation for Development: Participation and Control in Tanzania', *Journal of African Studies*, 6/4: 182–92.

Hyden, Goran (1980), *Beyond Ujamaa in Tanzania: Underdevelopment and an Uncaptured Peasantry*, London: Heinemann.

IDS Bulletin (1995), 'Towards Democratic Governance', 26/2.

Jonakin, Jon (1996), 'The Impact of Structural Adjustment and Property Rights Conflicts on Nicaraguan Agrarian Reform Beneficiaries', *World Development*, 24/7: 1179–91.

Jonas, Susan, and Stein, Nancy (1990), 'The Construction of Democracy in Nicaragua', *Latin American Perspectives*, 17/3: 20–37.

Kaiser, Paul J. (1996), 'Structural Adjustment and the Fragile Nation: The Demise of Social Unity in Tanzania', *Journal of Modern African Studies*, 34/2: 227–37.

Kasfir, Nelson (1992), 'Popular Sovereignty and Popular Participation: Mixed Constitutional Democracy in the Third World', *Third World Quarterly*, 13/4: 587–605.

Kothari, Rajni (1988), *State against Humanity: In Search of Human Governance*, Delhi: Ajanta.

Leogrande, William M. (1996), 'Making the Economy Scream: US Economic Sanctions against Sandinista Nicaragua', *Third World Quarterly*, 17/2: 329–48.

Lijphart, Arend (1977), *Democracy in Plural Societies: A Comparative Exploration*, New Haven: Yale University Press.

—— (1996), 'The Puzzle of Indian Democracy: A Consociational Interpretation', *American Political Science Review*, 90/2: 258–68.

Lofchie, Michael (1989), *The Policy Factor: Agricultural Performance in Kenya and Tanzania*, Boulder, Colo.: Lynne Rienner.

Loomis, C. Douglas (1991), 'Development against Democracy', *Alternatives*, 16/1: 31–66.

Luanda, Nestor N. (1994), 'The "Uncaptured Forms" of Democratization in Tanzania', Department of History, University of Dar es Salaam (unpublished).

Luciak, A. Ilja (1990), 'Democracy in the Nicaraguan Countryside: A Comparative Analysis of Sandinista Grassroots Movements', *Latin American Perspectives*, 17/3: 55–75.

McHenry, Dean E., Jr. (1994), *Limited Choices: The Political Struggle for Socialism in Tanzania*, Boulder, Colo.: Lynne Rienner.

Macpherson, C. B. (1966), *The Real World of Democracy*, Oxford: Oxford University Press.

Maliyamkono, T. L., and Bagachwa, M. S. D. (1990), *The Second Economy in Tanzania*, London: James Currey.

Mamdani, Mahmoud (1990), 'The Social Basis of Constitutionalism in Africa', *Journal of Modern African Studies*, 28/3: 359–74.

—— (1996), *Citizen and Subject: Contemporary Africa and the Legacy of Late Colonialism*, Princeton: Princeton University Press.

Miller, David (1993), 'Deliberative Democracy and Social Choice', in Held (1993).

Mmuya, Max, and Chaligha, Amon (1992), *Towards Multiparty Politics in Tanzania*, Dar es Salaam: Dar es Salaam University Press.

Molyneux, Maxine (1985), 'Women', in T. W. Walker (ed.), *Nicaragua: The First Five Years*, New York: Praeger.

Mouffe, Chantal (ed.) (1992), *Dimensions of Radical Democracy: Pluralism, Citizenship, Community*, London: Verso.

Mwansasu, Bismark U., and Pratt, Cranford (eds.) (1979), *Towards Socialism in Tanzania*, Toronto: University of Toronto Press.

Nursey-Bray, Paul (1983), 'Consensus and Community: The Theory of African One-Party Democracy', in Graeme Duncan (ed.), *Democratic Theory and Practice*, Cambridge: Cambridge University Press.

Nyerere, Julius (1965), 'Democracy and the Party System', in J. Nyerere, *Freedom and Unity*, Dar es Salaam: Oxford University Press.

—— (1968), *Freedom and Socialism*, Dar es Salaam: Oxford University Press.

—— (1973), *Freedom and Development*, Dar es Salaam: Oxford University Press.

Nzomo, Maria (1995–6), 'The Political Economy of the African Crisis: Gender Impacts and Responses', *International Journal*, 51/1: 78–102.

Parekh, Bikhu (1993), 'The Cultural Particularity of Liberal Democracy', in Held (1993).

Pateman, Carol (1970), *Participation and Democratic Theory*, Cambridge: Cambridge University Press.

Pratt, Cranford (1979), 'Tanzania's Transition to Socialism: Reflections of a Democratic Socialist', in Mwansasu and Pratt (1979).

Presidential Commission on Single Party or Multiparty Systems in Tanzania, 1991 (1992), vol. i: *Report and Recommendations of the Commission on the Democratic System in Tanzania*, Dar es Salaam: United Republic of Tanzania (Nyalali Commission).

Pretty, Jules N. (1995), 'Participatory Learning for Sustainable Agriculture', *World Development*, 23/8: 1247–63.

Prevost, Gary (1995), 'The Role of the Sandinista Revolution in the Process of Democratization in Nicaragua', *Democratization*, 2/2: 85–108.

—— (1996), 'The Nicaraguan Revolution: Six Years after the Sandinista Electoral Defeat', *Third World Quarterly*, 17/2: 307–27.

Przeworski, Adam (1991), *Democracy and the Market: Political and Economic Reforms in Eastern Europe and Latin America*, Cambridge: Cambridge University Press.

Putnam, Robert (1993), *Making Democracy Work: Civic Traditions in Modern Italy*, Princeton: Princeton University Press.

Robinson, I. William (1992), *A Faustian Bargain: US Intervention in the Nicaraguan Elections and American Foreign Policy in the Post-Cold War Era*, Boulder, Colo.: Westview Press.

Rueschemeyer, Dietrich, Stevens, Evelyne Huber, and Stevens, John D. (1992), *Capitalist Development and Democracy*, Cambridge: Polity Press.

Schumpeter, Joseph A. (1965), *Capitalism, Socialism and Democracy*, London: Allen & Unwin, 1st pub. 1943.

Seligson, Mitchell A., and Booth, John A. (1993), 'Political Culture and Regime Type: Evidence from Nicaragua and Costa Rica', *Journal of Politics*, 55/3: 777–92.

Serra, Luis (1993), 'Democracy in Times of War and Socialist Crisis: Reflections Stemming from the Sandinista Revolution', *Latin American Perspectives*, 20/2: 21–44.

Shivji, Issa G. (1976), *Class Struggles in Tanzania*, London: Monthly Review Press.

—— (1991), 'The Democracy Debate in Africa: Tanzania', *Review of African Political Economy*, 50: 79–81.

Sklar, Richard L. (1987), 'Developmental Democracy', *Comparative Studies in Society and History*, 29/4: 686–714.

Spoor, Max (1994), 'Neoliberalism and Institutional Reform in Post-1990 Nicaragua: The Impact on Grain Markets', *Bulletin of Latin American Research*, 13/2: 185–202.

Stahler-Sholk, Richard (1995), 'Sandinista Economic and Social Policy: The Mixed Blessings of Hindsight', *Latin American Research Review*, 30/2: 235–50.

Stiefel, Mathias, and Wolfe, Marshall (1994), *A Voice for the Excluded: Popular Participation in Development*, London: Zed Books.

Sundet, Geir (1994), 'Beyond Developmentalism in Tanzania', *Review of African Political Economy*, 21/59: 39–49.

Swantz, Marja Liisa, and Tripp, Aili Mari (eds.) (1996), *What Went Right in Tanzania: People's Response to Directed Development*, Dar es Salaam: Dar es Salaam University Press.

Tungaraza, Casta (1998), 'The Transformation of Civil–Military Relations in Tanzania', in E. Hutchful and A. Bathily (eds.), *The Military and Militarism in Africa*, Dakar: CODESRIA.

Utting, Peter (1991), *Economic Adjustment under the Sandinistas: Policy Reform, Food Security and Livelihood in Nicaragua*, Geneva: UNRISD.

van Cranenburgh, Oda (1990), *The Widening Gyre: The Tanzanian One-Party State and Policy towards Rural Co-operatives*, Delft: Eburon.

Vanden, Harry E., and Prevost, Garry (1993), *Democracy and Socialism in Sandinista Nicaragua*, Boulder, Colo.: Westview Press.

Vellinga, Menno (ed.) (1993), *Social Democracy in Latin America*, Boulder, Colo.: Westview Press.

Vilas, Carlos (1991), 'Nicaragua: A Revolution that Fell from the Grace of the People', *Socialist Register 1991*, London: Merlin Press: 302–21.

—— (1996), 'Are There Left Alternatives? A Discussion from Latin America', *Socialist Register 1996*, London: Merlin Press: 264–85.

Wangwe, S. M. (1996), *Economic Reforms and Poverty Alleviation in Tanzania*, Employment Paper no. 7, Geneva: ILO Employment and Training Department.

Warren, Bill (1980), *Imperialism: Pioneer of Capitalism*, ed. J. Sender, London: Verso.

Whitehead, Laurence (1993), 'The Alternatives to "Liberal Democracy": A Latin American Perspective', in Held (1993).

Williams, Philip J. (1994), 'Dual Transitions from Authoritarian Rule: Popular and Electoral Democracy in Nicaragua', *Comparative Politics*, 26/2: 169–86.

Williamson, John (1993), 'Democracy and the Washington Consensus', *World Development*, 21/8: 1329–63

Wright, Bruce E. (1990), 'Pluralism and Vanguardism in the Nicaraguan Revolution', *Latin American Perspectives*, 17/3: 38–54.

Index

access 22, 40–1, 43, 47, 105, 142–3,
  155, 162–3, 167, 169, 176, 180–1,
  289
accountability:
  balance and 135, 137
  capacity and 85–8, 90, 95–8, 102,
    106–7, 109–10
  democracy and 21, 23, 26
  developmental democracies and
    30–4, 36–7, 41, 44
  government 308, 314, 336–7
  participation and 151–2, 165,
    169–70, 177, 179, 181–2
  rural poor 284, 294, 302
  South Africa 232, 236
  women 248, 251, 275
administration 29–30, 138–9, 142,
  237, 251–3, 321, 323, 325, 327
Africa 26, 38–40, 44, 46, 91, 103–4,
  128, 152, 164–8, 217, 248, 253,
  307, 320, 329
  see also South Africa; sub-Saharan
    Africa
African National Congress (ANC)
  (South Africa) 61, 216–20, 222–4,
  227–8, 230, 236–7, 239, 257–61,
  264–7, 272
agriculture 71, 164, 208, 217, 262,
  270, 320, 324–6, 328–9, 331–2,
  336
aid 21, 74, 84–110, 334
Ajam, T. 233
Angola 91, 281, 289
apartheid 74, 166, 215, 224, 235, 237,
  257–8, 272
Argentina 34, 190, 192, 307
Arusha Declaration (1967) (Tanzania)
  316, 318, 321, 325, 327, 333, 337
Asia 18, 20, 22–3, 26–7, 30, 39, 42,
  44, 46, 88, 103–4, 152, 164, 251,
  287, 307

authoritarianism:
  democracy and 164, 191, 193, 307
  developmental democracies
    17–18, 22–8, 30, 42, 44–5, 53,
    65, 144
  Middle East 91
  in Nicaragua 319, 323
  participation and 150–1, 180
  rural poor and 281, 287–8, 292–3,
    296, 301
  women and 248, 253
authority 18, 29–30, 34, 64, 190, 212,
  215–16
autonomous participation 158, 162–3
autonomy:
  developmental democracies 30–1,
    38, 44, 61–6, 69–70, 73–4, 77
  government 169
  India 189, 197
  Philippines 136
  state 19, 233, 252, 275
  women 246, 250, 256, 260

balance of development and democracy
  125–48
Bangladesh 44, 89
Bangura, Y. 289, 296
Bardhan, Pranab 61, 195, 202
bargaining 32, 66, 91, 97, 104, 130,
  145, 147
Barnes, J. 236, 237, 239
Bayart, Jean-François 60, 134, 291,
  293, 295
Bhorat, H. et al. 226
Bigombe, Betty 262
Blumenfeld, J. 221
Boadway, Robin et al. 189
Bolivia 155, 170, 173, 174–82
Booth, D. et al. 173, 174, 175, 177,
  179
Botswana 38–9, 52–4, 63–6, 168–9

bottom-up approach 23, 125–6, 138–41, 145, 218, 329
Bratton, M. 165, 286, 288, 289, 293, 301
Brazil 34, 39, 190, 192
Brecht, Bertolt 306
Breslin, E. et al. 232
Brinkerhoff, D. W. 164, 165, 166, 167, 300
Britton, Hannah 268
budgeting 85, 87, 106–10, 190, 220–2, 233, 235–6
bureaucracy 63, 65, 73, 94, 102, 105–7, 136–7
Byanyima, Winnie 264

capacity:
  centralization 282
  community 175
  corporatism and 223
  democratic states 52–78
  developmental democracies 28, 38, 44
  Indian state 203, 205
  institutions in South Africa 230–2, 235–7
  interest groups 160, 162
  market 18
  poor 169, 288
  state 23, 25, 63, 77–8, 188, 190–2, 194, 245–6
  state in Fourth World 84–110
  women 252, 254, 266, 269, 272, 275
capital-intensive states 95–7
capitalism 62, 71–2, 75, 217, 309–13, 315–20, 325–6, 335
Caribbean 88, 103
caste 68, 172, 175–6, 178, 181–2
centralization 73, 144–5, 164, 189, 196–9, 202–3, 206–11, 216, 219–22, 236, 239, 290
Chama Cha Mapinduzi (CCM) (Tanzania) 317, 319, 321, 325, 327, 330–5
Chatterjee, Somnath 206
Chile 34, 39, 46, 56, 70, 315
China 18, 57, 62, 76, 110, 190, 212
citizen influence 85–6, 97–8, 104–5, 110
citizenship 21, 28, 47, 288–9, 297, 313, 316

civil society:
  accountability 23
  democracy and 310–14
  developmental democracies 31–3, 36, 39–42, 45–6
  equality 28
  formal and informal 280, 282, 284–5, 292–302
  manipulation 129, 135, 142, 146–7
  Nicaragua 324–5
  participation 150
  South Africa 219, 223
  Tanzania 321, 333
  weak and development 63–5
  women 251, 253–61, 267–8, 271–2, 274–5
class, social:
  developmental democracies 35, 39, 64–5, 67–8, 77
  elites 280, 284, 286–7, 291, 302
  empowerment 310–11, 313, 315
  equality 245
  Nicaragua 332
  participation 160
  policy 252
  Tanzania 334
class-compromise non-developmental democracies 63, 67, 70–4
clientelism 22, 37, 41, 285–7, 301, 315
coalitions 35–8, 42, 45–7, 60–1, 63, 66–70, 78
coercion 96, 127–8, 144–5
Cold War 91, 104, 306, 312, 316–17
collective action 156–61
colonialism 68, 75, 103–4, 108, 283, 300, 311
commandism 126–7, 144–7, 219, 222, 315
communism 18, 160, 311, 317
community:
  balance and 127, 135, 138–42, 145–7
  government 153
  participation 170–9
  rural poor 282, 286–7, 291, 293, 297, 300
  South Africa 218, 227, 229–30, 232, 236, 239
  women 256, 262

competition:
  donor 85–7, 107–10
  Indian intra-state 198–9, 202, 205, 207
  political 19, 126–31, 134, 146, 250, 274–5
  value system 299–300
confidentiality 125, 142–4, 146–7
conflict:
  consensus and 36, 42, 125
  order and 125–9, 145, 147
Congo 91, 134
Congress Party (India) 77, 171–2, 195–6, 201–2, 209
consensus 30, 34–5, 44, 56, 59–61, 67–9, 75–6, 125, 164, 206, 223, 225–6, 281, 283, 300
consent and effectiveness 30, 36, 125
conservatism 56, 60, 72, 74
consolidation 24–5, 34, 39–40, 43, 46, 55–63, 65–7, 70, 73, 76–8, 152–3
constitution 30, 33, 59–61, 71, 196, 233, 238, 245, 256, 260, 262–4, 266, 274–5, 294, 308–10, 320, 322–3
consultation 41, 166–9, 180
continuity 66, 76, 86, 125–6, 141–2, 145
control 103–5, 127, 133–4, 153, 170, 190, 308, 312
coordination 219–20, 222, 230, 232, 236, 238–9
corporatism 41–2, 164, 167, 170, 223–30, 239, 249, 273–4, 322
corruption 18, 22, 138–40, 143, 146, 179, 199–203, 210, 256–7, 330
Costa Rica 39, 46, 52–4, 58–9, 61, 63, 75–6
Côte d'Ivoire 72, 91, 133–5
Coulon, C. 300
Cruise O'Brien, D. 300
Cuba 57, 62, 76
culture 60, 67, 74, 152, 160
Czech Republic 39, 46

Davies, Susanna 280–303, 315
de-localization 264–5
decentralization 129, 134, 138–44, 146, 153, 164, 170, 172–3, 178–9, 181, 189, 195, 216, 229–30, 233, 236, 239, 327

decision-making:
  balance and 130, 141
  capacity and 98
  consensual 318
  conservative 56
  democracy and 308–9, 312, 315
  developmental democracies and 33, 41
  federalism 189
  globalization 307
  India 196
  participation 151–4, 156–9, 162, 164–6, 168–70, 172, 174–6, 180–2
  South Africa 218, 223, 225, 229
  women 249, 253–4, 256, 259, 262, 268–9, 275
Degnbol, T. 300, 302
delivery of development 230–3
departmentalism 219–22, 238
dereservation 199–201
design of developmental democracies 32–42
developmental democracies 52–3, 55–61
  balance of 125–48
  capacity and 84–110
  construction of 17–47
developmental democracies, states 61–77
Diamond, Larry 25, 36, 53, 56, 125
dictatorship 164, 311, 319, 337
donors 85, 89, 95, 107–9, 173, 221, 280–1, 283, 285–6, 288, 314–15, 317, 321, 329–30

'earnedness' of state income 85–7, 94–9, 106
Eastern Europe 18, 23, 29, 33, 43–4, 46, 247–8, 330
economy:
  Bolivia 174
  efficiency and development 306
  Fourth World 88–90
  growth and democracy 17–18, 20, 22–3
  growth as development 281, 283, 285, 288, 301
  growth and developmental democracies 28–9, 38, 44, 52–3, 56–7, 61–2, 64–6, 68–70, 74–6, 78

economy (*cont.*):
  growth in South Africa 215, 219–22, 225, 227–9
  liberalization 130, 146–7, 166–7, 313
  liberalization in India 172, 187–8, 191–208, 210–12
  management 316
  Nicaragua 319, 324, 327, 329, 331–7
  participation 165
  reform and democracy 151–2
  Tanzania 329–30, 333–4, 336
  women and planning 245–50, 267–75
education 108, 152, 159–61, 163, 181, 233, 236, 246, 269, 289, 333, 335
effectiveness 19, 29, 32–3, 36, 73, 77, 106, 125, 151, 156–7
efficiency 21, 26, 187–92, 196, 198–9, 212, 230
elections:
  Côte d'Ivoire 134
  balance 128–9, 136
  Bolivia 174, 177
  democracy and 150, 152–3, 156–9, 192, 308
  developmental democracies 38, 55–6, 59, 65
  India 175, 195–6, 201, 209, 212
  Nicaragua 317, 322–3, 331–2, 334
  participation 165, 172–3, 181
  rural poor 285–7
  South Africa 215–16, 224, 228, 238–9
  Tanzania 317, 320, 333
  Venezuela 72
  women 248, 255, 260–1, 263–5
elites:
  Bolivia 173
  democracy and 22, 86, 88, 103, 308, 315, 336
  developmental democracies 30–1, 37–43, 45, 52, 56, 58, 60–2, 66, 69, 71–3
  India 188, 197–203, 207, 210–11
  manipulation 129–30, 139
  participation 150, 153–4, 162–7, 169, 174–5, 180, 314
  rural democracy 280, 284, 289, 292
  South Africa 224, 238
Elson, Diane 262, 269, 270

emancipation, democracy as 308–9, 312, 315
embeddedness 30–1, 43
employment 66, 75, 165, 217, 219, 221–3, 226–7, 230, 232, 238, 289
empowerment 21, 131, 136, 142, 156–7, 172, 177, 216, 218, 286, 293, 310–14, 327, 337
environment 20, 43, 66, 283
equality 159, 162, 187–90, 207–12, 308, 312, 322
Ethiopia 101, 281, 289, 337
Europe 42, 44, 58, 96–7, 102–3, 167
Evans, Peter 2, 53, 65, 126, 164
Evers, Barbara 262, 269, 270
exclusion:
  apartheid and 224
  corporatism and 229
  decision-making 98
  developmental democracies 28, 67
  participation 153–5, 157, 159–65, 167, 169–76, 178–82, 182, 309, 311, 313–15
  rural poor 286–7, 289, 292, 296, 300, 302
  women 246–7, 252, 256, 259–60, 264, 269
expectations 24–5, 138–41, 281, 288
expenditure, public 85, 107–8, 165, 170–1, 173, 175, 177–9, 181–2, 189, 194, 210, 215, 217, 235–6, 269, 272–3

Fatton, Robert 39, 294, 295
federalism 35, 73, 187–212
feminism 245–7, 250–3, 255–6, 260, 262–3, 266, 268–9, 274–5
Fiji 64, 68
finance, public 90–8, 110
fiscal federalism 189–91, 233–8
forces, external and internal and development 58
forms of state 52–78
Fourth World state capacity 84–110
Fowler, A. 286, 293, 295, 296, 297, 301
Fox, L. 282, 296, 297
France 95–6, 249
freedom 27, 56, 60, 74, 248, 274–5, 288, 294, 309, 318
Fukuyama, Francis 19
funding development 73, 108, 140, 142

GDP 194, 219, 331–2
Ghana 25, 38, 46, 166, 307, 311
Ghosh, Arun 200
Ghosh, B. 175, 178
globalization 18–19, 21, 77, 307, 313, 315, 336
GNP 52–5, 62, 69, 329
Goetz, Anne Marie 245–76
governance 25–6, 33–7
Gramsci, Antonio 309, 312
grants 107–8, 173
Great Britain 42, 95–6, 281
Greer, Germaine 251
Grindle, M. S. 162–3
Guhan, S. 209

Haggard, Stephan 34, 65, 191, 192, 224, 225
Hangana, Nomatyala 265
health 108, 233–4, 236, 246, 269, 328, 330
Heredia, Blanca 130
Houphouet-Boigny, Felix 133–4
Human Development Index 53–4, 281
Hungary 39, 46
Huntington, Samuel P. 2, 23, 24, 53, 55, 156, 158, 159, 161

ideology 64, 72, 74–5, 160
inappropriateness of democracy 282, 287–8, 291–2
income providers 93–5, 98, 104, 106
incomes:
    developmental states 66, 75
    distribution 53
    Fourth World 88
    India 207
    participation 159, 161
    South Africa 217, 226–8, 233–4
    state 85–7, 100–2, 105–6, 202
India 38, 44, 46, 52–4, 61, 63, 73, 76–7, 99–100, 131, 139, 141–3, 166
    federalism in 187–212
    Panchayati Raj 155, 170–82
Indonesia 18–19, 26, 53
industrialization 18, 20, 61, 75, 224
industry 193, 197–201, 204, 326
inequality:
    alleviation of 20, 29
    in Botswana 66

civil society and 40
    in Costa Rica 75
    democracy and 28, 43, 60, 292, 299, 310, 312
    elites and 22
    empowerment and 313
    levels of 24, 288
    markets and 146, 325
    in Philippines 137
    in South Africa 74, 215–18, 222, 225–7, 229–30, 233, 238
    in Tanzania 333
    in Venezuela 73
infrastructure 29, 43, 93, 101, 103, 106, 178, 193, 199–202, 216, 232
innovation and continuity 125–6, 141–2, 145
institutions:
    democracy and 19–20, 86, 88, 95, 97, 307–9, 311–14
    democracy in post-apartheid South Africa 215–39
    developmental democracies 29–36, 41, 43–4, 46–7, 63, 69, 77
    federalism in India 187–212
    formal and informal 125, 135–7, 145
    liberalization 17
    participation and public policy 150–82
    self-interest and 125, 128–35, 137
    structural development 52, 55, 60
    sustainable development 281–4, 289–90, 292–6, 298–302
    Tanzania 320, 326, 333
    women and gendered 245–9, 251–3, 255, 260–1, 269, 271–5
instrumentalism 151–2, 154, 156–7
intensity of participation 154, 158–60, 171, 182
interests:
    rural poor 282, 292–3, 302
    women's 243–7, 250, 259–60, 262–4, 267, 269, 272–4
intermediation 37, 153–4, 158, 160, 162–3, 171, 174, 182
International Monetary Fund (IMF) 68, 73, 76, 194, 321, 329, 331, 333
internationalism 31, 46, 102–6
investment 74, 193, 198–9, 201–2

Jamaica 52–4, 56–7, 63, 75–6, 168
Japan 38, 41–2, 58, 64, 249
Jenkins, Rob 128, 130, 131, 187–212
Jiménez, Marcos Pérez 71
justice, social 146, 227, 246, 251, 283, 309

Karnataka (India) 170–2, 175–8, 181–2, 209–11
Kaufman, Robert 34, 191, 224, 225
Kazibwe, Specioza Wandira 262
Keemar, G. 175, 178
Konaré, Alpha 286
Korea 36, 38–9, 41, 55, 58, 61, 110, 164

labour:
  gendered division of 247, 249, 251–2, 254, 269–70
  relations in South Africa 216–17, 222–9, 238
land 61, 136–7, 172, 175, 178, 182, 200–2, 211, 216–17, 297, 324, 328, 331, 336
Latin America 18, 22, 26, 29, 33–4, 37, 39, 43–6, 58, 65, 75, 104, 140, 152, 164, 248, 313, 316, 335
Lee Kuan Yew 22–3
Leftwich, Adrian 1, 3, 6, 23, 52–78, 252
legislature 245, 248–9, 253, 261–2, 267, 308, 321–3, 331
legitimacy:
  consolidation 58–9
  democracy 24–5, 156, 230
  local government 177, 181
  political 286, 290, 292, 295, 301
  political systems 73, 127–8, 132, 147
  state 61, 63, 151–2, 165, 171
  state of Tanzania 321, 330
  women 251, 257, 259, 263, 265–6, 269, 275
liberal democracy 17–21, 23–4, 26–7, 37, 44, 66, 151, 156, 215, 222, 238, 246, 259, 275, 290, 292, 296
  alternatives to 306–38
literacy 54, 217, 256, 270, 289, 320, 328
livelihood:
  contemporary states 98–102
  democracy 302, 315
  democratization and sustainable 280–303

lobbying 139, 157–9, 167, 203, 227–8, 299
low-intensity democracies 22, 78, 152
Lozada, Sanchez de 173
Luckham, L. 152
Luckham, Robin 2, 3, 27, 104, 292, 306–38
Lund, C. 298, 300

Macpherson, C. B. 307
macro-economic policy 151–2, 159, 165–6, 168, 180
Maderna, Paras Ram 206–7
Madison, James 308, 312
Malaysia 18–19, 27, 52, 54, 63, 67, 69, 74
Mali 38, 281, 286, 300
Mandela, Nelson 219, 222
Mandela, Winnie 265, 266
Manley, Michael 168
Manor, James 125–48, 172, 176, 177, 178, 179, 195, 282
Marcos, Gill 273
marginalization 41, 229, 281, 291–2, 294, 309, 312
  see also exclusion
market:
  economy 29
  liberalization 129–30, 146, 270
  orientation 215, 217, 222, 309, 311, 329, 333–7
  orientation in India 187, 191, 193–4, 197, 201–2, 206–7, 212
  preserving federalism 189–91
  women and 246, 248, 250
marketization 17–19, 21
Marx, Karl 309
Mauritius 52–4, 57, 63–4, 67–9, 74
Mbeki, Thabo 222
Medard, Jean-François 91
mediated participation 158, 162–3
Metcalfe, S. 290
Middle East 91, 101, 104–5
military 59, 65, 71–3, 76, 78, 102–5, 108
mobilization, political 21, 41, 151, 169, 229, 329, 337
mobilized participation 158, 160, 162–3
Moily, Veerappa 209–10
Moore, Mick 2, 22, 84–110, 167, 210

Morris, M. 236, 237, 239
Moyser, G. 157, 160, 162
Mozambique 165, 281, 289
multi-party organization 25, 37–8,
    285, 288
  Eastern Europe 248
  Nicaragua 317–18, 322, 334, 336
  South Africa 257, 259
  Tanzania 317–18, 330–1, 333
  Uganda 255
multiple aid 85, 107–9
Museveni, Yoweri 255, 257, 261,
    262
Myrdal, Gunnar 22

Naidoo, Jay 219, 222
National Economic, Development, and
    Labour Council (NEDLAC) 223,
    225–9, 237, 239, 273
Nattrass, Nicoli 215–39
natural resources 101, 104, 198, 290,
    300
Ndegwa, S. 286, 293
Nelson, J. M. 156, 158, 159, 161
networks 105, 295–7
Nicaragua 59, 307, 311, 315, 316–38
Nie, N. H. 156, 159, 160, 161
Niger 38, 281, 294, 299–300
Nigeria 64, 91, 166
Nkrumah, Kwame 311
non-developmental democracies 53,
    57, 62–4, 67, 70–7
non-governmental organizations
    (NGOs) 135, 142, 146, 153, 221,
    231–2, 284, 286, 293–4, 296,
    314
Nyerere, Julius 311, 317, 318, 320,
    321, 327, 329, 330, 333, 334

Obote, (Apollo) Milton 255
one-party system 20, 38, 64–5, 134,
    164, 318, 320–1, 327, 329
open and closed political systems
    163–4
order 18–19, 29, 125–9, 145, 147
organizations:
  Bolivia 175, 177, 179, 181–2
  civil society 39–40
  development and 64–5, 71, 218,
    224, 227
  grass-roots and democracy 23

grass-roots and popular democracy
    311, 315–17, 320–2, 325, 328,
    330, 332–4, 336, 338
interest groups 151–3, 158, 160,
    163–4, 167–9, 228
interest groups and development
    balance 128–32, 135, 140, 142,
    146
interest groups in India 202–5, 210
non-official 135
participation 150, 173
poor in South Africa 216, 238
rural poor 284–5, 288, 293–302
social 313, 315
state earned incomes 94
women 250, 253–60, 262–4, 266–7,
    270, 273–4, 322, 330

Pakistan 44, 61, 89
Panchayati Raj (India) 155, 170–82
parliamentarianism 33–5
Parry, G. 157, 160, 162
partial democracy 45, 56–7, 78
participation:
  active 218, 225, 236
  balance and 140, 147
  development and 72–3, 78
  development and rural poor 281,
    285–91, 296
  developmental democracies and 41,
    44, 55–6
  popular 306–11, 313–18, 322–3,
    325–9, 334–5, 337
  public policy 150–82
  women in Uganda and South Africa
    245–76
party, political:
  alternation non-developmental
    democratic states 63, 67, 70,
    74–7
  balance and 128
  Bolivia 173
  Botswana 168–9
  civil society 293–4
  competition 20, 150, 188, 308
  democracy and 192, 196
  developmental democracies 30,
    34–9, 41–3, 46
  dissidence 205–7
  dominant developmental democratic
    states 63–6, 70, 78

party, political (*cont.*):
    gender equity and 249, 254, 257–8,
        260, 263, 265–7, 275
    as institution 135, 137
    as mediation 162–3
    participation 165
    South Africa 219, 239
patriarchy 246, 250, 252, 261, 275, 310
patronage 74, 76, 131–5, 197, 202,
        210, 285–7, 294, 296, 301, 321
Pawar, Sharad 204
penetration, authoritative 30–1
people-centred development 216–22
people's democracy 306–7, 310–12,
        316, 322, 337
performance 24–5, 45, 57, 63,
        187–9, 191, 197, 199, 212, 230,
        247, 252
Peru 26, 34
Philippines 34, 58, 136–7, 139, 307,
        310
Phillips, Anne 160, 241, 249–50
pluralism 17, 23, 67–9, 74, 294, 302,
        319
policy:
    conservative 56, 59–61
    democracy and 188, 191–2, 206–7,
        212
    implementation 192
    India 196
    participation and public 150–82
    rural poor 281, 285–7
    South Africa 216, 222, 225, 227,
        229, 239
    women's participation 245–7, 251–3,
        257, 260, 267–75
political society:
    democracy and 311, 314
    developmental democracies 32–3,
        36, 40–1, 46
    Nicaragua 322, 324
    South Africa 223
    women 253–61, 267–8, 275
political systems:
    balance and 127–8, 131–2, 135
    democracy and 23, 26–7
    Fourth World 88–9
    global 19
    legitimacy of 73, 127–8, 132, 147
    policy and 163
    rural poor 280, 282, 285, 293, 301

politics:
    democracy and 18, 21, 23
    development and 55–7, 62–3, 67,
        70–4, 77–8
    developmental democracies and
        31–3, 36, 43, 47
poor:
    democracy 22
    developmental democracies 28, 38,
        40, 140
    empowerment 312, 314
    India 207–11
    Nicaragua 332
    participation 153–5, 157, 160–1,
        163, 167, 169–70, 172–82, 309,
        313–15
    rural and livelihood democracy
        280–303
    in South Africa 216–17, 219, 223,
        226, 229, 232–3, 235, 238–9
    women 269
popular democracy as alternative to
        liberal 306–38
Popular Participation Law (Bolivia)
        155, 170, 173–5, 177–82
poverty:
    alleviation 20, 23, 29, 43, 52, 61,
        140–1
    authoritarianism and 287
    democracy and 28, 60, 281, 291,
        300, 310
    extreme 24, 288
    gender and 252
    in India 172, 179
    participation and 152
    in South Africa 215–17, 221–2,
        226–7, 230, 233–4
    sustainable development and 283
    in Uganda 270
    in Venezuela 73
power:
    control and 59–60
    democracy 24, 27
    developmental democracies 30, 35
    elite 86, 286–7, 302
    Nicaragua 322
    participation 159–60, 162–3, 169,
        174, 180–1
    pluralism 308
    political 150, 157
    relations 311, 313, 332

rights and 289, 291–2
state 62, 64–5, 67, 73, 96–8,
    103–4, 187–8, 192, 196, 238–9,
    294
Tanzania 321
use of 129, 134–6, 144
women 247, 249–50, 260, 266,
    268–9, 273
Pratt, Cranford 317, 320
presidentialism 33–5, 37
private sector 17, 62, 65, 74, 76,
    129–30, 146, 166–8, 193,
    199–200, 206
projects, development 127, 132, 135,
    138–9, 141–2, 144, 151–3, 157,
    176, 178–9, 182
proportional representation 35, 238–9,
    249–50, 264–6
protest 73, 157, 165
Przeworski, Adam 29, 60, 70, 72, 308,
    311
public/private spheres 246, 250, 313

quota and women 249, 251, 265

race 35, 39, 60, 64–5, 67–9, 74, 161,
    174, 215, 217, 272, 312, 316, 323
radical democracy 60–1, 156, 313
Ramirez, Sergio 319, 322
Ramos, Maria 273
Rao, Narasimha 171, 194, 195
Rasheed, S. 281, 285, 288, 300
reciprocity 94, 97, 295
Reconstruction and Development
    Programme (RDP) (South Africa)
    216–23, 229, 231, 236, 239
redistribution 29, 40, 43–4, 74, 106,
    215–18, 221, 223, 227, 229–30,
    233, 235
regionalism 35, 64, 67–8, 77,
    195–211
regulation 29, 42, 58–60, 72, 78,
    136–7, 189, 193
religion 35, 39, 60, 67–9, 74, 77, 161
representation:
    decentralization and 229
    governability and 36
    marginalization and 174–7, 180–2
    mediation and 158
    origins of 95–8, 102
    participation and 164, 168, 172

of rural poor 284, 289, 294
of women 245–8, 250–1, 253, 259,
    261–4, 267–9, 271, 273–4
representative democracy 34–5, 215,
    307, 309–10, 316
reproduction, social 246–8, 254, 275
resistance to democracy 25, 197, 199,
    202–7, 210–11
resources:
    balance and 130–4, 138–42
    capacity and 103
    development and 29, 56, 60, 64
    developmental democracies 40–1
    distribution 310, 326–8, 332
    India 196, 198, 205, 210–11
    in India 216, 218, 220, 226, 233,
        235–6, 238
    mobilization 316
    participation 153–4, 157, 160–3,
        169, 171–2, 176, 178, 180–1
    rural poor 281, 283, 286–92, 300–2
    women 246–7, 250, 254, 272
responsiveness 26, 85, 90, 95–8
revenue-raising 85, 90, 92–3, 99–102,
    105–6, 108, 110
revolution:
    Nicaragua (1979) 316–17, 319, 322,
        328, 333
    transformation and 310, 312, 315
rights:
    civil 19, 24–5, 27, 56, 60, 66,
        288–92, 295, 297, 299, 302
    democracy and 312, 315–16, 318,
        320, 322
    human 54, 78
    political 38
    property 247, 309
    rural poor 284
    women 246, 248, 255, 260–1, 263,
        266, 271, 273–4
Rosberg, Carl G. 144
Rousseau, Jean-Jacques 309
Rueschemeyer, Dietrich 39, 53, 57,
    311
rule by the people, democracy as 308,
    336
Russia 42, 192

Sandanistas (Nicaragua) 311, 315,
    317, 319–20, 322–5, 327–9, 331–7
Scandinavia 42, 248–9, 251, 253, 274

Schumpeter, Joseph A. 55, 56, 308, 309, 336
scope of participation 154–5, 158–60, 171, 181–2
Seaga, Edward 76
seats, reserved 172, 176–7, 181, 251, 261–3, 265
Seekings, Jeremy 215–39
Seers, Dudley 22
self-interest 43–4, 125, 128–35, 137, 156, 162, 170, 197, 286, 292
Sellars, C. 228
Senegal 134, 165, 299–300
services, social 73, 152, 178, 216, 221, 233, 237, 289, 293, 325, 333
Sierra Leone 91, 281
Simkins, C. 217, 233, 235
Singapore 26–7, 38–9, 52, 54, 63–6, 74
Singer, Hans 22
Singh, Manmohan 171, 172, 206
Sisulu, Albertina 265
Sklar, Richard L. 5, 27, 32, 46, 52, 312
social democracy 44–5, 66, 227, 250, 308, 313, 316
socialism 19–20, 26–8, 62, 310–12, 316–20, 325–30, 333–6
socio-economic development 17, 19–24, 26–32, 35, 40–1, 44–6, 64–5, 72–3, 75, 154, 159–63, 180, 182
Somalia 106, 289, 310
Soros, George 19
South Africa 46, 57–9, 61, 63–5, 67, 70, 74, 166, 245–76, 315, 337
  institutions and democracy in post-apartheid 215–39
sovereignty 19, 78, 107, 109–10, 252, 308, 310–11
Soviet Union 18, 20, 28, 62, 88, 307
stability, political 28, 39, 41, 61, 68, 70, 74–6, 106, 156, 161, 223–4, 281–2, 284, 290, 302, 318, 334
state–society relations:
  balance and 126, 129–31, 133–5, 141, 146–7
  capacity and 85, 90–8, 102–3
  developmental democracies 47, 62
  rural poor 282, 284, 292–8, 301
  Uganda 256

strategic interaction 92–3, 102
Stretton, Hugh 56
structural adjustment 18, 68, 76, 134, 194, 269–70, 285, 289, 321, 333–4
sub-Saharan Africa 18, 25–6, 39, 58, 88–9, 103–5, 144, 164–5, 217
  livelihood democracy 280–303
subsidies in India 193–4, 208–10
survival 56–8, 66, 72, 75, 283–4
sustainability 24, 29, 52, 56, 62, 127, 141–2, 196–7, 230
  livelihood and 280–303

Taiwan 39, 46, 53, 58, 110, 164
Tamale, Sylvia 256, 257, 262, 263, 268, 271
Tanzania 20, 38, 165, 307, 311, 316–38
taxation 91–7, 99, 101, 105–6, 139, 173, 189–90, 193, 210–11, 219, 223, 238
Third World 17, 22–3, 45, 55, 61, 63, 78, 88, 90–1, 103–4, 160, 309
Tilly, Charles 96, 102–3, 104
time constraints and activism 160–1, 250, 254, 289
top-down approach 125–6, 138–41, 145, 172, 182, 285, 323
trade unions 71, 168, 173, 175, 182, 204–5, 211, 218, 223–4, 226, 228, 239, 273, 321, 330, 335
transition to democracy:
  development and 29
  developmental democracies 25, 42–3, 55, 57–62, 64
  federalism and 191
  nature of 307
  participation 165, 170
  rural poor 282, 285, 289, 293–4, 300
  women 248, 253, 257, 272
transparency 125, 142–4, 146–7

Uganda 25, 165, 245–76, 337
ujamaa villagization (Tanzania) 318, 320–1, 325–7, 337
underdevelopment 88–90
unrest, social 29, 39, 59, 67, 75–6, 105–6, 127, 281, 284, 289, 293, 299, 302
Uruguay 34, 39
USA 76, 110, 249, 317, 322–3, 331–2

van Cranenburgh, Oda 321, 325, 326, 327
van de Walle, N. 165, 286, 288, 289, 293, 301
Venezuela 41, 46, 52–4, 57–9, 63–5, 67, 70–5, 167–8
Verba, S. 156, 159, 160, 161
Villalón, L. 299, 300
violence, domestic 263–4, 267, 271, 274–5
voice 43, 137, 141, 165, 175, 182, 216, 219, 229, 233, 238–9, 256, 266, 269, 289
voting 35, 153, 157–8, 160, 164–5, 169, 181, 285–6, 324
vulnerability 52, 281, 283, 295

Wangusa, Hellen 270
war 281, 284, 289, 310, 319, 329, 331–2
wealth 159, 161, 163, 174, 180
Webster, N. 172, 175, 176, 178, 179

welfare 52, 61, 66, 68, 75, 105, 140, 147, 178, 217, 226, 233–6, 246, 248–9, 251–2, 267, 269, 275, 283, 296, 330
West Bengal (India) 136–7, 170–2, 175–6, 178–9, 182, 197, 206
Wolpe, H. 218
women:
  empowerment 311–13, 316, 324
  participation 160, 172, 174–7, 179, 182, 245–76
  rights 246, 248, 255, 260–1, 263, 266, 271, 273–4
Women's National Coalition (WNC) (South Africa) 258–9, 266
World Bank 68, 194, 208, 270, 281

Young, Crawford 60, 92, 144
Yugoslavia 59

Zambia 20, 25, 38, 164–5
Zimbabwe 59, 290